Progress in
Psychobiology and
Physiological Psychology

Volume 15

Progress in
PSYCHOBIOLOGY AND
PHYSIOLOGICAL PSYCHOLOGY

Edited by ALAN N. EPSTEIN

Leidy Laboratory
Department of Biology
University of Pennsylvania
Philadelphia, Pennsylvania

ADRIAN R. MORRISON

Department of Animal Biology
School of Veterinary Medicine
University of Pennsylvania
Philadelphia, Pennsylvania

Volume 15

ACADEMIC PRESS, INC.
Harcourt Brace Jovanovich, Publishers
San Diego • New York • Boston
London • Sydney • Tokyo • Toronto

This book is printed on acid-free paper. ∞

Academic Press, Inc.
1250 Sixth Avenue, San Diego, California 92101-4311

United Kingdom Edition published by
Academic Press Limited
24–28 Oval Road, London NW1 7DX

Library of Congress Catalog Number: 66-29640

International Standard Book Number: 0-12-542115-X

PRINTED IN THE UNITED STATES OF AMERICA
92 93 94 95 96 97   QW   9 8 7 6 5 4 3 2 1

Contents

Suckling Physiology and Behavior of Rats: An Integrated Theory of Ingestion and Satiety

Dennis N. Lorenz

Brain Neuronal Unit Discharge in Freely Moving Animals: Methods and Application in the Study of Sleep Mechanisms

Dennis McGinty and Jerome M. Siegel

Sleep—Wake States, Sucking, and Nursing Patterns in Young Rats

Harry N. Shair and Myron A. Hofer

Taste, Feeding, and Pleasure

Thomas R. Scott

Contributors

Numbers in parentheses indicate the pages on which the authors' contributions begin.

Myron A. Hofer, Department of Developmental Psychobiology, New York State Psychiatric Institute, New York, New York 10032, and Department of Psychiatry, College of Physicians and Surgeons, Columbia University, New York, New York 10032 (141)

Dennis N. Lorenz, Human Development, University of Wisconsin–Green Bay, Green Bay, Wisconsin 54311 (1)

Dennis McGinty, Sepulveda Veterans Administration Medical Center, Sepulveda, California 91343, and Department of Psychology, University of California, Los Angeles, Los Angeles, California 90024 (85)

Thomas R. Scott, Department of Psychology, University of Delaware, Newark, Delaware 19716 (231)

Harry N. Shair, Department of Developmental Psychobiology, New York State Psychiatric Institute, New York, New York 10032, and Department of Psychiatry, College of Physicians and Surgeons, Columbia University, New York, New York 10032 (141)

Jerome M. Siegel, Sepulveda Veterans Administration Medical Center, Sepulveda, California 91343, and Department of Psychiatry, University of California, Los Angeles, Los Angeles, California 90024 (85)

This preface opens on an unusual, very sad note: I must announce that my friend and co-editor, Alan Epstein, died tragically in a traffic accident in Mexico on January 9, 1992. At the time, Alan was taking a vacation in the company of his wife, Fifi, and some old friends en route to a developmental psychobiology conference.

Alan had a remarkable scientific career that began when he entered Eliot Stellar's laboratory as an undergraduate at Johns Hopkins. One way that we, his friends, will mark his career will be in the next volume of this series. It will contain articles representing each of his lines of research. For the forthcoming special volume, I am inviting James Sprague and Eliot Stellar, the originators of this series, and Steven Fluharty to join me as editors. Eliot edited the first five volumes with Jim Sprague and then turned his editorship over to Alan. Jim continued for six more volumes before asking me to carry on with Alan. After the special volume, the series will continue with Steve Fluharty, one of Alan's students, as co-editor. (More will be said about Steve in Volume 17.)

I enjoyed Alan's supportive friendship for 31 years. We first met in Eliot's office when I came to Pennsylvania as an aspirant for a fellowship at the Institute of Neurological Sciences, and Alan was about to begin his career in the Department of Biology. Alan depicted the INS in glowing terms; it did not take long for me to realize that he had not exaggerated. We spent many pleasurable times together: INS dinners, seminars, parties, conversational walks to the 30th Street train station, and Phillies' games. I will particularly miss, though, our leisurely planning sessions for this series in Alan's office, discussed over deli sandwiches, kosher dill pickles, and tea.

Alan was passionate about behavioral neuroscience, and "P4," as we referred to this series, allowed him to display its wares in a scholarly, congenial way. Authors are encouraged to write about their work and their particular area of interest in a personal way. The articles vary greatly in style, format, and length; they can be weighted heavily toward data or toward speculation. Practically the only requirement—and it is an important one—is that the articles focus on behavior as it expresses brain mechanisms. The articles in the present volume provide good examples of this editorial philosophy.

Dennis Lorenz chose to present a comprehensive theory of ingestion and satiety. He first reviews separately the topics of lactation, nipple attachment, stimulation of the mammary gland, ingestion of milk, and sleep and thermoregulation in infant rats, emphasizing innate and developing internal controls. Lorenz then builds on this presentation by discussing the motivated process of ingestion, including the deprivation, appetite, consumption, and satiety phases. The evidence presented suggests that sucking, ingesting, sleeping, and thermoregulating are interactive processes, modified in unison by typical events in the nest. Lorenz's theory emphasizes the symbiostatic balance achieved between the dam and her offspring.

Harry Shair and Myron Hofer have taken another, but related tack; for they too are concerned with the interaction of sleeping and feeding in the young. However, they have elected to present original experiments and to discuss their results in greater depth than journal articles allow. They report that, contrary to general belief, rat pups are asleep much of the time while nursing and that sucking occurs at appreciable levels while rat pups sleep. Interestingly, although sucking increases following deprivation from the dam, sucking rates in wakefulness, slow wave sleep, and paradoxical sleep do not increase; instead, the proportion of time spent in those states with the highest sucking rates (wakefulness and slow wave sleep) increases. The experiments of Shair and Hofer provide one of the first demonstrations of an organized, essential behavior that is embedded in sleep.

Sleep is the sole focus of the article by Dennis McGinty and Jerome Siegel. Not only do they provide us with insights into the neural regulation of sleep gained from chronic single-unit studies, but they also include a thorough description of the microwire technique which they have so ably used to relate neuronal activity to behavior. In effect, they have included a handy little "how to do it" manual. McGinty and Siegal illustrate how data from neuronal unit recording studies using the microwire technique have been absolutely critical in assessing the validity of hypotheses concerning the localization of sleep control systems. Long-term stability of recordings and relative freedom of movement of the animal subject have permitted the testing of hypotheses in a way that other methods could not.

In his article, Tom Scott reviews the neural circuitry of the gustatory system in the omnivorous rat, and compares its anatomical and physiological features to that of the monkey, a species whose food selection has evolved with greater reliance on vision. Scott proceeds to describe the overlapping central projections, and likely coprocessing, of viscerotropic and gustatory information at virtually all levels of the neural hierarchy. Scott hypothesizes that such shared neural topography underlies the important relationship between ingestion and metabolism, wherein taste provides the first interoceptive cues about the likely metabolic consequences of a food or toxin. In this context, he reviews data demonstrating that gustatory processing of sapid stimuli can be modified by metabolic surfeits and deficits. In the end, Scott offers a unique viewpoint on the relationship between gustation and vicero–metabolic reflexes, proposing that what tastes good is good for us. Could it have been otherwise?

I close by assuring you that this series will continue, and that Alan's influence will still be felt. Many authors of future articles will be those pursuing areas of research to which Alan contributed significantly, and his former student, Steve Fluharty, will be an editor for this series. Together, we will strive to emulate the considerable editorial skills and dedication that Alan Epstein brought to his volumes.

Adrian R. Morrison

Contents of Recent Volumes

Suckling Physiology and Behavior of Rats: An Integrated Theory of Ingestion and Satiety

Dennis N. Lorenz
Human Development
University of Wisconsin–Green Bay
Green Bay, Wisconsin 54311

False facts are highly injurious to the progress of science, for they often endure long; but false views, if supported by some evidence, do little harm, for every one takes a salutary pleasure in proving their falseness: and when this is done, one path towards error is closed and the road to truth is often at the same time opened.

Charles Darwin, 1874

I. Introduction

A. OVERVIEW

Shortly following birth, neonatal mammals attach to a nipple and ingest their first nutrients. They also display periods of activity and inactivity while body temperature fluctuates throughout the day. These conditions, typifying newborn eutherian mammals, including human infants, change quickly with the rapid development of the brain. At some time between birth and weaning, infant mammals begin to control ingestion of their food, the sleep–wake cycles stabilize, and homeothermy develops through physiological and behavioral mechanisms. At first glance, these homeostatic systems appear to be quite autonomous in their development and function. However, recent evidence suggests that they are linked through the distinctively mammalian behaviors of suckling.

Suckling rats are emphasized in this article because of the extensive data available regarding these young mammals. Basic research into the physiology and behavior of the laboratory rat has revealed substantial information about species-typical behaviors, as well as basic principles applicable to many mammals in general.

The following evidence suggests that sucking, ingesting, sleeping, and thermoregulating are interactive processes modified in unison by typical events in the

1

nest. A cyclic pattern of behavior begins with the deprivation of milk and the lack of maternal care. This natural form of privation accelerates heat loss, eventually reduces sleep, and creates a state of hunger and distress in young pups. Evidence also indicates that rat pups communicate their distress during times of emergency by emitting ultrasounds, but the link between ultrasounds and the lack of milk has not been made. The need for milk is revealed by rhythmic sucking and ingestion of milk when pups are presented with the opportunity to suckle. The dam responds by providing a sufficient amount of milk and heat to alter the internal state of the pups. Ingestion of warm milk and contact with the dam reverses most, if not all, of the physiological perturbations of the internal state that occurred during her absence. This orderly cyclic process constitutes the first series of motivated behaviors in infant rats.

This article focuses on evidence gathered through a variety of experiments involving the natural nursing/suckling situation and, to a lesser extent, conditions in which the dam has been anesthetized. Some methodological procedures are critically reviewed, and areas lacking in information are described. Certain disparate facts and interpretations of seminal reports are reevaluated in terms of an overall integrated theory. The theory is proposed to explain many of the behaviors and underlying physiological events related to ingestion during the suckling phase, and to provide us with a framework from which hypotheses can be generated and tested. This is the first attempt to bridge three fields often considered separate: ingestion, sleep, and thermoregulation in developing animals. Much of the theory is based on fact; the remainder is speculative but heuristic. Readers interested in the development of "independent" feeding may refer to several relevant reviews (Blass and Cramer, 1982; Hall and Williams, 1983; Hall, 1985, 1990).

B. Basic Terms

There is interest and enlightening debate, coupled with genuine confusion and strong opinions, about whether or not infant rats control their ingestion of milk from the mother (Hall and Rosenblatt, 1977; Lorenz *et al.*, 1982; Hall and Williams, 1983). The problem is directly related to the more central issue of understanding basic physiological and behavioral processes responsible for ingestion in general. The confusion has stemmed, in part, from the multiplex use of the word "suckling," from the incorporation of a variety of new methodological procedures, and from rigid interpretations of a limited number of studies. These points are elaborated on below.

Investigators working directly on the problems as described, and other individuals interested in the documentation of developmental changes in ingestive behavior, may benefit from a discussion of the major terms as well as the issues.

The terms "suckling" and "nursing" are defined at this point to clarify their usage throughout this article.

It is now possible to delineate and categorize some of the events associated with the process of suckling. There is an unambiguous beginning and end to this encounter for all rodents: nipple attachment and detachment. Thus, a general category of suckling emerges through identification of several tightly linked subcategories of behaviors occurring between the initiation and completion of the suckling act. After rooting behaviors, when the nipple has been identified by olfactory cues (Pedersen and Blass, 1982), the act of suckling commences. It includes (1) positioning a nipple in the oral cavity, (2) sucking the nipple and pausing between sucks, (3) mechanically stimulating the teat, (4) ingesting milk (including the "stretch response"), and (5) releasing the nipple. Subcategories are considered separate primarily because each process has been or can be narrowly defined through independent physiological and behavioral measures. The behaviors composing each subcategorical area are affected by a different set of stimuli. Some of the behaviors can be classified as motivated; others cannot. This theme is developed more thoroughly here.

A general term is warranted because the subcategorical behaviors are arranged in a highly predictable unambiguous sequence that can be viewed as a complete unit. The term "suckling" is an obvious choice to denote the entire sequence of behaviors and underlying physiological events of infant rodents and eutherian mammals that occur while they are in direct oral contact with the mother's nipples. By selecting "suckling" as the undiminished inclusive term, it remains open for expansion within the boundaries of nipple attachment. More subcategories can be added and current ones can be elaborated on as our understanding of the phenomena progresses.

In this article, the term "suckling" is used to indicate all naturally related behaviors and physiological processes of infant mammals only during the time of nipple attachment. The term connotes nursing by the mother because of the dyadic nature of the process, but ultimately its utility depends on distinguishing the behaviors of the offspring from those of the mother. It does not refer to the age of an animal. "Suckling," as interpreted etymologically, also excludes rooting in the mother's fur, nipple-shifting, and other possibly related behaviors and underlying physiological events occurring while pups are not attached to a nipple. The term has more restrictions here than was previously recommended (Cowie et al., 1951; Blass et al., 1979; Drewett, 1983; Hall et al., 1988). The distinctions made here permit more circumscribed discussions of infant behaviors during the unambiguous detection of nipple attachment without introducing speculation about behaviors possibly relevant to initiating the act, or about the purpose and aim of an infant in close proximity to a nipple.

The term "nursing" is used to indicate all of the reciprocal natural behaviors and physiological processes of the mother while infants suckle. Milk letdown (ejection) and lactation are included in the process only if they occur when at least one pup is attached to a nipple.

The term "nursing" does not include the withdrawal of milk by suckling infants, as implied previously (Hall *et al.*, 1988). The transfer of milk is made possible through a synchrony of processes, including previous and/or current galactopoiesis (synthesis of milk within alveoli), nursing including milk let-downs (providing milk), and suckling (which may include taking milk). The transfer of milk is a consequence of the collective process of lactation, nursing, and suckling, just as normal growth and development of the pups are consequences of this collective process.

The act of nursing, by definition, does not include what the pups are doing (suckling) or any putative preparatory behaviors of the mother prior to nipple attachment by the pups. Although maternal behaviors such as grooming her ventral surface, her nipples, and the pups are important to engage pups in the act of suckling (Pedersen and Blass, 1982), these behaviors occur at other times as well and for various reasons that may not be related to the acts of nursing and suckling.

Finally, there are many behavioral and physiological events concurrent with the nursing/suckling act, such as ventilation and bruxism (chattering of the teeth), that have not been demonstrated to be directly involved in the act.

II. Rat Lactation and Milk Supply

A. FLEXIBILITY, PARITY, AND LIMITATIONS

The biology and behavior of suckling are enormously diverse among eutherian mammals. Nursing and suckling positions, as well as the frequency and duration of bouts, can vary greatly between and within species (Blaxter, 1961). Despite the diverse arrangements elaborated during evolution, there are basic principles that transcend species differences. One of these relates to the general process of lactation: Milk supply is flexible. It is regulated over the long term by the number of infants suckling (Blaxter, 1961). Furthermore, the mother is best able to supply an ample amount of milk for the normal growth and development of her offspring when the number of suckling infants does not exceed the number of nipples available (parity)[1] (Wurtman and Miller, 1976; Edwardson and Eayrs, 1967).

[1]The term "parity" or phrase "pup/nipple parity" is used here to indicate that the mother has one functional nipple per offspring. The term "hyperparity" refers to the situation in which there are more pups than functional nipples; conversely, "hypoparity" refers to fewer pups than functional nipples. "Disparity," a general term, refers to situations in which there are either more or fewer pups than functional nipples and mammary glands. A more conventional use of the term "parity" has been to indicate the state of having given birth to one or more infants, alive or dead.

B. Adjustable Milk Supply

The flexibility of milk supply in situations of parity and disparity has been reported for rats (Kumaresan *et al.*, 1967) and mice (Falconer, 1947). For example, in lactating mice in which parity is 10, litters ranging in size from one to 10 pups gained weight at approximately the same rate (Falconer, 1947). Average body weights ranged from 5.4 g for pups in litters of one to 5.3 g for pups in litters of 10 at 12 days postpartum. Although the average individual body weights did not differ more than 10%, the total litter weight increased substantially from 5.4 g for one pup to 52.9 g for 10 pups (Falconer, 1947). Subtraction of birth weights (estimated at 1 g per pup) still indicated an enormous increase in total litter weight at 12 days by the larger litter. Greater weight gained by the larger litter was probably made possible by an increase in the supply of milk.

The rate of milk production in rats has been studied through various measures by different investigators. Some weighed the litter on a daily basis and corrected for metabolic losses (Brody and Nisbet, 1938), others weighed the stomach contents of the pups (Grosvenor and Turner, 1959), and still others weighed mammary tissue (Hanwell and Linzell, 1972). Several factors varied among experiments, including the duration of separation from the litter (from not stated to 10 hr), litter size (six to 12 pups), weight of the dam (260–303 g), and day of lactation (10–14). The average estimated milk yield ranged from 14.9–43.0 g/day within these reports. [For more details, see Hanwell and Linzell (1972).] The large variability in the average daily production of milk was likely due to the litter size and the dam's ability to produce and release milk, as well as the test conditions and methods of assessment. The results reinforce our understanding of lactation as a multifaceted flexible phenomenon. They also remind us that different methods reveal different aspects of the lactational process.

C. Litter Size Factors

If milk supply is flexible, why are pups from small litters often larger than pups of the same age from large litters? A number of factors may contribute to this frequent observation, including lighter birth weights of rat (Leon and Woodside, 1983) and mouse pups (Parkes, 1926) born into large litters, greater competition for nipples, and possibly a limited supply of milk, on which many investigators have focused (Heggeness *et al.*, 1961; Kumaresan *et al.*, 1967; Edwardson and Eayrs, 1967).

The size of a litter suckling the dam from the first day postpartum can have a substantial impact on weight gained by the litter as a whole. The reciprocal relationship between litter size and litter weight has been documented unambiguously in an experiment in which litter size was varied from one to 25 rat pups (Edwardson and Eayrs, 1967). When litter weights were determined 16 days after parturition, the average gain in weight per pup was reduced as a function of the original size of the litter. Conversely, the average gain in weight of the whole litter increased linearly until the unit reached 10–12 pups. Beyond parity, the average litter weight remained constant from 12 to 25 pups, but the average weight of the pups plummeted (see Fig. 1).

The total number of nipples sucked and presumably the amount of sensory information provided to the dam play a vital role in the magnitude of lactation (Edwardson and Eayrs, 1967). From experiments including complete denervation of selected nipples by dorsal root rhizotomy, investigators discovered that two newborn pups suckling only two innervated teats of their unanesthetized dam fared poorly (functional hyperparity because lactation was not well established). However, a repetition of the experiment starting at 5 days of age did not alter the growth of the pups (functional parity because lactation was well established).

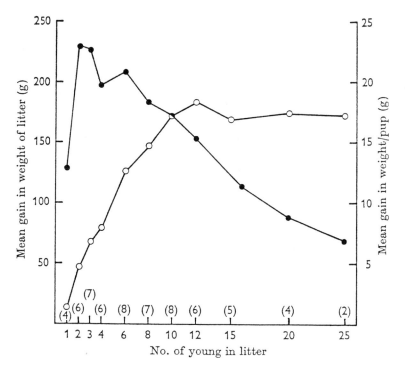

FIG. 1.   Relationship between the size of the litter and maternal milk yields as measured by the weight gain of the litter during the 16 days after parturition (○) and the mean weight gain of each pup (●). Numbers in parentheses refer to the numbers of litters at each level of treatment (Edwardson and Eayrs, 1967). Reproduced with permission from the *Journal of Endocrinology, Ltd.*

Furthermore, two newborn pups flourished when given access to all nipples of an intact unanesthetized dam (hypoparity) (Edwardson and Eayrs, 1967).

In an experiment designed to evaluate the effects of anesthesia on milk ejections and weight gained by pups, investigators found anesthetized dams to be refractory while stimulated by the suckling of one to six pups, but moderately responsive to the suckling of eight to 10 pups. In contrast, unanesthetized dams at the same phase of lactation provided an ample amount of milk to litters ranging from one to 12 pups (Drewett and Trew, 1978). Although the level of anesthesia was not well documented, the results from this set of experiments are consistent with the idea that rat dams must receive a certain critical amount of sensory input from nipple and teat stimulation to promote lactation and milk letdowns.

Since pups do not begin to shift nipples until approximately 10 days of age (Hall *et al.*, 1977; Drewett and Trew, 1978; Cramer *et al.*, 1980), and since nipple preference is not a typical behavior of rat pups, the experiments described above suggest that two pups randomly stimulating different nipples during separate bouts of suckling are able to provide the critical amount of sensory stimulation necessary and sufficient to initiate and sustain lactation in the rat. The threshold for milk letdown declines with the progression of lactation, as indicated by the fact that the sucking stimulus of one pup is sufficient to elicit milk letdowns in experienced lactating dams at day 10, but not at day 1.

Once underway, lactation progresses as a function of the number of nipples stimulated (Edwardson and Eayrs, 1967). This means that two pups stimulating more than two nipples in hypoparity will increase milk yield. Sucking different nipples increases the availability of the current milk supply to all participants. Twelve pups sucking all 12 of the dam's nipples will stimulate what appears to be the maximum production of milk before nipple-shifting begins. Any pups added beyond parity must compete with other pups for the milk supply and the opportunity to obtain it. Hyperparity increases the relative importance of several factors likely to influence lactation, including milk distribution within the main litter or sublitters, the frequency and duration of nursing behaviors, and maternal nutrition.

There appear to be two reasons that pups in hypoparity gain weight more quickly than pups in parity or hyperparity situations. First, due to the random selection of nipples, pups in hypoparity as early as day 1 are selecting different nipples during different suckling bouts, resulting in the stimulation of more nipples than there are pups. Thus, the lack of nipple preference is likely to increase milk yield and enhance the distribution of a relatively larger volume of milk produced per pup on a daily basis. Note, however, that pups from smaller litters do not receive the maximum amount of milk the dam is capable of producing (Edwardson and Eayrs, 1967), and litter growth, often attributed solely to milk yield, must include the pups' decision to ingest milk (Lorenz *et al.*,

1982) and their genetically inherent capacity for development, which cannot be exceeded by an overabundance of milk (Grosvenor and Turner, 1959).

Second, nipple-shifting within bouts, starting at about 10 days of age, is likely to maximize lactation because of the extensive repetitive stimulation of most, if not all, of the nipples. Moreover, frequent withdrawal of milk from the mammary glands is a strong stimulus for the production of milk (Bateman, 1957; Blaxter, 1961).

Regulatory mechanisms responsible for milk production and distribution develop postnatally. Although birth weight is inversely related to the number of fetuses, as stated above, the fetuses appear to exert little influence on the prenatal development of mammary glands in mice (Cole, 1933). The amount of milk produced by the mother, primarily dependent on pup demand, increases daily in proportion to the overall sucking stimulus and the amount of milk removed from the teats (Bateman, 1957; Blaxter, 1961).

Milk production increases in response to increases in the size of the litter (Kumaresan et al., 1967), but milk production is not in direct proportion to litter size in rats (Kumaresan et al., 1967) or mice (Bateman, 1957).

Growth rates, described as varying inversely with litter size in rats (Widdowson and McCance, 1960; Kumaresan et al., 1967) and mice (Parkes, 1926), can be remarkably stable in litters in which parity has not been exceeded, and in which pups of equal body weight on day 1 suckle one dam throughout the suckling phase. Under these controlled conditions, mean body weights of rat pups at 21 days of age were approximately the same, regardless of their being raised in litters of two, four, eight, or 12. However, pups raised in litters of 16 (four beyond parity) were significantly lighter (Wurtman and Miller, 1976).

It should not be surprising to find that the optimal balance between milk production and growth rate for the litter occurs when the number of pups in the litter approaches the number of nipples possessed by the mother (Edwardson and Eayrs, 1967). In extreme situations of one or 24 offspring per litter, rat (Edwardson and Eayrs, 1967; Russell, 1980) and gerbil pups (Elwood and Broom, 1978) fared poorly. However, some exceptions have been documented for gerbils (Elwood and Broom, 1978) and mice (Parkes, 1926; Falconer, 1947). For example, a single mouse pup raised by its natural mother gained weight more rapidly than pups in litters of two to 10 (Parkes, 1926). In addition, some dams from certain strains of mice accommodated litters from one to 15 without distorting the weight gain of the pups (Falconer, 1947).

These apparently contradictory results indicate that factors influencing the growth of the litter must include more than just litter size. Note that maternal behavior does not appear to be diminished when the dam attends to a small litter. In fact, the amount of time lactating dams spend with their pups is greater in smaller litters of rats (Grota, 1973), mice (Priestnall, 1972), and gerbils (Elwood and Broom, 1978).

D. SUBLITTERS

Lactating rodents gradually increase their total milk supply, depending on the number of pups suckling from the time of parturition. Larger natural litters that extend beyond parity present a different level of complexity for lactating rodents. Some rat dams attempt to nurse 13 or more pups at the same time. This tends to exclude the weakest, least aggressive, pups. Thus, hyperparity can result in runtiness. Other dams divide the original nest into two or more nests, permitting sublitters to be nursed at different times of the day (Galler and Turkewitz, 1975; Russell, 1980). Cannibalism also occurs in large litters, but the reasons are not entirely obvious (Parkes, 1926).

The sublitter strategy increases the likelihood of survival of all of the pups. In addition to the number of nests, the size of the litter, the age of the pups, the lactational status of the dam (Grota, 1973), and maternal experience (Rosenblatt, 1975) are some of the variables affecting maternal behaviors. However, little is known about the limits of the lactation process, or about the relevant cues responsible for educing various methods of maternal care within the hyperparity nursing situation.

E. "WET NURSE" PHENOMENON

The lactational response and nursing frequency in rodents are fine examples of a flexible efficient system that accommodates small or large litters. The "wet nurse" phenomenon, consistent with the flexibility of this system, emphasizes the importance of the sucking stimulus and the withdrawal of milk. The typical lactation period of 3–5 weeks in rats has been prolonged for long periods (Bruce, 1958; Nicoll and Meites, 1959), in some instances for as long as 12 months, by providing lactating dams with young foster pups (Nicoll and Meites, 1959).

The wet nurse phenomenon is also significant because it demonstrates the influence of young pups over the dam. Provided that the signals for weaning have not appeared, many dams are willing to continue nursing, apparently because the stimuli are compelling. During the decline of the nursing phase, changes in the mammary glands can be rapid if weaning is abrupt. For example, partial involution of all glands due to reduced sucking occurred within 2 days and was complete by 12 days in mice (Cole, 1933).

Reliable rates of growth and the flexibility of lactation indicate regulatory processes. One principal question regarding the process of regulation in the ontogeny of ingestive behavior is where the locus of control resides. Do individual pups control their intake, does the dam control the pups' intake, or is there an interaction within the dyad that determines the amount of milk consumed by each pup during a bout of suckling? This central issue is developed throughout this article.

F. Milk Availability and the "Ceiling Effect"

The ill-defined concept of the "ceiling effect"[2] occupies an unusual position in the assessment of factors affecting the ingestion, growth, and rate of development of suckling rodents.

A ceiling effect explanation has been used by several authors to attribute control of individual bouts of ingesting to the nursing dam (Heggeness *et al.*, 1961; Friedman, 1975; Drewett and Trew, 1978; Blass *et al.*, 1979; Henning, 1980; Lau and Henning, 1984, 1989). Although evidence abounds for the long-term adjustment of milk supply, there is no convincing evidence that milk supply is altered during individual bouts or that pups take the total volume of milk during each bout in the natural suckling situation. Thus, at this time, the ceiling effect explanation is merely a proposal.

The validity of the ceiling effect explanation, in reference to a mechanism used by the dam to control the intake of her pups, can be challenged on at least three levels.

First, as yet, no methods are available to measure the total immediate milk supply directly and unambiguously in rodents in the natural nursing situation. A sudden increase in the number of pups suckling the dam invariably results in less milk per pup (Bateman, 1957), but this artificial situation reveals nothing about the possibility of a ceiling effect operating during each bout within suckling/nursing symbiostasis.[3]

When provided with a series of unanesthetized milk-laden foster dams, deprived pups continued to ingest much more milk than pups supplied with recently suckled dams (Friedman, 1975). These results suggested that the litters' intakes were limited in some way by the first dam in the series. It raised the possibility that the mother controls the volume of milk distributed to the entire litter during each bout, but other factors must be considered regarding the litter both as a whole and as individual pups. The pups may have been satiated with the amount of milk taken from the first dam, approximately 7% of their body weight. Satiety,

---

[2]The phrase "ceiling effect" has been used to connote one or more of the following: (1) the lack of mother's receptivity to continue to nurse biological or foster pups; (2) the relative refractory state of the maternal neuroendocrine system, responsible for the synthesis and release of hormones stimulating galactopoiesis and galactokinesis; (3) the reduction in sensitivity of mammary tissue for the hormones of lactation; (4) the reduced volume of milk available for excretion; and (5) the reluctance of pups to ingest more milk due to optimal filling of the gut.

[3]The term "symbiostasis" (a conjugate of "symbiosis" and "homeostasis") is introduced to describe the harmonious balance that develops during the suckling phase between the physiology and behaviors of pups and the physiology, lactational status, and behaviors of the biological unanesthetized mother. It denotes the progressive adjustments in milk supply and maternal behaviors throughout the nursing phase, as well as a myriad of rapidly changing demands for milk, heat, and hygiene created by the litter. Although our understanding of symbiostasis is far from complete, data gathered through the use of lactating foster rats and anesthetized dams cannot be assumed as evidence of symbiostasis unless adequate time has been allowed for dyadic adjustments and appropriate comparisons have been made.

however, was not measured. Then, the pups were artificially aroused with the presentation of each new dam. Novel odors and gustatory stimuli may have temporarily interfered with the satiety state. This would permit the resumption of rhythmic sucking. Although presumably brief, the sucking behaviors apparently were sufficient to elicit milk letdowns from the relatively sensitive milk-engorged dams, and the litters ingested more milk.

Some important distinctions to be made here concern the amount of milk available from each dam and the level of analysis. In this regard, the dams' milk supply was not measured. Thus, the measure of milk intake by the pups is an indirect and possibly inaccurate assessment of the dams' milk supply, resulting in a circular argument which, by itself, will never resolve the issue. On a different level, this seminal experiment revealed that litters deprived for longer periods collectively ingested more milk from the series of dams. The experimental design limited the assessment of internal controls to the litter as a group. In contrast to group controls, assessment of individual controls has been demonstrated through other methods by preloading pups with different volumes of milk (Lorenz *et al.*, 1982) and by fasting some pups but not others (Jakubowski and Terkel, 1986) prior to the simultaneous suckling of an unanesthetized dam.

The failure of deprived pups to ingest more milk when placed with recently suckled foster dams (Friedman, 1975) was a convincing demonstration that procurement of milk by the litter as a whole can be quite limited following previous nursing engagements by the dams. There was either a reduction in the rate of synthesis of milk or a refractory period for oxytocin release, or a combination of these and other factors in this particular situation, that reduced the production and/or availability of milk. But are these factors normally operating to control ingestion by individual suckling pups in symbiostasis with the biological mother?

In separate experiments of a similar nature, pups deprived of milk (for 24 hr) ingested significantly more milk (155%) than nondeprived pups, regardless of whether the dams previously nursed underfed hungry pups or nondeprived pups (Jakubowski and Terkel, 1986) (See Table I).

Thus, in contrast to the earlier report by Friedman (1975), the internal state of the pups can be a more salient factor in determining milk intake for individuals than the lactational status of the dam. Obviously, the ceiling effect hypothesis must be tested under a variety of conditions in the natural suckling situation before we can determine its relative importance. It is a formidable challenge to test our ingenuity against the uncertainty created by experimental artifact.

G. SURFEITS AND DEFICITS IN IMMEDIATE MILK SUPPLY

The addition of pups to a litter that already established symbiostasis generally results in the inability of the dam to provide sufficient milk for the normal growth and development of biological or fostered pups (Bateman, 1957). This is consis-

TABLE I

Mean ± SEM Weight Gain of Hungry or Satiated Test Pups and Frequency of Milk
Ejections in Mother Rats That Had Previously Nursed Either Underfed Pups
(Experimental Rats) or Normally Fed Pups (Control Rats)[a]

Parameter	Experimental rats $(n = 11)$	Control rats $(n = 10)$	Significance[b]
Litter weight gain (g/4 hr)			
Hungry test pups	3.4 ± 0.4[c]	3.3 ± 0.3[d]	NS
Satiated test pups	2.2 ± 0.2[c]	2.2 ± 0.2[d]	NS
No. of milk ejections/hr			
Hungry test pups	9.8 ± 0.6[e]	14.3 ± 1.0[f]	$p < 0.01$
Satiated test pups	9.4 ± 0.6[e]	13.7 ± 0.8[f]	$p < 0.02$

[a]Tests were conducted between days 12 and 14 of lactation. Litters were removed at 1030 hr and
new sets of five pups, 6–10 days old, were introduced at 1100 hr. Each female was tested twice, once
with hungry pups and once with satiated pups. Weight gain of test pups was determined after they
were suckled for a net period of 4 hr, and frequency of milk ejections was determined over a net
period of 1 hr of suckling. (From Jakubowski and Terkel, 1986.) Reproduced with permission from
Williams & Wilkins. ©1986 The Endocrine Society.

[b]By Student's t test. NS, Not significant.

[c]$p < 0.01$.

[d]$p < 0.02$.

[e]NS (by paired t test).

[f]NS (by paired t test).

tent with the idea of a ceiling effect due to a limited supply of milk, but a
reasonable alternative explanation lies in the relative inertia of lactation.

Setting aside the argument of inertia for a moment, this facet of the ceiling
effect proposal has another obvious weakness, which forms a second challenge.
If the dam controls the intake of her suckling rats by the immediate volume of
milk available, then removal of some of the pups from a litter established in
symbiostasis should result in excessive filling of those that remain. This prediction has never been substantiated. In fact, the removal of mouse pups from a
litter did not result in engorgement of those that remained (Bateman, 1957).
Similarly, rat pups, from litters of 10 temporarily reduced in numbers ranging
from 10 to one, ingested an average of 1.6 g during a single nursing bout
(Drewett and Trew, 1978) (see Fig. 2). Although the total amount of milk that
each dam was capable of producing and delivering was never determined, pups
in litters of 10 ingested a total of 16 g on average (1.6 g per pup), while nipple-
shifting pups in litters consisting of one pup ingested a total of 1.6 g. The
equality of intake per pup across all litters (1.6 g), regardless of the wide range of
the total intake by litters of different sizes, could be explained if each pup
ingested to the point of satiety, then stopped. Thus, the ceiling effect argument

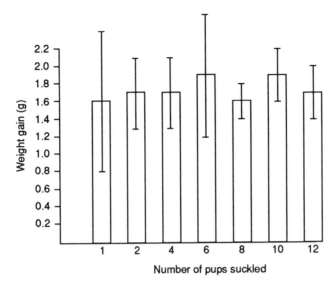

FIG. 2.   Weight gain (per pup) of pups suckled in litters of different sizes. Mean ± SD. $N = 8$ in each case (Drewett and Trew, 1978). Reproduced with permission from Animal Behaviour.

often breaks down when experimental emphasis is shifted away from the intake by the litter as a group to the intake by individuals.

The experiments just described included an artificial shift away from symbiostasis, and therefore are viewed with caution. Nonetheless, the results call into question the singular emphasis placed on the total immediate milk supply of the dam as the determining factor controlling ingestion by individual pups. In order for the ceiling effect argument to remain viable, investigators must succeed at their attempts to measure the milk supply (volume) while considering a variety of factors, including symbiostasis and the lactational and nutritional status of the dam, and the nutritional status, number, and age of pups willing to remove milk from their unanesthetized mother.

H. "LOST PUP" PROCEDURE

The "lost pup" procedure revealed that an 8-day-old deprived pup ingested more milk when returned with nondeprived littermates to a nondeprived foster dam (Lau and Henning, 1984). These results were interpreted by the experimenters to mean that the lost pup ingested more milk because the mother's immediate supply contained a reserve of milk. Although the data may be viewed as evidence against the ceiling effect hypothesis, additional experiments must be conducted to determine the extent of the milk supply and the limits for individuals as well as the litter as a group.

In the context of symbiostasis, the results of the lost pup experiment complement the results of preload experiments reported earlier (Houpt and Epstein, 1973; Drewett and Cordall, 1976; Lorenz *et al.*, 1982). The preload and lost pup experiments indicate the reliable reciprocal relationship between the amount of milk in the gut and the amount of milk the pup ingests in the immediate bout. Pups ingest less as the gut fills in the natural suckling situation (Lorenz *et al.*, 1982). However, neither experimental procedure revealed the limits of the dam's milk supply or the possibility of a milk reserve, or lack of one, as a controlling factor in the natural nursing situation in which littermates of similar nutritional status suckle simultaneously. Furthermore, the results described above do not preclude the possibility that nondeprived or preloaded littermates suckled differently than lost pups or sham-loaded pups. A reduction in sucking vigor by satiated pups is likely to reduce the amount of milk they extract from the dam. Conversely, an increase in sucking vigor by deprived and sham-loaded pups would maximize the amount of milk ingested when it is made available during letdowns. Therefore, the results of the preload and lost pup experiments in relation to the control of ingestion could be explained by the amount of milk within the pups, rather than by an undetermined amount of milk that may or may not have been available from the dam.

I. INVESTIGATOR-INDUCED MILK LETDOWNS

Several attempts have been made to determine the amount of milk immediately available to the pups by administering exogenous oxytocin to anesthetized dams (Grosvenor and Turner, 1957; Cramer and Blass, 1983, 1985; Lau and Henning, 1984). In one study, the supply of milk appeared to be greatest during the first hour of letdowns after deprivation when determined by these artificial methods (Lau and Henning, 1984). However, the validity of these procedures as representing natural suckling or nursing conditions has never been established (Grosvenor and Turner, 1957).

The measure of maternal milk volume becomes especially difficult when considering our limited of knowledge regarding the salient internal and external stimuli that may affect the production and release of milk. Furthermore, the ever-present uncertainty of experimenter artifact during procedures in which the dam is anesthetized raises serious questions of technical problems that challenge our ability to make precise measurements of the natural transfer of milk from the dam to her pups. It will be very difficult to incorporate the concept of a ceiling effect as part of an explanation of the dam's control over her pups until we learn more about the parameters controlling the production and distribution of milk in the unanesthetized biological mother.

Regardless of the methods used to determine the relative flow of milk from the mother, there is no evidence indicating that female rats can sense their supply or use this information to limit the amount of milk dispersed to individual pups or to the litter, or to count the number of letdowns.

J. MILK PRODUCTION AND DISTRIBUTION

The third challenge to the ceiling effect hypothesis is that many factors in disparity situations are unknown and consequently excluded when investigators draw conclusions or interpret reports by others. Aside from the obvious importance of malnutrition, the diminished opportunities for nipple attachment and sucking created by hyperparity may have contributed to certain developmental delays, such as eye-openings and the growth of fur, as described in one study (Galler and Turkewitz, 1975). The problem is now elaborated on in detail because alternative interpretations appear to be necessary at this time.

Weight gained by over- and undernourished preweanling rats was the subject of a report published in 1961 (Heggeness et al., 1961). Within this study, newborn rats were placed into one of six foster groups. For simplicity, only two groups are described here. The litters in group 1 were culled to six pups, which were then nursed consecutively by one of three milk-laden foster mothers, rotated every 8 hours. Group 6, at the opposite extreme, was enlarged at birth with foster pups to total 18 pups per litter. Each litter in group 6 was attended by a single lactating dam. The results revealed that pups at 21 days of age in group 1 weighed an average of 52.8 g, which totaled 316.8 g for the litter. Pups in group 6 weighed an average of 19.5 g. The litter weighed 351.0 g. The only obvious difference in body weights between the groups was in fat content. The developmental aspects of the pups appeared normal, except for the number of deaths in the large litters. Deaths occurred only in experimental group 6, which exceeded parity. Pups from replacement litters were added to this group when needed to keep the original number of pups at 18, but the replacements were not included in the data analyses. The investigators concluded that the differences between groups 1 and 6 and other intermediate groups were due to the supply of milk.

A supplementary interpretation is that pups in group 6 failed to thrive because they had fewer opportunities to suckle; thus, presumably, they spent less time suckling, and therefore ingested less milk. The severity of this situation is indicated by the mortality figures for group 6 (mean, 3.4 per litter versus zero for all other groups). Although milk supply was the intended focus of the study, the failure of the pups to grow rapidly in litters beyond parity suggests that a problem in distributing milk may have contributed to the outcome as much as or more than the actual supply (volume) of milk. In fact, the net weight gained by 18 pups in the overcrowded condition (243 g) indicates that a greater volume of milk was produced to sustain the runts than to fatten pups in smaller liters of 12 (170 g) and six (175 g), even after initial body weights of 6.3 g per pup were subtracted from each group.

In addition to the unequal distribution of milk between groups, the reduced amount of time spent suckling, not assessed in this or other reports of this nature, may have contributed to the poor development and attrition of subjects in large litters. Another complication in this report, as noted previously (Priestnall, 1983), is that the rotation of pups between pup-deprived and recently suckled dams versus nonrotated dams seriously confounded the variables of milk supply, maternal behaviors, nipple availability, and the demand for milk by the pups. Finally, there was no control for the addition of pups to group 6 as the experiment progressed.

Even if it becomes possible to measure the total available milk supply per bout, this alone will not prove that a ceiling effect mechanism is in operation, nor will it diminish the fact that rat pups have internal controls that regulate their ingestion of milk from the dam. Evidence supporting the existence of internal controls for ingestion in suckling pups is presented below and in Section V.

K. ADDITIONAL FACTORS AFFECTING MILK DISTRIBUTION

Other problems that deserve our consideration are whether the dam synthesizes milk immediately on demand during a nursing bout, as suggested (Lau and Henning, 1984), whether pups are able to alter the rate of milk letdowns, and whether the dam has any control over the oxytocin-induced contraction of myoepithelium surrounding mammary alveoli.

Neuroendocrine studies indicate that suckling increases plasma prolactin levels in lactating rats within 15–30 minutes of the start of a bout (Blake, 1974; Voogt and Carr, 1974; Jakubowski and Terkel, 1986). This is well within the limits of a typical nursing bout. In fact, prolactin levels in the plasma are typically elevated at the time milk letdowns begin, and the suckling by milk-deprived pups stimulates more prolactin release in the dam than the suckling by satiated pups (Jakubowski and Terkel, 1986). These correlations would suggest that some milk is synthesized for immediate consumption during each nursing bout. However, this is doubtful. Other reports indicate quite clearly that there is a delay of several hours between the release of prolactin and its galactopoietic effects (Grosvenor and Mena, 1973; Grosvenor et al., 1975). Therefore, adjustments in the production of milk according to pup demands are rapid but not instantaneous and not likely to affect consumption by pups during the immediate bout.

Even though the volume appears to be set during a given bout, the number and rate of letdowns can be altered by a variety of factors. For example, larger litters tend to increase the rate of letdowns by the dam (Russell, 1980), but the importance of the frequency is questionable when focusing on the amount of milk ingested by each pup. In a separate report (Jakubowski and Terkel, 1986), the number of letdowns actually decreased in dams nursing underfed pups, but the deprived pups ingested more milk than controls under these conditions, and again ingested more than nondeprived subjects in a situation in which milk letdowns were much more plentiful (see Table I). Thus, the relative number of letdowns appears to have little effect, within limits, on the amount of milk pups ingest.

Is it possible for the dam to modify the neuroendocrine reflex of milk letdown? The meager evidence available in this area does suggest that the dam has some control over the tonus of the duct system, which permits more or less milk to flow (Deis, 1968; Grosvenor et al., 1972). Auditory stimuli are capable of eliciting oxytocin release in rats (Ogle and Lockett, 1966). Exteroceptive stimuli, probably auditory, prior to a nursing bout enhanced the amount of milk released from the dam (Deis, 1968). Collectively, these results suggested that the response likely included the release of oxytocin before suckling began, but it also included another mechanism, because injection of the hormone alone prior to a suckling bout had little effect on milk taken from the dam by the litter (Deis, 1968). Thus, the dam may be able to influence muscle tone in the teats through neural pathways independent of the actions of oxytocin. The importance of this putative mechanism for the release of milk remains to be determined. More information on this topic is presented in Section IV.

The reports discussed above suggest that, once the dam commits herself to a nursing bout, she plays a permissive and supportive role in supplying the pups with milk. This assessment is not meant to diminish the role of the mother; rather, it reflects the current limited set of facts regarding maternal responses within the natural nursing situation. The immediate volume of milk made available by the dam during a bout of nursing must be the consequence of her physiological status and behaviors as well as the nutritional and developmental status and behaviors of the pups. A variety of maternal factors are relevant. Even the dam's diet is important. Lactating dams provided with a diluted or high-quality diet were able to defend their body weights, but the litters gained more weight suckling during the first 2 weeks when the dams were fed the high-quality diet (Leon and Woodside, 1983).

L. SUMMARY

Several points deserve reemphasis. The sucking stimulus and nutritional demands of the litter gradually but persistently direct the magnitude and duration of lactation, at least during the early and middle segments of the suckling phase.

It is not unusual for pups in smaller litters to gain weight more rapidly than pups in larger litters. This observation has often been attributed solely to the mother's milk supply, with little consideration of other important factors affecting pups, such as birth weight, access to nipples, and the duration of sucking.

Additional factors of maternal experience, age, and nutrition probably contribute to nursing strategies, and consequently to weight gain and management of the litter. The frequent observation of larger pups found in smaller litters cannot be explained entirely by a larger milk supply, and clearly does not argue against the controls of ingestion in individual pups.

Although milk supply (volume) and distribution may be factors affecting the litter as a whole throughout the suckling phase, their impact on intake by individual pups during each bout is a separable process deserving closer scrutiny. Suckling pups in hypoparity symbiostasis typically gain weight more rapidly than pups in a parity or hyperparity situation. This suggests that, in the long term, litters in hypoparity stimulate more nipples per pup and consequently have greater access to more milk. However, in the short term, symbiostatic litters placed temporarily in hypoparity situations did not overingest. This emphasizes the function of internal controls of ingestion by the pups in the presence of a putative surplus of milk. Therefore, interpretations of the control of milk ingestion in suckling rats emphasizing the concept of milk supply as an immediate mechanism available to the dam are inappropriate and possibly misleading, especially in reports in which parity or the long-term nature of the lactational response is ignored.

Milk supply and its availability may prove to be important factors regarding the growth of the litter as a group during the nursing phase, but there is no convincing evidence at this time that the dam controls the immediate intake of each pup by the amount of milk she provides.

Several investigators have used foster mothers to assess the importance of milk volume and availability, but methods including the rapid substitution of foster mothers or foster litters may have inherent confounding variables that preclude the direct application of their results to events in the natural situation in which symbiostasis has been established.

Currently, there is no evidence that the dam can selectively alter the distribution of milk flowing from individual teats, nor is there evidence that rat pups prefer to suckle a particular teat. The demonstration of a limited supply of milk for the litter during a given bout, if possible within the natural nursing situation, still would not explain or supersede the control of intake displayed by the individual pup. Within the normal constraints imposed by a mother, each pup appears to take more or less milk when it is provided during separate milk letdowns.

A variety of factors affect milk yield and the growth rate of the entire litter, including prolactin plasma levels of the lactating dam during nursing, possibly neural control of milk released from the mammary glands, and the diet of the mother. The difficult task is to assess the relative importance of each factor and factor interactions determining the rate of growth and development of each individual.

Collectively, at this time, the reports of natural suckling in rodents suggest that after the dam agrees to nurse, she plays a permissive and supportive role in supplying the pups with milk. This assessment may be revised after procedures have been perfected to examine the dam's behaviors and her production and distribution of milk within the natural nursing situation. Experimental results thus far also support the thesis that individual mouse and rat pups control their intake of milk in the natural suckling situation, as well as suggesting some limits in the provision of milk. Our understanding of the dominating factors controlling the amount of milk ingested by a pup in any bout of suckling is still incomplete. Future investigation of these factors will provide a formidable challenge for developmental psychobiologists and physiologists.

III. Nipple Attachment

A. INNATE MOTIVATED RESPONSE

Rooting, nipple attachment, and ingestion of milk are innate behaviors that typify newborn mammals. The common anatomical structures involved and the close temporal relationships linking this sequence of behaviors have led to some erroneous conclusions regarding their interactions in rat pups. While nipple attachment behavior is a prerequisite for the ingestion of milk during suckling, current evidence suggests that the controls of nipple attachment and ingestion operate independently in young pups. The motivational aspects of nipple attachment are assessed in this section in reference to the subsequent but separate process of ingestion.

Preparatory behaviors to the cyclic nursing/suckling process start when the rat dam approaches her litter. After making contact with the pups, grooming them and herself, the dam is encouraged to initiate the nursing posture when her ventral surface is stimulated by the pups (Stern and Johnson, 1989). The pups, aroused by the presence of the dam, use olfactory and tactile cues to locate and attach to a nipple (Hofer *et al.,* 1976; Blass *et al.,* 1979; Pedersen and Blass, 1982; MacFarlane *et al.,* 1983). They mouth and moisten the nipple with saliva, then begin to suck, creating a sustained vacuum seal (Epstein *et al.,* 1970). Once their lips are sealed around a nipple, neonatal pups remain attached for long periods, but ingestion occurs intermittently. Prolonged bouts of attachment during the initial postnatal period may involve as much as 75–100% of the time the rat dam spends with her litter (Grota and Ader, 1969), 70% for the mouse dam (Bateman, 1957). Gerbil pups remain attached to the dam as much as 75% of the time during the first 8 days (Elwood and Broom, 1978).

The motivated process of nipple attachment has been revealed by a number of recent experiments. Investigators demonstrated that the lack of contact with the mother, apparently tactile contact with her fur, enhanced rooting behaviors in pups (Terry, 1988; Hall, 1990). Moreover, rooting behaviors, elicited by tactile stimuli from furry objects, increased in the absence of the goal (nipple), and decreased gradually with prolonged exposure to the furry stimulus, or abruptly in the presence of a nipple (Terry, 1988; Hall, 1990).

Nipple-grasping behaviors, like rooting behaviors in young pups, are not affected by the deprivation of nutrients and maternal care prior to day 10 (Hall *et al.*, 1977) (see Fig. 3), by the deprivation of nutrients alone (Henning *et al.*, 1979), or by gastrointestinal preloads of milk (Lorenz *et al.*, 1982). However, the time spent attached to a nipple and sucking is monitored in some manner. Extended periods of sucking (20–24 hr) in the absence of ingesting milk (nonlactating dam) have been shown to reliably increase the latency to attach to a nipple at 11–13 days of age (Brake *et al.*, 1979, 1982).

Nipple-grasping and sucking also have profound effects on the internal state of young pups. They rapidly shift from the awake state during rooting and searching

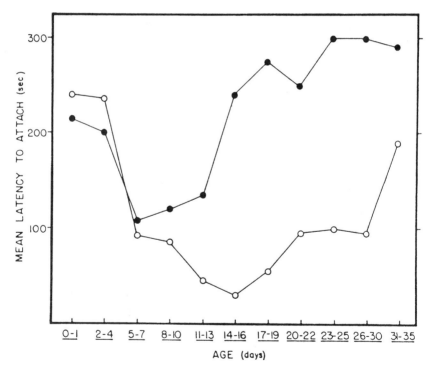

FIG. 3. Mean latency to attach to the nonlactating teats of anesthetized rat dams by their 22-hr-deprived (○) and nondeprived (●) young of various ages (Hall *et al.*, 1977). Reproduced with permission from the American Psychological Association.

behaviors to slow-wave sleep within seconds of attaching to a nipple (Shair *et al.*, 1984; Lorenz, 1986a). These data suggest an orderly motivated sequence that can be described in conventional terms. The deprivation state is characterized by pups' actively searching for a nipple (the goal) when exposed to furry stimuli. The speed with which pups attach to a nipple is determined in part by the amount of time they have recently spent in contact with the fur and the nipple. Finally, the satiety state for this motivated process is reflected by an abrupt change in internal state from arousal to slow-wave sleep.

Two remarkable features must be emphasized here. First, consummation of the goal (nipple attachment and sucking) and a prolonged satiety state (slow-wave sleep) are relatively weak in deterring this motivated process, because young pups readily attach under most conditions and remain attached to the dam for relatively long periods. Second, the presence or absence of milk in the gut are not among the many factors influencing nipple searching and attaching behaviors. Nipple attachment and consumption of milk appear to be governed by separate systems of controls in pups younger than 10 days. More information on this issue is given below.

Nipple attachment provides infant rodents with more than a conduit for milk. It is the basis of a life-sustaining heat-exchange process. The transfer of heat from the dam's ventral surface to poikilothermic pups is optimal during suckling contact for most infant rodents and mammals in general. Furthermore, nipple attachment is vital for rapid transportation in times of emergency for many cricetid rodents (King, 1963). This multiplicity of function forces us to reconsider the prominent notion that nipple attachment occurs solely for the purpose of ingestion.

B. Latency to Attach as a Measure of Hunger

The difficulty involved in assessing ingestion by suckling rats prompted investigators to establish different, independent, methods to measure hunger. The latency to attach to a nipple of an anesthetized dam was the first method to be used (Drewett *et al.*, 1974). In the original study, pups 8–10 days old were either deprived of milk and maternal care for 16 hr or left in the care of a lactating foster dam. At test time, each pup was held against a recently sucked nipple of the anesthetized natural mother. Pups deprived of milk and maternal care attached to a nipple much more quickly than pups that had been cared for and presumably nursed by the lactating foster dam. During the second experiment, deprived pups were fed artificially by suckling an anesthetized dam infused with oxytocin. The pups attached less quickly (mean, 10.8 sec) than deprived control subjects (mean, 6.5 sec) that sucked nipples for the same amount of time but were not fed. The differences among groups were small in the second experiment, in which the recency of sucking experience was controlled. Nonetheless, the results of the new procedure convinced the investigators that hunger could be measured by the speed with which rat pups grasp and suck nipples of the anesthetized dam.

Different types of experiments that followed produced results consistent with the original hypothesis, confirming the reliability of the latency to attach under certain conditions (Drewett and Cordall, 1976; Henning et al., 1979). Other investigators using this technique demonstrated that newborn rats were relatively slow to attach to an anesthetized dam, but the pups became more adept toward the end of their first day, independent of milk acquisition (Dollinger et al., 1978). The pups may have been reinforced with olfactory or tactile stimuli, because, by 12 hr of age, pups attached more quickly to anesthetized foster dams that had been lactating for 12 hr than to dams whose lactational status differed (Holloway et al., 1978). Regardless of the sensorimotor issue described here, warmed pups, deprived of milk and maternal care for long periods (22 hr) attached to an anesthetized dam more quickly than nondeprived pups as early as day 1 (Dollinger et al., 1980). Thus, the reliability of the phenomenon has been reaffirmed many times, but the validity of latency to attach as a measure of hunger has never been confirmed in suckling rats younger than 10 days.

There are criticisms of the methods described, some of which have been addressed, while others have not. One initial problem was the failure of the method to dissociate the primary independent variable, deprivation of milk, from other variables, such as deprivation of sucking and maternal care as well as heat loss by pups in most of the studies that followed the original report. Did the deprived pups attach more quickly because of their interest in sucking or ingesting, or in something else?

Subsequent experiments helped to clarify and resolve the issue. Investigators fasted 10-day-old pups 16 hr with nipple-ligated lactating foster mothers (Henning et al., 1979; Gisel and Henning, 1980). Assuming that the adult females administered typical maternal care under these conditions, the pups were deprived only of milk. Their latencies to attach to an anesthetized dam were similar to those of pups that were deprived of milk and maternal care. In neither of the deprived conditions did pups attach more or less quickly than recently fed pups at day 10.

Additional results were gathered in an experiment designed to test the effects of ambient temperature. Pups deprived of milk and maternal care in isolation at 34°C attached with latencies similar to those of pups placed with the ligated dam, but cooler deprived pups attached more quickly (Henning et al., 1979). Thus, body temperature is a crucial factor in this situation, as others have demonstrated in similar situations (Johanson and Hall, 1980). The failure of milk deprivation to influence nipple attachment latency corroborates a previous report in which pups were deprived of milk and maternal care in a warm environment (Hall et al., 1977) (see Fig. 3), but is contrary to the original report (Drewett et al., 1974).

To summarize, with the exception of the original report by Drewett et al.

(1974), other investigators controlling the same variables regarding maternal presence have been unable to demonstrate that deprivation of milk alone prior to 10 days postpartum alters the speed with which rat pups attached to a nipple. Therefore, latency to attach to a nipple as described thus far is not an appropriate measure of hunger for pups younger than 10 days. Moreover, rooting and nipple attachment behaviors appear to be a motivated process independent of milk acquisition (Hall *et al.*, 1977; Dollinger *et al.*, 1978; Terry, 1988).

Nonetheless, the concept of latency to attach to a nipple is still deeply entrenched. Instead of eliminating the measure as an index of hunger in young pups, some claimed that because there were no differences in the latencies to attach, there is no hunger in rat pups prior to 10 days of age, but there is satiety because pups in this age range respond to filling of the gut (Henning *et al.*, 1979).

The existence of a satiety system without a hunger system is a provocative but perplexing idea. It raises a familiar semantic issue regarding the ethereal constructs of "hunger" and "satiety." The statement also reminds us of a fundamental problem in the psychobiology of motivation. The problem of a hunger/satiety system cannot be resolved solely by facts indicating the pups' willingness to ingest more or less milk. Although pups as early as day 1 adjusted their intake of milk in proportion to the amount of milk present in the gut (Lorenz *et al.*, 1982), we are unable to state with any certainty that the motivation to ingest is controlled through a satiety system operating alone, a hunger system that waxes and wanes, or a combination of both. Reification of these basic terms, essential for progress in the general area of feeding behavior, will continue as we collect physiological, biochemical, anatomical, and behavioral facts that direct a consensus of the definitions of "hunger" and "satiety."

At approximately 17 days of age, latency for pups to attach to an anesthetized dam is affected by the deprivation of milk (Henning *et al.*, 1979). The degree of hunger has not yet been quantified by varying the deprivation period, but the more mature experienced pups associate the nipple of an anesthetized dam with their primary source of nutrition by 2 weeks of age (Kenny *et al.*, 1979).

There have been only a few attempts to evaluate the latency-to-attach measure in the natural suckling situation. Rat pups at 1, 10, and 20 days of age deprived of milk and maternal care for 9 hr displayed reliable age-related attachment latencies to the unanesthetized biological mother (Lorenz *et al.*, 1982) (see Fig. 4).

Nipple attachment latencies were not altered by small (2% of body weight) or moderate (4% of body weight) preloads of an artificial bitch's milk, but ingestion of milk from the mother was suppressed at all ages, especially by volumes of 4% or larger (Fig. 4). Therefore, processes controlling nipple attachment and those controlling ingestion of milk are separable, especially during the first 10 days, when the latency to attach is inappropriate as a measure of hunger. An additional

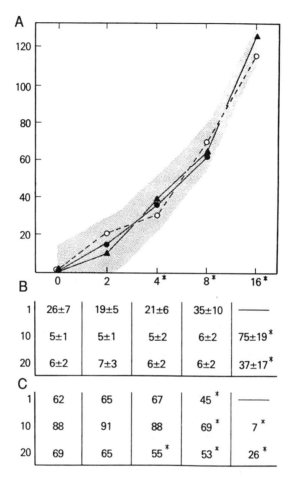

FIG. 4. (A) Percentage of suppression of weight gain, (B) latency to attach (minutes ± SE), and (C) percentage of incidence of attachment for pups at 1 (●), 10 (○), and 20 (▲) days during a 2-hr suckling bout. Preloads of an artificial milk ranging up to 16% of body weight are represented in columns. The stippled area indicates the standard error of the nearest mean. ∗, Significantly different from 0% preload data ($p < 0.05$) (Lorenz *et al.*, 1982). Reproduced with permission from John Wiley & Sons, Inc.

fact in support of this idea is that acute subdiaphragmatic vagotomy substantially increased ingestion of mother's milk during the first bout after surgery without affecting the latency to attach to a nipple (Lorenz, 1983) (see Fig. 5). Gut loads at 8% and 16% of body weight (Lorenz *et al.*, 1982) and certain manipulations of the viscera, such as pyloric ligation plus preloading, increased the latency with which pups attached to a nipple (Lorenz, 1983) (see Fig. 5).

Collectively, these results indicate that the controls for nipple attachment and

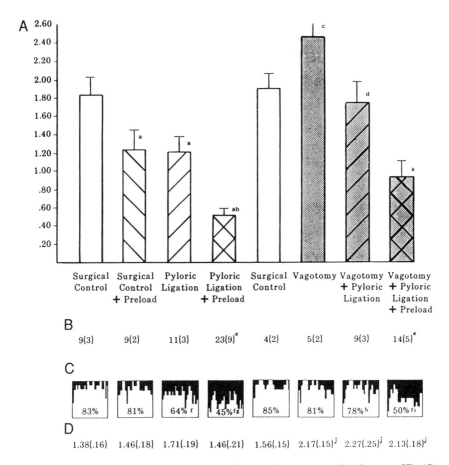

FIG. 5. (A) Mean weight gain (grams ± SE), (B) mean latency to attach (minutes ± SE), (C) incidence of attachment, and (D) mean weight of gastric contents (grams ± SE) are displayed according to each visceral manipulation. The incidence of attachment equals the number of pups attached during each 5-min interval of the 2-hr suckling period. The open bars indicate attachment by one to eight pups; the solid bars represent detachment. Shown are the percentages of pups attached during the 24 observations. a, Compared with surgical control, $p < 0.05$; b, compared with pyloric ligation, $p < 0.05$; c, compared with surgical control, $p < 0.05$; d, compared with vagotomy, $p < 0.05$; e, compared with surgical control, $p < 0.01$; f, compared with surgical control, $p < 0.05$; g, compared with pyloric ligation, $p < 0.01$; h, compared with pyloric ligation, $p < 0.01$; i, compared with vagotomy plus pyloric ligation, $p < 0.01$; j, compared with surgical control, $p < 0.01$. $N = 8$ pups per group (Lorenz, 1983). Reproduced with permission from John Wiley & Sons, Inc.

ingestion are separable but not mutually exclusive in the natural suckling situation. Under certain circumstances, including the extreme conditions described above, both behaviors were affected prior to day 10. Large gut loads elicited a relatively nonspecific suppression of behaviors in the suckling rat. The latency to attach to a nipple in the natural suckling situation following deprivation of milk, without depriving pups of maternal care, has not been investigated.

In summary to this point, the latency for pups to attach to a nipple of an anesthetized dam is a reliable phenomenon under several conditions. However, the experiments conducted to elaborate and refine latency to attach as a measure of hunger in the last decade revealed that olfactory, temperature, and chronological variables together with recentness of the suckling experience are the most salient factors affecting the process. Hunger, when not confounded by other variables, does not appear to influence the speed with which rat pups attach to an anesthetized dam during the first 10 days. More experiments are required to assess the latency-to-attach measure using the unanesthetized natural dam.

The idea that nipple attachment is inextricably linked to the motivated process of ingestion has been fostered unwittingly by methods involving the use of tongue cannulas and anesthetized dams. The methods include surgically equipping pups with a plastic tongue cannula that delivers small amounts of milk to the posterior region of the mouth. Pups are fed while sucking a nipple of an anesthetized dam. The level of anesthesia is sufficient to block her milk letdowns. Exogenous milk delivered through the cannula in this manner causes involuntary reflexive swallowing of each infusion (Hall and Rosenblatt, 1977). Young pups at 5 days of age tested in this way ingested every infusion of milk to the point of gross abdominal distension and respiratory distress before relinquishing their hold on the nipple. Pups that detached were picked up by the investigators and reintroduced to the nipple. Most of the pups at 5 days of age reattached. The tenacity to remain attached and the will to reattach to a nipple were interpreted by the investigators as a sign that the pups were willing to ingest more milk, and the infusions continued.

Finally, the failure of grossly engorged pups to reattach to the dam was interpreted as a lack of direct and specific control of suckling in young pups (Hall and Rosenblatt, 1977). Thus, the criterion used in an attempt to reveal the existence of direct internal controls of ingestion was whether or not the pups were willing to attach and remain attached to the dam. Milk infusions, eliciting reflexive swallowing, continued as long as the pups agreed to attach to a nipple. Pups at day 15 and older rejected the nipple and refused to reattach before reflexively ingesting abnormally large amounts of milk. Therefore, according to the operational definition of suckling created by Hall and Rosenblatt (1977), including nipple attachment and reflexive swallowing, young pups (5 days and some at 10 days) had no control of ingestion, whereas older pups (15 days and older) demonstrated control by refusing to attach to a nipple.

The method and results of this experiment have been very instructive; the controversy resides in their interpretation. The data indicated that, under certain conditions, pups at 5 days of age would rather swallow milk reflexively to the point of almost drowning than detach from the nipple. This is the most severe and best experimental test of the tenacity of nipple attachment behavior in young rat pups reported thus far. It indicates, without question, the priority of nipple attachment behavior in young pups even under a life-threatening situation. Because pups do not ordinarily drown while ingesting milk in the natural suckling situation, we are led by this compelling demonstration to conclude either that pups have no control over ingestion at this age, and they are saved from drowning because the dam never supplies them with such a large amount of milk, as the authors proposed, or that the results were due primarily to the unusual methods used.

The Hall and Rosenblatt (1977) experiments raised two questions that must be addressed. First, to what extent do the anesthetized dam preparation and the posterior tongue cannula mimic the natural suckling paradigm? Judging by the fact that these results do not resemble information obtained from natural suckling, one is forced to view the reflexive ingestion data generated by these methods as highly instructive artifacts, or to place strong emphasis on the milk supply hypothesis, which lacks empirical support. The mere fact that swallowing proceeded under these conditions is not sufficient evidence that natural events of suckling were being investigated, nor do the methods justify a shift away from the natural suckling paradigm. Nevertheless, the technique has been used to assess suckling by other investigators (Williams and Blass, 1987).

Second, the results of Hall and Rosenblatt (1977) raised the question: To what extent are the controls of nipple attachment and ingestive behavior the same in neonatal pups? These investigators proceeded under the assumption that the controls of nipple attachment are combined with the controls regulating the ingestion of milk. This inevitably led them to an indefensible conclusion: Rat pups have no direct control over ingestion of milk while suckling the dam during the first 2 weeks of life (Hall and Rosenblatt, 1977). It is indefensible in principle because their negative results were used to induce a general conclusion.

This interpretation also fails to explain the fact that suckling pups younger than 10 days suppressed their intake of milk following small and moderate volumes of milk (2–4% of body weight) preloaded into the upper gastrointestinal tract, without altering nipple attachment behaviors (Lorenz et al., 1982). Unusually large preload volumes of milk at 8–16% of body weight resulted in a profound suppression of ingestion as well as a marked reduction in nipple attachment behavior (Lorenz et al., 1982). Thus, the reduction of milk intake that occurred without disrupting other behaviors suggests the existence of a specific mechanism(s) capable of altering the motivation to ingest. Furthermore, an obviously nonspecific suppression effect was demonstrated in the same experiment by increasing the stimulus (gut load) to an exaggerated level not typically experienced. This resulted in the state of nimiety: discomfort as a result of overstimulating a satiety mechanism (Kulkosky, 1985).

The laudable attempt by Hall and Rosenblatt (1977) to isolate and investigate the pup's contribution to milk intake by neutralizing the dam resulted in a distorted representation of the pup's behavior by the very fact that the dam no longer provided milk in her typical manner. This report, however, did present us with valuable information about nipple attachment, as well as insights into technological limitations of our ability to explore suckling. The willingness of pups to voluntarily ingest mother's milk while attached to an unanesthetized dam remains the optimal situation for the exploration of suckling ingestive behaviors. Alternative methods must be validated by successfully challenging the utility of the natural suckling/nursing paradigm.

A more recent interpretation is that milk withdrawal is controlled by the young pup, but the control is achieved indirectly during suckling by changes in the sleep–wake state (Hall, 1990). This interpretation accommodates a greater number of reports. The emphasis is shifted away from whether or not the pups have control of their intake, and redirected toward the issue of direct versus indirect mechanisms influencing milk intake from the mother.

Eventually, the two motivated systems of nipple attachment and ingestion merge briefly during the second week of life. The latency to attach to a nipple is affected at this time by the nutritional status of the pup. Nipple attachment may still occur for reasons other than ingestion of milk, but the pups clearly associate the nipple with a source of nutrition at this time and thereafter.

C. INCIDENCE OF ATTACHMENT AS A MEASURE OF HUNGER

The second alternative method for assessment of hunger in rat pups is the numeration of pups attached to nipples at various times during a test period. Investigators reported that milk deprivation increased the number of pups sucking during the first 30 min of a test (Drewett and Cordall, 1976).

Evidence gathered in the natural suckling situation tends to support the idea that the incidence of attachment reflects deprivation of milk, but the sensitivity of the method is not optimal, and crucial experiments have not been performed. In one report, rat pups at 1, 10, and 20 days of age deprived of milk and maternal care for 9 hr were preloaded and returned to the dam to suckle. The incidence of attachment was recorded very 5 min during a 2-hr bout of suckling (Lorenz et al., 1982). As shown in Fig. 4, the results revealed the incidence-of-attachment measure to be as sensitive at day 1 and more sensitive at days 10 and 20 than the latency to attach. The incidence of attachment decreased as a function of the volume of milk filling the upper gastrointestinal tract. Pups spent less time attached as the volume of milk in the gut increased beyond 4% of the pup's body weight. At day 20, even the 4% load decreased the incidence of attachment. This was probably related to the fact that older pups recognize the nipple as a source of nutrients. Thus, the incidence of attachment is more sensitive as a predictor of ingestion than the latency to attach in the natural suckling situation, but neither measure of attachment is as sensitive as the volume of milk in the upper gastrointestinal tract for predicting the amount of milk to be ingested by rat pups. Furthermore, the incidence measure, like the latency-to-attach measure, is inappropriate as an index of hunger for pups under 10 days of age, because they typically remain attached to the dam for long periods between bouts of ingesting milk. The incidence of attachment in the natural suckling situation following deprivation of milk alone has not been investigated.

D. SUMMARY

Nipple attachment, an innate behavior in young pups, is guided by appropriate stimuli. Evidence suggests that neonatal nipple attachment is motivated in the traditional sense of having appetitive, consumptive, and satiety phases, but observations of persistent nipple attachment suggest that the process cannot be equated with adult motivated behaviors, which are deferred during the satiety state. Although nipple attachment is controlled initially by specific stimuli, it is likely susceptible to secondary reinforcement as the animal develops and is closely linked to the motivated process of ingestion by 2 weeks of age.

Dissociation of prerequisite attachment behaviors from the independent motivated process of ingestion in young suckling rats has been an arduous task. Attempts to establish valid alternative measures of hunger by recording nipple attachment parameters were thoughtful and creative, but they failed because nipple attachment and ingestion are consecutive processes, rather than integral components of a single appetitive system prior to 10 days of age in the rat pup. In the neonatal pup, nipple attachment is affected by a number of variables, but deprivation of milk does not appear to be one of them. Nipple attachment parameters can be used to identify the urge for milk beyond the first 2 weeks, but these measures have never been proven to be more sensitive than the amount of milk the individual pup is willing to ingest.

The difficulty in relinquishing the idea that nipple attachment must reflect hunger if hunger exists in neonatal rats stems, in part, from a misunderstanding of the importance of the natural suckling situation, from ignoring multiple purposes of the innate process of nipple attachment, and by assuming that appetitive behaviors leading to ingestion in suckling infants must resemble appetitive behaviors in hungry adult rats.

Suckling is the main event for young rats as well as other infant mammals. The chronological development of nipple attachment and ingestion are natural processes extending from immature anatomical, physiological, and behavioral systems. As complexity emerges, systems diverge and converge in the relative phases of growth. The present challenge is, first, to identify the constraints and controls of suckling as a uniquely mammalian characteristic, then to explore the dominant processes affecting behaviors during transitions into adolescence and adulthood as they occur in the rapidly developing rodent.

IV. Stimulation of the Mammary Gland

A. SUCKING, PADDLING, AND PINCHING

Sucking behaviors typically commence after a pup attaches to a nipple. Investigators have categorized three types of sucking patterns by recording digastric muscle potentials from the jaws of pups sucking nipples of anesthetized dams (Brake *et al.*, 1979). The first type included rhythmic negative pressure waves. Each wave, lasting approximately 3 sec, occurred repetitively (rhythmic run), depending on the status of the pups. A second type of sucking included a brief irregular series of negative pressure waves (bursts), each lasting about 0.5 sec and repeated in series lasting only 2–3 sec. These were often accompanied by teat-paddling behaviors with the forepaws, described as "treadles" (Brake *et al.*, 1979). Treadles characterize the third type of suckling. However, there is some question about whether the sucking performed during treadling movements is substantially different from the burst type of sucking (for more information, see the article by Shair and Hofer in this volume). Sucking behaviors were also labeled as nutritive or nonnutritive, depending on the presence or absence of milk in the mouth (Wolff, 1968; Brake *et al.*, 1979).

Rhythmic run sucking increased as a function of maternal deprivation. Specifically, pups deprived of the dam for 20–24 hr displayed substantial increases in rhythmic run sucking, in treadling behaviors, and in the intensity of electromyographic (EMG) recordings when compared with pups deprived for 2–6 hr at 3–5 days of age (Brake and Hofer, 1980) and at 11–13 days of age (Brake *et al.*, 1979). Furthermore, nonnutritive rhythmic sucking was increased specifically by deprivation of oral stimulation and decreased consequently as pups sucked without milk reward (Brake *et al.*, 1979). Nutritive rhythmic sucking was increased by deprivation of nutrients and decreased substantially by filling the gut with milk (Brake *et al.*, 1982). Specific alteration of the vigor of nutritive sucking according to nutritional status is one criterion indicating a motivated response. It is important to note that both types of rhythmic sucking diminished during a bout of ingestion in which oral stimulation and gastric filling occurred simultaneously. Therefore, the type of sucking that pups engage in at any moment is determined by complex interaction among oral factors, gut factors, and internal state (Brake *et al.*, 1982).

The precise origin and function of bursts of sucking are unknown. This atypical type of sucking is not affected by deprivation and repletion conditions (Brake *et al.*, 1982). It may be generated by a separate independent brain stem mechanism responsible for arousing the pup. A burst of sucking followed by paddling behaviors may reinstate nonnutritive sucking for a variable period, depending on the status of the pup. Bursts of sucking may also represent ingestion of small amounts of milk forced from the mammary gland as the result of low levels of oxytocin stimulating weak contractions of the myoepithelium (Grosvenor and Mena, 1982). Regardless of the specific origin of either type of sucking, stimulation of the sensitive receptors surrounding the nipple during a series of bursts and nonnutritive rhythmic sucking by the litter ultimately elevate afferent sensations beyond a threshold culminating in milk letdowns.

Nipple attachment in rats, like other mammals, including humans, is sufficient but not necessary for sucking to occur. EMG recordings of jaw muscle activity indicate that pups occasionally engage in sucking-like activity when away from the dam (Brake *et al.,* 1979). This may serve to perpetuate the response. The robust phenomenon of suckling is innate, but it must be practiced to a certain extent or the behavior is lost (Stoloff *et al.,* 1980). Although a hallmark of mammalian behavior, suckling is not essential for the survival of rats after the first day. Pups provided with milk through intragastric infusions appeared to develop normally (Hall, 1975).

Sucking constitutes only part of the stimulus directed toward the mammary gland during suckling. Rat pups, as well as most other infant rodents, knead or rhythmically paddle the teat as they suckle between letdowns. This gentle treadling with open paws is replaced by steady pressure from extended forelimbs during the initial part of the milk letdown. As the letdown begins to wane, older pups often treadle vigorously, then clench their forepaws in a sustained pinching grip with claws turned into the dam's ventral surface, usually a teat (personal observation of pups at day 20).

Treadling and pinching stimulate contraction of the myoepithelium only within the teat directly manipulated (Grosvenor, 1965). Other glands are affected, but by a reflex process. For example, mechanical stimulation of two thoracic mammary glands initially inhibited intramammary pressure in abdominal glands, apparently through a spinal sympathetic reflex mechanism that restricted blood flow to the glands. Then, within approximately 10 min, pressure increased in the abdominal glands for a prolonged period (Grosvenor and Mena, 1979). Although mechanical stimulation prepares the teats for milk letdowns, and sensory information from mammary glands appears to enhance the release of oxytocin (Lincoln and Wakerley, 1975), vigorous suckling by pups results in the withdrawal of negligible amounts of milk between letdowns. The letdown reflex is crucial for the transfer of most of the milk in rodents, because the dam lacks large storage cisterns necessary for a separate phase of milk release found in other mammals, such as ungulates (Zaks, 1962).

Overall, the present data suggest that pups receive milk during letdowns because stimulation of the teat causes local as well as central effects. Stimulation of the teat causes contraction of the local myoepithelium as well as oxytocin release, then the partially contracted myoepithelium constricts even more when oxytocin reaches the site. Gradually, impedance to the flow of blood is reduced throughout all mammary tissue. This physiological scenario remains to be proved under natural suckling and nursing conditions. Nonetheless, the suckling sequence, including sucking, treadling, and pinching, is a complex stimulus having central as well as local effects on the dam, culminating in the transfer of milk to the pups.

B. SUCKING COMMUNICATION

The nonnutritive rhythmic type of sucking by pups may be of primary importance in communicating their willingness to ingest milk. The sucking code has not been deciphered at this time, but afferent stimulation of the mammary nerve in the lactating rat, using 1-msec pulses, 10–20 per second at 5–30 V, reliably elicited a rise in intramammary pressure similar to an intravenous infusion of oxytocin (Mena *et al.*, 1978). Furthermore, the intramammary pressure responses, presumably oxytocin-induced contractions, increased with either increased frequency or voltage of electrical stimuli. This is consistent with the observation that temporal and spatial summation of the collective sucking stimulus appears to determine the amount of oxytocin released from the pituitary gland (Grosvenor and Mena, 1982). Similarly, prolactin is released from the pituitary gland in proportion to the intensity of the sucking stimulus (Grosvenor and Mena, 1971).

The number of pups sucking does not change during oxytocin release from the pituitary gland of anesthetized dams (Wakerley and Drewett, 1975). This demonstration led to the broad premature conclusions that milk letdowns were not elicited by changes in the behaviors of the pups, and that the litter applied a constant stimulus that elicited intermittent letdowns. However, the null results of this experiment cannot be considered conclusive because the specific nature of individual sucking responses was not measured. Furthermore, results were gathered with the use of anesthetized dams. The anesthetized dam preparation can be valuable in some situations but misleading in others. For example, a moderate level of anesthesia under urethan permits milk letdowns in the rat, but the letdowns can be significantly delayed (Lincoln *et al.*, 1973). This raises the possibility that the behavioral events occurring before milk letdown in anesthetized dams may not reflect the chronology of behavioral events occurring in the natural suckling situation. As discussed above, more recent data obtained by EMG techniques indicate that pups engage in different types of sucking while attached to a nipple, and at least one type is affected by the nutritional state of the pup (Brake *et al.*, 1982). Thus, it is possible that the type and duration of sucking provide the salient temporal and spatial characteristics of stimulation affecting milk letdowns, regardless of any sucking events that may or may not immediately precede oxytocin release in the unanesthetized dam.

The unique features of the sucking code are problematic at this time, but further investigation may reveal that they include a type of neurophysiological activation common to the reproductive system. Exploration of the anatomical pathways responsible for lactation and milk letdown revealed central nervous system pathways that also overlap with neuroendocrine reflexes involved in reproduction. The final unifying process includes sleep. For example, oxytocin is released during slow-wave sleep in the nursing rat (Lincoln, 1969), and vaginal distension induces activity in oxytocin neurons in adult rats (Negoro *et al.,* 1987). In addition, vaginal stimulation results in hormonally induced ovulation during slow-wave sleep in the rabbit (Sawyer and Kawakami, 1959). Thus, suckling-induced sleep in adult rats following periodic stimulation of the teats, and postcoital satiety sleep following stimulation of the vagina, probably include common brain mechanisms in the female. The neuroendocrine reflex resulting in oxytocin release during slow-wave sleep in the rat is discussed below.

C. MILK LETDOWN

The classic neuroendocrine reflex resulting in milk letdown has been investigated actively since the middle of the 19th century (Cross, 1961). A number of terms have been used to describe the process. The term "ejection" is a misnomer, to some degree, for the rat. It refers to milk being forced out of the alveoli into the sinuses or cisterns of the teat (Cowie *et al.,* 1951), but nipple sphincters prevent milk from squirting out of unoccupied nipples in the rat. "Letdown" is also a misnomer, to some degree, for the rat because the term implies a passive process. However, "letdown" also implies that the availability of milk is optional for each pup, which fits current experimental evidence. This is why the phrase "milk letdown" has been selected for use here.

The reflex is initiated by sensory stimulation of the mother, resulting in the release of pituitary hormones, which promote the production of and force the release of milk from the alveoli. Nipple-sucking is the salient stimulus for milk letdown in the lactating rat (Edwardson and Eayrs, 1967; Lincoln *et al.,* 1973). Specific afferent nerves have been assessed for their relative contribution of sensory information from each set of nipples (Edwardson and Eayrs, 1967).

Auditory stimuli prior to and during a suckling bout are also sufficient to release oxytocin (Ogle and Lockett, 1966), which may result in greater amounts of milk ingested by the pups (Deis, 1968). The amount of oxytocin stimulating the mammary glands is a crucial factor determining the amount of milk made available to the pups (Grosvenor and Turner, 1959), but it is not the only factor. Evidence suggests that the dam can modify the effect of oxytocin at the mammary gland, probably by affecting ductal contractility and vascular smooth muscle tone through afferent arousal of the sympathetic nerves (Grosvenor *et al.*, 1972). However, the precision of control in distributing milk by altering muscle tone has not been determined at this time.

The sucking pattern of the litter includes alternative sucking by pups in a random way such that at least one pup in the litter is actively sucking at any one time (Wakerley and Drewett, 1975). Within approximately 10–15 min, hypothalamic paraventricular and supraoptic neurons of the lactating rat fire rapidly, precipitating the release of oxytocin from the pituitary gland. Subsequently, oxytocin is released intermittently in a pulsatile manner (Lincoln *et al.*, 1973). This occurs only when the dam is in slow-wave sleep (Lincoln, 1969; Lincoln *et al.*, 1980; Voloschin and Tramezzani, 1979). The significance of the dam's restful state is discussed in Section VII. Consequently, milk letdown occurs 12–15 sec after oxytocin is released from the brain (Lincoln and Wakerley, 1975). Milk letdowns occur with a mean frequency of 6 min (Lincoln *et al.*, 1973), some within as short an interval as 45 sec (personal behavioral observation of the stretch response by pups). There is considerable variation in the interletdown interval among different nursing dams, which is probably related to the refractory nature of the system demonstrated in anesthetized and unanesthetized subjects. The latency to milk letdown, the intervals between letdowns, and the number of letdowns by the dam are affected by the duration of separation from the litter (Lincoln *et al.*, 1973). Recent evidence also suggests that the body temperature of the dam alters milk letdown parameters (Jans and Woodside, 1987).

Oxytocin-producing neurons in the hypothalamus increase in mass as a function of the size of the litter and the stage of lactation (Russell, 1980). In concert with this adaptation, the amount of oxytocin released per letdown and the proportional rise in intramammary pressure are directly related to the number of pups suckling an anesthetized dam (Lincoln and Wakerley, 1975). Similar results were obtained by observing unanesthetized dams (Mena and Grosvenor, 1968), which suggests that the collective sucking stimulus of the litter regulates the extent of lactation in the dam and influences the amount of milk made available for ingestion during each letdown.

Regardless of the nature of the collective sucking stimulus, pups in groups of one, two, four, six, eight, 10, or 12 were able to withdraw the same amount of milk from the dam, approximately 1.7 g per pup in a natural suckling bout lasting 2 hr (Drewett and Trew, 1978). The time factor is crucial in this regard, because small litters limited to 30-min bouts of suckling do not fare as well as larger litters (Mena and Grosvenor, 1968). Given a sufficient amount of time (2 hr) and an unanesthetized dam, smaller litters were able to obtain as much milk from the dam as larger litters, possibly by eliciting fewer milk letdowns of larger volume. The larger litters may elicit more letdowns of smaller volume (Russell, 1980). More recent evidence suggests that milk-deprived pups increase their intake by increasing the volume taken from the dam per letdown, not by increasing the number of letdowns (Jakubowski and Terkel, 1986). The limits of the flexibility of this part of the system must be examined in greater detail.

D. Summary

The pattern, duration, and intensity of sucking generated by different numbers of pups appear to affect the frequency and total number of letdowns within a single bout of natural suckling, as well as the magnitude of lactation. The amount of milk provided by the dam depends, to a great extent, on the collective complex stimulus from the litter. However, the amount of milk taken from the dam is not tightly linked with the frequency of letdowns. This is an exciting prospect, because it contributes to the explanation of how some pups ingest more than others during the same bout, but many facts remain to be demonstrated in the natural suckling situation.

Current evidence suggests that there are at least three mechanisms by which suckling vigor by pups alters the amount of milk they ingest during a bout. First, suckling stimuli of the litter collectively affect the amount of oxytocin released from the pituitary gland. Consequently, the myoepithelium surrounding mammary alveoli contracts as a function of the amount of oxytocin present, and milk letdown is crucial for the transfer of milk in rats. Second, on an individual basis, the amount of milk forced from a teat following contraction may be determined in part by local mechanical stimulation. Finally, the amount of milk withdrawn from a teat depends on the amount of milk available and the eagerness of the pups to extract it. Pups actively engage in nutritive sucking when milk is available, especially after they have been deprived of nutrients. The control of ingestion is discussed in greater detail in Section V.

Clearly, the pups' sucking pattern and vigor are no more important for milk letdown than the relative refractory condition of the dam. Hungry pups suckling a refractory dam are no more likely to obtain large amounts of milk than satiated pups suckling a dam that has been deprived of her litter for several hours. Beyond the general constraints of the interaction between the dam and her litter affecting letdowns, the internal controls of ingestion govern milk intake by individual suckling rats.

V. Ingestion

A. Obstacles and Challenges

Suckling, a uniquely mammalian behavior, presents an unusual set of problems for investigators interested in the biological and motivational aspects of ingestion. Three obstacles compound the challenge. First, young pups remain attached to the dam for long periods without ingesting milk. Bouts of ingestion during the neonatal period are especially difficult to discern. This has stifled attempts to assess intake in terms of discrete meals. Second, the amount of milk available from the dam and the amount ingested by each pup are not immediately obvious. Direct measures of the flow of milk into receptive offspring have remained elusive. Third, the distribution of milk through intimate contact with an essential provider, the lactating dam, raises questions regarding locus of control and doubts about the pups' motivation to ingest. With these issues in mind, the present discussion is focused on measurements used to evaluate ingestion and to determine the pup's ability to control its intake of milk while suckling an un-anesthetized dam.

B. ORIGINAL MEASURE OF INTAKE AND OTHER METHODS

The original measure of ingestion by suckling rats was accomplished indirectly by recording body weight gain after a bout of nursing. This technique has been used successfully by several investigators (Grosvenor and Turner, 1957; Morag, 1970; Lytle et al., 1971; Houpt and Epstein, 1973; Friedman, 1975; Lorenz et al., 1982; Lorenz, 1983), and the validity of the measure remains strong. Attempts have been made to increase its accuracy by controlling or monitoring weight lost through elimination (Drewett, 1978b; Lau and Henning, 1984), but there have been no successful major challenges of the premise. Direct measurement of the volume of milk flowing into the stomach of the pup has not yet been accomplished.

Other methods incorporating tritiated water have been used in studies of the recycling of water between the litter and the dam (Baverstock and Green, 1975; Friedman and Bruno, 1976). However, pulmocutaneous water exchange among the pups became a source of measurement error (Friedman and Bruno, 1976), and the method was not designed to detect milk transference on a short-term basis.

Labeling the mother's food with radioactive isotopes and subsequently measuring the radioactivity of the pups provided information regarding the long-term changes in litter weight (Babicky et al., 1970), but, again, this technique has never been used to determine milk intake during individual bouts of ingestion.

C. EXTRACTION OF MILK AND THE "STRETCH RESPONSE"

Extraction of milk from a teat depends on the pup's response at the time of each letdown. Positive pressure builds briefly within the mammary gland during oxytocin-induced contraction, but negative pressure must be applied by each pup to overcome resistance to the flow of milk established by the nipple sphincters (Wakerley and Drewett, 1975). The amount of milk withdrawn from the teat is determined by the volume of milk squeezed from the alveoli (an unknown factor at this time) and by the will of each pup to ingest. The will to ingest cannot be overemphasized as an essential factor, because negative pressure developed during nipple attachment alone does not ensure equal distribution of milk throughout the litter. Pups loaded with milk by gavage at 2%, 4%, or 8% of their body weight will remain attached to the dam throughout a bout of nursing but ingest much less than nonloaded pups (0%) (Lorenz et al., 1982) (see top of Fig. 4). The amount of milk ingested by the pups per letdown can vary substantially, depending on a host of factors involving the dam and her litter. One estimate of the volume of milk transferred during letdowns ranged from 5–30 mg per teat in the rat (Lincoln et al., 1973).

Pups typically engage in the stretch response while ingesting milk (Vorherr et al., 1967; Lincoln et al., 1973; Drewett et al., 1974; Lau and Henning, 1985). Apparently, they are alerted to the impending letdown by changes in the shape of the nipple (Lau and Henning, 1985). An erect body posture during the stretch, including extension of the forelimbs against the teat, is maintained for approximately 10 sec while milk is transferred quickly into the posterior region of the oral cavity and down the esophagus. There is no indication at this time that gulping or swallowing is necessary for pups to ingest.

Following the brief but intense offering of milk from the dam, pups younger than 10 days remain attached to a nipple. Older pups often display nipple-shifting immediately after the stretch response (Lincoln et al., 1973; Cramer et al., 1980). It appears that nipple-shifting behaviors permit pups to ingest more milk. Nipple-shifting also helps to keep all of the teats functioning when there are fewer than 12 pups in the litter. As few as two pups are sufficient to promote milk production in all of the dam's teats (Edwardson and Eayrs, 1967).

D. Deprivation and Preloading Effects

Studies of ingestive behavior within the natural suckling situation indicate that pups increase or decrease their intake, depending on their deprivation status. Pups as young as 1–7 days increased their intake of mother's milk following deprivation of milk in the care of foster dams (Lytle et al., 1971; Houpt and Epstein, 1973). Moreover, pups deprived of milk and maternal care for different periods ingested proportionately greater or lesser amounts of milk in the natural suckling situation when nursed at the same time (Morag, 1970; Lau and Henning, 1984). However, attempts to demonstrate increases in milk intake as a function of the duration of deprivation have not always met with success (Houpt and Epstein, 1973; Houpt and Houpt, 1975). Conversely, pups decreased their intake of mother's milk in the natural suckling situation following gastrointestinal preloads of a variety of solutions and suspensions (Houpt and Epstein, 1973; Houpt and Houpt, 1975; Friedman, 1975; Drewett, 1978b; Lorenz et al., 1982).

The search for a mechanism to account for the preload suppression effect in suckling rats has produced different types of experiments, and consequently different interpretations. In a preliminary study, a preload of bovine heavy cream (3% of body weight) remained in the stomach and did not suppress intake, whereas a preload of skimmed milk (3% of body weight), which emptied rapidly from the stomach, reduced intake in rat pups (Friedman, 1975). The investigator concluded that stomach distention and gastric emptying are not important determinants of ingestion in suckling rats. Although the importance of gastric distention was questioned as a putative mechanism controlling intake in this report, the variable of preload volume was not manipulated.

In a subsequent experiment in which the volume of the preload of warmed milk was varied systematically, investigators discovered that the suppression of milk intake during suckling was related directly to the amount of milk filling the upper region of the gut (Lorenz et al., 1982) (see top of Fig. 4).

The threshold preload volume for suppression of ingestion was 4% of the pup's body weight, an amount slightly larger than the ineffective preload volume of bovine heavy cream (3%), described above. The suppression was specifically related to ingestive behavior in the younger pups that received the small and moderate gut loads, because other behaviors, including the latency to attach to a nipple (middle of Fig. 4) and the incidence of attachment (bottom of Fig. 4) during the bout, were not altered (Lorenz et al., 1982). Larger preloads decreased nipple attachment behaviors and suppressed intake as well, which indicated that the two processes can be affected simultaneously if the stimulus is sufficiently strong. The fact that young pups typically do not detach from the nipple during a suckling bout indicated that the large preloads caused an unusual response, probably nimiety (Kulkosky, 1985).

One putative mechanism for the preload suppression effect appears to be distension of the stomach. A preload of water at 4% of the pup's body weight restricted to the stomach by acute pyloric ligation was very effective for the suppression of ingestion (Lorenz, 1983) (see mean weight gain in Fig. 5). However, pyloric ligation altered attachment behaviors (Fig. 5), which, once again, raised the question of whether the pups experienced satiety, nimiety, or some other state. This ambiguity accentuated the importance of identifying the normal postingestive state. Further advances in the investigation of the internal controls of ingestion will depend on a reliable index of satiety. Postingestive satiety, a major issue in this article, is discussed in greater detail below.

Obviously, preloading by gavage is not a natural event, as we have been cautioned (Friedman, 1975). The validity of the technique is based on the fact that a pup's stomach is normally filled with milk periodically throughout the day, and it empties in a reliable manner as a function of volume (Lorenz, 1985) (see Fig. 6). The validity of the procedure can be jeopardized by the methods of execution, including the handling routine, rate of gavage, preload volume, and

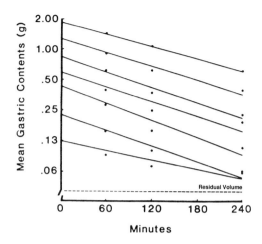

FIG. 6. Gastric emptying of rat's milk by 10-day-old pups deprived for 17–20 hr, then intubated with one of seven loads, ranging in volume from 0.06 to 2.00 g. Residual volume indicates the average amount of gastric contents found in pups after the deprivation period. Each point represents the mean of six to 10 pups from five or more litters (Lorenz, 1985). Reproduced with permission from the American Physiological Society.

preload substance. Other factors, including the duration of deprivation of the subject, the length of the test period, plus the volume and type of stomach contents at the time of preloading, may confound experimental results. Consequently, direct comparisons between different reports may be meaningless.

Regardless of methodological differences, the positive results from deprivation and preload experiments revealed the capacity for pups to respond to depletion and repletion conditions within the suckling situation. This fulfills one criterion demonstrating a motivated process.

E. VAGAL DENERVATION: SHORT-TERM EFFECTS

Filling the upper region of the gut with rat's milk reliably suppressed ingestion by suckling pups (Lorenz *et al.*, 1982). If mechanoreceptors are involved, the sensory information carried from the gut to the brain is likely to travel along visceral nerves. Recent evidence revealed the importance of such a mechanism. The vagus nerve, containing afferent and efferent parasympathetic fibers, is necessary for normal ingestive responses, as well as normal gastric filling and emptying in suckling rats (Lorenz, 1983). Acute subdiaphragmatic bilateral vagotomy resulted in hyperphagia and exaggerated gastric filling during the first postsurgical bout of ingestion (see the vagotomy group in Fig. 5). Vagotomy also attenuated the suppression effect of restricting contents to the stomach (cf. the vagotomy + pyloric ligation group and the vagotomy + pyloric ligation +

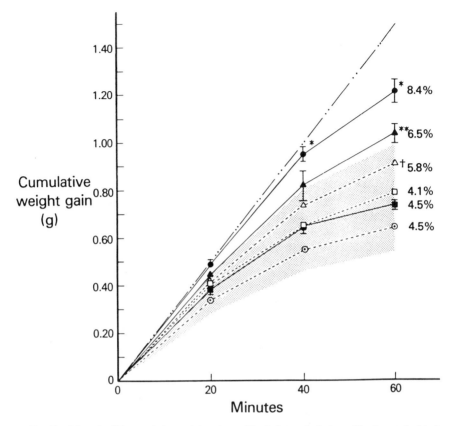

FIG. 7.   Mean (± SE) cumulative weight gains at 20-min intervals during a 60-min test. Isolated pups were fed an artificial milk through an anterior mouth catheter. ●, Spinal cordotomy plus vagotomy; ▲, vagotomy; △, sham surgical vagotomy; □, sham surgical cordotomy; ■, spinal cordotomy; ⊙, intact controls. *, Significantly different from vagotomized and normal pups at equivalent time ($p < 0.05$). **, Significantly different from sham-vagotomized pups at equivalent time ($p < 0.05$). †, Significantly different from normal pups at equivalent time ($p < 0.05$) (Lorenz *et al.*, 1982). Reproduced with permission from John Wiley & Sons, Inc.

preload group in Fig. 5). The data thus far suggest, but do not prove, that the stomach is one alimentary compartment involved in the internal control of milk intake, and the vagus is primarily responsible for relaying information from the gut to the brain in suckling rats. Vagotomy also greatly reduced the amount of paradoxical sleep, a putative marker of postingestive satiety (see Fig. 15 and Section VI,C).

Splanchnic nerves may also be involved in the control of ingestion because spinal cordotomy plus vagotomy (solid circles in Fig. 7) resulted in a synergistic hyperphagia and massive distension of the gut (Lorenz *et al.*, 1982) (see Fig. 7). However, the pups in this experiment were fed though an anterior mouth catheter. The results of this type of denervation on ingestive behavior have not been validated in the natural suckling situation.

F. Vagal Denervation: Long-Term Effects

The chronic effects of vagotomy provided some insights into the importance of vagal mechanisms in the control of ingestion, weight gain, and growth in rat pups (Lorenz, 1983). The subjects, vagotomized at day 10, were challenged with deprivation of milk and maternal care, then tested in the natural suckling situation at day 20. Weaning occurred on day 22, and the pups were killed on day 41, followed by measurements of body weight, body length, and gastric contents. Several physical and behavioral changes were observed. Permanent gastric distention and consequent abdominal swelling became obvious soon after surgery. Behavioral measures revealed that vagotomized pups ingested less milk from the dam when the number of milk letdowns was high (see Fig. 8). They also detached from the nipple and rested more frequently than shams and controls, suggesting an unusually rapid satiety response (see Table II).

The postmortem results suggested that the large abdomens of the vagotomized pups were the result of gastric stasis, probably a consequence of the lack of gastric tone. The pups also failed to gain weight at a normal rate (see Fig. 9) and failed to grow at a normal rate (see Fig. 10). Collectively, the results indicated that the vagus is necessary for normal suckling behavioral patterns, normal

TABLE II

PUP BEHAVIORS RELATED TO THE HIGH AND MODERATE NUMBER OF MILK EJECTIONS
DURING THE 2-HR SUCKLING TEST

	High No. MLD (median = 23)		Moderate No. MLD (median = 13)	
	Controls and shams	VX	Controls and shams	VX
Median (range) incidence of behaviors[a]:				
Attached	21 (20–24)[b]	14 (9–18)[c]	18 (12–23)[d]	15 (12–20)[e]
Detached–active	3 (0–4)[f]	4 (3–6)[g]	5 (1–11)[h]	6 (4–11)[i]
Detached–resting	0 (0–1)[j]	6 (2–11)[k]	0 (0–1)[l]	2 (0–8)[m]
N	9	6	25	12

[a]The total number of behavioral observations per suckling test is 24. b–m, Comparisons within high and moderate milk letdown (MLD) categories: b compared with c, $p < 0.01$; d compared with e, $p < 0.01$; f compared with g, $p < 0.02$; h compared with i, $p =$ not significant; j compared with k, $p < 0.01$; l compared with m, $p < 0.01$. Comparisons were made using the Mann–Whitney U test (Kumaresan et al., 1967). VX, Vagotomized pups. (Lorenz, 1983). Reproduced with permission from John Wiley & Sons, Inc.

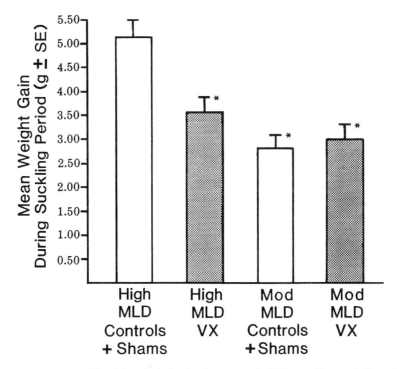

FIG. 8.   Mean (± SE) weight gains indicating the amount of milk ingested by pups in the suckling situation in which milk letdowns (MLD) were high or moderate in number. VX, Vagotomized pups. *, Compared with controls and shams in the high-MLD situation ($p < 0.05$) (Lorenz, 1983). Reproduced with permission from John Wiley & Sons, Inc.

processing of milk in the stomach, and normal growth and development (Lorenz, 1983).

Additional experiments must be performed to determine precisely the chronological appearance of the functioning vagal autonomic sensory system of the gut in relation to the development of somatosensory, olfactory, and gustatory modalities (Gottlieb, 1971). The appearance of the gut sensory system before the functional appearance of auditory or visual sensory systems is valuable in predicting the ontogeny of general sensory capabilities in rats and in describing homologous neuroanatomical pathways of other vertebrates. It may also be useful in the assessment and management of premature human infants.

G. Cholecystokinin Effects

The intestinal hormone cholecystokinin (CCK) has been described as a satiety agent for food in adult rats (Smith and Gibbs, 1979) and adult humans (Kissileff et al., 1981). Consequently, the hormone continues to be used to explore the process of ingestion in adult as well as infant rats.

In the initial reports of its use in rat pups, single-dose injections of the hormone suppressed ingestion of food in weanling rats (Bernstein *et al.*, 1976) and milk intake in suckling rats (Houpt and Houpt, 1979; Anika, 1983). However, the dose–response characteristics of this phenomenon, as investigated more recently, revealed surprising results. Deprived rat pups were tested in the suckling mode at day 10 and in adult and suckling modes at days 19–22 (Lorenz, 1986b). The older pups were tested with CCK-8 during the weaning transition because they naturally ingest in both modes at this time. The data revealed low-level

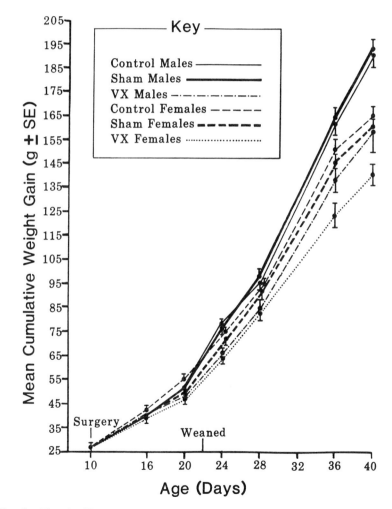

FIG. 9. Mean (± SE) cumulative weight gains by male and female controls, shams, and chronically vagotomized (VX) pups from days 10 to 40. $N = 7$–10 pups per group (Lorenz, 1983). Reproduced with permission from John Wiley & Sons, Inc.

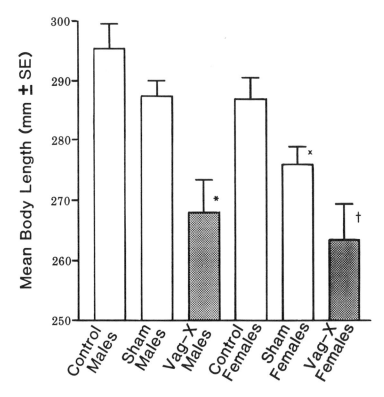

FIG. 10.   Mean (± SE) body lengths at day 41 for male and female controls, shams, and chronically vagotomized (Vag–X) pups. *, Compared with sham or control males, $p < 0.05$. x, Compared with control females, $p < 0.05$. †, Compared with sham or control females, $p < 0.05$. $N = 7$–10 pups per group (Lorenz, 1983). Reproduced with permission from John Wiley & Sons, Inc.

suppression of ingestion within the natural suckling situation following intra-peritoneal injections or intravenous infusions of the octapeptide across doses ranging from 2 to 16 µg/kg, regardless of age (see Fig. 11).

Conversely, pups ingesting in the adult mode (lapping from the substrate) suppressed their intake in a dose-related manner following administration of CCK at 1 day of age (Robinson et al., 1985). Lapping pups also reduced their intake of milk at 10–12 days of age after a single intragastric dose of soybean trypsin inhibitor (STI) (Weller et al., 1990), which has been shown to release endogenous CCK. Subsequently, the same investigators demonstrated that the STI suppression effect could be blocked by pretreatment with the specific CCK-A receptor blocker, MK-329. However, because the relatively high dose of MK-329 was somewhat nonspecific, and because the receptor blocker substance alone did not enhance ingestion beyond control intake, the investigators sug-

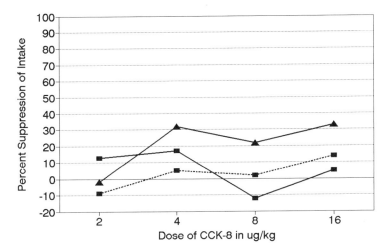

FIG. 11.   Mean percentage of suppression of ingestion of milk from the dam within the natural suckling situation. Pups at 10 (– ▲ –) or 19–22 (–■–) days of age were injected intraperitoneally with cholecystokinin-8 (CCK-8) prior to suckling, or 19–22 (···■···) days of age infused intravenously (30 min) with the peptide during the suckling act. Negative numbers indicate an increase in intake (Lorenz, 1986b).

gested that perhaps endogenous CCK is not involved in the control of milk intake under these conditions (Weller *et al.,* 1990). More information is necessary before conclusions can be drawn in this area. Regardless of the eventual conclusions regarding the effects of endogenous CCK during independent feeding, the hormone has little effect on young pups during the act of suckling.

Weanling-aged pups (19–22 days) ingesting in the adult mode by chewing pellets or lapping bovine milk from a dish also suppressed their intake as a function of the dose (Lorenz, 1986b) (see Fig. 12). Clearly, the mode of ingestion is the critical variable in these experiments. Age, dose, and route of administration of CCK-8 did not alter the low-level suppression effect on ingestion in the natural suckling situation. In striking contrast, pups of the same age ingesting in the adult mode responded to the octapeptide by suppressing their intake in a dose-related manner, like adults, regardless of the type of food or social context. These results are consistent with previous reports in which investigators administered single doses of the hormone to pups in the suckling mode (Houpt and Houpt, 1979; Anika, 1983).

H. GLUCOPRIVATION AND KETOPRIVATION

Glucose, the major energy metabolite in adults, has been implicated in the control of ingestion in adult rats. Infusions of glucose reduced food intake under

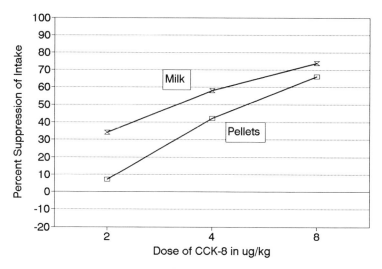

Fig. 12.   Mean percentage of suppression of food intake while ingesting in the adult mode. Pups at 19–22 days of age, in the company of littermates, were injected intraperitoneally with cholecystokinin-8 (CCK-8) prior to ingesting rat chow pellets or lapping bovine half-and-half prepared commercially (Lorenz, 1986b).

certain conditions (Russek, 1970), and glucoprivation induced by insulin (Adolph, 1957; Booth and Brookover, 1968; Smith and Epstein, 1969) or the glucose antimetabolite 2-deoxy-D-glucose (2-DG) enhanced feeding in adult rats (Smith and Epstein, 1969; Miselis and Epstein, 1975).

Similar methods used to evaluate ingestion by suckling rats elicited most of the anticipated physiological responses, but proved to be remarkably ineffective for altering ingestive behavior. Insulin failed to increase milk intake in suckling rats at 1 and 20 days (Lytle *et al.*, 1971), but did increase food intake in weanling pups starting at day 25 (Lytle *et al.*, 1971; Bernstein *et al.*, 1976). All pups, regardless of age or ingestive mode, presumably exhibited insulin-induced glucoprivation (Shapiro, 1968).

Pups as young as 5 days responded to insulin after a 6-hr delay by increasing their intake of milk from an anesthetized dam given oxytocin injections (Williams and Blass, 1987). The effects of this delayed testing procedure on young pups in the natural suckling situation is not known.

2-DG, when injected peripherally into pups at 3–7 days of age in doses ranging from 300 to 2000 mg/kg caused elevated blood glucose levels, but failed to enhance ingestion of milk from the dam (Houpt and Epstein, 1973). In fact, pups never responded to the challenge during the suckling phase. Gradually, weaned pups between 4 and 5 weeks of age began to respond to the 2-DG-induced glucoprivation by ingesting more solid food (Houpt and Epstein, 1973).

The developmental lag in the ingestive response to glucoprivation was first thought to be related to the fact that lipid, rather than glucose, is the main source of energy during the suckling phase (Hahn and Koldovsky, 1966; Gil-ad *et al.*, 1975). However, pharmacological blockade of free fatty acid oxidation (functional ketoprivation) failed to alter intake in suckling pups (Leshem *et al.*, 1990). Furthermore, in the same series of experiments, combined glucoprivation and ketoprivation produced similar null results on milk intake by suckling pups.

Therefore the data, with one possible exception (Williams and Blass, 1987), suggest that the inability of young pups to respond to standard insulin and 2-DG challenges or to ketoprivic plus glucoprivic challenges is not related to the metabolism of cellular fuels per se, but rather to the underdeveloped mechanisms that inform the infant brain of surfeits and deficits of saccharides and free fatty acids.

I. CEPHALIC PHASE OF INSULIN RELEASE

The ontogeny of the cephalic phase of insulin release in rats is thought to occur some time between birth and weaning (Bernstein and Woods, 1980). Just hours after birth, rat pups tested for the cephalic phase of insulin release to oral infusions of saccharin (0.1%) revealed no changes in immunoreactive insulin from plasma samples. However, at days 21–22, weaned pups displayed an enhanced insulin response to oral saccharin which resembled the adult response (Bernstein and Woods, 1980). The results were interpreted as evidence against an innately functioning cephalic phase system in neonatal rats. This was substantiated by other reports of delayed development of taste buds in rat pups (Mistretta, 1972), suggesting that afferent elements of the system do not function initially, but mature during the suckling phase. The existence of the cephalic phase and its importance for ingestion have not been demonstrated in the natural suckling situation.

J. THIRST CHALLENGES

Milk is a complete nutritional substance. It contains proteins, fats, and carbohydrates in proportions tailored during evolution to meet the demands of growing infants (for a more complete discussion, see Blaxter, 1961). Milk also contains water, minerals, and electrolytes in appropriate concentrations to hydrate and to balance corporeal tonicity. The complex nature of milk and the unitary process of ingestion through suckling provides still another challenge for investigators interested in the ontogeny of consumptive behaviors. Do rodents eat or drink milk while suckling?

Setting aside the artificial nature of this question, investigators discovered that certain standard thirst challenges affected ingestion of milk by rats in the natural suckling situation. Pups at 10 days of age deprived of the dam for 2 hr, then preloaded by gavage with water or 0.1 M NaCl at 3% of their body weight, suppressed their intake of mother's milk by approximately 90% following the water preload, and approximately 20% following isotonic saline over the course of a 4-hr suckling period (Friedman, 1975). The reduction of milk intake following the saline preload was not statistically significant, which suggested that the relevant factor was the lack of osmolality in the water preload. However, preloads of isotonic saline in larger volumes reliably suppressed ingestion by pups (Lorenz *et al.*, 1982). The larger preloads may have affected a distention mechanism. Other investigators preloaded pups with a variety of substances, but failed to find a consistent relationship between the osmolality of the preload and the suppression of milk intake (Houpt and Epstein, 1973; Houpt and Houpt, 1975). The issue appears to be complicated by methods that do not dissociate among putative distention, osmotic, and caloric receptors in preabsorptive or postabsorptive compartments.

A preload of water confined to the stomach by pyloric ligation was twice as effective in suppressing ingestion as either the preload or pyloric ligation alone (Lorenz, 1983) (see top of Fig. 5). Vagotomy also attenuated the suppression effect of the pyloric ligation and the combination of pyloric ligation plus the preload of water, which suggests that sensory information from the upper gastrointestinal tract, possibly related to hydration, is sent to the brain through the vagal afferents. This remains to be demonstrated using other techniques as well.

Hypovolemic challenges with polyethylene glycol and formalin reliably reduced blood volume and increased ingestion of milk by suckling pups, whereas hypertonic NaCl increased blood volume and reduced intake (Friedman, 1975). Deprivation of milk by placing pups with galactophore-ligated foster dams produced a similar hypovolemia (Friedman, 1975). Additional experiments in this area confirmed that plasma volume is labile in suckling rats. Plasma volume expanded rapidly after a suckling bout, but contracted substantially within 2 hr (Friedman, 1979). Furthermore, hypovolemia is exacerbated in warm ambient temperatures. Pups deprived of their mothers in a chamber at 35°C became more hypovolemic than those kept at 30°C (Friedman, 1979). Enhancement of hypovolemia under these conditions appeared to be the result of evaporative water loss, rather than increased urine formation (Friedman, 1979). The results suggest that extracellular dehydration during deprivation is sufficient to enhance milk intake in suckling rats.

Preloads of water effectively reduce milk intake in deprived pups, but the reason for this response is not clear, because water distends the gastrointestinal compartments and rapidly enters the vascular space. Water confined to the stomach by pyloric ligation reduced intake, but may have done so by causing discomfort. When preloads of isotonic saline were allowed to clear the stomach over a period of 4 hr prior to testing, milk intake was not altered during the subsequent suckling bout (Drewett, 1978b). This suggested that expansion of plasma volume is not important for the control of milk intake (Drewett, 1978b), but unfortunately, plasma volume was not measured during the experiment. Additional studies are required to determine the necessary and sufficient conditions of hydration affecting the control of ingestion and postingestive satiety in suckling rats.

Intracerebroventricular injections of renin failed to alter milk intake in suckling rats between 1 and 20 days of age (Leshem *et al.*, 1988). However, similar injections of renin increased milk intake in pups between 5 and 11 days of age and increased water intake in pups 7–20 days of age ingesting through an anterior mouth catheter (Leshem *et al.*, 1988). These results are consistent with several reports suggesting that most mechanisms, with the exception of gastric distention, known to control ingestion of food and water in weaned pups and adult rats are present but inoperative within the natural suckling situation.

K. SUMMARY

The most widely accepted method of assessing ingestion in suckling pups is the indirect method of weight gain during a controlled bout with the nursing dam.

Suckling pups actively remove milk from the dam when they are alerted to its presence during milk letdown. Typically, pups will display the stretch reflex while ingesting milk. The brief rigid stance of the reflex is often used as a behavioral confirmation of ingestion, but the posture does not reveal the amount consumed.

Evidence from several laboratories investigating ingestion of milk by rat pups in the natural suckling situation suggest that pups are able to regulate their intake of mother's milk under a variety of depletion and repletion conditions. As early as day 1, pups responded to deprivation by increasing their intake of mother's milk, and suppressed ingestion in direct proportion to the volume of milk loaded into the gut. This indicates that at least one system capable of detecting the presence and absence of milk matures prenatally.

Young pups have the capacity to control their intake of milk in the natural suckling situation by monitoring and responding to sensations from the gut. The mechanism appears to involve distension of the stomach mediated by the vagus nerve. Although no single controlling mechanism has ever been demonstrated convincingly in the natural suckling situation, filling the upper gastrointestinal tract with milk or other substances reliably and specifically reduced intake in suckling rats. In addition, the vagus is necessary for the normal control of ingestion because acute subdiaphragmatic truncal vagotomy produced hyperphagia, without affecting nipple attachment behaviors, and reduced paradoxical sleep. Chronic vagotomy produced a syndrome of weight loss and prolonged abdominal distention similar to that observed in adult rats following the same surgical procedure.

The suppression of ingestion is one criterion implying satiety, but alone it may be very misleading. Ingestion can be disrupted by a variety of physiological and behavioral events that have nothing to do with postingestive satiety. Therefore, additional measures of the change in motivation indicating postingestive satiety are mandatory for a complete assessment of the controls of ingestion in suckling pups. This idea is developed further in Sections VI and VII.

Exploration of the suckling mode of ingestion in rats revealed a unique response to the satiety hormone CCK. Suckling attenuated the suppression effect of exogenous CCK. The biologically active octapeptide elicited only a low-level non-dose-related suppression of milk intake in suckling rats, regardless of age. This is the first evidence of a natural blockade of the exogenous CCK satiety effect during ingestion, emphasizing once again the unique nature of the suckling situation.

Similar null results were obtain following administration of insulin and 2-DG. Standard glucoprivic challenges known to produce glucoprivation and feeding in adult rats produced glucoprivation in young rats with little effect on ingestive behavior. These results were initially explained by the fact that young pups, in contrast to adults, oxidize lipids rather than glucose for energy. However, recent evidence suggests that suckling pups are not defending the concentration of free fatty acids either. Thus, the presence or absence of metabolic fuels, if monitored at all during this early stage of development, is not sufficient to alter milk intake in suckling pups. The lack of a cephalic phase of insulin release during the suckling phase supports this contention.

Thirst challenges revealed that suckling pups respond to hypovolemia by ingesting more milk. The state of hypovolemia, whether derived from deprivation of milk or experimental manipulation, enhanced milk intake, whereas cellular challenges with hypertonic saline had the opposite effect. Renin did not alter milk intake while pups were suckling, but increased intake of young pups in nonsuckling situations.

Attempts to satisfy hunger and slake thirst may be closely coordinated in suckling rats. Due to the unique nature of milk and its acquisition by suckling pups, it would not be surprising to find that hunger and dehydration coincide during deprivation. Nor would it be unusual to find that ambient temperature affects these integrated systems. Additional experiments are required to dissociate the various control mechanism and to determine the importance of interactions between systems.

Although pups respond to gut filling by curtailing their intake in response to volume like adults, not all of the adult internal controls of ingestive behavior are present, functioning, or revealed during the suckling phase. The results described above clearly divide the question of the physiological basis of ingestive controls in pups into three categories: physiological controls known to suppress ingestion during suckling and nonsuckling feeding modes in young pups; those that are effective during the nonsuckling feeding mode in young pups; and those present and functioning in older weanling pups, resembling adult controls. Internal mechanisms that operate exclusively to control ingestion during the suckling mode have not yet been demonstrated. This leads one to believe that suckling and independent feeding provide separable, but not totally unique, conditions for exploring the motivated processes of ingestion. The original dichotomy of suckling versus independent feeding was useful to draw our attention to the differences (Drewett, 1978a; Hall and Williams, 1983; Hall, 1985), but strict interpretation of this proposal is no longer tenable. Gastric distention, a putative control mechanism, appears to operate at every level throughout the rat's life.

Given that suckling (an unanesthetized dam) is the only natural form of ingestion in rats during the first 10 days, the existence of incipient inactive systems capable of controlling independent feeding during this time raises provocative questions about the nature and evolution of suckling, as well as the development of feeding and drinking mechanisms. [For a detailed discussion of these issues, see Hall and Oppenheim (1987), Epstein (1986), and Drewett (1978a).]

VI. Sleep and Thermoregulation

A. TERMS, LIMITATIONS, AND INTERACTIONS

The behavioral repertoire of neonatal rats is relatively limited, but their immaturity, implied by the term "altricial," belies the fact that pups are capable of recognizing, locating, and attaching to a nipple at close range, sucking, and ingesting milk from the time of birth. Neonatal rats also display discrete periods of sleeping and waking (Hofer and Shair, 1982), although the basic rest–activity cycle has not yet been reported in rats as it has in other mammals (Kleitman, 1963; Sterman, 1979). Superimposed on the rapid physiological and behavioral changes occurring at this time is the gradual development of thermoregulatory mechanisms.

The ontogeny of these biobehavioral mechanisms has been revealed primarily by investigating each process separately. This strategy was essential in the beginning. Now it is important to consider how these mechanism interact. The evidence that follows suggests that innate sucking, ingesting, and sleeping behaviors are modified and directed in part by sensory cues from the alimentary tract. Furthermore, these behaviors are organized into a specific sequence by deprivation of milk, and they are altered by body temperature.

The developmental changes of sleep in pups are described in Table III. "Active sleep," identified by body twitches, implies paradoxical sleep. "Quiet sleep" implies slow-wave sleep. The terms "active sleep" and "quiet sleep" are operational definitions based on behavioral descriptions. This terminology is

TABLE III

ELECTROENCEPHALOGRAPHIC AND BEHAVIORAL MEASURES OF SLEEP AND WAKEFULNESS
IN ISOLATED RATS DURING DEVELOPMENT[a]

Age (days)	Electroencephalogram		State as a percentage of total recorded time[b]		
	Frequency (c/sec)	Amplitude (μV)	Wake or active	Slow-wave or quiet sleep	Paradoxical or active sleep
1–4	Unreliable		33 A	1 QS	66 AS
5–6			24 A	1 QS	75 PS
7	12–17	20–80	20 W		
	12–15	20–50		1 QS	
	17–19	30–80			79 PS
9	—	—	26 W		
	12–15	50		2 QS	
	20–22	50–100			72 PS
11	—	—	25 W		
	12–15	50		15 QS	
	20–22	50–100			60 PS
12	—	—	23 W		
	3–5	100		27 SWS	
	—	—			50 PS
15	17–20	50–100	27 W		
	—	—		32 SWS	
	17–20	50–100			41 PS
17	—	—	25 W		
		100–200		35 SWS	
	—	—			40 PS
26	—	—	40 W		
	7–8	100–250		48 SWS	
	—	—			12 PS
Adult	25–40	39–75[c]	44 W		
	7–25	50–350		48 SWS	
	20–25	40–80			8 PS

[a]Data are from Jouvet-Mounier et al., (1970) unless stated otherwise. Reproduced with permission from John Wiley & Sons, Inc.

[b]A, Active; W, wake. Sleep is defined primarily by rapid eye movement and behaviors until the electroencephalogram becomes reliable: QS, quiet sleep; AS, active sleep; PS, paradoxical sleep; SWS, slow-wave sleep.

[c]The adult ranges are from Mansbach and Lorenz (1983) and Timo-Iaria et al., (1970).

used when electroencephalographic recordings are unreliable, nonexistent, or not attempted in neonatal subjects, including humans. Gross cortical electrical potentials are sufficiently strong and reliable for recording electroencephalograms beginning at approximately 11–13 days of age in rats (Jouvet-Mounier et al., 1970; Gramsbergen, 1976).

B. DEPRIVATION EFFECTS

Depriving rat pups from the dam has profound effects on sleep–wake states of the pups. During separation, slow-wave sleep and paradoxical sleep are reduced, whereas wakefulness and sleep transitions increase (Hofer, 1976; Hofer and Shair, 1982). Young pups also have difficulty maintaining body heat throughout the day. The absence of milk and maternal care appear to exacerbate heat loss (Bignall et al., 1974; Johanson, 1979). The changes in internal states as a result of deprivation can be prevented by periodic intragastric infusions of milk formula under warm ambient conditions, as described below (Hofer and Shair, 1982). Thus, some of the physiological and behavioral changes that occur during maternal deprivation strongly suggest a need for sleep and milk as well as heat.

C. SLEEP AS AN INDEX OF ALIMENTARY SATIETY

If ingestion of milk from the teat is a motivated process, then it should be possible to identify the postingestive state of satiety in suckling pups. Sleep may indicate satiety, because there is a high probability of the event after a successful bout of ingestion; however, information on this topic is far from complete.

The first report of postingestive sleep in the neonatal rat was presented as a single observation. A 4-day-old pup quickly entered active sleep following tube feeding and grooming while in isolation (Jouvet-Mounier et al., 1970). More recently, pups 13–14 days of age were equipped with cortical electrodes and monitored under *ad libitum* conditions in the natural suckling situation (Shair et al., 1984). The pups quickly entered slow-wave sleep after attaching to a nipple. They were awakened briefly by the milk letdowns, but returned to slow-wave sleep within a few seconds after ingesting milk. The investigators noted that rhythmic sucking occurred during slow-wave sleep, but the incidence of rhythmic sucking during paradoxical sleep was greatly reduced or eliminated. They also noted similarities in time spent in the awake state, in slow-wave sleep, and in paradoxical sleep for pups attached to a teat or away from the dam. Moreover, the rates of the three types of sucking (rhythmic, bursts, and sucking with treadles) did not change between the first and second halves of nursing bouts. The results by Shair et al. suggested that levels of arousal do not change in the pups as nursing bouts progress, and they concluded that arousal level does not explain the termination of ingestion.

This was a valuable informative report introducing innovative technical procedures for recording physiological events in the natural suckling situation. However, it did not address any of the questions regarding motivation or postingestive satiety. For example, there was no indication of the pups' nutritive status prior to testing. In addition, intake by the pups during the experiment was not controlled or measured. The pups received milk through as few as one or as many as eight milk letdowns. Furthermore, no distinction was made between time spent in paradoxical sleep versus slow-wave sleep as a function of milk letdowns. Some of the issues of motivation have been explored in detail in controlled experiments, as described below.

Several important relationships between environmental and alimentary stimuli and their effects on sleep–wake states of infant rats were demonstrated in an earlier controlled experiment (Hofer and Shair, 1982). The reduction of paradoxical sleep proved to be a prominent feature among the variety of changes in internal state during the deprivation of milk and maternal care in infant rats. Continuous intragastric infusions of bovine milk failed to normalize sleep–wake states in warm infant rats, even in the presence of a nonlactating dam. Only periodic infusions of an enriched milk formula resembling rat's milk under warm ambient conditions reduced all sleep disturbances to the point at which the sleep–wake states resembled those displayed by pups in the natural nesting situation. Periodic infusions of the enriched milk formula under the appropriate conditions also resulted in greater weight gain during the test period (Hofer and Shair, 1982).

The ineffective continuous gastric infusions were not coordinated with sucking bouts, nor did the effective periodic gastric infusions stimulate the oropharyngeal region, as described above. These results raise several questions about the importance of sucking and oropharyngeal stimulation for normal sleep–wake states. Apparently, sucking is not necessary for normal sleep–wake states, and yet the rhythmic periodic processes of nipple attachment and sucking are sufficient to elicit slow-wave sleep under certain conditions (Lorenz, 1986a; Shair *et al.*, 1984), and they may contribute to the postingestive state of satiety in the natural suckling situation.

Ingestive controls suggest a motivated process likely to include a postingestive state of satiety. To explore this possibility, the sleep–wake states of pups were investigated recently by manipulating one or more variables, including the option to attach to a nipple and suck, loading of rat's milk into the gut, or a combination of these factors (Lorenz, 1986a). Rat pups, equipped with cortical and neck muscle electrodes, were placed into one of four groups: no sucking and no milk, no sucking and milk intubation, sucking and no milk, and sucking and milk intubation. The results indicated that nipple attachment and sucking elicited slow-wave sleep almost immediately in pups deprived of milk and maternal care (see hatched bars, C1 and D1, Fig. 13). Paradoxical sleep occurred sporadically,

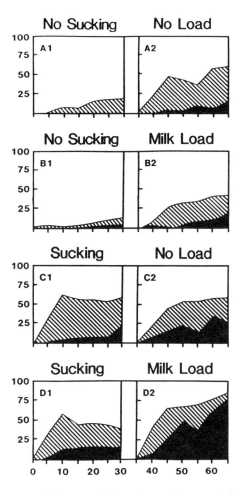

FIG. 13.   Mean percentage of time spent in the awake state (open area), slow-wave sleep (hatched area), and paradoxical sleep (solid area) during two consecutive 30-min periods in the presence of the anesthetized dam. Nipple attachment and suckling were permitted for some pups (sucking) but not others (no sucking). Pups were intubated between periods (minutes 30–35) with nothing (no load) or rat's milk at 4% of their body weight (milk load) (Lorenz, 1986a).

but did not constitute much of the total sleep time (see solid bars, C1 and D1, Fig. 13). Warmed rat's milk loaded into the pups by gavage at 4% of their body weight had no effect on either type of sleep when the pups were prevented from attaching and sucking (see C2, Fig. 13). This result was predictable in light of the fact that there was no periodic stimulation of the alimentary canal. In marked contrast, paradoxical sleep increased dramatically in pups when the milk load was administered in the context of sucking (see solid bars, D2, Fig. 13).

A more recent series of experiments has provided us with the ability to distinguish between the satiety sleep state and nimiety in pups using methods described previously (Lorenz *et al.*, 1982; Lorenz, 1986b). Young pups between 12 and 14 days of age were surgically equipped with cortical and neck muscle electrodes. After 9–12 hr of separation from their mothers, the pups were preloaded with milk (Esbilac, Pet-Ag Inc., Hampshire, IL) at 0%, 2%, 4%, 8%, or 16% of their body weight, then allowed to attach and suckle the anesthetized dam. The pups displayed a preload-related increase in paradoxical sleep as the gastric volume increased from the 0% load to the 4% load. Paradoxical sleep began to decline beginning with the 8% gut load, and almost disappeared following the 16% gut load (Lorenz, 1991) (see the black histograms in Fig. 14).

These data support the results from earlier reports indicating that the 4% preload is most effective for reducing milk intake without affecting nipple attachment (Lorenz *et al.*, 1982; Lorenz, 1983). In fact, paradoxical sleep was at its peak following this gut load. In addition, the larger preloads of 8% and 16% that caused a reduction in nipple attachment and the concomitant reduction in paradoxical sleep suggest malaise, probably nimiety brought about by exaggerated distention of the gut.

The demonstration of experimental control over sleep states by varying the volume of milk in the gut is strong evidence suggesting that postingestive satiety in suckling rats is driven in part by alimentary receptors. If such a mechanism includes distension of the gut, then denervation of the gut should eliminate the phenomenon. To test this hypothesis, pups equipped with cortical and neck muscle electrodes underwent either vagotomy (subdiaphragmatic, bilateral trun-

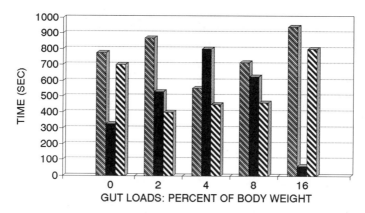

FIG. 14.   Mean time (in seconds) spent in the awake state (lightly hatched bars), slow-wave sleep (black-hatched bars), and paradoxical sleep (solid bars) following gut loads of Esbilac milk administered to suckling rats as a percentage of body weight (Lorenz, 1991).

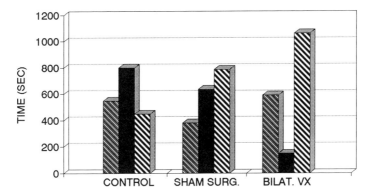

FIG. 15. Mean time (in seconds) spent in the awake state (lightly hatched bars), slow-wave sleep (black-hatched bars), and paradoxical sleep (solid bars) following no surgery (control), laparotomy (sham surg.), and bilateral subdiaphragmatic truncal vagotomy (bilat. VX). All subjects were preloaded with milk at 4% of their body weight prior to this 30-min test (Lorenz, 1991).

cal) or sham surgery (laparotomy). The pups were then deprived of milk and maternal care in a warm environmental chamber for 9–11 hr. At test time, the pups were returned to their anesthetized dam and allowed to attach to a nipple. Thirty minutes into the test, each pup was intubated with milk using a volume equal to 4% of its body weight, then returned to the dam to suckle. The results indicate that paradoxical sleep was greatly attenuated in the vagotomized pups (Lorenz, 1991) (see Fig. 15).

The reduction of paradoxical sleep in vagotomized pups resembled that in intact pups following the large obtunding preloads of milk. Although this initially created a dilemma, the distinction between the lack of satiety and the presence of nimiety became obvious when the nipple attachment behaviors were analyzed. Most intact pups that received the large preloads (16% of body weight) failed to attached to the dam and remained immobile for most of the test, which suggests malaise. In marked contrast, most vagotomized pups were eager to attach to the dam and suckled in a manner that appeared quite normal. The nipple attachment behaviors proved to be crucial for interpreting the internal states of the pups. Vagotomy blocked the enhancement of paradoxical sleep, thus blocked or delayed postingestive satiety, whereas the large gut loads resulted in malaise, or nimiety (Lorenz, 1991). The results suggesting the lack of satiety in vagotomized pups are also corroborated by the enhanced intake of milk by vagotomized pups in the natural suckling situation (Lorenz, 1983) (see Fig. 5).

Experimental results of this type permit us to speculate on the nature of the gut–brain axis controlling ingestion and sleep in infant rats. Milk acting on the gut in the appropriate behavioral context of suckling was sufficient to trigger and sustain paradoxical sleep, suggesting a gating mechanism between the alimentary

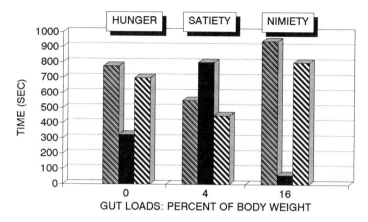

FIG. 16.   Internal states can be inferred by physiological measures, especially paradoxical sleep. A hunger profile was established by recording (for 30 min) the duration of sleep–wakes states in suckling rats deprived of milk and mother for 9–12 hr. Pups spent about 17% of their time in paradoxical sleep. The satiety profile represents the duration of sleep–wake states in pups deprived of milk and mother for 9–12 hr, then loaded with warm milk (4% of body weight) just before testing. Pups spent about 44% of their time in paradoxical sleep. The nimiety profile was established by intubating deprived pups with a large obtunding volume of milk (16% of body weight) prior to testing. Pups spent about 3% of their time in paradoxical sleep (Lorenz, 1991). Lightly hatched bars, awake state; black-hatched bars, slow-wave sleep; solid bars, paradoxical sleep.

canal and the hindbrain sleep system mediated by the vagus nerve. Although paradoxical sleep appears to be an integral part of postingestive satiety in suckling rats, more experiments under more natural suckling conditions must provide positive results before conclusions can be drawn. Nonetheless, selective enhancement of paradoxical sleep following a gut load of rat's milk in the context of suckling has many ramifications.

The fact that milk in the gut enhances paradoxical, rather than slow-wave, sleep may have special significance for developing rats as well as other infant mammals, as described in the next section (Lorenz, 1986a). Furthermore, the reduction in nipple attachment, together with the striking reduction of paradoxical sleep following the larger gut loads or vagotomy, suggests that investigators now have the ability to distinguish between postingestive satiety and other states in suckling rats (see Fig. 16).

D. SIGNIFICANCE OF SLEEP FOR SUCKLING ANIMALS

The role of either type of sleep in infants or adults is not completely understood at this time, but it is possible to speculate on a physiological mechanism and its significance for young mammals in view of several facts. For example, protein synthesis is accelerated in the brain during paradoxical sleep, but not during slow-wave sleep (Drucker-Colin *et al.*, 1975; Stern and Morgane, 1977). Furthermore, protein synthesis inhibitors specifically inhibit paradoxical sleep (Drucker-Colin *et al.*, 1979; Rojas-Ramirez *et al.*, 1977), and, conversely, paradoxical sleep deprivation greatly decreases protein synthesis in the brain (Voronka *et al.*, 1971). Protein synthesis in the brain during paradoxical sleep in developing infants is likely to be related to structural growth (Roffwarg *et al.*, 1966), possibly the formation of new synapses. If this is true, then milk in the gut, triggering the paradoxical sleep of postingestive satiety, would coordinate at least some, perhaps many, of the anabolic processes of the developing neonatal brain (Lorenz, 1986a).

Slow-wave sleep may reflect a different type of satiety. The abrupt change in internal state from arousal in the rooting pups to slow-wave sleep following nipple attachment and sucking has been described in separate reports (Shair *et al.*, 1984; Lorenz, 1986a). The urge to suck and sucking behaviors, not to be confused with rooting and nipple attachment behaviors, may be considered a motivated process, because sucking behaviors vary as a function of deprivation and gastrointestinal events, as described in Section IV (Brake and Hofer, 1980; Brake *et al.*, 1979). This also deserves further exploration.

Regardless of the events and conditions leading to slow-wave sleep during suckling, the reliability of the phenomenon is remarkable. Sucking has a soothing soporific effect on young rats. Oral stimulation of the type experienced while the nipple is positioned deep within the pup's mouth appears to be a prerequisite for prolonged periods of paradoxical sleep. Recall that warmed rat's milk in the gut did not enhance paradoxical sleep in the pup when it was denied the opportunity to suck a nipple (see Fig. 13). Sucking and concomitant slow-wave sleep may serve to coordinate physiological and metabolic events in the developing pup. Although sufficient in this regard, suckling after day 1 is not essential for what appears to be normal growth and development (Hall, 1975).

Somnolence and hypoactivity have been reported following ingestion of milk by rat pups in other experimental situations involving the use of tongue cannulas and anesthetized dams (Blass *et al.*, 1979; Hall and Rosenblatt, 1977). However, the authors interpreted the reduced activity as an indirect nonspecific effect unrelated to the direct control of ingestion found in adult rats. The issues of ingestive control, postingestive satiety, and methodological procedures are discussed in Section VII.

E. THERMOREGULATION: INTERNAL AND EXTERNAL FACTORS

Altricial rat pups are poikilothermic (Adolph, 1957). The development of homeothermy is a gradual process extending through at least the first 3–4 weeks of life (Conklin and Heggeness, 1971). During this time, behavioral and physiological mechanisms of thermoregulation can be dissociated. Behaviors involved in seeking an environmental heat source (Johanson, 1979; Kleitman and Satinoff, 1982) and retaining heat through huddling (Alberts, 1978) appear to be implemented before internal physiological mechanisms of heat conservation have matured (Fowler and Kellogg, 1975). For example, 1-day-old rats (Kleitman and Satinoff, 1982) and mice (Ogilvie and Stinson, 1966) were able to move toward warmth on a thermocline, provided they were given ample time. Rudimentary heat-seeking behaviors are present at day 1, and mechanisms for the production of body heat develop within the first two weeks (Conklin and Heggeness, 1971). Before this, rat pups have little control over heat loss, which makes them susceptible to hypothermia during the suckling phase (Conklin and Heggeness, 1971; Hahn and Koldovsky, 1966).

Poikilothermic pups deprived of maternal warmth in cool ambient temperatures display reliable changes in behaviors and internal states. Heat loss, combined with the absence of nutrition and maternal care, resulted in the greatest disruption of sleep, notably by increasing the frequency of awakenings (Hofer and Shair, 1982). Pups also increased locomotor responses under certain starvation conditions (Moorcroft, 1981). Thus, one would anticipate that young pups deprived of heat and milk will become more alert and active as the period of deprivation increases. This prediction also includes the eventual reduction in movement as the bodies become markedly hypothermic and depleted of nutrients. None of this has yet been verified.

F. ULTRASONIC COMMUNICATION

Rat (Okon, 1972; Allin and Banks, 1971), mouse (Okon, 1970), hamster (Okon, 1972), and gerbil (McCauley and Elwood, 1984) pups emit ultrasounds during hypothermic conditions. Ambient temperatures, specifically cool ambient temperatures, appear to be more effective than isolation conditions in eliciting ultrasounds by distressed pups (Allin and Banks, 1971). Ultrasonic emissions during cool ambient conditions for rodents are rare during the first few days of life, but become progressively more frequent during the next 2 weeks, and taper off during the third week (Okon, 1972; Noirot, 1972). Although ultrasonic cries may not provide explicit information (Bell, 1974; Oswalt and Meier, 1975), they appear to be functional in the nesting situation because they elicit searching behaviors by the dam (Allin and Banks, 1972). Emergency signaling of this nature shortens the latency for the dam to return to her nest, but it is not known to occur routinely in laboratory situations in which the dam frequently visits the nest site (Jans and Leon, 1983).

Sonic as well as ultrasonic cries also occur within the nest when young pups are jostled or stepped on (Noirot, 1972). This usually causes the dam to shift her position, but the impact of ultrasonic vocalizations by pups on the attending dam extends beyond the realm of behavior. Increased prolactin levels in lactating female rats and, to a lesser degree, in virgin female rats have been reported following exposure to pup ultrasounds (Terkel et al., 1979). However, other investigators have not been able to reproduce this response and suggest that the release of prolactin by the dam may have been a conditioned response, rather than a reflex (Stern et al., 1984). Contradictory reports of this nature indicate that further studies are necessary to determine the extent to which rat mothers are affected by the vocalizations of young pups.

Heat loss and the deprivation of milk usually coincide in pups when the mother leaves the nest during the first 2 postnatal weeks. However, these conditions may occur independently. When they are separated, heat loss, rather than the lack of milk, appears to force parental action. For example, gerbil pups, deprived of their dam and left in the care of their father for 3 hr did not vocalize, provided they experienced contact and warmth (McCauley and Elwood, 1984). Deprivation of milk, including the loss of body heat, elicited vocalization sooner than deprivation of milk within the warm nest (McCauley and Elwood, 1984). Thus, ultrasonic vocalization is used to communicate distress to caretakers, especially heat loss, which may or may not accompany the absence of milk in gerbils. These two conditions are most likely to occur simultaneously in rat pups, because the adult male does not usually exhibit maternal nesting behaviors. The distress calls appear only during severe conditions, because sibling interactions within the nest tend to blunt the responses (Hofer and Shair, 1978). The deprivation of milk has not been investigated as a separate factor in the elicitation of ultrasounds by rat pups.

Young poikilothermic pups are reheated on a regular basis by contact with the dam and by ingesting her warm milk. Heat from these sources is retained by different methods to ensure survival and optimal growth for young rats. One method includes the proper construction of a nest. The preparturient rat engages in nest-building activities about 24 hr before the birth event (Rosenblatt, 1975). The nest serves to insulate, shelter, and contain the litter (Leon et al., 1985). Evidence suggests that most nesting behaviors are influenced by an increase in ovarian estradiol (Terkel and Rosenblatt, 1972; Moltz et al., 1970).

After the pups are born, the mother ingests the placentas (Kristal et al., 1986), retrieves stray pups, grooms them, and crouches over them in a nursing posture typical of this early phase (Rosenblatt, 1975). There is a transition in factors affecting maternal behaviors during the first 1.5 days. Behaviors initially educed during pregnancy (estrogen as the mediator) are enhanced by the pups after their arrival (Rosenblatt, 1975). A variety of stimuli from the pups, including contact (Stern and Johnson, 1989), ultrasonic vocalization, and suckling, begin to play an important role in regulating the dam's behavior (Rosenblatt, 1975).

G. Mother–Young Reunions and the Tilt-Box Apparatus

The frequency with which the dam visits the nest and attends to her offspring is governed by internal factors as well. The mother is forced to leave the nest more frequently in search of food and water as the pups' need for milk increases and their need for an external heat source decreases (Leon and Woodside, 1983).

The frequency and duration of mother–young reunions have been documented using a tilt-box apparatus (Croskerry et al., 1976). Observations generated through the use of the apparatus, consistent with the original report (Grota and Ader, 1969), indicated that the mean duration of each nesting bout is gradually shortened as the pups develop, but the frequency of maternal visits remains unchanged (Leon et al., 1978).

This reliable phenomenon encouraged investigators to search for causal factors. The search began with a number of assumptions related to previous reports of nipple attachment and ingestion (Leon et al., 1985). These authors noted that other investigators observed young pups clinging incessantly to nipples when the dam was anesthetized (Hall et al., 1975). They also noted that pups remained attached to the dam even when drowning with milk supplied through a posterior tongue catheter (Hall and Rosenblatt, 1977). This suggested to them that mother rats control the duration of contact bouts. Also implicit in this suggestion was the assumption that the mother controls the ingestive behavior of her pups by limiting the contact time with her litter.

The tilt-box procedures (Leon et al., 1978), used to investigate only factors involved in the frequency and duration of nesting bouts, revealed that rat dams spent more time with cool pups than with control or warm pups. Although the mean nesting time was approximately the same for control and warm pups, the frequency of the dam's visits was significantly elevated for warm pups, while the duration of each visit was sharply reduced. Conversely, cool pups were visited infrequently, but the dam stayed for significantly longer periods. Unfortunately, maternal and pup behaviors within the nest were not described.

In a separate experiment in the same report (Leon et al., 1978), the investigators clearly demonstrated that rat dams spent more time with pups in cool rooms than with pups in control or warm rooms. The results were interpreted as evidence indicating that the maternal thermal state limits nest bout duration. This applied only to dams in control and warm room conditions. Core temperatures were elevated at the termination of bouts in these environments, whereas core temperatures were significantly reduced in dams at the termination of bouts in the cool room. If the rise in maternal temperature is a factor controlling milk intake by pups, then nesting behavior as well as ingestive bouts, and consequently milk intake by rat pups, should vary as a function of long-term ambient temperatures. This type of experiment may help us to distinguish certain thermoregulatory variables from other factors nested in nursing, but the current dilemma remains:

How are ingestion of milk and thermoregulation accomplished? This issue is discussed further in Section VII.

Does the dam visit the nest to deliver milk to her litter? In an attempt to answer this question, the nipples of rat dams were sealed by cauterization on the day they gave birth (Leon *et al.*, 1978). This prevented the dams from delivering milk to their pups, but the dams continued to visit their nests for the same amount of time as control dams, and displayed the typical age-related decrease in nesting time. Foster dams nursed the pups in the morning. This experiment suggested to the investigators that stimuli associated with milk delivery do not play a critical role in the regulation of nesting activity (Leon *et al.*, 1978).

Another way to view these data, not incompatible with the original interpretation, is that mechanisms controlling the frequency and duration of nesting visits can, under certain circumstances, operate independently of the transference of milk. The investigators' procedures ruled out the possibility that the pups received milk from the teat-sealed dam, but did not eliminate the possibility that the pups, nursed by a lactating foster dam, communicated their satiety status to the teat-sealed natural dam through a reduction in rhythmic sucking. This type of communication could have coordinated the normal pattern of maternal visits. No information was provided in reference to the nutritional status of the pups during the biological mothers' visits, or in regard to whether the pups attached and suckled normally during these reunions. The experiment raised several interesting questions about what might be necessary and sufficient regarding the control of suckling and nursing activities, but it did not provide compelling evidence for or against nesting time as a factor regulating milk intake in pups, nor does it conflict with the present theory described in Section VII.

The tilt-box apparatus and continuous sampling technique provided valuable information regarding mother–young reunions, but the information is limited in certain aspects. Nesting time cannot be equated directly with nursing time, as originally implied (Croskerry *et al.*, 1976), because a rat mother typically grooms the litter and herself before pups attach to the nipples (Pedersen and Blass, 1982). Another important consideration is that the latency to attach is a function of age. Older pups attach to the dam quicker than younger pups (Lorenz *et al.*, 1982). In addition, nursing time is not equivalent to an ingestive bout. Ingestion of milk by young pups occurs intermittently while they suckle the dam for long periods. Often, pups are sleeping while attached to the dam (Bolles and Woods, 1964; Shair *et al.*, 1984). Thus, the tilt-box measure of nesting time is an accurate measure of the time the dam spends in the nesting area, but not an optimal measure of nursing time, and clearly not a direct index of hunger, ingestion, or satiety by individual pups.

A variety of internal and external events may affect the initiation and termination of a nesting bout. These events may also interfere with or augment the nursing period. Ingestion of milk by pups must be related in some manner to the dam's behaviors, and the link is probably through the temperature-sensitive milk letdown process. Investigators recently demonstrated that the rise in ambient temperature correlates with a reduced latency for the first milk letdown within a bout (Jans and Woodside, 1987). Their work also demonstrated that successive milk letdowns occurred more rapidly under warmer ambient conditions. Thus, it is possible, as the authors suggested, that a warmer dam enters into slow-wave sleep sooner than a cooler dam. The sooner the dam enters slow-wave sleep, the sooner the ingestive bout begins and the quicker the bout is completed. The question of how the rising temperature of the dam is integrated into the final signal for terminating a bout independent of the milk letdown process remains open for investigation.

H. SUMMARY

Investigation of the ontogeny of separate homeostatic processes has provided us with a basic, albeit incomplete, understanding of each mechanism. Knowing that regulatory mechanisms involving ingestion, sleep, and temperature control develop concurrently and are frequently altered simultaneously, it is appropriate to view changes within these systems as interrelated and probably dependent. Depriving pups of maternal milk, warmth, and stimulation has a gradual but profound effect on their behaviors and internal states. They soon become hypo-thermic, they experience sleep loss, and they vocalize and engage in a variety of behaviors to advertise and terminate their abandoned condition, some of which may promote the rapid return of the dam.

When the pups' needs for milk and heat are met, there is a reliable shift in internal state toward sleep. Paradoxical sleep was the dominant form of sleep demonstrated in an experiment in which rat's milk was loaded into the gut, followed immediately by suckling behaviors in warm ambient conditions. Nipple attachment and paradoxical sleep were greatly reduced when gut loads became relatively large. Paradoxical sleep was also reduced in vagotomized pups that attached and suckled the dam. Thus, it was possible to make the distinction between the lack of satiety (vagotomy condition) and the presence of nimiety (large gut load conditions) by observing nipple attachment behaviors and gross body movements. Currently, the data suggest that paradoxical sleep can be used as a marker for postingestive satiety and nimiety. However, more information is required in this area, because the preferential shift into paradoxical sleep has not yet been demonstrated in pups under natural suckling conditions or in controlled situations in which the amount of milk in the gut, behavioral activation, and ambient temperatures have been manipulated systematically.

Questions regarding the significance of sleep in developing mammals have arisen as the result of research in several laboratories. The poikilothermic nature of young rats is a demanding condition for the dam and her pups alike. Successful growth during the initial phase of development depends on symbiostatic interactions. Cool pups are motivated to seek and retain body heat. They accomplish this task in a number of ways, with the cooperation of the dam. Under extreme situations of hypothermia, isolation, and other noxious conditions, pups announce their distress through sonic and ultrasonic cries. Hunger has not been investigated as a condition sufficient for the elicitation of ultrasonic distress calls in young rats.

The data clearly indicate that rat dams are sensitive to ambient temperature, to litter temperature, and to ultrasounds elicited by distressed pups. Lactating dams respond in a reliable manner by returning more quickly to vocal pups and by spending more time with cool pups than warm pups. The time spent in the nest may be determined by the dam's assessment of the rise in her body or brain temperature. This phenomenon appears to operate only in neutral or warm ambient temperatures. The issue of whether the dam's nesting time is a direct or indirect method for regulating pup temperature has not been resolved. The dam's body temperature, ingestion by the pups, and nesting duration may be linked through the temperature-sensitive milk letdown process.

Use of the tilt-box apparatus to describe mother–young reunions has been very helpful in revealing the effect of heat on maternal behaviors, but it was not designed to indicate the amount of milk transferred by the dam to her litter, nor does it indicate the amount of milk ingested by individual pups.

Although the emphasis of this article is on the pups' abilities to cope with perturbations in external and internal environments, the role of the caretaker is vital. The interaction of regulatory systems united by symbiostatic behaviors presents a large and challenging area of research for developmental psychobiologists.

VII. An Integrated Theory of Ingestion and Satiety

A. Introduction

The results of several recent experiments provide essential information for the proposal of a theory of motivation that integrates the internal control of ingestion with other regulatory processes culminating in sleep and brain growth. This theory defines conditions under which the control of ingestion is operating, and describes the importance of body temperature that promotes postingestive satiety, primarily paradoxical sleep.

In order for a series of behaviors to qualify as a motivated response in suckling pups as well as adults, it is necessary to identify the state of deprivation, one or more drive behaviors evoked by deprivation, the goal of the behaviors, and the state of satiety. Each of these phases has been described for ingestion by suckling rats in separate experiments and is presented now in its natural order.

B. Deprivation State

The internal state of rat pups changes as a function of time since the last ingestive episode. During deprivation, the awake state gradually becomes more pronounced (Hofer and Shair, 1982), slow-wave sleep and paradoxical sleep decrease (Hofer, 1976), and rhythmic sucking is greatly enhanced when nipples are made available (Brake et al., 1979). There is no evidence at this time that pups are able to communicate their state of hunger at a distance, thereby encouraging the dam to return to the nest.

On returning to the nest, the dam's maternal behaviors are piqued by pups generating auditory stimuli (Okon, 1972), olfactory and gustatory stimuli (urine) (Moore, 1981), and tactile stimuli (Stern and Johnson, 1989). She arouses her pups by grooming them. Pups less than 10 days old then respond by quickly attaching to a nipple, regardless of their nutritive status (Hall et al., 1977; Brake et al., 1979; Henning et al., 1979).

Nipple attachment creates an essential avenue of communication between the pups and their dam. After the pups attach, they engage in nonnutritive sucking (Brake et al., 1979). Rhythmic sucking is likely to be the relevant collective signal pups use to inform the dam of their intent to ingest (Grosvenor and Mena, 1982). Additional stimulation of mechanoreceptors in the mammary glands resulting from pups paddling the teats may also contribute to the afferent signal for milk delivery (Lincoln and Wakerley, 1975). The longer the deprivation period, the more the pups are motivated to suck rhythmically (Brake et al., 1979). The sucking, probably rhythmic sucking, has a direct soporific effect on the dam. As a consequence, the dam relaxes within a few minutes, then enters slow-wave sleep (Voloschin and Tramezzani, 1979). Milk letdowns occur only while the dam is in slow-wave sleep (Lincoln, 1969; Lincoln et al., 1980; Voloschin and Tramezzani, 1979). Milk is made available during the periodic letdowns, but the pups are not forced to ingest (Lorenz et al., 1982). They ingest according to their individual needs. This is the goal.

C. Consumption

The ingestive behavior of the pups is influenced by deprivation of milk. Pups deprived of milk will ingest more than nondeprived pups in the natural suckling situation (Houpt and Houpt, 1975; Lau and Henning, 1984). Furthermore, intake decreases in direct proportion to the volume of milk in the gut (Lorenz et al., 1982), even when they suckle the dam at the same time (Morag, 1970; Lorenz et al., 1982).

The regulation of ingestion in individual pups is not readily apparent by casual observation, because they tend to ingest at the same time and a bout is terminated at approximately the same time. Pups are generally deprived at the same time for the same duration, and milk empties from the stomachs of the pups at a consistent rate, depending on volume (Lorenz, 1985). Therefore, their internal states are likely to be synchronized, which generally masks the existence of individual controls of ingestion. One could argue teleologically from the dam's point of view that this routine is the most efficient method of distributing large amounts of milk to many pups over a short period. As a group, the hungry litter probably sustains rhythmic sucking longer, or the litter may suck more vigorously, eliciting larger milk letdowns, resulting in the presentation of more milk than is offered to a litter that has fed more recently.

Regardless of the collective process of the litter, the preload and deprivation experiments clearly demonstrated that, on an individual basis, a pup having very little milk in its gut will evacuate more milk from the dam per bout than a nearby pup that has a moderate or large volume of milk in its gut (Lorenz *et al.*, 1982).

The visceral denervation studies corroborate the fact that internal mechanisms are involved in the individual control of milk intake in the natural suckling situation (Lorenz, 1983). Although many factors influence the rates of growth and weight gain in normal suckling rats, the internal controls for ingestive behavior in each pup must be partially responsible for the differences in body weights of littermates found in a typical litter. The dam's milk supply during conditions of adequate nutrition is also likely to be a crucial factor in determining the growth and development of suckling pups. However, the amount of milk made available during a nursing bout is unknown at this time.

Suckling is not a camouflaged form of adult feeding. It is a unique natural method of ingestion for eutherian mammals that involves the acquisition and transportation of food through the alimentary canal. All of the compartments along the canal involved in processing milk eventually process adult foods as well. Therefore, it should not be surprising to find that at least one of the gut mechanisms responsible for controlling intake and processing milk in suckling infants develops prenatally, and is elaborated as encephalization and development progress. The gastric distension phenomenon appears to be consistent with this prediction. Gastric distension, one of the putative mechanisms involved in the internal control of ingestive behavior during the suckling phase, continues to operate through weaning, adolescence, and adulthood.

D. POSTINGESTIVE SATIETY STATE

The concept of "postingestive satiety" in suckling rats can be viewed, in a broad sense, as (1) a marked reduction in or elimination of ingestive behaviors, (2) a demonstrable predictable change in internal state, and (3) a reliable shift toward behaviors not immediately related to ingestion.

The results from several experiments support the idea of postingestive satiety in suckling pups, and permit us to go beyond these general descriptions. More specifically, the postingestive state in suckling rats includes the voluntary reduction of milk intake as a function of the volume of milk filling the gut (Lorenz, 1983).

The predictable change in internal state appears to be the shift from predominantly slow-wave sleep to prolonged periods of paradoxical sleep (Lorenz, 1986a). However, the return of relatively large amounts of paradoxical sleep may be viewed by some as a rebound phenomenon. The term "rebound" in sleep studies has the connotation of an exaggerated sleep state following an abnormal type of deprivation (Dement, 1978). This description does not appear to be appropriate when recording the sleep–wake patterns of pups deprived of milk and maternal care for 9–12 hr, then intubated with warm milk and allowed to suckle. The amount of paradoxical sleep has rarely exceeded 50% of the test period under these conditions (see Figs. 13 and 14).

The issue here is whether paradoxical sleep after ingestion represents a typical shift in internal state as part of an ongoing cyclic event, one that would be labeled "satiety," or an exaggerated sleep state resulting from an unusual or prolonged deprivation, one that would be labeled a "rebound event." The transition point at which satiation becomes a rebound event will be difficult to determine. These physiological and semantic issues deserve further exploration.

The return of paradoxical sleep in substantial amounts is not incompatible with the notion of satiety. Both are fragile states that require optimal conditions for their fullest expression. The occurrence of paradoxical sleep soon after a bout of ingestion and at times beyond the immediate ingestive bout may represent the activity of two overlapping systems that promote a common state. Gut mechanisms that promote paradoxical sleep seem to enhance an obligatory process of the brain that operates regardless of nutritive status. Understanding the differences between minimal and optimal sleep state conditions will provide us with a better understanding of how ingestion and nutrition contribute to the processes of brain growth and maturation.

Paradoxical sleep increases to a certain limit as a function of milk loaded into the upper gastrointestinal tract (Lorenz, 1991), and is substantially reduced by truncal vagotomy (Lorenz, 1991). These results, demonstrating experimental control over the phenomenon of gut-regulated paradoxical sleep, were obtained by using subjects suckling an anesthetized dam. Thus, they suggest, but do not prove, that pups in the natural suckling situation will show similar changes in their sleep–wake states following more natural events.

When nutritive needs have been met, the current theory predicts that the suckling pup will shift its attention away from ingestion and engage in other typical behaviors. Several independent reports support this contention. EMG recordings of jaw movements during sucking by pups in a controlled experiment using an anesthetized dam revealed that nutritive and nonnutritive rhythmic sucking subside when milk enters the upper gastrointestinal tract (Brake *et al.*,

1982). Furthermore, rhythmic sucking is virtually eliminated during paradoxical sleep while pups remain attached to their dam (Shair *et al.*, 1984). Occasionally, the dam will move, which awakens the pups and elicits bursts of sucking and treadling. But toward the end of a bout, the present theory predicts that rhythmic sucking occurs in nonsignificant amounts before the young pups quickly reenter paradoxical sleep. Note that the shift from slow-wave sleep to predominantly paradoxical sleep has not yet been observed in nondeprived pups suckling their unanesthetized dam (Shair *et al.*, 1984).

The integrated theory of suckling also predicts that the cessation of rhythmic sucking during paradoxical sleep eliminates the pups' soporific influence over the dam. Milk ejections stop and the dam awakens. Often, she leaves the litter at this time. The signal to leave appears to be related to her rise in body temperature (Leon, 1979; Leon *et al.*, 1985), but other factors may be involved as well.

The most obvious shift in behaviors after milk letdowns cease is that pups older than 14 days relinquish the nipples and begin to aggregate. For pups younger than this age that tend to cling to the dam, the theory predicts that the force necessary to dislodge them during paradoxical sleep will be minimal, but not zero. Thus, if the dam moves very little at this time, the young pups will remain attached to her nipples. If she decides to vacate, few, if any, of the pups will be dragged from the nest site as she leaves. Regardless of the presence or absence of the dam, the warmed replenished nestlings of all ages are soon twitching in paradoxical sleep. This state, indicating postingestive satiety for suckling rats, is likely to be common to all mammals at an early age.

If rhythmic sucking communicates a pup's internal state, stemming from the lack of milk to a surfeit of milk, then many apparently discrepant results in the field today could be explained. The transfer of milk from the dam to her offspring occurs through a sequence of physiological and behavioral changes involving *both* parties. The dam and her pups enter into the natural nursing/suckling situation with separate goals and different internal states. After attaching, the pups communicate with the dam through an innate but motivated rhythmic suck-ing pattern. When the dam is anesthetized, as part of an experimental procedure, sucking communication is blocked. Consequently, the natural internal control of ingestion is no longer possible. Pups placed in this experimental situation tend to overingest, which has been interpreted as a lack of direct internal control of ingestion (Hall and Rosenblatt, 1977; Blass *et al.*, 1979; Blass and Cramer, 1982; Cramer and Blass, 1983, 1985).

An alternative interpretation to this "noncontrol" thesis is that the degree of overingestion depends on the method by which milk is provided to the pups. When milk was infused through a cannula located in the posterior region of the tongue, pups, attached to an anesthetized dam, swallowed every infusion reflex-ively to the point of gross distension and respiratory distress (Hall and Rosen-blatt, 1977). Although presumably satiated, the state of satiety, including the elimination of rhythmic sucking and the enhancement of paradoxical sleep, was not evident, because the investigators did not measure the appropriate responses. They observed nipple attachment, and as long as the pups remained attached to the dam, the investigators provided them with milk, which was swallowed reflexively.

In a different experiment, when milk was made available through the nipples of an anesthetized dam given repeated intravenous injections of oxytocin, pups showed more control over the amount consumed, but still overingested (Cramer and Blass, 1983), probably because the pups were unable to control the amount of oxytocin circulating in the dam, and thus were not able to exercise control over milk letdowns in their usual manner.

Pups, presumably satiated, also overingested when provided with a series of unanesthetized milk-laden foster dams (Friedman, 1975). Once again, the natural symbiostatic balance was shifted toward the ingestion of milk. Pups in the experimental litters ingested more milk than controls, but the reason for this response is not clear. Milk supply was interpreted as the limiting factor, but, as described above, this unknown factor, along with the probable confound of different maternal behaviors, generated data that led to more questions than explanations.

Postingestive sleep is typical, not ineluctable. The optimal expression of internal control over ingestive behavior occurs in the natural suckling situation when the pups have established sucking communication with an unanesthetized dam and are not aroused by unusual events or animals other then their siblings and the dam that initiated the bout.

The resumption of sucking following artificial stimulation is not evidence of the lack of internal control by the pups; rather, it is evidence indicating that satiety can be disrupted easily. Like satiated adult rats aroused by a mild tail pinch (Antelman, 1975), young suckling rats briefly revert to ingesting when satiation has been disrupted.

Innate behaviors at this young age, probably arranged hierarchically, emanate from the hindbrain and possibly from the hypothalamus (Moran, 1986). As the forebrain develops, postingestive satiety is less likely to include sleep, and interruption of satiation is less likely to reinstate ingestive behaviors. The degree of overingestion by suckling pups under unnatural conditions in which sucking communication or maternal neuroendocrine reflexes have been circumvented appears to be related to the strength of the arousing stimuli, physical limits of the gut, and the age of the pups.

E. THERMOREGULATION

There is substantial evidence suggesting that body heat is an essential component permitting the natural postingestive state, although body temperatures of individual pups in the suckling situation have not been measured directly. Heat radiated from the dam, heat from the ingested milk, and possibly heat from the rise in basal metabolic rate, together with heat-conserving behaviors, contribute to the postingestive state by promoting paradoxical sleep in pups. This deduction is supported by the fact that warm ambient temperatures promote paradoxical sleep in infant rats (Kleitman and Satinoff, 1982) as well as adult rats (Szymusiak and Satinoff, 1981).

The nudging and shuffling for position in the huddle by poikilothermic pups are likely to occur when the dam leaves the litter, exposing the pups to a cooler ambient temperature (Barnett, 1963; Alberts, 1978). The present theory predicts that pups that are able to get to the bottom of the huddle will retain more heat, which permits them to experience more paradoxical sleep. This must be documented. The cooler pups on top eventually work their way to the bottom of the huddle (Alberts, 1978). Perpetual redistribution of bodies within the huddle is likely to distribute the heat, and therefore periods of paradoxical sleep, evenly among the pups. Additional research is required to determine whether paradoxical sleep diminishes as a function of the interaction between the duration of milk deprivation and the degree of heat lost from the litter.

Elevated body temperature alone is not sufficient for the satiety state, because rat pups deprived of milk in a warm environment still show an increase in time spent in the awake state and a decrease in paradoxical sleep (Hofer and Shair, 1982). Moreover, enhancing heat loss in rat pups during maternal deprivation does not increase the consumption of milk (Henning and Romano, 1982). Therefore, the body temperature of the pup plays an essential supportive role in the normal postingestive state, but internal temperature does not appear to control ingestive behavior during suckling.

The increases in body temperature (Leon et al., 1978; Leon, 1979) and brain temperature (Leon et al., 1985) of the dam have been correlated with the cessation of contact with the litter. The fact that a dam spends proportionately less time with the litter as her temperature rises suggests that body heat may contribute to her motivation to leave, but it is not a complete explanation of the circumstances that determine her stay at the nest site (Leon et al., 1978), nor does it address the issue of internal control of ingestion apparent in each pup. Heat may alter the nursing bout just as heat quickens many biological and physiological events (Jans and Woodside, 1987).

F. Brain Anabolism

The behavioral and physiological events described above are accompanied by metabolic events in the brain which are no less remarkable. Paradoxical sleep and slow-wave sleep occur for similar durations throughout a bout of suckling in nondeprived pups (Shair et al., 1984). However, deprived pups tested in an experimentally controlled situation displayed slow-wave sleep quickly after grasping the nipple, and paradoxical sleep primarily when sucking occurred while warm rat's milk distended the upper gastrointestinal tract (Lorenz, 1986a). This suggested a postingestive satiety state in suckling rats. Additional evidence suggested that paradoxical sleep, probably triggered by moderate loads of milk in the gut (Lorenz, 1991), permits or enhances protein synthesis in the brain (Drucker-Colin et al., 1975; Stern and Morgane, 1977). Protein synthesis appears to be tightly linked to paradoxical sleep, because deprivation of this state also inhibits protein synthesis (Voronka et al., 1971), and drugs that block protein synthesis inhibit paradoxical sleep (Rojas-Ramirez et al., 1977; Drucker-Colin et al., 1979).

There are other observations in humans suggesting that paradoxical sleep is the sleep state most appropriate for postingestive satiety. For example, although sleep is a time when most individuals believe they are oblivious to internal and external events, adult humans are capable of integrating sensory information into ongoing dreams during paradoxical sleep (Dement, 1978). If infant animals are as sentient, then internal events in the gut as well as on the surface of the skin may influence transitions from paradoxical sleep to the awake state and vice versa, depending on the amount of milk in the gut and the current ambient temperature or temperature of the skin. Signals from the gut and the skin may have preferential access through existing channels to the hindbrain during paradoxical sleep that is unparalleled at any other time. The quasi-alert state of the brain during paradoxical sleep is consistent with the fact that sleeping humans are more easily aroused from paradoxical sleep than the deeper stages of slow-wave sleep (Dement, 1978). The ability of a young animal to adjust its internal environment by ingesting more milk and its external environment by diving deeper into the huddle may be necessary to maximize brain growth and development during the suckling phase.

The sequence of events in which the alimentary canal is stimulated is important for postingestive satiety. The suckling stimulus alone, or filling the gut by preloading out of context, is not sufficient to elicit the relatively large amounts of paradoxical sleep that characterize postingestive satiety (Lorenz, 1986a). Furthermore, greatly distending the gut (Lorenz, 1991) and filling the gut continuously (Hofer and Shair, 1982) are not the best methods of activating this gut–brain system. Normalization of sleep–wake states and optimal weight gain occur only while warm pups receive periodic gut infusions of a formula resembling rat's milk (Hofer and Shair, 1982). Collectively, the evidence suggests, but does not prove, that suckling pups periodically warmed, hydrated, and filled with nutrients quickly enter into prolonged periods of paradoxical sleep, which appear to promote protein synthesis in the brain. The protein synthesis may include neuronal growth and synaptogenesis (Roffwarg et al., 1966), but the details regarding long-term alterations during paradoxical sleep remain to be determined.

G. SUMMARY

The current theory proposes that different systems in the pup (e.g., hunger, thermoregulation, sucking urge, and arousal, as well as others yet to be described) are affected simultaneously during the absence of the dam. When the dam returns, she initiates nursing behaviors, and the motivated pups ingest milk. Gradually, the behavioral and physiological changes in the pups brought about during her absence are reversed.

Specifically, the theory predicts that, once the dam agrees to nurse, she places herself in the position of being influenced by the suckling behaviors of the pups. The altricial pups take charge of the bout when they attach to the dam and suckle.

Deprivation-induced rhythmic sucking by the pups puts the dam to sleep. Milk letdowns occur only while she is in slow-wave sleep. Individual pups control their intake of milk from day 1 within the natural suckling situation. They do this by altering the intensity or frequency of their rhythmic sucking, which communicates their hunger state to the dam, and by extracting various amounts of milk made available during and immediately after letdowns.

Pups continue to ingest until milk filling the upper gastrointestinal tract signals a change in nutritional status to the brain through the vagus nerve and possibly other systems as well. The signal, probably from distension of the gut, promotes a change in internal state. As milk fills the stomachs of the pups their rhythmic sucking slows, then completely stops when they enter paradoxical sleep. This is the postingestive satiety state for young suckling rats, and the culmination of the motivated urge to ingest milk.

The fact that protein synthesis in the brain is greatly enhanced during paradoxical sleep is not merely coincidental. It probably represents rapid brain growth during an opportune period coordinated by the presence of proteins and fats soon to be available from the gut.

The appropriate and predictable reduction in rhythmic sucking, synchronized with satiety, heralds the end of the pups' soporific influence on the dam, and she awakens. At this time she may decide to end her nursing bout and leave the nest for a variety of reasons, including the desire to dissipate heat, to seek food and drink, or to engage in social interactions.

Clearly, some of these events have been documented more thoroughly than others. The most speculative part of the theory predicts that postingestive satiety, especially paradoxical sleep, is a vital process linking ingestive behaviors with the rapid growth and development of the infant brain.

The motivation for pups to ingest milk has been the focus of this article, but we are now faced with several provocative possibilities regarding the driving force within the system. The progressive development of the brain, specifically protein synthesis, may motivate the animal to suckle for milk. Perhaps paradoxical sleep is a goal in itself, and periodic filling of the gut with milk is an important rate limiting factor. Another consideration is that the behavioral and physiological mechanisms of thermoregulation, although not directly involved in the control of ingestion, may be crucial for the expression of postingestive satiety.

The theory is built on the symbiostatic relationship between a mother and her offspring, a relationship in which the controlling party and events are not always obvious at any one moment. It remains essential to discuss certain events from the point of view of the dam or her pups to indicate what each is capable of doing at certain times, but finding proof of controlling factors in freely behaving subjects is our foremost challenge.

VIII. Conclusions

The proposed theory is the first attempt to encompass three major areas of research in developing pups: Ingestion, sleep, and thermoregulation. Although some parts of the theory are not as well established as others, we can begin to explore and anticipate certain interrelated behavioral responses, internal states, endocrine effects, metabolic events, and anatomical changes that contribute to, or are the results of, the suckling/nursing cycle. Many rules governing individual processes have been described, yet many more remain to be discovered.

A privileged form of ingestion occurs during suckling. The dam dispenses milk by attending to the collective stimulation of rhythmic sucking provided by the litter, and each pup exerts individual control over its intake. The motivated process driving ingestion in pups has been documented through the use of some, but not all, of the standard feeding challenges. The striking contrast between the controls of milk intake displayed during suckling versus intake during adult modes of ingestion in pups of the same age defies our preconceptions. The data force us to conclude that, within this symbiostatic relationship, a unique set of rules governs ingestion of milk during suckling.

The theory itself allows us to look even further into the scheme of suckling. Has evolution circumscribed conditions of suckling to promote rapid maturation of the brain? Evidence implies that it has, because of the dramatic changes that occur within the brain during postingestive paradoxical sleep. Although the evidence described thus far hardly constitutes proof, it presents an exciting springboard for new hypotheses and experiments that may significantly alter our view of biological priorities controlling development during the suckling phase.

Forces of natural selection supported rapid growth and development of the sophisticated brain that insured a position for rats, rodents, and other mammals in their respective niches. Perhaps the integrated approach of investigating the internal controls of ingestion and satiety will help us to discern a variety of mechanisms controlling the rates of growth and development in suckling mammals.

Finally, the heuristic value of this integrated theory, predicated on the validity of the natural suckling situation, will be realized, not so much by the accuracy of the proposal at this time, but by the generation of new facts describing each basic regulatory process, and by the recognition of complex biobehavioral interrelationships in suckling rodents and other mammals.

Acknowledgments

The integrated theory of suckling was presented, in detail, at the annual meeting of the International Society for Developmental Psychobiology in Annapolis, Maryland, 1986. The author's research cited in this article was supported by National Institute of Mental Health Institutional Training Grant 15092, National Institute of Child Health and Human Development (NICHHD) Grant 15720, University of Vermont Institutional Grants PHS 07125 and BSCI83-9, NICHHD Academic Research Enhancement Award Grant 24350, and Gettysburg College Institutional Grant 90-00-04086-30000.

References

Adolph, E. F. (1957). Ontogeny of physiological regulations in the rat. *Quarterly Review of Biology* **32,** 89–137.

Alberts, J. R. (1978). Huddling by rat pups: Group behavioral mechanisms of temperature regulation and energy conservation. *Journal of Comparative and Physiological Psychology* **92,** 231–245.

Allin, J. T., and Banks, E. M. (1971). Effects of temperature on ultrasound production by infant albino rats. *Developmental Psychobiology* **4,** 149–156.

Allin, J. T., and Banks, E. M. (1972). Functional aspects of ultrasound production by infant albino rats, *Rattus norvegicus. Animal Behaviour* **20,** 175–185.

Anika, S. M. (1983). Ontogeny of cholecystokinin satiety in rats. *European Journal of Pharmacology* **89,** 211–215.

Antelman, S. M. (1975). Tail pinch induces eating in sated rats which appears to depend on nigrostriatal dopamine. *Science* **189,** 731–733.

Babicky, A., Ostadalova, I., Parizek, J., Kolar, J., and Bibr, B. (1970). Use of radioisotope techniques for determining the weaning period in experimental animals. *Physiologia Bohemoslovaca* **19,** 457–467.

Barnett, S. A. (1963). "The Rat: A Study in Behavior," pp. 75–76. Aldine, Chicago.

Bateman, N. (1957). Some physiological aspects of lactation in mice. *Journal of Agricultural Science* **49,** 60–77.

Baverstock, P., and Green, B. (1975). Water recycling in lactation. *Science* **187,** 657–658.

Bell, R. W. (1974). Ultrasounds in small rodents: Arousal-produced and arousal-producing. *Developmental Psychobiology* **7,** 39–42.

Bernstein, I. L., and Woods, S. C. (1980). Ontogeny of cephalic insulin release by the rat. *Physiology and Behavior* **24**, 529–532.

Bernstein, I. L., Lotter, E. C., and Zimmerman, J. C. (1976). Cholecystokinin-induced satiety in weanling rats. *Physiology and Behavior* **17**, 541–544.

Bignall, K. E., Heggeness, F. W., and Palmer, J. E. (1974). Effects of acute starvation on cold-induced thermogenesis in the preweanling rat. *American Journal of Physiology* **277**, 1088–1093.

Blake, C. A. (1974). Stimulation of pituitary prolactin and TSH release in lactating and proestrous rats. *Endocrinology (Baltimore)* **94**, 503–508.

Blass, E. M., and Cramer, C. P. (1982). Analogy and homology in the development of ingestive behavior. *In* "Changing Concepts of the Nervous System: Proceedings of the First Institute of Neurological Sciences Symposium in Neurobiology" (A. R. Morrison and P. L. Strick, eds.), pp. 503–523. Academic Press, New York.

Blass, E. M., Hall, W. G., and Teicher, M. H. (1979). The ontogeny of suckling and ingestive behaviors. *Progress in Psychobiology and Physiological Psychology* **8**, 243–299.

Blaxter, K. L. (1961). Lactation and the growth of the young. *In* "Milk: The Mammary Gland and Its Secretion" (S. K. Kon and A. T. Cowie, eds.), Vol. 2, pp. 305–361. Academic Press, New York.

Bolles, R. C., and Woods, P. J. (1964). The ontogeny of behaviour in the albino rat. *American Journal of Physiology* **12**, 427–441.

Booth, D. A., and Brookover, T. (1968). Hunger elicited in the rat by a single injection of bovine crystalline insulin. *Physiology and Behavior* **3**, 439–446.

Brake, S. C., and Hofer, M. A. (1980). Maternal deprivation and prolonged suckling in the absence of milk alter the frequency and intensity of sucking responses in neonatal rat pups. *Physiology and Behavior* **24**, 185–189.

Brake, S. C., Wolfson, V., and Hofer, M. A. (1979). Electromyographic patterns associated with non-nutritive sucking in 11–13-day-old rat pups. *Journal of Comparative and Physiological Psychology* **93**, 760–770.

Brake, S. C., Sager, D. J., Sullivan, R., and Hofer, M. A. (1982). The role of intra-oral and gastrointestinal cues in the control of sucking and milk consumption in rat pups. *Developmental Psychobiology* **15**, 529–541.

Brody, S., and Nisbet, R. (1938). Growth and development with special reference to domestic animals—XLVII. A comparison of the amounts and energetic efficiencies of milk production in rat and dairy cow. *Research Bulletin—Missouri, Agricultural Experiment Station* **285**, 1–30.

Bruce, H. M. (1958). Suckling stimulus and lactation. *Proceedings of the Royal Society of London, Series B: Biological Sciences* **149**, 421–423.

Cole, H. A. (1933). The mammary gland of the mouse, during the oestrous cycle, pregnancy and lactation. *Proceedings of the Royal Society of London, Series B: Biological Sciences* **114**, 136–160.

Conklin, P., and Heggeness, W. F. (1971). Maturation of temperature homeostasis. *American Journal of Physiology* **220**, 333–336.

Cowie, A. T., Folley, S. J., Cross, B. A., Harris, G. W., Jacobsohn, D., and Richardson, K. C. (1951). Terminology for use in lactational physiology. *Nature (London)* **168**, 421.

Cramer, C. P., and Blass, E. M. (1983). Mechanisms of control of milk intake in suckling rats. *American Journal of Physiology* **245**, R154–R159.

Cramer, C. P., and Blass, E. M. (1985). Nutritive and nonnutritive determinants of milk intake of suckling rats. *Behavioral Neuroscience* **99**, 578–582.

Cramer, C. P., Blass, E. M., and Hall, W. G. (1980). The ontogeny of nipple-shifting behavior in albino rats: Mechanisms of control and possible significance. *Developmental Psychobiology* **13**, 165–180.

Croskerry, P. G., Smith, G., Leon, M., and Mitchell, E. A. (1976). An inexpensive system for continuously monitoring maternal behavior in the laboratory rat. *Physiology and Behavior* **16,** 223–225.

Cross, B. A. (1961). Neural control of lactation. *In* "Milk: The Mammary Gland and Its Secretions" (S. K. Kon and A. T. Cowie, eds.), Vol. 1, pp. 229–277. Academic Press, New York.

Deis, R. P. (1968). The effect of an exteroceptive stimulus on milk ejection in lactating rats. *Journal of Physiology (London)* **197,** 37–46.

Dement, W. C. (1978). "Some Must Watch While Some Must Sleep." Norton, New York.

Dollinger, M. J., Holloway, W. R., and Denenberg, V. H. (1978). Nipple attachment in rats during the first 24 hours of life. *Journal of Comparative and Physiological Psychology* **92,** 619–626.

Dollinger, M. J., Holloway, W. R., and Denenberg, V. H. (1980). The development of behavioral competence in the rat. *In* "Maternal Influences and Early Behavior" (R. Bell and W. Smotherman, eds.), Spectrum, pp. 27–56. Holliswood, New York.

Drewett, R. F. (1978a). The development of motivational systems. *Progress in Brain Research* **48,** 407–417.

Drewett, R. F. (1978b). Gastric and plasma volume in the control of milk intake in suckling rats. *Quarterly Journal of Experimental Psychology* **30,** 755–764.

Drewett, R. F. (1983). Sucking, milk synthesis, and milk ejection in the Norway rat. *In* "Parental Behavior of Rodents" (R. W. Elwood, ed.), pp. 181–204. Wiley, New York.

Drewett, R. F., and Cordall, K. M. (1976). Control of feeding in suckling rats: Effects of glucose and of osmotic stimuli. *Physiology and Behavior* **16,** 711–717.

Drewett, R. F., and Trew, A. M. (1978). The milk ejection of the rat, as a stimulus and a response to the litter. *Animal Behaviour* **26,** 982–987.

Drewett, R. F., Stratham, C., and Wakerley, J. B. (1974). A quantitative analysis of the feeding behaviour of suckling rats. *Animal Behaviour* **22,** 907–913.

Drucker-Colin, R. R., Spanis, C. W., Cotman, C. W., and McGaugh, J. L. (1975). Changes in protein in perfusates of freely moving cats: Relation to behavioral state. *Science* **187,** 963–965.

Drucker-Colin, R. R., Zamora, J., Bernal-Pedraza, J., and Sosa, B. (1979). Modification of REM sleep and associated phasic activities by protein synthesis inhibitors. *Experimental Neurology* **63,** 458–467.

Edwardson, J. A., and Eayrs, J. T. (1967). Neural factors in the maintenance of lactation in the rat. *Journal of Endocrinology* **38,** 51–59.

Elwood, R. W., and Broom, D. M. (1978). The influence of litter size and parental behaviour on the development of Mongolian gerbil pups. *Animal Behaviour* **26,** 438–454.

Epstein, A. N. (1986). The ontogeny of ingestive behaviors: Control of milk intake by suckling rats and the emergence of feeding and drinking at weaning. *In* "Feeding Behavior: Neural and Hormonal Controls" (R. C. Ritter, S. Ritter, and C. D. Barnes, eds.), pp. 1–25. Academic Press, New York.

Epstein, A. N., Blass, E. M., Batshaw, M. L., and Parks, A. D. (1970). The vital role of saliva as a mechanical sealant for suckling in the rat. *Physiology and Behavior* **5,** 1395–1398.

Falconer, D. S. (1947). Milk production in mice. *Journal of Agricultural Science* **37,** 224–235.

Fowler, S. J., and Kellogg, C. (1975). Ontogeny of thermoregulatory mechanisms in the rat. *Journal of Comparative and Physiological Psychology* **89,** 738–746.

Friedman, M. (1975). Some determinants of milk ingestion in suckling rats. *Journal of Comparative and Physiological Psychology* **89,** 636–647.

Friedman, M. (1979). Effects of milk consumption and deprivation on body fluids of suckling rats. *Physiology and Behavior* **23,** 1029–1033.

Friedman, M., and Bruno, J. P. (1976). Exchange of water during lactation. *Science* **191,** 409–410.

Gallen, J. R., and Turkewitz, G. (1975). Variability of the effects of rearing in a large litter on the development of the rat. *Developmental Psychobiology* **8,** 325–331.

Gil-ad, I., Udeschini, G., Cocchi, D., and Muller, E. E. (1975). Hyporesponsiveness to glucoprivation during postnatal period in the rat. *American Journal of Physiology* **229**, 512–517.

Gisel, E. G., and Henning, S. J. (1980). Appearance of glucoprivic control of feeding behavior in the
developing rat. *Physiology and Behavior* **24**, 313–318.

Gottlieb, G. (1971). Ontogenesis of sensory function in birds and mammals. *In* "The Biopsychology
of Development" (E. Tobach, L. R. Aronson, and E. Shaw, eds.). Academic Press, New York.

Gramsbergen, A. (1976). The development of the EEG in the rat. *Developmental Psychobiology* **9**,
501–515.

Grosvenor, C. E. (1965). Contraction of lactating rat mammary gland in response to direct mechanical stimulation. *American Journal of Physiology* **208**, 214–218.

Grosvenor, C. E., and Mena, F. (1971). Effect of suckling upon the secretion and release of prolactin
from the pituitary gland of the lactating rat. *Journal of Animal Science* **32** (Suppl. 1), 115–136.

Grosvenor, C. E., and Mena, F. (1973). Evidence for a time delay between prolactin release and the
resulting rise in milk secretion rat in the rat. *Journal of Endocrinology* **58**, 31–39.

Grosvenor, C. E., and Mena, F. (1979). Alterations in the oxytocin-induced intramammary pressure
response after mechanical stimulation of the mammary gland of the anesthetized lactating rat.
Endocrinology (Baltimore) **104**, 443–447.

Grosvenor, C. E., and Mena, F. (1982). Regulating mechanisms for oxytocin and prolactin secretion
during lactation. *In* "Neuroendocrine Perspectives" (E. F. Muller and R. M. MacLeod, eds.),
pp. 69–102. Elsevier/North-Holland, Amsterdam.

Grosvenor, C. E., and Turner, C. W. (1957). A method for evaluation of milk "let down" in lactating
rats. *Proceedings of the Society for Experimental Biology and Medicine* **94**, 816–817.

Grosvenor, C. E., and Turner, C. W. (1959). Effect of growth hormone and oxytocin upon milk yield
in the lactating rat. *Proceedings of the Society for Experimental Biology and Medicine* **100**,
158–161.

Grosvenor, C. E., DeNuccio, D. J., King, S. F., Miaweg, H., and Mena, F. (1972). Central and
peripheral neural influences on the oxytocin-induced pressure response of the mammary gland
of the anesthetized lactating rat. *Journal of Endocrinology* **55**, 299–309.

Grosvenor, C. E., Whitworth, N., and Mena, F. (1975). Milk secretory response of the conscious
lactating rat following intravenous injections of rat prolactin. *Journal of Dairy Science* **58**,
1803–1807.

Grota, L. J. (1973). Effects of litter size, age of young, and parity on foster mother behaviour in
Rattus norvegicus. *Animal Behaviour* **21**, 78–82.

Grota, L. J., and Ader, R. (1969). Continuous recording of maternal behaviour in *Rattus norvegicus*.
Animal Behaviour **17**, 722–729.

Hahn, P., and Koldovsky, O. (1966). "Utilization of Nutrients during Postnatal Development."
Pergamon, New York.

Hall, W. G. (1975). Weaning and growth of artificially reared rats. *Science* **190**, 1313–1315.

Hall, W. G. (1985). What we know and don't know about the development of independent ingestion
in rats. *Appetite* **6**, 333–356.

Hall, W. G. (1990). The ontogeny of ingestive behavior: Changing control of components in the
feeding sequence. *Handbook of Behavioral Neurobiology* **10**, 77–123.

Hall, W. G., and Oppenheim, R. W. (1987). Developmental psychobiology: Prenatal, perinatal, and
early postnatal aspects of behavioral development. *Annual Review of Psychology* **38**, 91–128.

Hall, W. G., and Rosenblatt, J. S. (1977). Suckling behavior and intake control in the developing rat
pup. *Journal of Comparative and Physiological Psychology* **91**, 1232–1247.

Hall, W. G., and Williams, C. L. (1983). Suckling isn't feeding, or is it? A search for developmental
continuities. *In* "Advances in the Study of Behavior" (J. S. Rosenblatt, R. A. Hinde, R. A.
Beer, and M. Busnell, eds.), Vol. 13, pp. 219–254. Academic Press, New York.

Hall, W. G., Cramer, C. P., and Blass, E. M. (1975). Developmental changes in suckling of rat pups. *Nature (London)* **258**, 318–320.

Hall, W. G., Cramer, C. P., and Blass, E. M. (1977). The ontogeny of suckling in rats: Transitions toward adult ingestion. *Journal of Comparative and Physiological Psychology* **91**, 1141–1155.

Hall, W. G., Hudson, R., and Brake, S. C. (1988). Terminology for use in investigations of nursing and suckling. *Developmental Psychobiology* **21**, 89–91.

Hanwell, A., and Linzell, J. L. (1972). A simple technique for measuring the rate of milk secretion in the rat. *Comparative Biochemistry and Physiology A: Comparative Physiology* **43A**, 259–270.

Heggeness, F. W., Bindschadler, D., Chadwick, J., Conklin, P., Hulnick, S., and Oaks, M. (1961). Weight gains of overnourished and undernourished preweanling rats. *Journal of Nutrition* **75**, 39–44.

Henning, S. J. (1980). Maternal factors as determinants of food intake during the suckling period. *International Journal of Obesity* **4**, 329–332.

Henning, S. J., and Romano, T. J. (1982). Investigation of body temperature as a possible feeding control in the suckling rat. *Physiology and Behavior* **28**, 693–696.

Henning, S. J., Chang, S. S. P., and Gisel, E. G. (1979). Ontogeny of feeding controls in suckling and weanling rats. *American Journal of Physiology* **237**, R187–R191.

Hofer, M. A. (1976). The organization of sleep and wakefulness after maternal separation in young rats. *Developmental Psychobiology* **9**, 189–205.

Hofer, M. A., and Shair, H. (1978). Ultrasonic vocalization during social interaction and isolation in 2-week-old rats. *Developmental Psychobiology* **11**, 495–504.

Hofer, M. A., and Shair, H. (1982). Control of sleep–wake states in the infant rat by features of the mother–infant relationship. *Developmental Psychobiology* **15**, 229–243.

Hofer, M. A., Shair, H., and Singh, P. (1976). Evidence that maternal ventral skin substances promote suckling in infant rats. *Physiology and Behavior* **17**, 131–136.

Holloway, W. R., Dollinger, M. J., and Denenberg, V. H. (1978). Differential nipple attachment by the neonatal rat. *Behavioral Biology* **24**, 428–441.

Houpt, K. A., and Epstein, A. N. (1973). Ontogeny of controls of food intake in the rat: GI fill and glucoprivation. *American Journal of Physiology* **225**, 58–66.

Houpt, K. A., and Houpt, R. T. (1975). Effects of gastric loads and food deprivation on subsequent food intake in suckling rats. *Journal of Comparative and Physiological Psychology* **88**, 764–772.

Houpt, K. A., and Houpt, R. T. (1979). Gastric emptying and cholecystokinin in the control of food intake in suckling rats. *Physiology and Behavior* **23**, 925–929.

Jakubowski, M., and Terkel, J. (1986). Prolactin release and milk ejection in rats suckling underfed pups. *Endocrinology (Baltimore)* **118**, 8–13.

Jans, J. E., and Leon, M. (1983). Determinants of mother–young contact in Norway rats. *Physiology and Behavior* **30**, 919–935.

Jans, J. E., and Woodside, B. (1987). Effects of litter age, litter size, and ambient temperature on the milk ejection reflex in lactating rats. *Developmental Psychobiology* **20**, 333–344.

Johanson, I. B. (1979). Thermotaxis in neonatal rat pups. *Physiology and Behavior* **23**, 871–874.

Johanson, I. B., and Hall, W. G. (1980). The ontogeny of feeding in rats: III. Thermal determinants of early ingestive responding. *Journal of Comparative and Physiological Psychology* **94**, 977–992.

Jouvet-Mounier, D., Astic, L., and Lacote, D. (1970). Ontogenesis of the states of sleep in rat, cat, and guinea pig during the first postnatal month. *Developmental Psychobiology* **2**, 216–239.

Kenny, J. T., Stoloff, M. L., Bruno, J. P., and Blass, E. M. (1979). Ontogeny of preference for nutritive over nonnutritive suckling in albino rats. *Journal of Comparative and Physiological Psychology* **93**, 752–759.

King, J. A. (1963). Maternal behavior in Peromyscus. *In* "Maternal Behavior in Mammals" (H. L. Rheingold, ed.), pp. 58–93. Wiley, New York.

Kissileff, H. R., Pi-Sunyer, F. X., Thornton, J., and Smith, G. P. (1981). C-terminal octapeptide of cholecystokinin decreases food intake in man. *American Journal of Clinical Nutrition* **34,** 154–160.

Kleitman, N. (1963). "Sleep and Wakefulness." University of Chicago Press, Chicago.

Kleitman, N., and Satinoff, E. (1982). Thermoregulatory behavior in rat pups from birth to weaning. *Physiology and Behavior* **29,** 537–541.

Kristal, M. B., Thompson, A. C., Heller, S. B., and Komisaruk, B. R. (1986). Placenta ingestion enhances analgesia produced by vaginal/cervical stimulation in rats. *Physiology and Behavior* **36,** 1017–1020.

Kulkosky, P. J. (1985). Conditioned food aversions and satiety signals. *Annals of the New York Academy of Sciences* **443,** 330–347.

Kumaresan, P., Anderson, R. R., and Turner, C. W. (1967). Effect of litter size upon milk yield and litter weight gains in rats. *Proceedings of the Society for Experimental Biology and Medicine* **126,** 41–45.

Lau, C., and Henning, S. J. (1984). Regulation of milk ingestion in the rat. *Physiology and Behavior* **33,** 809–815.

Lau, C., and Henning, S. J. (1985). Investigation of the nature of the "stretch response" in suckling rats. *Physiology and Behavior* **34,** 649–651.

Lau, C., and Henning, S. J. (1989). Mutualism in mother–offspring interaction: Its importance in the regulation of milk release. *In* "CRC Handbook of Human Growth and Developmental Biology" (E. Meisami and P. S. Timiras, eds.), Vol. II, Part B. CRC Press, Boca Raton, Florida.

Leon, M. (1979). Mother–young reunions. *Progress in Psychobiology and Physiological Psychology* **8,** 301–334.

Leon, M., and Woodside, B. (1983). Energetic limits of reproduction: Maternal food intake. *Physiology and Behavior* **30,** 945–957.

Leon, M., Croskerry, P. G., and Smith, G. (1978). Thermal control of mother–young contact in rats. *Physiology and Behavior* **21,** 793–811.

Leon, M., Adels, L., and Coopersmith, R. (1985). Thermal limitation of mother–young contact in Norway rats. *Developmental Psychobiology* **18,** 85–105.

Leshem, M., Boggan, B., and Epstein, A. N. (1988). The ontogeny of drinking evoked by activation of brain angiotensin in the rat pup. *Developmental Psychobiology* **21,** 63–76.

Leshem, M., Flynn, F. W., and Epstein, A. N. (1990). Brain glucoprivation and ketoprivation do not promote ingestion in the suckling rat pup. *American Journal of Physiology* **258,** R365–R375.

Lincoln, D. W. (1969). Correlation of unit activity in the hypothalamus with EEG patterns associated with the sleep cycle. *Experimental Neurology* **24,** 1–18.

Lincoln, D. W., and Wakerley, J. B. (1975). Factors governing the periodic activation of supraoptic and paraventricular neurosecretory cells during suckling in the rat. *Journal of Physiology (London)* **250,** 443–461.

Lincoln, D. W., Hill, A., and Wakerley, J. B. (1973). The milk-ejection reflex of the rat: An intermittent function not abolished by surgical levels of anesthesia. *Journal of Endocrinology* **57,** 459–476.

Lincoln, D. W., Hentzen, K., Hin, T., van der Schoot, P., Clarke, G., and Summerlee, A. J. S. (1980). Sleep: A prerequisite for reflex milk ejection in the rat. *Experimental Brain Research* **38,** 151–162.

Lorenz, D. N. (1983). Effects of gastric filling and vagotomy on ingestion, nipple attachment, and weight gain by suckling rats. *Developmental Psychobiology* **16,** 469–483.

Lorenz, D. N. (1985). Gastric emptying of milk in rats. *American Journal of Physiology* **248,** R732–R738.

Lorenz, D. N. (1986a). Alimentary sleep satiety in suckling rats. *Physiology and Behavior* **38,** 557–562.

Lorenz, D. N. (1986b). Cholecystokinin effects on ingestion in infant rats. Paper presented at the Ninth International Conference on the Physiology of Food and Fluid Intake, Seattle.

Lorenz, D. N. (1991). Preload and vagotomy effects on paradoxical sleep in infant rats. Paper presented at the Developmental Psychobiology Winter Conference, Cancun, Mexico.

Lorenz, D. N., Ellis, S. B., and Epstein, A. N. (1982). Differential effects of upper gastrointestinal fill on milk ingestion and nipple attachment in the suckling rat. *Developmental Psychobiology* **15**, 309–330.

Lytle, L. D., Moorcroft, W. H., and Campbell, B. A. (1971). Ontogeny of amphetamine anorexia and insulin hyperphagia in the rat. *Journal of Comparative and Physiological Psychology* **77**, 388–393.

MacFarlane, B. A., Pedersen, P. E., Cornell, C. E., and Blass, E. M. (1983). Sensory control of suckling-associated behaviours in the domestic Norway rat, *Rattus norvegicus*. *Animal Behaviour* **31**, 462–471.

Mansbach, R. S., and Lorenz, D. N. (1983). Cholecystokinin (CCK-8) elicits prandial sleep in rats. *Physiology and Behavior* **30**, 179–183.

McCauley, P. J., and Elwood, R. W. (1984). Hunger and the vocalizations of infant gerbils. *Developmental Psychobiology* **17**, 183–189.

Mena, F., and Grosvenor, G. E. (1968). Effect of number of pups upon suckling induced fall in pituitary prolactin concentration and milk ejection in the rat. *Endocrinology (Baltimore)* **82**, 623–626.

Mena, F., Pacheco, P., Aguayo, D., Clapp, C., and Grosvenor, G. E. (1978). A rise in intramammary pressure follows electrical stimulation of mammary nerve in anesthetized rats. *Endocrinology (Baltimore)* **103**, 1929–1956.

Miselis, R. R., and Epstein, A. N. (1975). Feeding induced by intracerebro ventricular 2-deoxy-D-glucose in the rat. *American Journal of Physiology* **29**, 1438–1447.

Mistretta, C. M. (1972). Topographical and histological study of the developing rat tongue, palate and taste buds. *In* "The Third Symposium of Oral Sensations and Perception: The Mouth of the Infant" (J. F. Bosma, ed.), pp. 163–187. Thomas, Springfield, Illinois.

Moltz, H., Lubin, M., Leon, M., and Numan, M. (1970). Hormonal induction of maternal behaviour in the ovariectomized nulliparous rat. *Physiology and Behavior* **5**, 1373–1377.

Moorcroft, W. H. (1981). Heightened arousal in the 2-week-old rat: The importance of starvation. *Developmental Psychobiology* **14**, 187–199.

Moore, C. L. (1981). An olfactory basis for maternal discrimination of sex of offspring in rats (*Rattus norvegicus*). *Animal Behaviour* **29**, 383–386.

Morag, M. (1970). Estimation of milk yield in the rat. *Laboratory Animals* **4**, 259–272.

Moran, T. H. (1986). Environmental and neural determinants of behavior in development. *Handbook of Behavioral Neurobiology* **8**, 99–128.

Negoro, H., Uchide, K., Tadokoro, Y., Honda, K., and Higuchi, T. (1987). Vaginal distension induces milk ejection-related burst of oxytocin neurones interacting with suckling stimuli in lactating rats. *Brain Research* **404**, 371–374.

Nicoll, C. S., and Meites, J. (1959). Prolongation of lactation in the rat by litter replacement. *Proceedings of the Society for Experimental Biology and Medicine* **101**, 81–82.

Noirot, E. (1972). Ultrasounds and maternal behavior in small rodents. *Developmental Psychobiology* **5**, 371–387.

Ogilvie, D. M., and Stinson, R. H. (1966). The effect of age on temperature selection by laboratory mice (Mus musculus). *Canadian Journal of Zoology* **44**, 511–517.

Ogle, C. W., and Lockett, F. M. (1966). The release of neurohypophysial hormone by sound. *Journal of Endocrinology* **36**, 281–290.

Okon, E. E. (1970). The effect of environmental temperature on the production of ultrasounds by isolated nonhandled albino mouse pups. *Journal of Zoology* **162**, 71–83.

Okon, E. E. (1972). Factors affecting ultrasound production in infant rodents. *Journal of Zoology* **168**, 139–148.

Oswalt, G. L., and Meier, G. W. (1975). Olfactory, thermal and tactual influences on infantile ultrasonic vocalization in rats. *Developmental Psychobiology* **8**, 129–135.

Parkes, A. S. (1926). The growth of young mice according to size of litter. *Annals of Applied Biology* **13**, 374–394.

Pedersen, P. E., and Blass, E. M. (1982). Olfactory control over suckling in albino rats. *In* "Development of Perception: Psychobiological Perspectives" (R. N. Aslin, J. R. Alberts, and M. R. Peterson, eds.), Vol. 1, pp. 359–381. Academic Press, New York.

Priestnall, R. (1972). Effects of litter size on the behaviour of lactating female mice (*Mus musculus*). *Animal Behaviour* **20**, 386–394.

Priestnall, R. (1983). Postpartum changes in maternal behavior. *In* "Parental Behavior of Rodents" (R. W. Elwood, ed.), pp. 67–94. Wiley, New York.

Robinson, P. H., Moran, T. H., and McHugh, P. R. (1985). Gastric cholecystokinin receptors and the effect of cholecystokinin on feeding and gastric emptying in the neonatal rat. *Annals of the New York Academy of Sciences* **448**, 627–629.

Roffwarg, H. P., Muzio, J. N., and Dement, W. C. (1966). Ontogenetic development of the human sleep–dream cycle. *Science* **152**, 604–619.

Rojas-Ramirez, J. A., Aguilar-Jimenez, E., Posadas-Andrews, A., Bernal-Pedraza, J. G., and Drucker-Colin, R. R. (1977). The effects of various protein synthesis inhibitors on the sleep–wake cycle of rats. *Psychopharmacology (Berlin)* **53**, 147–150.

Rosenblatt, J. S. (1975). Prepartum and postpartum regulation of maternal behavior in the rat. *Ciba Foundation Symposium* **33**, 17–32.

Russek, M. (1970). Demonstration of the influence of an hepatic glucosensitive mechanism on food intake. *Physiology and Behavior* **5**, 1207–1209.

Russell, J. A. (1980). Milk yield, suckling behavior and milk ejection in the lactating rat nursing litters of different sizes. *Journal of Physiology (London)* **303**, 403–415.

Sawyer, C. H., and Kawakami, M. (1959). Characteristics of behavioral and electroencephalographic after-reactions to copulation and vaginal stimulation in the female rabbit. *Endocrinology (Baltimore)* **65**, 622–630.

Shair, H., Brake, S. C., and Hofer, M. A. (1984). Suckling in the rat: Evidence for patterned behavior during sleep. *Behavioral Neuroscience* **98**, 366–370.

Shapiro, S. (1968). Adrenal catecholamine response of the infant rat to insulin-provoked hypoglycemia. *Endocrinology (Baltimore)* **82**, 1065–1067.

Smith, G. P., and Epstein, A. N. (1969). Increased feeding in response to decreased glucose utilization in the rat and monkey. *American Journal of Physiology* **217**, 1083–1087.

Smith, G. P., and Gibbs, J. (1979). Postprandial satiety. *Progress in Psychobiology and Physiological Psychology* **8**, 179–242.

Sterman, M. B. (1979). Ontogeny of sleep: Implications for function. *In* "The Functions of Sleep" (R. Drucker-Colin, M. Shkurovich, and M. B. Sterman, eds.), pp. 207–232. Academic Press, New York.

Stern, J. M., and Johnson, S. K. (1989). Perioral somatosensory determinants of nursing behavior in Norway rats (*Rattus norvegicus*). *Journal of Comparative Psychology* **103**, 269–280.

Stern, W. C., and Morgane, P. J. (1977). Sleep and memory: Effects of growth hormone and sleep, brain biochemistry and behavior. *In* "Neurobiology of Sleep and Memory" (R. R. Drucker-Colin and J. L. McGaugh, eds.), pp. 373–410. Academic Press, New York.

Stern, J. M., Thomas, D. A., Rabii, J., and Barfield, R. J. (1984). Do pup ultrasonic cries provoke prolactin secretion in lactating rats? *Hormones and Behavior* **18**, 86–94.

Stoloff, M., Kenny, J. T., Blass, E. M., and Hall, W. G. (1980). The role of experience in suckling maintenance in albino rats. *Journal of Comparative and Physiological Psychology* **94**, 847–856.

Szymusiak, R., and Satinoff, E. (1981). Maximal REM sleep time defines a narrower thermoneutral zone than does minimal metabolic rate. *Physiology and Behavior* **26**, 687–690.

Terkel, J., and Rosenblatt, J. S. (1972). Humoral factors underlying maternal behavior at parturition: Cross transfusion between freely moving rats. *Journal of Comparative and Physiological Psychology* **80**, 365–371.

Terkel, J., Damassa, D. A., and Sawyer, C. H. (1979). Ultrasonic cries from infant rats stimulated prolactin release in lactating mothers. *Hormones and Behavior* **12**, 95–102.

Terry, L. M. (1988). An early appetitive response: I. Ontogeny of response form and sensitivity to maternal and nutritional deprivation. Ph.D Dissertation, Duke University, Durham, North Carolina, pp. 4–48.

Timo-Iaria, C., Negrao, N., Schmidek, W. R., Hoshino, K., Lobato de Menezes, C. E., and Leme da Rocha, T. (1970). Phases and states of sleep in the rat. *Physiology and Behavior* **5**, 1057–1062.

Voloschin, L. M., and Tramezzani, J. H. (1979). Milk ejection reflex linked to slow wave sleep in nursing rats. *Endocrinology (Baltimore)* **105**, 1202–1207.

Voogt, J. L., and Carr, L. A. (1974). Plasma prolactin levels and hypothalamic catecholamine synthesis during suckling. *Neuroendocrinology* **16**, 108–118.

Vorherr, H., Kleeman, C. R., and Lehman, E. (1967). Oxytocin-induced stretch reaction in suckling mice and rats: A semiquantitative bioassay for oxytocin. *Endocrinology (Baltimore)* **81**, 711–715.

Voronka, G. A., Demin, N. N., and Pezner, L. Z. (1971). Total protein content and quantity of basic proteins in neurons and neuroglia of the supraoptic and red nuclei of the rat brain in natural sleep and deprivation of rapid eye movement sleep. *Doklady Akademii Nauk SSSR* **198**, 974–977.

Wakerley, B. J., and Drewett, R. F. (1975). Pattern of sucking in the infant rat during spontaneous milk ejection. *Physiology and Behavior* **15**, 277–281.

Weller, A., Smith, G. P., and Gibbs, J. (1990). Endogenous cholecystokinin reduces feeding in young rats. *Science* **247**, 1589–1591.

Widdowson, E. M., and McCance, R. A. (1960). Some effects of accelerating growth: I. General somatic development. *Proceedings of the Royal Society of London, Series B: Biological Sciences* **152**, 188–206.

Williams, C. L., and Blass, E. M. (1987). Development of postglucoprivic insulin-induced suckling and feeding in rats. *American Journal of Physiology* **253**, R121–R127.

Wolff, P. H. (1968). Suckling patterns of infant mammals. *Brain, Behavior and Evolution* **1**, 354–367.

Wurtman, J. J., and Miller, S. A. (1976). Effect of litter size on weight gain in rats. *Journal of Nutrition* **106**, 697–701.

Zaks, M. G. (1962). *In* "The Motor Apparatus of the Mammary Gland" (A. T. Cowie, ed.; D. G. Fry, transl.). pp. 1–26. Oliver and Boyd, London.

Brain Neuronal Unit Discharge in Freely Moving Animals: Methods and Application in the Study of Sleep Mechanisms

Dennis McGinty* and Jerome M. Siegel †

Sepulveda Veterans Administration Medical Center
Sepulveda, California 91343
and
Departments of Psychology* and Psychiatry†
University of California, Los Angeles
Los Angeles, California 90024

I. Introduction

In the evolution of hypotheses concerning brain mechanisms of behavior, few techniques have had more influence than the study of neuronal discharge in awake behaving animals. The basic principles behind this approach are simple. Any set of neurons hypothesized to be involved in a particular function can be expected to exhibit altered discharge in temporal relationship to the occurrence of the function. In addition, the details of the temporal patterns of discharge correlated with the function could provide specific information about the kind of complex coding in the neural circuitry underlying the associated brain mechanisms. Well-known examples include movement-related cells in the precentral cortex and stimulus "edge" detectors in the visual cortex.

Outside of delineated sensory or motor pathways, many brain areas appear to have multiple functions, possibly reflecting the various specializations of closely adjacent or overlapping subsets of neurons or the convergence or integration of multiple functions by individual neurons. The functions of any particular neuron encountered either electrophysiologically or histologically may be unknown. In these cases, unit-recording techniques may allow us to identify such functions. For example, we may ask whether certain hypothalamic neurons show changes related to satiety, hunger, or food ingestion, or physiological stimuli related to feeding (e.g., blood glucose), rather than to any of several other hypothalamic functions.

85

Even certain concepts with a primarily neurochemical basis may be studied by examining neuronal unit discharge. This approach is based on the concepts that the release of neurotransmitters is initiated by nerve impulse flow and that the neuronal discharge rate is, therefore, one measure of the rate of transmitter release. This method can be used when chemically defined neurons (e.g., serotoninergic neurons) are clustered such that they may be localized using conventional histology, or they have unique identifiable electrophysiological properties, inputs, or projections. The role of monoaminergic mechanisms in sleep was studied by recording the discharge patterns of identified monoamine-releasing neurons. Examples of this type of experiment are summarized below (Section IV,D,G).

Clearly, a variety of methods play essential roles in the analysis of brain functions, and each has both uses and limitations. Neuronal recording, in comparison to lesion, stimulation, biochemical correlative, pharmacological, or imaging techniques, can provide more specific information concerning anatomical localization and temporal features of control mechanisms. Motor control systems may provide the clearest example. A lesion study of a particular part of the brain may reveal a motor deficit, but a unit-recording study could reveal discharge related to a specific element of movement, such as initiation or termination of movement, movement velocity or force, to learned or unlearned aspects, or even to certain motor fiber types. Neurons with a specific relationship to movement may be localized in a specific subregion or layer of a structure. Thus, neuronal unit recording provides unique information about both detailed temporal and spatial coding and relationships to subunits or elements of a behavior. We may refer to this information as the "behavioral functional neuroanatomy of a brain site."

On the other hand, neuronal unit-recording methods are essentially correlative in nature. It is very difficult to know whether activity in a particular neuronal type is generating a process, or only responding to some input which is the true generator. When events or processes have abrupt onsets with latencies of responses in the millisecond range, as, for example, in the case of a startle response, it may be possible to make interpretations that include causal relationships. Such interpretations may be useful in the context of specific anatomical information concerning probable neuronal connections. However, in the case of behavioral events such as sleep–waking state changes, which occur over the course of several seconds or more, latency information is far less definitive relative to questions of causality.

Thus, lesion or stimulation methods have more often provided the bases for generating hypotheses about the role of a particular brain site in a function. However, neuronal activity studies may be used to verify and refine a hypothesis, to suggest particular ways in which a mechanism is regulated. Still more reductionistic methods, including analysis of receptors and membrane conductance mechanisms, neurochemical synthesis, release, binding, and inactivation, and details of neuronal structure, will eventually be brought to bear on any particular problem. However, it should be clear that understanding of the functions and mechanisms of any brain structure will also depend on knowing exactly when neuronal subtypes are active. We believe that this behavioral functional neuroanatomy in any site is as crucial to understanding of the site as the chemical anatomy or the identification of transmitters or projection patterns. It would seem that only with a combination of these approaches can the mechanistic basis of behavior be determined.

In this article, we examine the status of investigation of sleep mechanisms and assess the uses (and abuses) of chronic unit-recording studies for the larger goal of unraveling the nature of sleep mechanisms. From the start, we focus on attempts to understand behavior. In the case of sleep, we hope to determine what mechanisms explain processes such as the change in behavior defined by the onset and termination of sleep, the stages within sleep, including rapid eye movement sleep (REMS), the temporal features of sleep architecture, the regulation of the amounts of sleep, and the unique features of physiological processes within sleep. While these goals have not been achieved, the analysis of sleep mechanisms has developed to the point where specific mechanistic hypotheses are under study.

The study of brain mechanisms of sleep has evolved along a course not unlike that of other types of behavior. Initial beliefs that mechanisms might be associated with restricted cell groups such as norepinephrine- or serotonin-containing neurons have given way to more complex concepts. At the same time, there has been an astonishing growth in the knowledge of more basic neurophysiological mechanisms. We are now aware of dozens of neurotransmitters and neuromodulators, receptors with multiple components, complex pre- and postsynaptic modulatory events, and a variety of ionic processes regulating cellular excitability. Each cell seems to be capable of intricate adaptations. Each region of the brain contains numerous cell types. In the current context, it is not surprising that different methods used in the analysis of structure–function relationships have sometimes yielded conflicting results. Of particular interest to students of neuroscience may be a comparison of the conclusions obtained by different methodologies.

II. A Chronic Neuronal Unit-Recording Method

To apply neuronal recording techniques to the problems of behavioral functions, it was first necessary to study the unanesthetized animal. This approach was pioneered by Hubel (1960), Jasper *et al.* (1960), and Evarts (1968) in head-restrained animals. As researchers interested in certain slowly changing behaviors and sleep and waking states, we required a technique that would permit long-term stability of unit recording. Further, we were interested in brain areas thought to be involved in a wide variety of behavioral functions, and we anticipated that the use of head restraint would severely limit the kinds of behavior we could study. These were the technical issues we faced in 1970. We developed a simple technique that permitted chronic unit recording in unrestrained animals for hours, sometimes days. The method is based on the use of fine-wire recordings of unit discharge. This article summarizes the technical aspects as well as the applications of the method, using examples from our work in sleep neurophysiology. Among the most crucial findings have been the analysis of movement-related discharge in medial reticular formation neurons (Siegel, 1979a), the long-term cyclic REMS-off behavior of dorsal raphe serotonin-containing neurons (McGinty et al., 1973; McGinty and Harper, 1976), and the sleep-selective activity of neurons within the basal forebrain (Szymusiak and McGinty, 1986b). A review summarizing many of the findings of this approach in a wider range of behaviors is also available (McGinty and Szymusiak, 1988a).

Prior to our work, Strumwasser (1958) and Olds et al. (1972) had demonstrated the usefulness of chronically implanted, fixed-position, "floating" fine-wire electrodes in providing stable unit or multiunit recordings in unrestrained rodents. This method had also been used successfully in cats (Naka and Kido, 1967; O'Keefe and Bouma, 1969; Harper, 1971; Burns et al., 1974) and humans (Marg and Adams, 1967). However, fixed electrodes are obviously limited, since recordings are restricted to neurons close to final resting site of the electrode after implantation. One of us (D.M.) developed the simple, skull-mounted, lightweight microdrive that permitted the exploration of a track through a site, like that used with conventional rigid microelectrodes. This improvement made it possible to record from many more neurons in a single animal and to adjust electrode position to optimize isolation of action potentials from single neurons (Harper and McGinty, 1973).

Neurophysiologists who had struggled with the construction and use of very high-impedance microelectrodes were initially skeptical that electrodes with exposed tips several times larger than those of conventional microelectrodes could possibly isolate single units. However, results provided by fine-wire techniques have been completely consistent with those obtained using conventional microelectrodes; the method has stood the test of time. The long-term stability of unit recording with microwires has permitted certain types of experiments that were very difficult or impossible with conventional microelectrode techniques. This feature has led to a number of discoveries about the coding of behavior. While more complex variations of the microwire method have now been described (e.g., McNaughton et al., 1983), and these may be useful in some experimental problems, our particular method still offers an advantage in simplicity. A detailed discussion of the biophysical and other technical issues involved in chronic unit recording can be found in the monograph by Lemon (1984).

The features of our method for recording neuronal unit discharge in un-restrained animals are shown in Fig. 1. The electrodes consist of fine insulated wires, commonly called microwires, which are threaded into the brain through the barrels of stainless steel cannulae that are part of a microdrive. The microdrive is described in detail below. Unlike conventional electrodes, which are relatively thick except at the sharpened tip, microwires have the same small diameter throughout their length. This makes it possible to place several adjacent electrodes in a site, driven from one microdrive, without producing extensive damage to adjacent tissue. Since a cluster of microwires is used and calls can be studied from each wire, a single pass with the microwire bundle is equivalent to several passes with a conventional single microelectrode. In addition, it is often possible to record from two or more neurons in close proximity, permitting the analysis of interactions of adjacent cells (see below). The animal can be prepared with a variety of additional recording electrodes or other devices, such as for recording electroencephalographic (EEG) patterns, eye movements, and muscle activity and for brain stimulation (see Fig. 1 and further discussion below).

Additional advantages are derived from the fact that the microwire electrodes have a lower impedance compared to conventional microelectrodes. This means that recordings are less influenced by "antenna-derived" noise and by electrical artifacts generated by cable movements. Thus, study of discharge during all types of movement of animals is possible. Conventional microelectrodes can be used in unanesthetized animals with the head rigidly restrained, but this creates certain complications. The animal must be adapted to the restraint, but even with adaptation the procedure could remain stressful. Further, head restraint prevents head movements and locomotion, two basic classes of movement.

Stability of recording is usually the greatest difficulty encountered when using conventional microelectrodes. The stability of microwire unit recording is among its greatest advantages. Instability is thought to be caused by slight movements of brain tissue relative to the electrode tip, and may result from "pulsations" in blood flow or movements related to respiration. These effects are amplified if the skull cavity is open, as it is with conventional microelectrodes. However, with the microwire technique, electrodes are implanted chronically and the skull is sealed, minimizing such movements.

Two variations on the method for placing the microwires within a guide cannula are in use in our laboratories. The original method utilized a bundle of microwires prepared before surgery. The advantage of this method is that each wire can be soldered to an electrical connector prior to surgery, eliminating a difficult step during the surgical procedure. The bundle is lowered through the cannula as a unit. Histological inspection of electrode tracks indicates that wires of a bundle often remain in a compact cluster within the brain. It is not unusual to record the neuronal discharge of the same cell from two, presumably adjacent, wires. When 32-μm or finer wires are used in the bundle, it may be useful to add

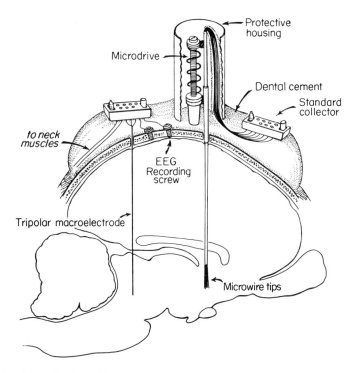

FIG. 1. Schematic view of the cat brain and overlying skull showing how the microwire unit-recording system is mounted. The microdrive is stereotaxically positioned in a selected brain site and fixed to the skull with dental cement. Additional recordings from cortical surface electroencephalographic and electromyographic electrodes or from depth electrodes may be made through separate electrical connectors.

stiffness to the bundle by including nonrecording 65-μm wires that end about 5 mm from the bundle tip.

A second method consists of lowering three to seven microwires individually through the guide cannula during surgery, which was done to achieve two goals. First, we found that bundles did not readily penetrate ependymal tissues in the floor of the fourth ventricle, because of the combined cross-sectional area of several wires. Individual wires could penetrate readily. When individual wires were cut on an angle, to provide a beveled tip, they penetrated tissue even more easily. However, individual 19– to 32-μm wires do not have sufficient stiffness to be threaded through a cannula into the brain. In order to insert single fine bevel-cut wires individually, it was necessary to attach a strengthening support wire. This was done by gluing 37-, 45-, or 65-μm support wires to the finer recording wires, the latter extending 1–4 mm beyond the end of the support wires (see below). The glued microwire pairs typically have a slight curvature. This yields a second advantage to this variation. The tips of the microwires tend to follow slightly different paths, providing some dispersion of the tips, and a slightly wider area of neuronal sampling under the cannula. A third use of individual microwires has been suggested (Chang *et al.*, 1988). In some species, during neck movements, the medulla moves longitudinally relative to the overlying cranial bones, to which the microdrive is fixed. Therefore, recordings of medullary unit discharge in unrestrained chronic animals are very unstable. Chang *et al.* proposed that the individual fine wires may "float" in the medulla even during longitudinal movements, permitting improved recording stability.

The disadvantage of the individual-wire method is that the fine wires must be soldered to a connector after placement in the microdrive, a critical but tedious and sometimes difficult task that must be added to the surgical procedure.

Formvar-insulated stainless steel microwire can be purchased in any diameter and in a variety of alloys from a commercial source.[1] It is important to order double- or triple-insulated wire that is "stress-relieved" and shipped on a 6-inch spool, to maximize wire straightness. We currently use type 304 stainless steel because it is relatively stiff and contains iron. The iron content permits the deposition of iron with an anodal current and the identification of the electrode tip with the Prussian Blue staining technique (Siegel, 1968). We use wires with diameters of 19, 25, 32.5, and 37.5 μm for electrodes, and 37.5, 45, or 62.5 μm for support wires, depending on the nature of the recording site. In many sites, the larger wires are as effective as smaller wires in achieving good recordings. In some sites, a combination of 32- and 65-μm wires has proved effective.

Wires to be placed in the brain as part of a bundle are prepared by cutting desired lengths (e.g., about 110 mm for the cat). If wires are to be introduced glued to support wires, several "coils" of electrode wire are wrapped on a jig (Fig. 2). The support wires are then glued to the suspended portions of the electrode wire. We use Epoxylite (Epoxylite Corp., S. El Monte, CA) enamel glue, which requires that the entire jig is baked for about 1 hr at 100°C. The glued pairs of wires are then cut free in 110-mm lengths, the support wire ending about 2–4 mm from one end. This end is prepared as the recording tip. The recording tip can be cut either at 90° or at a 45–60° angle to create a pointed electrode. The opposite end must be stripped of insulation (2–3 mm) to facilitate soldering to a head-mounted connector. Insulation is removed with fresh commercial enamel remover (Strip-X, GC Electronics, Rockford, IL) or by burning off insulation with a small flame (Chang *et al.*, 1988). It is also important to "tin" this end, using stainless steel solder and flux prior to surgery. We have recently started to electroplate gold on the recording tip[2] to produce a more

[1]California Fine Wire, 338 South Fourth Street, P.O. Box 446, Grover City, California 93433; (805) 489-6760.
[2]EutecSol Flux, type 682, Eutectic Corp., 7731 Oakport, Oakland, California 94621; (800) 662-0051.

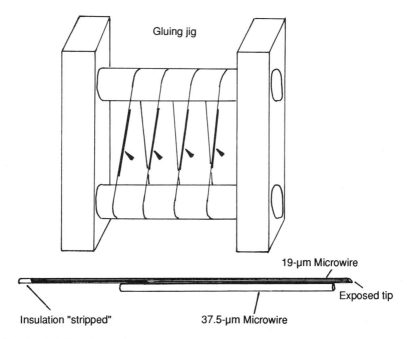

FIG. 2. Technique for making individual microwires with support wires. (Top) Several turns of the recording wire are firmly wrapped on a wood-gluing jig. Sections of the selected support wire (about 60 mm long for cats) are dipped in Epoxylite and positioned on the suspended sections of the recording wire. After "baking" for about 60 min at 100°C to harden the epoxylite, sections of wire are cut free (bottom).

chemically inert exposed surface, although we have not done a controlled study to determine whether this is important.

We emphasize that the preparation of the microwires is a crucial aspect of the procedure; microwire electrode failure is not uncommon. The most common types of failure appear to be (1) poor soldering of the very fine stainless steel wires to the connector, (2) insulation failure along the microwire, and (3) poor configuration of the electrode tip. It is important to use stainless steel solder and flux.[3] When using 25-μm or smaller wire, it may be useful to take additional steps to ensure a good solder joint such as soldering tiny pieces of tubing to the wires before surgery. The cutting of the recording tip should be done with very sharp scissors. The properties of microwire insulation and tip configuration may be indicated by the electrode impedance. We have begun pretesting the impedance of microwires after implantation to reduce the failure rate. A commercial

[3]Electrode impedence meter, model BL-2000, Winston Electronics, P.O. Box 638, Millbrae, California 94030; (415) 589-6900.

microwire impedance tester is available.[4] Wires with either too high or too low impedance should be replaced. Insulation failure typically develops over a period of 1–2 weeks. Diana *et al.* (1987) compared the effectiveness of different insulators *in vivo* and concluded that Parylene (Union Carbide) or lacquer were superior to Formvar, but they did not test double- or triple-layer Formvar, which we have found suitable.

The design of the microdrive was determined by the requirement for compactness; we wished to be able to mount several drives on one animal, while maintaining space for electrical connectors to accommodate each microwire plus stimulating and recording macroelectrodes. We also wished to avoid the need for specialized machine tools. We continue to use the original microdrive, built with less than $1 worth of readily available hardware items[4] in less than 30 min (Fig. 3). More refined, machine-made, microdrives can also be used. A small metal block can be drilled with adjacent holes serving as guide tubes and, after threading, providing the positioning of the machine screw. With this approach, the acquisition of the slight skills needed to master the construction procedure can be avoided, but there is little or no improvement in results. However, one advantage of machine-made microdrives is the possibility of creating three-dimensional arrays of cannulae, driven by the same machine screw.

The steps in constructing a microdrive are shown in Fig. 4. Using a grinding disk on a moto-tool, stainless steel tubing sections for both inner and guide cannulae can be cut to appropriate lengths, as determined by the depth of the recording site below the dorsal surface of the skull. Stainless steel tubing sizes (gauges) for the inner and guide cannulae can be 24TW and 21TW or 23TW and 20TW, respectively. Three to five stainless steel nuts are tightened (using fingertips) on a machine screw and soldered together to form the stack (Fig. 4B). After the outer cannulae are positioned in a suitable jig (Fig. 4C), the nut stack is soldered to them. The machine screw used during this soldering operation can then be removed and saved for the next fabrication. A new screw is inserted through a stack of three washers, and the spring is then threaded into the nut stack for several turns, the spring now being compressed against the washers. The inner cannulae are then slid through the outer cannulae into position and soldered to the washers (Fig. 4D). Microdrives can be constructed with one, two, three, or more cannulae. A final step is to cement in place a piece of flexible tubing that serves to maintain a path under the nut stack for the machine screw. Otherwise, this area may inadvertently be filled with dental cement during surgery. Microdrives built for use with rats, cats, and dogs are shown in Fig. 5.

An important advantage of the handmade microdrive is the ability to build a wide variety of configurations of the cannula positions in order to optimize

---

[4]Small Parts, Inc., 6891 NE Third Avenue, P.O. Box 381966, Miami, Florida 33238-1966; (305) 751-0856. Catalog available.

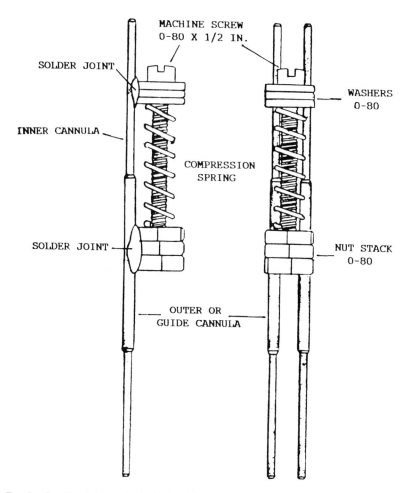

FIG. 3.   Details of the mechanical microdrive. Shown is a two-barrel microdrive with barrels separated by 2 mm. Both the number and the separation of barrels, as well as their length, can be varied according to the needs of the experiment. For additional details, see text and Fig. 4.

recording from neuronal groups with varying spatial dimensions. Additionally, it is possible to build microdrives with recording sites adjacent to sites for microinjection, measurement of temperature, and electrical stimulation or for any other implantable device. The adjacent device can move in parallel with the microwire tips, or not, according to the needs of the experiment. Figures 6 and 7 show two variations for microinjection adjacent to recording sites. Experiments utilizing cholinergic stimulation adjacent to recording sites are described below (Section IV,E). In this case, microinjections were made about 1 mm from recording sites and utilized an

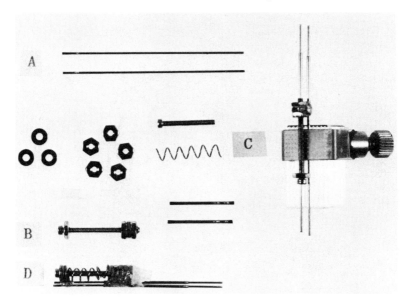

FIG. 4. Construction of a two-barrel mechanical microdrive. (A) The parts required include stainless steel tubing for the inner cannula and the outer or guide cannula (below spring), washers (size 0), nuts and machine screw (size 0–80), and compression spring. (B) Three to five nuts are tightened together on a machine screw and soldered to form the nut stack. (C) A stereotaxic electrode holder is used as a jig to hold the inner cannulae parallel at the desired separation. (D) Final configuration of the microdrive (see text).

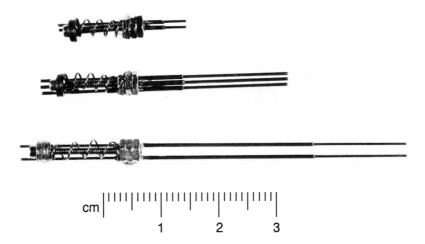

FIG. 5. Microdrives for deep recording sites in the rat, cat, and dog (note scale at bottom). Three different barrel configurations are shown.

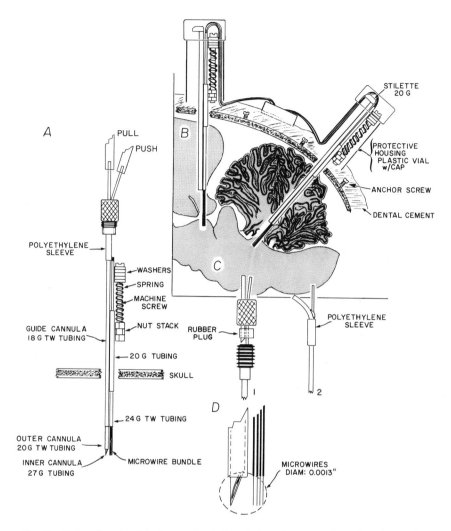

A

PULL
PUSH

POLYETHYLENE
SLEEVE

WASHERS
SPRING
MACHINE
SCREW

GUIDE CANNULA
18 G TW TUBING
NUT STACK

20 G TUBING

SKULL

24 G TW TUBING

OUTER CANNULA
20 G TW TUBING

INNER CANNULA
27 G TUBING
MICROWIRE BUNDLE

B

STILETTE
20 G

PROTECTIVE
HOUSING
PLASTIC VIAL
w/CAP

ANCHOR SCREW

DENTAL CEMENT

C

RUBBER
PLUG

POLYETHYLENE
SLEEVE

1

2

D

MICROWIRES
DIAM: 0.0013"

FIG. 6. System for microinjection or chemical perfusion adjacent to microwire unit-recording sites, illustrated for the cat midbrain (B) and pontine (C) sites. (A) Diagram of a push–pull cannula system attached to the microdrive. The push–pull system guide cannula is positioned beside the microdrive so that the tip is about 1 mm from the microwire tips. Note that this system can be used for either simple infusion or push–pull perfusion. (B) Microdrive push–pull guide cannula assemblies are implanted in two sites in a cat, but perfusion tips are not in position. (C) Construction details showing two types of "plumbing" for separating the infused solution and the extracted solution from the concentric tubes. (1) The inner cannula passes through the sealed chamber above the outflow of the outer cannula. Outflow collection is made from a separate tube passing into the chamber. (2) The outer cannula is bent, with a hole above bend. The inner cannula passes through the hole, which is then sealed with solder. Polyethylene sleeves can be adjusted to determine the depth of the cannula. (D) Field of diffusion to recording sites of perfused or infused substances. (From McGinty *et al.*, 1982.)

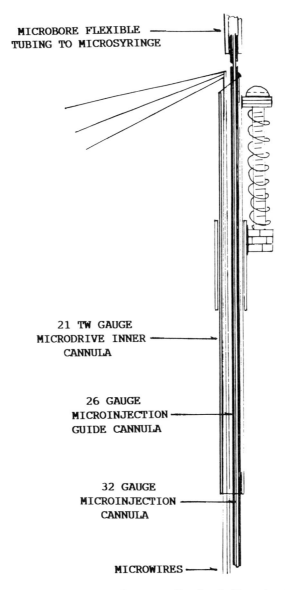

MICROBORE FLEXIBLE
TUBING TO MICROSYRINGE

21 TW GAUGE
MICRODRIVE INNER
CANNULA

26 GAUGE
MICROINJECTION
GUIDE CANNULA

32 GAUGE
MICROINJECTION
CANNULA

MICROWIRES

FIG. 7.   Method for microinfusion very close to recording sites. In this version of the microdrive, an infusion cannula and microwires pass through the same inner cannula, so that microinjections may be within 0.5 mm of the recording site.

injection volume sufficient to induce specific behaviors (Fig. 6). If the purpose is to approximate the goals of an iontophoretic injection study (i.e., application of a very small amount of chemical very close to the recording site), then the variation shown in Fig. 7 can be used. In this case, the microinjection cannula passes within the same guide as the microwires. However, injection volumes must be very small (~0.05 μl), and injections must be made slowly to avoid displacement of tissue away from the recording site, thereby disrupting the recording.

Finally, the need to make multiple passes through a site may apply in some situations, as when a neuronal group has little vertical depth, so that few cells of a type can be encountered on one pass, or in extremely valuable animals in which it is essential to record the maximum number of cells. For these applications, we have devised a microdrive variation for making multiple passes along slightly different paths through a single site. This is accomplished by making the inner cannula with a slight bend and incorporating a method for withdrawing the microwires and rotating the cannula after completion of one vertical penetration (Fig. 8).

Although the crucial value of this system is the ability to record unit activity in unrestrained animals for extended periods, a secondary virtue is the relative ease of application. No special instruments or tools or outside assistance is needed to make electrodes or microdrives. Thus, less of the experimenters' effort needs to be devoted to these technical matters.

Figure 9 shows a schematic recording and behavioral study facility including two channels of unit data as well as other polygraphic variables. Connections to the experimental subject are supported by a counterweighted boom. Microwire signals are led to selector switches that permit scanning of each wire for suitable recordings. The amplified and filtered signal is displayed on an oscilloscope, and may be stored on a tape recorder for future analysis. The window discriminator converts unit signals into standard pulses that may be detected by a laboratory computer interface or displayed on a polygraph. The integrator accumulates the pulses in a convenient time interval for additional display on the polygraph and rapid rate estimation. There are several commercial versions of this equipment.

While recording unit discharge, it is possible to perform a wide variety of experimental manipulations, including microinjections, brain or chamber temperature control, brain stimulation, control of lighting, food delivery, introduction of complex behavioral contingencies, or sleep deprivation with a treadmill (Fig. 9). Good visibility or video monitoring is essential, as it is important to observe the animal closely. Changes in unit discharge that are detected may be related to an unexpected component of behavior elicited by the experimental treatment.

In the examples described below (Section IV,B), we demonstrate certain advantages of the microwire technique in comparison to the conventional stiff fine-tipped microelectrode technique used in head-restrained animals. The microwire technique provides far superior temporal stability of recording and the capability

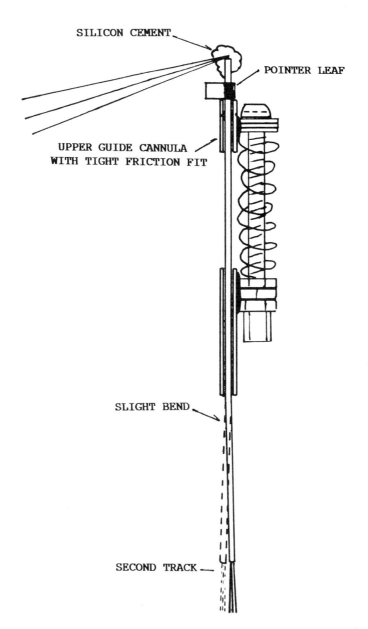

SILICON CEMENT

POINTER LEAF

UPPER GUIDE CANNULA
WITH TIGHT FRICTION FIT

SLIGHT BEND

SECOND TRACK

FIG. 8. Modification of the microdrive for multiple passes in one site. The lower portion of the inner cannula has a slight bend, so that when it is rotated, a new path is determined. Instead of being soldered tightly to the washers, the inner cannulae are connected by a tight friction-fitted tubing. A small metal pointer leaf, soldered to the top of the inner cannula, is used to turn the cannula and show the direction of the bend. Microwires are held in the cannula by a small glob of silicon seal. Before turning the inner cannula, the microwires are withdrawn to a position above the cannula tip. The rotating cannula tip will produce mechanical brain damage, but the diameter of the tip path may be only 1 mm.

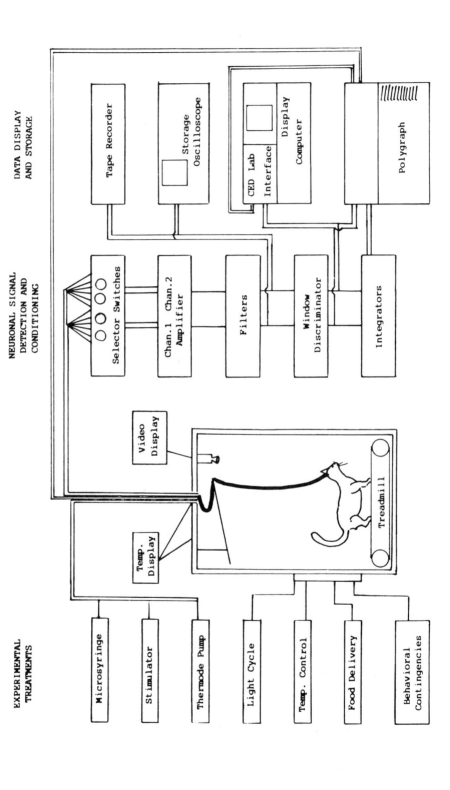

of correlating unit discharge with a wide range of behaviors. These advantages have permitted several important observations. On the other hand, the conventional stiff-electrode technique may provide superior isolation of single units, particularly in areas of high neuronal density, and better resolution of small neurons. A "stereotrode" system, in which subtle differences in wave forms recorded from adjacent microwires can be used to discriminate cells, has been developed for use in areas of high cell density (McNaughton et al., 1983). The microwire technique has been applied primarily in subcortical sites; applications in the neocortex have been demonstrated, but require further study (Lemon, 1984).

III. Overview of Sleep Mechanisms

Readers may refer to many excellent books for reviews of the complexities of sleep physiology and neurophysiology (Orem and Barnes, 1980; Borbely and Valatx, 1984; McGinty et al., 1985; Wauquier et al., 1985, 1989; Kryger et al., 1989). Here, we summarize only the important features of sleep that are crucial to understanding the search for neural substrates of sleep mechanisms.

Sleep in mammals and birds (i.e., homeotherms) shares crucial common features; it is composed of two distinct "states," namely, slow-wave sleep (SWS), and REMS. SWS is named for the higher-amplitude lower-frequency (slow-wave) EEG patterns that identify this state under normal conditions. During REMS, the EEG is "activated" or desynchronized as it is in waking. However, REMS periods can be identified by the absence of postural muscle tone in conjunction with EEG activation. These states alternate within extended periods of sleep, REMS occurring at roughly 10- to 100-min intervals, depending primarily on the species. SWS occurs initially at sleep onset, except in neonates, which may have sleep-onset REMS. Total sleep time varies with species and is correlated with the basal metabolic rate of the species, although the functional

---

FIG. 9.   Experimental apparatus used for unit recording and a variety of experimental manipulations. Microwire signals are conveyed in separate wires to selector switches which determine input to both amplifiers and filters. In this diagram, two unit recordings can be done simultaneously, but a three- or four-channel system may be useful. Filters are usually set to pass frequencies between 300 and 5000 Hz (-6 db), although it may be useful to compare electroencephalographic and unit recordings from the same electrodes in some types of experiments. Switches permit the scanning of all wires for suitable recordings, as seen on the oscilloscope. Unit signals of suitable amplitude, stability, and separation from other units are detected by window discriminators, which generate pulses for computerized data analysis and for display on a polygraph. Pulse integrations are also displayed on the polygraph for rapid quantification of data. Data may also be stored on a tape recorder for subsequent analysis. We use a Cambridge Electronic Design (CED) computer interface system, which includes a variety of spike-train analysis software, but several commercial systems are available. Separate cables are used to convey additional neurophysiological or physiological signals directly to the polygraph.

significance of this correlation continues to be debated (Zepelin and Rechtschaffen, 1974). The proportion of sleep which is REMS ranges from about 6% to 46% in adult mammals and, across species, is correlated with the maturity of the species at birth and an aspect of its ecological niche: Predators and animals with secure nests have more REMS (Allison and Cicchetti, 1976). Again, these correlations are not well understood in functional terms. Sleep in neonates may consist primarily of REM (e.g., Valatx *et al.*, 1964). Within SWS, there are more differentiated EEG-defined substates in higher primates and humans, a probable reflection of the elaboration of the neocortex.

Sleep in poikilothermic animals seems to be quite different from that in mammals. Although these animals may have clear sustained behavioral quiescence, the distinctive EEG features of both SWS and REMS are absent in reptiles, amphibians, and fish. The sleeplike state of poikilotherms is more dependent on environmental conditions; transitions between states are gradual. Some observers (e.g., Flanigan *et al.*, 1973) have suggested that toporlike states in reptiles and lower animals are most akin to SWS. However, the differences between poikilothermic and homeothermic sleep is striking, and it is reasonable to hypothesize that many of the specialized neuronal adaptations underlying both SWS and REMS are connected to the physiological adaptations found in homeotherms.

SWS and REMS are literally odd "bedfellows." They are very different states. SWS is associated with reduced cerebral metabolic rate, reduced (although not absent) neuronal activity in most brain regions, reduced cerebral blood flow, and a radically changed pattern of cerebral neural activity, compared to waking (see McGinty and Beahm, 1984). In contrast, REMS is characterized by an activated brain with an associated increase in cerebral metabolic activity. On the basis of neuronal discharge patterns, the brain seems as if it is awake in REMS, except for certain differences (see Section IV,D,G below). However, while upper motor neuronal systems are activated in REMS, most spinal motoneurons are paralyzed by potent hyperpolarization, producing the so-called muscle "atonia" of REMS. Although SWS and REMS are different in most physiologically measurable ways, it is important to remember that these two states provide continuity of behavioral sleep and reduced sensory responsiveness. The neurophysiological correlates of the behavioral and psychophysiological similarities of SWS and REMS are not established.

There is an important distinction between "phasic" and "tonic" components of REMS. Thus, although REMS is a sustained tonic state, as identified by EEG and motor criteria (i.e., atonia), there are superimposed phasic events such as REMs, twitches, and changes in heart rate. REMS-deprived animals have more phasic events in their recovery sleep, suggesting that the expression of phasic events is a critical regulated feature of this state. While phasic events tend to be "made up" in recovery sleep, total REMS time is not. The best-studied phasic event in the brain is the PGO wave, or "spike" (see Fig. 11), so named because of their recording sites: the dorsolateral pons, lateral geniculate nucleus, and occipital cortex (Jouvet, 1967). They begin 30 sec or more before the onset of tonic features of REMS and may have a role in triggering this state. PGO waves are also coincident with individual eye movements of REMS. PGO waves have been studied extensively because they are frequent, stereotyped, and discrete events susceptible to neurophysiological analysis and because they have been localized in structures that are hypothesized to be critical for generation of REMS. Transection studies have shown that regions caudal to the midpontine nucleus reticularis pontis oralis are not required for the generation of PGO activity released by reserpine (Laurent *et al.*, 1974). Spontaneous PGO waves in association with a REMS-like state persist in the forebrain of undrugged chronically maintained animals with transections at the pontomedullary junction (Siegel *et al.*, 1984). Cytotoxic lesions placed within the dorsolateral pontine region between these transections eliminate PGO spikes or greatly reduce their amplitude (Webster and Jones, 1988). Stimulation of the dorsolateral pons triggers PGO spikes with a latency similar to the latency difference between the spontaneous and lateral geniculate nucleus PGO waves (Sakai *et al.*, 1976). This evidence indicates that pontine mechanisms are the critical substrate for PGO wave generation.

A PGO-like potential can be elicited in the alert wakefulness by intense stimulation (Bowker and Morrison, 1976; Wu *et al.*, 1989), indicating that the potential is related to alerting or startle. Since the brain in REMS is in many ways similar to the waking brain, it has been hypothesized that the presence of PGO waves in REMS represents an endogenous activation of the startle network (Morrison and Bowker, 1975; Morrison, 1979).

The word "state" is sometimes applied to SWS and REMS. A "state" is defined as a physiological condition which is identified by a constellation of parameters, rather than by one particular parameter. Indeed, it has not been possible to find a single physiological parameter that unambiguously defines either SWS or REMS under all conditions. Key features of a given state may occur in the absence of the state, or the state may occur without the key features (see McGinty and Siegel, 1983). For example, characteristics of the cortical or thalamic EEG normally define SWS; the words "slow wave" are derived from the normal EEG correlates of the state. However, neonatal and neodecorticate animals appear to have the quiet sleep state in the absence of EEG synchrony. After treatment with muscarinic blocking agents such as atropine, the EEG may exhibit normal sleeplike patterns in a behaviorally awake animal (e.g., Szymusiak *et al.*, 1990a). Similarly, after lesions of a specific area in the dorsal pons, cats may have what appears to be fully developed REMS, but without exhibiting the usual motoneuron paralysis, indicating that the atonia or REMS is not sufficient to define REMS under all conditions.

Thus, none of the usual correlates of either SWS or REMS can be used alone to identify the state under all conditions. Under certain experimental conditions, they may appear independently of the sleep–waking state in which they normally appear. This implies that the neural generators of each of these correlates of sleep states are mediated by separate neuronal circuits; they may function in the absence of the parent state. An important concept is that the neural basis of both SWS and REMS must include processes that recruit these separate component generators to the symphony of conditions that constitute the state. In summary, sleep state mechanisms would seem to include the sum of their correlated parts, plus the mechanism that recruits or integrates the partially independent component networks.

Another aspect of sleep state physiology is the sensitivity of state patterns to certain physiological variables (McGinty, 1985). SWS is augmented while REMS is reduced at mildly elevated body temperatures, at elevated blood pressure, and in a hypoxic atmosphere (hypoxia with hypocapnia). The occurrence of SWS under these conditions tends to reduce the physiological stress by reducing temperature, blood pressure, and metabolism. Thus, sleep appears to participate in overall homeostatic processes. Further, sleep also modulates neuroendocrine function. SWS is known to gate or trigger the release of growth hormone and prolactin. Sleep onset inhibits the release of corticotropin and thyroid-stimulating hormone. These hormonal changes are appropriate for a condition of rest (McGinty and Beahm, 1984).

Also, sleep directly alters physiological regulatory systems. For example, sleep onset changes the gain of the chemoreceptor control of ventilation and induces heat-loss mechanisms, reflecting a lowered thermoregulatory set point (see McGinty and Beahm, 1984). These physiological changes affect the sleep control mechanisms, as noted above. Thus, sleep both changes and is changed by physiological variables, establishing a feedback control loop. For example, sleep onset lowers the regulated temperature set point, which would establish a heat-loss condition (relative heat load), until temperature falls to the sleep-associated set point. This heat load may facilitate SWS. Similar regulatory loops may apply to blood gas and blood pressure regulation. The existence of such feedback loops implies that each sequential state must establish an equilibrium on the basis of these sleep state–homeostatic physiological interactions.

States undergo sequential changes in a cyclic pattern. Within sustained sleep, SWS and REMS alternate in nonrandom patterns. In humans and monkeys, the cycle is quite predictable. For example, in humans, REMS reappears at 90- to 100-min intervals. In other mammals, the REMS–REMS interval is quite irregular, but has clear modal values. Sleep–waking is also cyclic, particularly in strongly circadian animals. However, elimination of circadian rhythmicity by making lesions of the hypothalamic circadian "clock" pacemaker in the suprachiasmatic nucleus changes only the 24-hr patterning of sleep and has little effect on the amount of sleep or short-term SWS–REMS architecture (see McGinty and Beahm, 1984). Thus, the 24-hr cycle affects the timing, but not the generation, of SWS and REMS.

The point of this brief review is to provide perspective on the issue of searching for the neural basis of sleep. In this search, we must be aware of the possibilities of misinterpretation of data because:

1. An experimental manipulation may change one of the correlates of sleep, rather than the state itself. For example, muscarinic blockers do not induce sleep, even though they induce a sleeplike EEG (see McGinty and Beahm, 1984).

2. Experimental manipulations may alter physiological variables, modifying the equilibrium between sleep and physiology. This, in turn, could cause an apparent state instability unrelated to state-generating mechanisms.

3. Neurophysiological events that appear to be correlated with a sleep state may only be correlated with a physiological concomitant of sleep and could be seen in the absence of the state if the appropriate physiological variable is changed to the critical level.

4. Sleep is easily prevented by discomfort or stress, or any stimulus that may increase the arousal level of the animal. REMS is blocked by a very wide variety of drugs and chemical agents; in many cases, this may only reflect physiological stress or disequilibrium, rather than a specific action of the agent in question. For example, the suppression of REMS by the α-adrenoreceptor antagonist phentolamine is secondary to the hypothermia caused by the drug, and can be prevented simply by maintaining the animal's body temperature (Kent et al., 1987).

5. Sleep and waking states do not appear in an all-or-none fashion. Scoring manuals describe the defining characteristics of REMS and SWS in order to facilitate communication among investigators. However, it is naive to interpret such definitions as indicating an abrupt event susceptible to latency analysis in the same way that evoked unit responses are. For example, REMS onset can be defined as the point at which the first burst of REMs occur in conjunction with EEG desynchrony and muscle atonia. If one takes this definition too literally, it is tempting to see any antecedent change in neuronal activity as causing this state change. In fact, there is a regular progression of physiological changes preceding "scoring manual-defined" REMS onset. For example, EEG desynchrony usually precedes the first REM, typically by 10–30 sec in the cat. EEG desynchrony itself is always preceded by the appearance of PGO spikes 30–60 sec earlier. These spikes show a regular reduction in amplitude and an increase in frequency prior to the appearance of EEG desynchrony. It would be erroneous to argue that EEG desynchrony "causes" the REMs, or that PGO spikes "cause" EEG desynchrony or the REM sleep state itself. However, precisely the same argument has been made for neurons showing activity changes before the manual-defined onset of REMS and waking (Hobson et al., 1974). Therefore, it is important to

appreciate the continuous nature of the spontaneous transitions into and out of sleep states in evaluating the role of any neuronal group in state transitions. Of course, events that occur earlier, rather than later, in a transition are more likely to be related to the control of the transition, but timing itself is not a sufficient argument.

This brings us to a second issue with regard to neural changes preceding physiological states. One can use statistical techniques to compare the latency of antecedent changes in various cell groups. The approach is to find the group with the earliest change, and then make the argument that this group has a causal role in the state transition. This approach is preferable to that of attributing a causal role to any neuron with activity changes prior to scoring manual-defined sleep state onsets. However, it can be equally misleading. The point at which a change in neuronal activity becomes statistically significant is determined by two variables. One is to point at which that cell group receives excitatory or inhibitory input, or autochthonously generates a change in activity; this is the variable of interest. The second variable is the amount of noise in the system. This may be a function of other inputs arising in the system, the noise caused by the recording technique, the aspect of spike discharge parameters used (e.g., simple rate, modal spike interval per unit of time, the duration of the sample used, the "baseline" firing rate of the cell in question, use of membrane potential measurements versus extracellular measurements, and use of cell pairs versus single-cell measurements). It is often difficult to separate the variable of interest from the noise involved in the measurement process. Latency measures are useful in the analysis of events occurring on the order of milliseconds, in which only a few synapses can be involved. However, latencies are usually quite unconvincing when analyzing state transitions occurring over a period of tens of seconds or minutes.

IV. Evaluation of Hypotheses Concerning Sleep Control

A. LOCALIZATION OF REMS MECHANISMS

Studies by French investigator Michel Jouvet and colleagues using chronically maintained animals with brain stem transections suggested that a neural generation of the REMS-like state could be localized in the lower brain stem. One can cut through the midbrain in the coronal plane, so as to separate the caudal brain stem from the diencephalon and telencephalic structures. Animals with such lesions manifest all of the brain stem signs of REMS that can be observed *caudal to the cut*. Atonia, REMs, and PGO spike bursts, as well as a REMS-like activation of reticular formation units occur in a regular ultradian rhythm (Jouvet, 1962; Villablanca, 1966). Therefore, one may conclude that structures rostral to the midbrain are not required for REMS, and that structures caudal to the midbrain contain neurons that are sufficient to generate REMS. Transection at the junction of the spinal cord and the medulla does not prevent all of the signs of REMS from occurring rostral to the cut (Adey *et al.*, 1968; Puizillout *et al.*, 1974). Thus, spinal mechanisms are not essential for the generation of REMS. From the above, we may conclude that structures caudal to the midbrain and rostral to the spinal cord are necessary for REMS.

This technique has been carried one step further by transecting between the medulla and the pons and maintaining the animals for extended periods to allow the fullest possible recovery from the transection (Siegel *et al.*, 1986). As was the case with midbrain sections, the brain regions rostral and caudal to the cut produce independent physiologically defined states. The medulla cycles regularly between an activated and a quiescent state. The activated state is characterized by high levels of muscle tone, identical to those seen in active waking, and by accelerated respiration and heart rate. The quiescent state is characterized by lower levels of muscle tone, resembling those seen in SWS, and by slow regular respiration. Periods of muscle atonia are not seen. Unit activity, recorded with our microwire technique, in the medial medulla during the quiescent state of the medullary animal resembles that seen in this region in SWS in the intact animal (i.e., it is slow and regular) (Fig. 10). Unit activity increases, but remains regular during the activated state. Thus, the respiratory regularity, the low level of muscle tone, and the unit activity during the quiescent state are similar to the conditions of SWS. The increased muscle tone and the unit activity during phasic arousal are similar to the conditions of waking. Periods of increased unit activity alternate in a regular ultradian rhythm with periods of quiescence with tonic regular discharge. Periods of irregular unit discharge, like those usually seen in normal REMS, do not occur. This indicates that the medulla and the spinal cord, disconnected from rostral structures, show spontaneous variations in levels of arousal and SWS-like states, but do not show the medullary signs of REMS. Structures caudal to the pons are not sufficient to generate REMS.

A very different picture is seen in rostral structures after transection between the pons and the medulla (Siegel *et al.*, 1984). Three states can be distinguished rostral to the transection. The first is a synchronized state without PGO spikes, resembling SWS. Thus, both the medulla and the forebrain show independent SWS-like states after these transections. The second state is a desynchronized state without PGO spikes, resembling waking. The third state is a desynchronized state with PGO spikes. The PGO activity occurs in irregular bursts and as isolated spikes in a manner very similar to that seen in REMS. Midbrain reticular units show irregular burst–pause patterns of discharge in conjunction with this third state (Fig. 11), as they do in REMS (Siegel, 1985).

From the above, one can see that when the pons is connected to mid- and forebrain structures, most of the defining signs of REMS are seen in these rostral

BASELINE

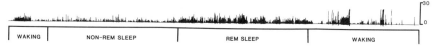

| WAKING | NON-REM SLEEP | REM SLEEP | WAKING |

TRANSECTED

5 MINUTES

FIG. 10. Medullary reticular formation (RF) unit activity during the sleep–waking cycle in an intact cat (baseline), and after brain stem transection at the pontomedullary junction. Tracing is the output of a digital counter resetting at 1-sec intervals. Note the long periods of accelerated and irregular RF unit discharge during waking and REMS in the intact cat. RF cells in transected cats had extremely regular discharge rates, interrupted by short periods of increased unit activity occurring in conjunction with movement arousals. Thus, unit-recording data supported the hypothesis that medullary mechanisms did not generate a REMS-like state. (From Siegel *et al.*, 1986.)

structures. When the pons is connected to the medulla and the spinal cord, as in the midbrain decerebrate animal, most of the defining signs of REMS are seen in caudal structures.

One can then transect through the middle of the pons and again ask the question "Which side has REMS?" (Siegel *et al.*, 1984, 1986). After this transection, the caudal pons and medulla shift between the aroused and quiescent states seen in the medullary animal (Siegel, 1985). No atonia or other signs of REMS are present. The rostral pons and forebrain show desynchronized waking-like states and synchronized SWS sleeplike states. The *synchronized* states may be accompanied by PGO spikes and PGO spike bursts, resembling those seen during desynchrony in REMS and REMS transitions. However, midbrain unit activity is greatly *decreased* at these times, in contrast to the activated pattern seen in REMS in the intact animal. PGO spikes do not occur in the desynchronized state. Therefore, with this midpontine transection, we reach the limit of the transection technique. The major defining characteristics of the REMS state are absent on both sides of the transection, even in chronically maintained animals.

While the foregoing indicates that the pons is necessary for the generation of REMS-like states in both rostral and caudal structures, one may ask, "Is the pons, in and of itself, sufficient to generate the pontine aspects of REMS?" One can monitor REMS signs after transecting *both* rostrally and caudally to the pons, producing an acute isolated pons preparation (Matsuzaki, 1969). In this case, the pons continues to generate periodic episodes of REMs and PGO spikes in a pattern which, in the intact animal, is seen only in REMS. This is impressive evidence of pontine control of these basic aspects of REMS.

B. REMS TRIGGERING AND THE MEDIAL PONTINE RETICULAR FORMATION (mPRF)

The next logical question was the identification of the critical cell groups for REMS generation within the pons. Hobson and colleagues hypothesized that mPRF cells were the critical neuronal elements. Cells in this area were found to have very high discharge rates in REMS, but were silent, or had relatively low discharge rates in SWS (Huttenlocher, 1961; Hobson *et al.*, 1974). In sleep-deprived cats adapted to the head restraint used during recordings, these cells have little waking activity, with waking rates comparable to those seen in SWS (Hobson *et al.*, 1974). They were also found to have a detectable increase in discharge 2 min before the "onset" of REMS (defined as the first REM burst), that is, "tonic latency."

However, in freely moving cats that were not sleep deprived, we found that virtually *all* mPRF cells discharge in waking at rates comparable to mean REMS rates (McGinty and Siegel, 1977; Siegel and McGinty, 1978; Siegel *et al.*, 1977). Discharge rates during active waking are positively correlated with REMS rates in a population of cells (Siegel *et al.*, 1979b). Figure 12 shows a continuous recording of a typical medial pontine unit during an extended period of waking and REMS. It is clear that the cells may be less active in waking than in REMS, but that during phasic episodes of activation, REMS and waking rates may be similar. During waking, periods of neuronal activation corresponded to periods of movement. Thus, the comparison of rates in different states depends on the behavior of animal during the sampling period.

POSTTRANSECTION
DAY 11

UNIT ACTIVITY DURING PGO

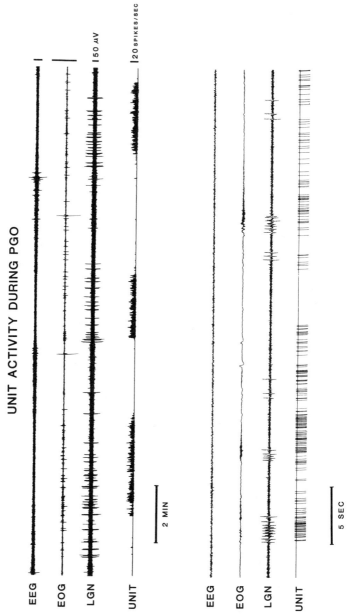

We devised a number of procedures for eliciting reflexes and testing with somatic, auditory, and visual stimuli. We also observed activity during spontaneous behaviors over periods averaging several hours. We quantified suspected movement relationships with a Hall-effect device [voltage induced in a conductor moving in a magnetic field (Nienhuis and Siegel, 1989)] and with photographic techniques (Siegel *et al.*, 1979a). We also devised a technique by which the animal could help us deduce the behavioral relationship. We reasoned that if the animal was reinforced for increasing discharge in the neuron of interest, it would increase the behaviors correlated with neuronal discharge. In this sense, the animal is required to determine the behavioral correlates of discharge in order to get reinforcement. The experimenter merely needs to observe the behavior that emerges and see whether it is the same as that observed during spontaneous firing and in response to appropriate stimuli. We accomplished this by reinforcing cats with hypothalamic stimulation for increasing discharge rate in these cells. We found that the animal quickly learned to produce the movement associated with maximal cell discharge repeatedly, much as an animal might learn to bar-press for reinforcement (Breedlove *et al.*, 1979). At the same time, with the photographic method, we could analyze the movement produced by the animal to obtain reinforcement (Fig. 13).

We found that most medial reticular cells discharge maximally in conjunction with a directionally specific movement of the head, neck, eyes, limbs, or facial musculature (Siegel and Tomaszewski, 1983). The most common correlate of increased discharge rate of cells in the mPRF is ipsilateral head movement. Such movements could be expected to occur in a variety of situations, especially those in which intense or noxious stimuli are applied.

One would expect centrally commanded skeletal movements (whose expression in REMS is blocked by motoneuron hyperpolarization) to accompany the REM bursts and muscle twitches of REMS. Thus, the apparent "selectivity" of discharge for REMS in cats recorded during head restraint can be seen as a consequence of the reduction in *waking* motor activity caused by the restraint, rather than indicating any essential role in REMS control for these cells (Siegel, 1979a). This conclusion is buttressed by studies showing no disruption of REMS

FIG. 11.   Midbrain reticular formation (RF) unit recordings with a cat with a pontomedullary transection. Unit activity during cortical electroencephalographic (EEG) desynchrony with PGO waves, or "spikes," shown at two different polygraph speeds. In the upper (slow) trace (see time calibration), the unit channel displays output of a digital counter resetting a 1-sec intervals. In the lower (faster) trace, individual unit potential signals trigger the deflections shown on the polygraph record. In contrast to the unit patterns recorded below the transection (Fig. 10), midbrain units showed sustained accelerated irregular discharge patterns like those normally seen in REMS, in conjunction with PGO waves. Thus, unit data supported the hypothesis that a REMS-like state could be generated by structures above the medullary RF. EOG, Electrooculogram; LGN, EEG patterns of the lateral geniculate nucleus, demonstrating PGO waves.

Waking

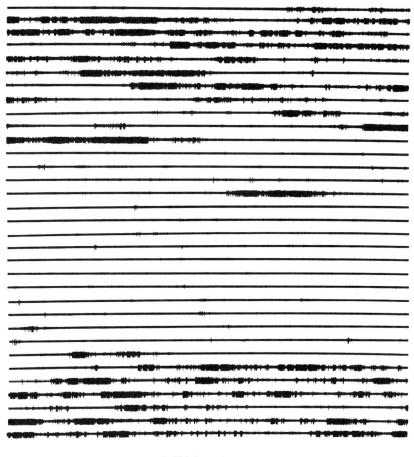

REM sleep

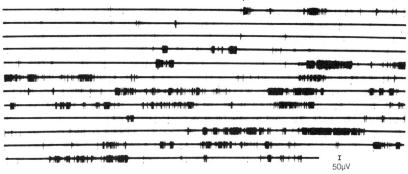

I
50μV

10 sec

when cytotoxins were injected into this region. Even though this manipulation totally removed all giant mPRF cells, REMS was not disturbed, appearing in normal amounts within 24 hr of the lesion (Sastre *et al.*, 1981; Drucker-Colin and Pedraza, 1983). However, such lesions do produce a persistent motor deficit, ipsilateral head movements being permanently impaired (Suzuki *et al.*, 1989). Conversely, chemical stimulation of this region produces a sustained contraction of the ipsilateral neck musculature (Suzuki *et al.*, 1989). Anatomical and physiological data indicating monosynaptic projections from this region to spinal motoneurons innervating neck muscles are consistent with our behavioral data (see Siegel, 1979a).

Thus, anatomical, stimulation, recording, and lesion data all agree in implicating mPRF cells in motor control. This finding, dependent on our ability to observe unit activity under normal behavioral conditions, has important implications not only for controversies over the role of mPRF cells in REMS control, but for literally several hundred previous studies (Siegel, 1979a). Early concepts of the reticular formation as a diffuse arousal system had led to many studies of unit activity in this area. Typically, these studies used anesthesia, or physical restraint. In the few cases in which the unrestrained preparation was utilized, little or no systematic observation of the animal was used. Investigators routinely found patterns of unit activity consistent with their arousal-related hypotheses. Thus, cells thought be to specifically related to "alertness," pain, reward anticipation, or attention were found virtually everywhere in the medial reticular formation. However, the assumption that the underlying relationship was to arousal-related processes blinded investigators to simpler relationships. Also lost in the literature were the underlying contradictions in much of this work. For example, one group of investigators reported a majority of mPRF cells discharged selectively in relation to pain in the same region that another group found cells discharging selectively in relation to REMS, while a third group found the majority of cells discharging in relation to reward (Siegel, 1979a). Only with the observation of these cells in the normally behaving animals could the underlying movement relationship be observed, explaining the unaddressed contradiction of how a single cell could be active in so many different behavioral situations.

In summary, since mPRF neuronal activity is not selective for REMS, it is unlikely to be critical for REMS generation. Detailed studies of these neurons

FIG. 12.   Continuous film record of amplified medial pontine reticular formation (mPRF) unit recording in waking (~11 min) and REMS (~4 min) in the freely moving animal. Note the variability of mPRF unit discharge in both states. Discharge bursts during waking were associated with specific movements. This is consistent with several types of evidence relating mPRF neuronal discharge to the control of movement (see text). We have hypothesized that the variability of REMS discharge reflects the internally programmed motor activity of this state. Also illustrated are quality and stability of unit recordings using the microwire method. (From Siegel *et al.*, 1977.)

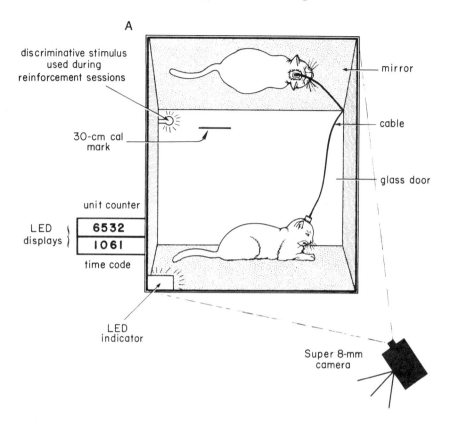

A

FIG. 13. (A) Arrangement of equipment used for the analysis of unit discharge–movement relationships. A film or video camera records the animal's movements, along with an LED display and incremental counter, which show each unit discharge. A second counter displays a time code, which is also written on the polygraph. (From Siegel *et al.*, 1979a.) (B) Unit discharge of a medial pontine reticular formation cell in which increased discharge was reinforced by hypothalamic stimulation. Each point represents total discharge in 2 min. B, Baseline (no reinforcement) periods; R,

showed that they participated in the regulation of movement. Subsequent studies showed that lesions of the mPRF had little or no effect on REMS, although subtle effects on motor control could be demonstrated. Thus, lack of selectivity established in unit-recording studies proved to be consistent with other findings. The original finding of REMS-selective discharge was an artifact resulting from restriction of movement. Reliance on correlational data to suggest a causal hypothesis proved to be incorrect. The tonic latency criterion that supported the REMS generation hypothesis was not sufficient, because it is difficult to define the initial event in a cascade of events lasting minutes, and in which there is little

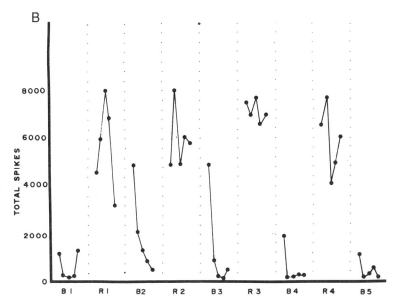

Fig. 13. (cont.)

reinforcement periods. The cat was presented with a discriminative stimulus signaling reinforcement periods. Note the increased discharge during reinforcement periods and successive "extinction" curves in the intervening baseline periods. Higher discharge rates were accompanied by repetitive directionally specific head movements, as determined by the photographic method shown in (A). (From Breedlove *et al.*, 1979.)

understanding of the critical onset processes. Below, we describe several additional cell types that appear to be part of a sustained cascade leading to REMS.

C. Dorsolateral Pontine and Medial Medullary Reticular Cells

A different picture has emerged in unit recordings from the lateral pontine and medial medullary reticular formation. Many cells in these regions have discharge profiles similar to those seen in medial pontine regions and may have similar involvement in motor control. However, these areas also contain a population of cells that discharge at a high rate throughout REMS and have little or no activity in SWS (Sakai, 1980). Figure 14 shows an example from our laboratories. In waking, these cells are generally silent, even during vigorous movement. However, some are active during head lowering and related postural changes involving reductions in tone in a number of muscles (Siegel *et al.*, 1979b). The pontine REMS-on cells are distributed throughout the region implicated by lesion studies in REMS control (Siegel, 1989; Sakai, 1980; Shiromani *et al.*, 1987). This

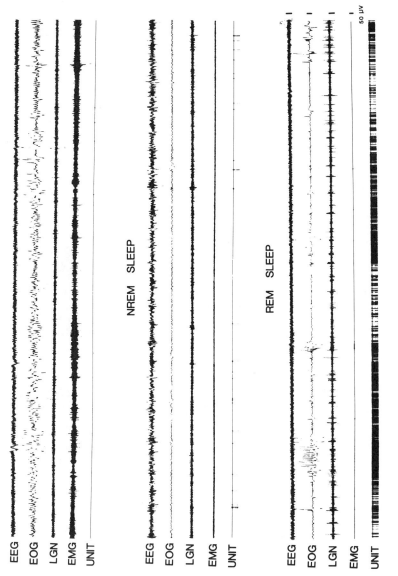

Fig. 14. Example of REMS-on cell recorded in the dorsolateral pons (B. N. Mallick and J. M. Siegel, unpublished observations). EEG, cortical electroencephalogram; EOG, electroculogram; LGN, EEG patterns of the lateral geniculate nucleus, demonstrating PGO waves; EMG, electromyogram.

distribution is significant, since it indicates that the critical lesion does not merely interrupt fibers of passage in the more ventrolateral portion of the critical area, but also removes the somas of cells that are selectively active in REM sleep. A recent paper (Shiromani *et al.*, 1988) reported that the REMS-on cells in this lateral region are not cholinergic, although it is likely that they are cholinoceptive. Aminergic cells are also not present in this region. Thus, the transmitter used by these cells remains unknown. The medullary REMS-on cells are located in an area receiving projections from the pontine REMS-on region (Sakai *et al.*, 1979).

D. NORADRENERGIC CELLS OF THE LOCUS COERULEUS COMPLEX

Noradrenergic cells [norepinephrine-containing, herein referred to as NE] in the locus coeruleus complex have relatively regular discharge patterns in waking, in contrast to the burst–pause discharge pattern seen in medial reticular neurons. During the initial stages of SWS, these cells slow slightly. During the "transition" to REMS (defined in the cat as the time at which PGO spikes begin appearing), discharge in both serotoninergic (serotonin-containing, herein referred to as 5-HT) and NE cells slows dramatically. During REMS, these cells have their lowest discharge rates, and many are completely silent (McGinty and Sakai, 1973; Aston-Jones and Bloom, 1981; Hobson *et al.*, 1975; Saito *et al.*, 1977). The significance of these unit activity patterns for REMS control and for the "function" of REMS is unclear. The slowing of discharge in these cells in SWS argues against the hypothesis that increased release of NE triggers REMS. The minimal discharge rate of these cells in REMS also argues against the hypothesis that NE maintains REMS. However, the complete absence of discharge in REMS does suggest that these cells may have a role in gating, inhibiting, or disinhibiting some aspect of REMS. The observation that pharmacological depletion of NE results in increased REMS amounts supports such a hypothesis (e.g., Hartmann *et al.*, 1971). In several models of REMS control, NE neurons are included in a neuronal network in which there are inhibitory interactions between REMS-excitatory and -inhibitory neuronal types (Hobson *et al.*, 1975; Sakai, 1985; Pompeiano and Valentinuzzi, 1976). However, lesions that destroy most of the NE cell group of the locus coeruleus have little effect on the amount of REMS (Jones *et al.*, 1977). Thus, the role of NE neurons in REMS is not understood. Siegel and Rogawski (1988) extended an earlier hypothesis (Hartmann, 1970) that the critical functional mechanism involves REMS effects on NE activity, rather than an effect of NE activity on REMS. They have advanced the hypothesis that, by suppressing NE discharge, REMS results in upregulation of receptor responses, with benefits in waking function.

E. Brain Stem Cholinergic Neurons

A variety of pharmacological and brain microinjection studies have supported a role for acetylcholine (ACh) in regulation of REMS. REMS is suppressed by systemic or pontine microinjection of muscarinic blocking agents such as atropine (but see below) and by the ACh synthesis inhibitor hemicholinium (e.g., Domino et al., 1968; Hazra, 1970). REMS-onset triggering may be accelerated in the decerebrate cat and in sleeping humans by intravenous administration of physostigmine (Pompeiano and Hoshino, 1976; Sitaram et al., 1976). Direct microinjection of cholinergic agonists, particularly carbachol, or an acetylcholinesterase inhibitor, neostigmine, into the dorsomedial pons elicits sustained episodes of REMS (George et al., 1964, and many others). Cholinergic receptors have been identified in this site, and fibers to this region have been traced to identified cholinergic cellular groups in the dorsolateral pontomesencephalic tegmentum, the pedunculopontine tegmental (PPT) area, and the laterodorsal tegmental nuclei, using double-labeling techniques (Shiromani et al., 1988). Further, in the cat, some PPT neurons discharge in discrete bursts beginning 30–40 msec before PGO waves, and these cells project to the thalamus, where PGO waves are most prominent (Sakai and Jouvet, 1980). PGO waves invariably precede REMS episodes in the cat. On the basis of such evidence, it has been proposed that cholinergic activation is an essential mechanism for triggering REMS, and that REMS is regulated by the interaction of cholinergic and aminergic (NE and 5-HT) neurons. These two classes of neurons are hypothesized to be mutually inhibitory, such that NE- and 5-HT-containing neurons must be off and acetylcholine-containing neurons must be active to produce REMS (Hobson et al., 1986).

The observation that often prolonged periods of REMS may be elicited by microinjection of the cholinergic agonist carbachol into the medial or central dorsal pontine tegmentum, often with very short latency, has been confirmed repeatedly since its first observation by George et al. (1964). On the other hand, as reviewed above, mPRF neurons are not selectively active in REMS. We wondered whether carbachol was acting via the mechanism that had been assumed (i.e., by activating mPRF neurons) or whether there was something unique or unexpected about the response of pontine tegmental neurons to the local application of carbachol. To answer this question, we utilized the method of microwire recording adjacent to the site of carbachol microinjection (Shiromani and McGinty, 1986).

This study showed that carbachol activated only slightly over one-quarter of mPRF neurons, all of which were also activated in spontaneous REMS periods. Twice as many cells exhibited *decreased* discharge during REM-like periods elicited by carbachol, although these same cells increased discharge in spontaneous REMS. Thus, while carbachol had a stimulatory effect on some cells, responses were not identical to the activity patterns found in normal spontaneous REMS periods. In another study, we recorded mPRF neuronal activity adjacent to microinjection of a protein synthesis inhibitor, chloramphenicol. Application of chloramphenicol reduced the frequency of REMS periods and suppressed discharge of adjacent mPRF neurons, particularly at the time of abortive REMS transitions (Drucker-Colin *et al.*, 1982). Injections of an inactive analog of chloramphenicol had no such effects. Thus, these studies supported the hypothesis that PRF activation could participate in the triggering of REMS, even if this was only a facilitatory role. On the other hand, as shown by recording unit activity during carbachol injections, massive mPRF activation is not essential for triggering REMS.

Experimental studies of cholinergic PPT neurons could also be used to assess hypotheses concerning the role of ACh in REMS. We may ask whether such PPT neurons are invariably active before and during REMS and whether they are selectively active in REMS? Researchers have also been concerned with the technical problem of identifying ACh-containing neurons, since the PPT area is not absolutely homogeneous. However, it has been reported that, within the PPT area, at least 80% of neurons projecting to the thalamus are either cholinergic or NE. The latter can be recognized by their characteristic REM-off discharge pattern, which is similar to that of 5-HT-containing neurons. Therefore, cholinergic neurons might be tentatively identified as those PPT neurons projecting to thalamus that are not REMS-off types. However, it should be noted that the interpretation that PPT neurons projecting to thalamus are all cholinergic has been questioned on the basis of *in vitro* neurophysiological studies. Recent studies of PPT slice preparations have suggested that neurons within the PPT area that have the membrane conductance bursting mechanisms (low-threshold slow depolarizations crowned by bursts) are not cholinergic (Kang and Katai, 1990). *In vivo* studies show that bursting PGO-related neurons may project to the thalamus. However, these constitute only about 5% of PPT neurons (Steriade *et al.*, 1990b).

There have been several studies of PPT neurons identified by antidromic activation from the thalamus, including some cells that exhibit the PGO burst discharge pattern. Figure 15 illustrates our results, which are in general agreement with those of others (McGinty and Szymusiak, 1988b). In our study, we distinguished groups of cells exhibiting PGO-related bursts (some of which were identified by antidromic activation), other antidromically activated cells, and cells showing generally similar discharge patterns, but which could not be activated antidromically. All of these cells were somewhat alike in that they were characterized by low discharge rates, even during peak activity. All showed very low discharge rates without bursting in SWS. Two of these groups showed increased discharge in the pre-REMS period (S-PGO), and all showed increased discharge in active REMS compared to SWS. However, these cells were not

Dennis McGinty and Jerome M. Siegel

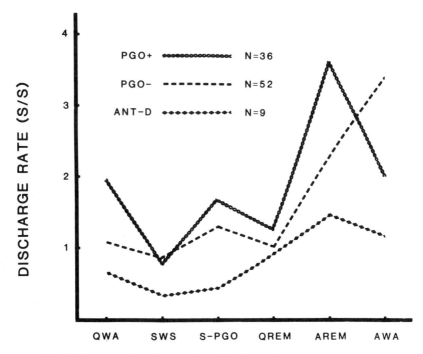

FIG. 15. Discharge rates in spikes per second (S/S) of cells recorded in the pedunculopontine tegmental (PPT) area in the cat during sleep and wakefulness. Separate rate profiles are provided for cells with discharge tightly coupled to PGO waves (PGO+) or not (PGO−), and for cells that could be antidromically activated from the thalamus (ANT-D). Rates were determined for active waking (AWA, far right), active REMS (AREM), quiet REMS (QREM), SWS with PGO waves (S-PGO), SWS, and quiet waking (QWA). All cell types exhibited relatively slow discharge in all states. PGO+ cells had higher rates in AREM than in AWA, but AWA rates were higher than QREM rates. In other cell types, AWA rates were equal or higher than those in REMS states. Discharge was low in SWS. These data do not provide strong support for the hypothesis of unique involvement in the control of both active and quiet REMS by PPT neurons, but suggest a more complicated mechanism. (From D. McGinty and R. Szymusiak, unpublished observations.)

selectively active in REMS. Active waking rates were higher than pre-REMS rates in each of these groups. Although PGO-related cells had higher rates in active REMS than in active wake, rates in quiet REMS and pre-REMS were comparable to awake rates. The only distinctive event related to REMS was the burst discharge; this seemed to be absent or rare during waking.

Steriade *et al.* (1990a,b) have completed more detailed studies in head-restrained cats in which they define a number PPT neuronal types. These include slowly discharging PGO-related "sluggish"-burst neurons, tonically discharging high-frequency PGO-related burst neurons, very slowly bursting PGO-related neurons, PGO-on single-spike neurons, PGO-off neurons, and post-PGO-on neurons. They hypothesized that the sluggish-burst neurons correspond to the PGO-related neurons described previously; they argued that these are probably not cholinergic on the basis of the *in vitro* studies summarized above. The other PGO-related neuronal types may mediate the cholinergic facilitation of REMS and PGO waves, while the sluggish-burst neurons would convey the specific PGO event to the thalamus. The Steriade *et al.* papers described a detailed model by which PPT neurons, in conjunction with other brain stem mechanisms, could facilitate REMS, PGO waves, and EEG activation.

These findings would be consistent with the following conclusions: (1) Since aminergic and cholinergic neurons both exhibit near-maximal rates during active waking, they cannot be regulated primary by mutually inhibitory interactions. Thus, the Hobson–McCarley model prediction (Hobson *et al.*, 1975) is not fulfilled. (2) Cholinergic activity does not occur selectively in REMS, but may also occur during waking. While such activity must be one facilitatory influence on REMS, it may not itself determine REMS onset. Indeed, there is some recent evidence that this is the case. We have found that the inhibitory effects of atropine on REMS seen at normal laboratory temperatures (23°C) are greatly attenuated in a warm ambient temperature (30°C) (Szymusiak *et al.*, 1990b). Thus, while there is little doubt that cholinergic input to the dorsal PRF may elicit REMS, this response may normally depend on some additional factors. One component may be the PGO sluggish-burst-cell input, and inhibitory gating by norepinephrine and 5-HT is also involved. Additional still unidentified dorsal pontine neuronal elements, including REMS-on cells could also be essential elements in a complex network that regulates REMS. Such a conclusion would be consistent with the survival of REMS after restricted lesions of ACh neuronal areas. However, after more extensive dorsal pontine lesions involving both cholinergic areas and adjacent areas, REMS may be suppressed for long periods (Webster and Jones, 1988).

F. NEURONAL BASIS OF SWS

Recent studies (see Steriade and Llinas, 1988) have strongly supported the hypothesis that the generation of synchronized or desynchronized EEG patterns depends on two primary mechanisms, which we summarize briefly here. First, individual neurons in many central nervous system (CNS) sites may generate sleeplike or waking-like neuronal discharge patterns on the basis of different voltage-dependent conductances. In particular, high-amplitude slow waves in the membrane potential with characteristic brief high-frequency bursts of neuronal discharge may be triggered by brief neuronal excitation during a hyperpolarized state. The slow depolarization results from activation of a so-called low-threshold CA^{2+}-dependent conductance. This slow depolarization is blocked if the membrane resting potential is relatively depolarized. In the latter case, excitatory inputs result, not in bursts, but in more sustained spike trains characteristic of the waking state. Whether or not thalamic neurons exhibit slow waves depends on the resting level of membrane polarization. This resting polarization level is hypothesized to be regulated by cholinergic and serotoninergic inputs from the brain stem. A second mechanism appears to account for the synchronization of neuronal pools associated with SWS. Intrathalamic circuits originating in the reticular nucleus and possibly the midline, intralaminar, and dorsomedial nuclei initiate feedforward and feedback inhibition of thalamic relay neurons to produce the critical hyperpolarized state and to "synchronize" groups of cells. Thus, with respect to the issue of the control of EEG synchronization in SWS (one aspect of the sleep process), it is necessary to understand how the resting potential of thalamic neurons is controlled.

Since behavioral sleep may occur after ablation of the thalamus, it is likely that the regulation of EEG control originates outside of the thalamus. The mechanisms regulating SWS would be expected to modulate motor and autonomic aspects of the state, in conjunction with EEG synchrony. Several SWS-regulating mechanisms have been proposed, including the medullary reticular formation, the serotoninergic system, and the basal forebrain–preoptic hypothalamus.

G. 5-HT AND SWS

A brilliant initial attempt to integrate sleep mechanisms with "chemical neurophysiology" was Jouvet's (1967) set of hypotheses involving 5-HT and SWS, on the one hand, and NE cells of the locus coeruleus and REMS, on the other. The development of the histofluorescent method and the anatomical localization of the 5-HT- and NE-containing nuclear groups had just been developed by Falck et al. (1962). Jouvet and co-workers found that, in the cat, lesions of the 5-HT-containing raphe nuclei, or chemical blockade of 5-HT synthesis, caused insomnia, as well as the release of PGO waves in waking (see Jouvet, 1967). Other pharmacological data were consistent with these findings. They interpreted these findings to mean that 5-HT was an essential element in the generation of SWS.

Our investigation of this issue was based on the premise that the actions of 5-HT would depend on the release of transmitter, as triggered by nerve impulse flow. Thus, knowing when 5-HT-containing neurons were active would indicate how this putative transmitter would influence sleep–waking states. The identification of 5-HT-containing neurons was based on their localization in the relatively homogeneous dorsal raphe nuclei and the distinct regular slow discharge pattern of these cells, as discovered in anesthetized animals. The identification of 5-HT-containing neurons in this fashion was confirmed in several subsequent studies (e.g., Trulson, 1985).

In contradiction to the prediction of the Jouvet theory, we found that 5-HT-containing neurons showed an approximately 50% reduction in discharge during

SWS compared to waking, and a dramatic near-total suppression of discharge during REMS (McGinty *et al.,* 1973; McGinty and Harper, 1976) (Fig. 16). Further, many, but not all, of these neurons exhibited phasic suppression of discharge prior to PGO waves during the pre-REMS period. The latter finding was consistent with observations that drugs depleting the brain of 5-HT resulted in the release of PGO waves during waking and SWS, when they are normally absent (e.g., Dement *et al.,* 1972). Thus, release of 5-HT may normally inhibit the occurrence of PGO waves. The finding of SWS-related neuronal slowing, with further slowing in REMS, was extended by Jacobs and co-workers (e.g., Heym *et al.,* 1982) to the other brain stem raphe nuclei that comprise the sites of 5-HT-containing neurons.

The inference that the release of 5-HT was reduced during sleep was subsequently confirmed by examining the release of 5-HT in target sites. This was accomplished by both perfusion and electrochemical detection techniques (Trulson, 1985). In addition, in the rat, 5-HT turnover is lowest during the light phase of the circadian day, when sleep is predominant (Agren *et al.,* 1986). Thus, the unit-recording findings are consistent with results from most other methods. There is one great advantage to unit recording, namely, the possibility of determining specific close temporal correlations between serotoninergic function and behavior. In the case of 5-HT-containing neurons, the awake behavioral data do not support a role for 5-HT in specific temporally discrete functions, including movements or responses to sensory stimuli. Only weak modulation in relation to movement or sensory input has been observed (Fig. 17). This finding can be contrasted with studies of mPRF neurons, discussed above (Section IV,B), that revealed a close relationship between neuronal discharge and specific behaviors.

We believe that these studies illustrate the great usefulness of chronic unit recording in the evaluation of theoretical hypotheses. In this case, lesion data were misleading. In the face of this and other evidence, Jouvet *et al.* (1989) have modified his theory to a version in which the release of 5-HT during *waking* may cause an indirect facilitation of SWS through actions in the hypothalamus. This modification of the theory would rationalize the findings of insomnia after 5-HT depletion and unit-recording studies. However, specific mechanistic details of this model or direct evidence for SWS facilitation by waking release of 5-HT have not been presented. An alternative view is that disruption of 5-HT-dependent processes resulted in some as yet unspecified physiological instability that interfered with sleep. The latter explanation would be consistent with the finding that, with sustained depletion of 5-HT, sleep returns to near-normality (Dement *et al.,* 1972). Cats may adapt to the physiological instability that initially disrupts sleep.

We introduced this article by noting that neuronal unit recording could be used both to test hypotheses and to suggest the nature of neural coding. For the latter application, we may consider what actions of 5-HT are indicated by the depres-

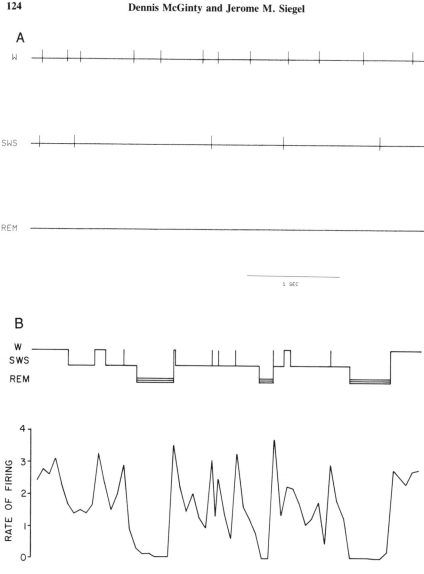

FIG. 16. (A) Oscilloscopic trace of amplified recording of dorsal raphe unit discharge in the cat. These neurons exhibit relatively regular discharge during waking (W), much slower discharge during SWS, and virtual silence during REMS. (From McGinty and Harper, 1976.) (B) Continuous record of dorsal raphe unit discharge during several waking–SWS–REMS cycles. Discharge is consistently stopped during REMS periods and elevated during waking, even during transient waking episodes. SWS discharge rates are intermediate. (From McGinty and Siegel, 1977.)

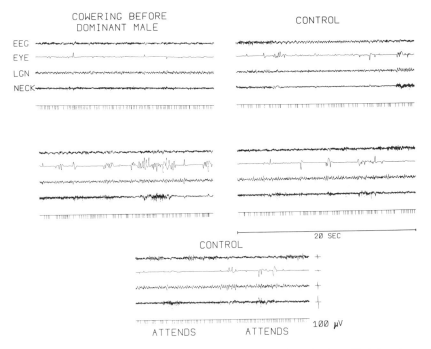

FIG. 17. An example of dorsal raphe unit during different waking behaviors. (Top) Samples on the left were obtained as the cat cowered in fearful submission and hissed in response to the presence of a dominant male cat, while control samples on the right were recorded during relaxed waking periods with eye movements. There may have been slightly increased unit discharge during intense arousal, but changes were much smaller than those occurring during each sleep cycle. (Bottom) There was no indication of altered discharge when the cat attended to a novel stimulus. EEG, Cortical electroencephalogram; EYE, electro-oculogram; LGN, lateral geniculate nucleus. (From McGinty *et al.*, 1973.)

sion of raphe unit discharge during sleep, particularly REMS. During waking, dorsal raphe discharge is unchanged by a wide variety of behavioral manipulations (McGinty *et al.*, 1973), so the sleep-related events are the most quantitatively significant naturally occurring changes in the release of 5-HT. Trulson *et al.* (1981) suggested that raphe unit discharge could be related to the central control of overall motor excitation. In this model, raphe discharge suppression during REMS is coupled with the atonia of REMS. They found that cats having pontine lesions resulting in REMS *without* atonia showed less reduction in dorsal raphe unit discharge in REMS. While this concept may have merit, the proposed 5-HT–motor tone relationship is not consistent under a wide range of conditions. Certainly, there is a weak relationship between motor activity and raphe unit discharge during waking behavior.

The functional significance of the release of 5-HT and its suppression during sleep continues to present a challenge to neuroscientists. The unusual features of the serotoninergic neuronal system may offer a guide to future experiments (see McGinty and Szymusiak, 1988a). This system projects diffusely to all regions of the CNS and make contacts with blood vessels as well as neurons. Moreover, most terminals on neurons are not conventional junctional synaptic contacts in either the cortex or the spinal cord. Iontophoretic studies indicate that 5-HT has primarily neuromodulatory actions. Pharmacological manipulation of 5-HT has been shown to affect virtually every type of behavior and basic regulatory function, including neuroendocrine function. At a neurophysiological level, 5-HT is often characterized as a neuromodulator, modifying responses to other inputs. Thus, 5-HT may regulate a nonspecific aspect of the state of the brain, rather than having a specific role in sleep control. The eventual understanding of the neuromodulatory role of 5-HT may tell us something about the nature of the state of the brain during sleep, rather than how sleep is controlled.

H. BASAL FOREBRAIN AND SWS

A hypothesis that basal forebrain (BF)–preoptic area–anterior hypothalamic (POAH) neuronal mechanisms facilitated SWS was first proposed on the basis of analysis of human encephalitic neuropathology, which sometimes produced insomnia as a result (von Economo, 1930). Subsequently, it was shown that insomnia could be produced in experimental animals with BF electrolytic or mechanical lesions (e.g., Nauta, 1946). Recently, we showed that cell-selective neurotoxin-induced lesions could have this effect (Szymusiak and McGinty, 1986a). Conversely, stimulation of this area using electrical, chemical, or thermal stimuli may induce sleep, as well as inhibit activity of the midbrain reticular areas thought to be involved in EEG arousal (e.g., Benedek et al., 1982; Bremer, 1973).

These studies suggested that it should be possible to identify BF neuronal units, which could convey the hypnogenic output of this region. The issue of neuronal identification was particularly important, since the BF region, including the POAH, is extremely complex and plays a role in a wide variety of behavioral, neuroendocrine, and autonomic functions. Recently, much interest has focused on the forebrain cholinergic cells localized in the magnocellular BF, including the diagonal bands of Broca, the lateral POAH (or substantia innominata), and the subpallial region. This cortically projecting cell group was found to have degenerated in patients with Alzheimer's disease (Whitehouse et al., 1982).

Using the microwire technique, we identified a diffuse subset of neurons, scattered throughout the magnocellular BF, which exhibited little or no discharge during waking and enhanced discharge during SWS and quiet REMS (Szymusiak and McGinty, 1986b). Sleep-active neurons (SANs), defined by having SWS discharge rates at least twice that of waking, were intermixed with other cell types that exhibited increased discharge during waking and REMS, much like neurons in a variety of CNS sites. SANs constituted 24% of the total sample in one study in cats. These cells exhibited an additional property that would be expected in neurons that play a role in the control of sleep. They exhibited increased discharge before the first spindle burst of sleep, thus anticipating the state transition (Szymusiak and McGinty, 1989b) (Fig. 18). This property does not prove a role in sleep control, as state transitions are difficult to define (see above), but such a finding, in conjunction with other types of data, supports the hypothesis that SANs participate in the hypnogenic role of the BF.

As noted above, the magnocellular BF contains neurons projecting to the neocortex as well as to the brain stem. In order to determine whether SANs were projection neurons, we attempted to activate these neurons antidromically by placing stimulating electrodes in the midbrain reticular formation and in the external capsule and the anterior cingulate bundle, two fiber bundles known to carry fibers to the neocortex from the BF. Antidromic responses were identified by the usual criteria (i.e., low variability in response latency and ability to respond to high-frequency paired pulse stimulation) and by the collision test. In the collision test, a spontaneous orthodromic spike discharge is used to trigger the stimulator eliciting the putative antidromic discharge. If the triggered pulse is

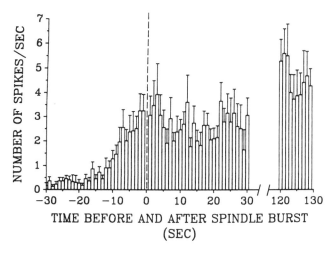

FIG. 18. Changes in basal forebrain sleep-active neuronal discharge in relationship to sleep onset, based on 22 sleep-active neurons. For each cell, transitions from alert waking to deep SWS were analyzed. The first high-amplitude spindle burst at sleep onset is indicated at time zero (vertical dashed line). Bars indicate the mean (±SEM) number of spikes for each second during the 30 sec before and after the spindle burst, and during 10 sec of sustained SWS 120 sec after sleep onset. These neurons showed increased discharge beginning 15–20 sec before the first spindle burst and a sustained increase in discharge during SWS. (From Szymusiak and McGinty, 1990.)

given within the interval of the antidromic response latency, an antidromically conducted pulse will "collide" with and be blocked by the refractory period produced by the orthodromic spike, and no antidromic spike will be observed. However, a pulse triggered after an interval that is slightly longer than the antidromic response latency will produce a response as usual.

About 30% of a sample of over 200 neurons recorded in the BF exhibited antidromic activation (Szymusiak and McGinty, 1989b). Both SANs and non-SANs could be driven antidromically from each of the three stimulation sites. For additional analysis, cells were divided into three groups: SANs, state-indifferent neurons (which exhibited very low discharge rates at all times), and waking-active neurons. This analysis showed that these subgroups of neurons could be discriminated on the basis of antidromic response latency. SANs and state-indifferent neurons invariably exhibited antidromic response latencies greater than 5 msec, averaging between 12 and 18 msec, depending on the stimulation site (Fig. 19). Waking-active neurons had antidromic response latencies from the same stimulation sites that were lower than 5 msec.

This study suggests that the population of BF projection neurons may consist of at least two subgroups with different conduction velocities and different state-related discharge profiles. It is plausible that these subgroups also utilize different neurotransmitters (Fisher et al., 1988). Since we are studying cortically projecting neurons in the magnocellular BF, it is very likely that one group includes the cholinergic neurons found in these areas. Some evidence supports the hypothesis that the waking-active neurons are cholinergic (Szymusiak and McGinty, 1990): (1) In our study, waking-active neurons tended to be located more dorsally, where cholinergic neurons are more numerous in the cat. (2) ACh is released in the cortex in EEG-activated states (Phillis, 1968). (3) EEG activation associated with waking is blocked by the muscarinic receptor-blocking agent atropine (e.g., Szymusiak and McGinty, 1990). (4) At the cortical and thalamic cellular levels, ACh has depolarizing effects (McCormick, 1989).

While there is strong evidence linking ACh release, and therefore waking-active neuronal discharge, to activated EEG states, the chemical identity of SANs remains uncertain. There are reports that GABAergic neurons are also localized in the magnocellular BF, and it is plausible that such an inhibitory agent would convey sleep-inducing output. However, definitive evidence for this hypothesis has not yet been presented. Histochemical identification of SANs is needed.

An additional study showed one mechanism by which sleep-active neurons may facilitate sleep onset (Szymusiak and McGinty, 1989a). We recorded neuronal discharge in the midbrain reticular formation (MRF), the hypothesized location of EEG-activating neurons projecting to the thalamus. We selected neurons in this area with a tonic discharge during waking. We found that single-shock stimulation in both the BF and the medial POAH suppressed MRF dis-

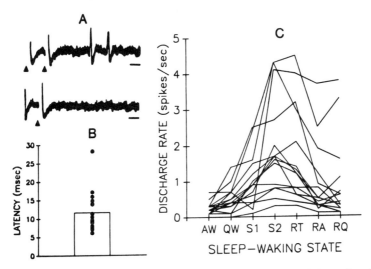

FIG. 19. Sleep-active neurons could be discriminated from neighboring cells by studies of anti-dromic activation. Shown are studies of basal forebrain (BF) neurons exhibiting antidromic activation with relatively long latency from the anterior cingulate bundle (ACB), a pathway from BF to the cerebral cortex. (A) Two standard tests for antidromic activation. (Top) BF neuronal discharges follow high-frequency (300-Hz) paired pulse stimulation (arrows) to the ACB. (Bottom) In the collision test, the ACB stimulation is triggered by a spontaneous unit discharge within the period of the response latency. The ACB stimulus fails to elicit a response, indicating "collision" with the orthodromically conducted spike. Calibration = 2 msec. (B) Mean and distribution of response latencies. (C) Sleep–waking discharge rate profiles of cells exhibiting response latencies greater than 5 msec. Slowly conducting neurons had sleep-active ($n = 9$) or state-indifferent ($n = 6$) discharge profiles. Waking-active neurons (not shown) had response latencies lower than 5 msec. For further details, see text. AW and QW, active and quiet awake, respectively; S1 and S2, Light and deep SWS, respectively; RT, transition period to REMS; RA and RQ, active and quiet REMS, respectively. (From Szymusiak and McGinty, 1989b.)

charge for 30–90 msec, sometimes preceded by a brief excitation. Thus, tonic discharge in the BF may inhibit the MRF, facilitating EEG synchronization. The chemical identity of the MRF neurons studied is not known.

Lesions of the medial POAH as well as the magnocellular BF (including the lateral POAH) have been found to result in sleep suppression (e.g., Szymusiak and McGinty, 1986a; Sallanon et al., 1986). The medial POAH is not a primary site of origin of long projection neurons and may play a different role in the SWS control system. The medial POAH is the site of thermoregulatory mechanisms and contains thermosensitive neurons, including primarily warmth-sensitive neurons. A relationship between thermoregulatory mechanisms of the medial POAH and hypnogenic mechanisms was noted in recent studies. Lesions of the medial POAH produce deficits in warmth sensitivity, probably reflecting the loss of warmth-sensitive neurons that predominate in this area. After lesions, there is an

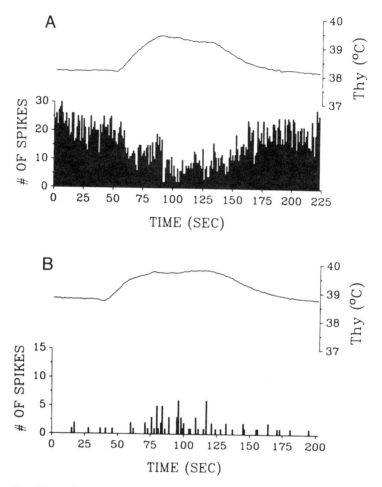

Fig. 20.   Effects of localized medial preoptic area–anterior hypothalamic (POAH) warming using a water-perfused thermode on neuronal discharge in lateral POAH–basal forebrain (BF) sites. The top traces show midline hypothalamic temperature. The bottom traces show the number of spikes in each successive 1-msec bin. (A) Example of suppression of discharge by medial warming in a lateral BF waking-active neuron. (B) Example of increased discharge in a sleep-active neuron. The cat was awake throughout the tests, so changes in discharge do not reflect passive effects of state change induced by warming. See text. (From Szymusiak and McGinty, 1990.)

elevated temperature threshold for heat-loss mechanisms such as panting. We have recently found that sleep suppression after medial POAH lesions can be reversed by placing animals in an elevated ambient temperature, suggesting that the temperature threshold for sleep as well as panting is elevated (Szymusiak *et al.*, 1991). This observation is congruent with a wide range of evidence indicating that SWS may be a thermoregulatory behavior, with a primary function of heat loss. Thus, warmth-sensitive neurons in the medial POAH are hypothesized to play a role in hypnogenesis as well as heat loss. It is well known that warming the medial POAH with a thermode may induce sleep onset (see McGinty and Szymusiak, 1990).

On the basis of these observations, we predicted that the SANs in the BF would be activated during waking by stimulation of warmth-sensitive neurons in the medial POAH. This prediction was tested by placing a water-perfused thermode with a thermocouple in the medial POAH and recording microwires in the lateral regions. A preliminary study confirmed our prediction (Fig. 20). By placing a very fine thermocouple within the microwire bundle, we showed that there was no direct thermal stimulation at the recording sites. Therefore, the activation of SANs in the lateral POAH was due to synaptic responses mediated by afferents from the medial POAH to the BF. We also found that discharge of waking-active neurons in the BF was suppressed by medial POAH warming (Szymusiak and McGinty, 1990). We expect that future studies will provide additional information about the mechanisms by which thermoregulatory mechanisms may regulate SWS (see McGinty and Szymusiak, 1990).

V. Conclusions

We have reviewed studies of the neural control of sleep, emphasizing those which applied the measurement of neuronal discharge in behaving animals. We described studies in which unit discharge during the sleep–wake cycle was recorded in conjunction with adjacent microinjection of chemical agents, adjacent thermal stimulation, antidromic activation, and orthodromic activation. We also reported studies of neurons in animals with brain transections. In these preparations, behavior was severely limited by lesions of sensory and motor pathways. Unit discharge served as an indicator of the state of the animal which was not expressed behaviorally. Because of the stability of the recordings, the microwire method provides a capability of carrying out hypothesis-testing studies, in addition to determining discharge rate changes during sleep–waking states. These studies have supported the following general conclusions:

1. Neuronal unit-recording methods have played a key role in the assessment of hypotheses concerning the localization of both SWS and REMS control systems. On the basis of studies of three brain regions, we have concluded that neuronal unit-recording studies agree with the "consensus" about the function of local populations of neurons reached after application of a wide variety of methods. Indeed, unit-recording studies sometimes produced findings that were inconsistent with initial theories, but eventually came to be widely accepted. If unit-recording studies are done with animals studied under a range of behavioral

conditions, this method, in contrast to other approaches, does not yield misleading results. Consequently, general hypotheses may be confirmed or refuted with such methods.

2. Mechanistic features of regulatory systems may be suggested or supported by neuronal unit-recording studies. For example, the finding of REMS-off behavior in 5-HT- and NE-containing neurons prior to REMS onset was consistent with the hypothesis that these cell types may normally inhibit REMS-related phenomena, such as PGO waves. This concept has been confirmed by other methods. In the case of the BF hypnogenic system, the fact that SANs project to the cortex and the MRF indicates that the hypnogenic output of the BF may be integrated at each of these levels. The discovery of specific movement-related discharge in mPRF neurons led to a reanalysis and a new concept of the functional output of this area. These details of neural activity, like anatomical details, provide a basis for mechanistic models of function.

3. By their nature, neuronal unit-discharge studies are correlational studies, and do not, by themselves, answer questions about "causal" regulatory mechanisms. However, unit-recording studies provide temporal detail that cannot be provided by any other technique. Temporal information can be so dramatic as to imply a discrete causal relationship. When unit discharge is discretely related to events in the millisecond range, as in the movement-related discharge of medial reticular formation neurons, or the PGO-related discharge of PPT neurons, it is possible to make inferences about function. However, most neuronal groups thought to be related to sleep have not displayed such specific correlations. Certainly, correlational information can be misleading, as in the case of initial development of the Hobson–McCarley theory that mPRF neurons were executive neurons for REMS (see Section IV,B above). A similar objection may apply to any model in which temporal relationships in the range of seconds or minutes is used to suggest causal relationships. In such cases, a wide variety of intervening processes may underlie the apparent correlation. Of course, temporal ordering may be consistent with causal models, but a variety of methods are needed to support such hypotheses. For example, in the case of the putative hypnogenic neurons of the BF, described above (Section IV,H), the hypothesized function of this site was also supported by lesion studies, several types of stimulation experiments, and analysis of interactions with brain stem reticular formation and medial POAH thermoregulatory systems. Nevertheless, it will still be necessary to examine alternative hypotheses, such as the possibility that SAN discharge is only a correlate of some autonomic process associated with sleep.

4. A few neuronal types have been identified that exhibit discharge occurring selectively in a particular state. These include the slow-wave SANs of the magnocellular BF and the REMS-on neurons of the lateral dorsal pontine reticular formation. However, lesions of these BF sites do not produce irreversible sleep suppression. Rather, it appears that this site regulates sleep through interaction

with medial preoptic, posterior hypothalamic, midbrain reticular, thalamic, and possibly cortical mechanisms, as well as involving thermoregulatory and possibly other homeostatic processes. Similarly, while the control of REMS is localized within the pontine reticular formation, it is unlikely that the few REMS-selective neurons are the only generators. REMS consists of several dissociable components which must be coupled to form the integrated state. REMS control seems to involve interactions of several neuronal types, utilizing ACh, NE, and probably other as yet unidentified transmitters. However, none of these regulating agents functions selectively in REMS. The lack of selectivity of neuronal discharge for one particular sleep–waking state argues strongly that the neuronal group under study does not regulate the state in a unitary way. On the other hand, lack of selectivity does not mean that a system plays no role in a mechanism. Thus, cholinergic neurons appear to facilitate REMS, although they are not selective. There may be some "cofactorial mechanisms" that operates in conjunction with ACh to trigger REMS. Similarly, mPRF neurons are not essential for REMS. However, activation of these neurons, in conjunction with other mechanisms, may facilitate REMS or some of the phenomena of this state. Thus, neurophysiological studies would seem to confirm the hypothesis that sleep states are determined by the interactions of several neuronal systems. Similar conclusions may apply to all complex behaviors.

This raises the critical problem of choosing methods for analyzing neural mechanisms underlying complexly controlled behaviors, in which no single neuronal type is essential and coregulation by several systems is likely. We must repeat the statement in the introduction that a variety of methods are required to analyze neuronal mechanisms. However, we suggest that data from neuronal unit-recording studies would seem to be critical, since no other methods can reveal the temporal coincidence of events or dynamic changes in excitability that must underlie behavioral regulation. The microwire method we have described is simple and applicable to problems in understanding complex behavioral control systems.

References

Adey, W. R., Bors, E., and Porter, R. W. (1968). EEG sleep patterns after high cervical lesions in man. *Archives of Neurology (Chicago)* **19**, 377–383.

Agren, H., Koulu, M., Saavedra, J. M., Potter, W. Z., and Linnoila, M. (1986). Circadian covariation of norepinephrine and serotonin in the locus coeruleus and dorsal raphe nucleus in the rat. *Brain Research* **397**, 353–358.

Allison, T., and Cicchetti, D. V. (1976). Sleep in mammals: Ecological and constitutional correlates. *Science* **194**, 732–734.

Aston-Jones, G., and Bloom, F. E. (1981). Activity of norepinephrine-containing locus coeruleus neurons in behaving rats anticipates fluctuations in the sleep–waking cycle. *Journal of Neuroscience* **1**, 876–886.

Benedek, G., Obal, F., Jr., Lelkes, Z., and Obal, F. (1982). Thermal and chemical stimulations of the hypothalamic heat detectors: The effects on the EEG. *Acta Physiologica Academiae Scientiarum Hungaricae* **60**, 27–35.

Borbely, A., and Valatx, J. L., eds. (1984). "Sleep Mechanisms." Springer-Verlag, Berlin.

Bowker, R. M., and Morrison, A. R. (1976). The startle reflex and PGO spikes. *Brain Research* **102**, 185–190.

Breedlove, S. M., McGinty, D. J., and Siegel, J. M. (1979). Operant conditioning of pontine gigantocellular units. *Brain Research Bulletin* **4**, 663–667.

Bremer, F. (1973). Preoptic hypnogenic area and reticular activating system. *Archives Italiennes de Biologie* **111**, 85–111.

Burns, B. D., Stean, J. P. B., and Webb, A. C. (1974). Recording for several days from single cortical neurons in completely unrestrained cats. *Electroencephalography and Clinical Neurophysiology* **36**, 314–318.

Chang, F. T., Scott, T. R., and Harper, R. M. (1988). Methods of single unit recording from medullary neural substrates in awake, behaving guinea pigs. *Brain Research Bulletin* **21**, 749–756.

Dement, W. C., Mitler, M. M., and Henriksen, S. J. (1972). Sleep changes during chronic administration of parachlorophenylalanine. *Revue Canadienne de Biologie* **31**, 239–246.

Diana, M., Garcia-Munoz, M., and Freed, C. R. (1987). Wire electrodes for chronic single unit recording of dopamine cells in substantia nigra pars compacta of awake rats. *Journal of Neuroscience Methods* **21**, 71–79.

Domino, E. F., Yamamoto, K., and Dren, A. T. (1968). Role of cholinergic mechanisms in states of wakefulness and sleep. *Progress in Brain Research* **128**, 113–133.

Drucker-Colin, R., and Pedraza, J. G. B. (1983). Kainic acid lesions of gigantocellular tegmental field (FTG) neurons does not abolish REM sleep. *Brain Research* **272**, 387–391.

Drucker-Colin, R., Bowersox, S. S., and McGinty, D. J. (1982). Sleep and medial reticular unit responses to protein synthesis: Effects of chloramphenicol and thiamphenicol. *Brain Research* **252**, 117–217.

Evarts, E. V. (1968). A technique for recording activity of subcortical neurons in moving animals. *Electroencephalography and Clinical Neurophysiology* **24**, 83–86.

Falck, B., Hillarp, N. A., Thieme, G., and Torp, A. (1962). Fluorescence of catecholamines and related compounds condensed with formaldehyde. *Journal of Histochemistry and Cytochemistry* **10**, 348–354.

Fisher, R. S., Buchwald, N. A., Hull, C. D., and Levine, M. S. (1988). GABAergic basal forebrain neurons project to neocortex: The localization of glutamic acid decarboxylase and choline acetyltransferase in feline corticopetal neurons. *Journal of Comparative Neurology* **272**, 489–502.

Flanagan, W. F., Jr., Wilcox, R. H., and Rechtschaffen, A. (1973). The EEG and behavioral continuum of the crocodilian, *Caiman sclerops. Electroencephalography and Clinical Neurophysiology* **34**, 521–538.

George, R., Haslett, W. L., and Jenden, D. J. (1964). A cholinergic mechanism in the brainstem reticular formation: Induction of paradoxical sleep. *International Journal of Neuropharmacology* **3**, 541–552.

Harper, R. M. (1971). Activity of single neurons during sleep and altered states of consciousness. *Psychophysiology* **7**, 312.

Harper, R. M., and McGinty, D. J. (1973). A technique for recording single neurons from unrestrained animals. *In* "Brain Unit Activity during Behavior" (M. I. Phillips, ed.), pp. 80–104. Thomas, Springfield, Illinois.

Hartmann, E. (1970). The D-state and norepinephrine-dependent systems. *International Psychiatry Clinics* **7**, 308–328.

Hartmann, E., Chung, R., Draskoczy, P. R., and Schildkraut, J. J. (1971). Effects of 6-hydroxydopamine on sleep in the rat. *Nature (London)* **233**, 425–427.

Hazra, J. (1970). Effect of hemicholinium-3 on slow-wave and paradoxical sleep of cat. *European Journal of Pharmacology* **11**, 395–397.

Heym, J., Steinfels, G. F., and Jacobs, B. L. (1982). Activity of serotonin-containing neurons in the nucleus raphe pallidus of freely moving cats. *Brain Research* **251**, 259–276.

Hobson, J. A., McCarley, R. W., Pivik, T., and Freedman, R. (1974). Selective firing by cat pontine brain stem neurons in desynchronized sleep. *Journal of Neurophysiology* **37**, 497–511.

Hobson, J. A., McCarley, R. W., and Wyzinski, P. W. (1975). Sleep cycle oscillation: Reciprocal discharge by two brainstem neuronal groups. *Science* **189**, 55–58.

Hobson, J. A., Lydic, R., and Baghdoyan, H. A. (1986). Evolving concepts of sleep cycle generation: From brain centers to neuronal populations. *The Behavioral and Brain Sciences* **9**, 371–448.

Hubel, D. H. (1960). Single unit activity in lateral geniculate body and optic tract of unrestrained cats. *Journal of Physiology (London)* **150**, 91–104.

Huttenlocher, P. R. (1961). Evoked and spontaneous activity in single units of medial brain stem during natural sleep and waking. *Journal of Neurophysiology* **24**, 451–468.

Jasper, H., Ricci, G. F., and Doane, B. (1960). Microelectrode analysis of cortical cell discharge during avoidance conditioning in the monkey. *Electroencephalography and Clinical Neurophysiology, Supplement* **13**, 137–155.

Jones, B. E., Harper, S. T., and Halaris, A. E. (1977). Effects of locus coeruleus lesions upon cerebral monoamine content, sleep wakefulness states and the response to amphetamine in the cat. *Brain Research* **124**, 473–496.

Jouvet, M. (1962). Recherches sur les structures nerveuses et les mécanismes responsables des differentes phases du sommeil physiologique. *Archives Italiennes de Biologie* **100**, 125–206.

Jouvet, M. (1967). Neurophysiology of the states of sleep. *Physiological Reviews* **47**, 117–177.

Jouvet, M., Denoyer, M., Kitahama, K., and Sallanon, M. (1989). Slow wave sleep and indolamines: A hypothalamic target. *In* "Slow Wave Sleep: Physiological, Pathophysiological, and Functional Aspects" (A. Wauquier, C. Dugovic, and M. Radulovacki, eds.), pp. 91–108. Raven, New York.

Kang, Y., and Kitai, S. T. (1990). Electrophysiological properties of pedunculopontine neurons and their postsynaptic responses following stimulation of substantia nigra reticulata. *Brain Research* **535**, 79–95.

Kent, S., Kaplan, R., and Satinoff, E. (1987). Decreases in REM sleep after phentolamine depend on the ambient temperature. *Brain Research* **415**, 169–171.

Kryger, M. H., Roth, T., and Dement, W. C., eds. (1989). "Principles and Practice of Sleep Medicine." Saunders, Philadelphia.

Laurent, J. P., Cespuglio, R., and Jouvet, M. (1974). Delimitation des voies ascendants de l'activité ponto-genicalo-occipitale chez le chat. *Brain Research* **65**, 29–52.

Lemon, R. (1984). Methods for neuronal recording in conscious animals. *In* "IBRO Handbook Series: Methods in the Neurosciences," (A. D. Smith, ed.) pp. 2–430. Wiley, Chichester, England.

Marg, E., and Adams, J. E. (1967). Indwelling multiple microelectrodes in the brain. *Electroencephalography and Clinical Neurophysiology* **23**, 277–280.

Matsuzaki, M. (1969). Differential effects of sodium butyrate and physostigmine upon the activities of para-sleep in acute brain stem preparations. *Brain Research* **13**, 247–265.

McCormick, D. A. (1989). Cholinergic and noradrenergic modulation of thalamocortical processing. *Trends in NeuroSciences* **12**, 215–221.

McGinty, D. J. (1985). Physiological equilibrium and the control of sleep states. *In* "Brain Mechanisms of Sleep" (D. J. McGinty, R. Drucker-Colin, A. R. Morrison, and P. L. Parmeggiani, eds.), pp. 361–384. Raven, New York.

McGinty, D. J., and Beahm, E. K. (1984). Neurobiology of sleep. *In* "Sleep and Breathing" (C. E. Sullivan and N. A. Saunders, eds.). Dekker, New York.

McGinty, D. J., and Harper, R. M. (1976). Dorsal raphe neurons: Depression of firing during sleep in cats. *Brain Research* **101**, 569–575.

McGinty, D., and Sakai, K. (1973). Unit activity in the dorsal pontine reticular formation in the cat. *Sleep Research* **2**, 33.

McGinty, D. J., and Siegel, J. M. (1977). Neuronal activity patterns during rapid-eye-movement sleep: Relation to waking patterns. *In* "Neurobiology of Sleep and Memory" (R. Drucker-Colin and J. McGaugh, eds.), pp. 135–158. Academic Press, New York.

McGinty, D. J., and Siegel, J. M. (1983). Sleep states. *In* "Handbook of Behavioral Neurobiology: Motivation" (E. Satinoff and P. Teitelbaum, eds.), pp. 105–181. Plenum, New York.

McGinty, D., and Szymusiak, R. (1988a). Neuronal unit activity patterns in behaving animals: Brainstem and limbic system. *Annual Review of Psychology* **39**, 135–168.

McGinty, D., and Szymusiak, R. (1988b). Discharge of pedunculopontine area neurons related to PGO waves. *Sleep Research* **17**, 9.

McGinty, D., and Szymusiak, R. (1990). Keeping cool: A hypothesis about the mechanisms and functions of slow wave sleep. *Trends in NeuroSciences* **13**, 480–487.

McGinty, D. J., Harper, R. M., and Fairbanks, M. K. (1973). 5-HT-containing neurons: Unit activity in behaving cats. *In* "Serotonin and Behavior" (J. Barchas and E. Usdin, eds.), pp. 267–279. Academic Press, New York.

McGinty, D. J., Drucker-Colin, R., and Bowersox, S. S. (1982). Reticular formation unit discharge modulation by local perfusion in behaving cats. *Experimental Neurology* **75**, 407–419.

McGinty, D. J., Drucker-Colin, R., Morrison, A. R., and Parmeggiani, P. L., eds. (1985). "Brain Mechanisms of Sleep." Raven, New York.

McNaughton, B. L., O'Keefe, J., and Barnes, C. A. (1983). The stereotrode: A new technique for simultaneous isolation of several single units in the central nervous system from multiple unit records. *Journal of Neuroscience Methods* **8**, 391–397.

Morrison, A. R. (1979). Brainstem regulation of behavior during sleep and wakefulness. *In* "Progress in Psychobiology and Physiological Psychology" (J. M. Sprague and A. N. Epstein, eds.), Vol. 8, pp. 91–131. Academic Press, New York.

Morrison, A. R., and Bowker, R. M. (1975). The biological significance of PGO spikes in the sleeping cat. *Acta Neurobiologiae Experimentalis* **35**, 821–840.

Naka, K., and Kido, R. (1967). Hypothalamic spike potentials recorded by chronically implanted tungsten microelectrodes. *Brain Research* **5**, 422–424.

Nauta, W. J. H. (1946). Hypothalamic regulation of sleep in rats. An experimental study. *Journal of Neurophysiology* **9**, 285–316.

Nienhuis, R., and Siegel, J. M. (1989). Analysis of head movement and position using Hall effect devices. *Physiology and Behavior* **45**, 199–203.

O'Keefe, J., and Bouma, H. (1969). Complex sensory properties of certain amygdala units in the freely moving cat. *Experimental Neurology* **23**, 384–398.

Olds, J., Disterhoff, J. F., Segal, M., Kornblith, C. L., and Hirsh, R. (1972). Learning centers of rat brain mapped by measuring latencies of conditioned unit responses. *Journal of Neurophysiology* **35**, 202–219.

Orem, J., and Barnes, C. D. (1980). "Physiology in Sleep." Academic Press, New York.

Phillis, J. W. (1968). Acetylcholine release from the cerebral cortex; its role in cortical arousal. *Brain Research* **7**, 378–379.

Pompeiano, O., and Hoshino, K. (1976). Tonic inhibition of dorsal pontine neurons during the postural atonia produced by an anticholinesterase in the decerebrate cat. *Archives Italiennes de Biologie* **114**, 310–340.

Pompeiano, O., and Valentinuzzi, M. (1976). A mathematical model for the mechanisms of rapid eye movements induced by an anticholinesterase in the decerebrate cat. *Archives Italiennes de Biologie* **114**, 103–154.

Puizillout, J. J., Ternaux, J. P., Foutz, A. S., and Fernandez, G. (1974). Les stades de sommeil de la préparation "encephale isolé": I. Déclenchement des pointes ponto-geniculo-occipitales et du sommeil phasique à ondes lentes. Rôle des noyaux du raphe. *Electroencephalography and Clinical Neurophysiology* **37**, 561–576.

Saito, H., Sakai, K., and Jouvet, M. (1977). Discharge patterns of the nucleus parabrachialis lateralis neurons of the cat during sleep and waking. *Brain Research* **134**, 59–72.

Sakai, K. (1980). Some anatomical and physiological properties of ponto-mesencephalic tegmental neurons with special reference to the PGO waves and postural atonia during paradoxical sleep in the cat. *In* "The Reticular Formation Revisited" (J. A. Hobson and M. A. Brazier, eds.), pp. 427–447. Raven, New York.

Sakai, K. (1985). Anatomical and physiological basis of paradoxical sleep. *In* "Brain Mechanisms of Sleep" (D. J. McGinty, R. Drucker-Colin, A. R. Morrison, and P. L. Parmeggiani, eds.), pp. 111–138. Raven, New York.

Sakai, K., and Jouvet, M. (1980). Brain stem PGO on cells projecting directly to the cat dorsal lateral geniculate nucleus. *Brain Research* **194**, 500–505.

Sakai, K., Petitjean, F., and Jouvet, M. (1976). Effects of ponto-mesencephalic lesions and electrical stimulation upon PGO waves and EMPs in unanesthetized cats. *Electroencephalography and Clinical Neurophysiology* **41**, 49–63.

Sakai, K., Sastre, J. P., Salvert, D., Touret, M., Tohyama, M., and Jouvet, M. (1979). Tegmentoreticular projections with special reference to the muscular atonia during paradoxical sleep in the cat: An HRP study. *Brain Research* **176**, 233–254.

Sallanon, M., Kitahama, K., Denoyer, M., Gay, N., and Jouvet, M. (1986). Insomnie de longue durée après lésions des perykarions d l'aire preoptique paramediane chez le chat. *Comptes Rendus Hebdomadaires des Seances de l'Academie des Sciences* **303**, 403–409.

Sastre, J. P., Sakai, K., and Jouvet, M. (1981). Are the gigantocellular tegmental field neurons responsible for paradoxical sleep? *Brain Research* **229**, 147–161.

Shiromani, P. J., and McGinty, D. J. (1986). Pontine neuronal response to local cholinergic infusion: Relation to REM sleep. *Brain Research* **386**, 20–31.

Shiromani, P., Armstrong, D. M., Bruce, G., Hersh, L. B., Groves, P. M., and Gillin, J. C. (1987). Relation of choline acetyltransferase immunoreactive neurons with cells which increase discharge during REM sleep. *Brain Research Bulletin* **18**, 447–455.

Shiromani, P. J., Armstrong, D. M., Berkowitz, A., Jeste, D. V., and Gillin, J. C. (1988). Distribution of choline acetyltransferase immunoreactive somata in the feline brainstem: Implications for REM sleep generation. *Sleep* **11**, 1–16.

Siegel, J. (1968). A rapid method for locating deep electrode placements. *Physiology and Behavior* **3**, 203–204.

Siegel, J. M. (1979a). Behavioral functions of the reticular formation. *Brain Research Reviews* **1**, 69–105.

Siegel, J. M. (1979b). Behavioral relations of medullary reticular formation cells. *Experimental Neurology* **65**, 691–698.

Siegel, J. M. (1985). Pontomedullary interactions in the generation of REM sleep. *In* "Brain Mechanisms of Sleep" (D. J. McGinty, R. Drucker-Colin, A. R. Morrison, and P. L. Parmeggiani, eds.), pp. 157–174. Raven, New York.

Siegel, J. M. (1989). Brainstem mechanisms generating REM sleep. *In* "Principles and Practice of

Sleep Medicine" (M. H. Kryger, T. Roth, and W. C. Dement, eds.), pp. 104–120. Saunders, Philadelphia.

Siegel, J. M., and McGinty, D. J. (1978). Pontine reticular formation neurons and motor activity. *Science* **199**, 207–208.

Siegel, J. M., and Rogawski, M. A. (1988). A function for rem sleep: Regulation of noradrenergic receptor sensitivity. *Brain Research Reviews* **13**, 213–233.

Siegel, J. M., and Tomaszewski, K. S. (1983). Behavioral organization of reticular formation: Studies in the unrestrained cat. I. Cells related to axial, limb, eye, and other movements. *Journal of Neurophysiology* **50**, 696–716.

Siegel, J. M., McGinty, D. J., and Breedlove, S. M. (1977). Sleep and waking activity of pontine gigantocellular field neurons. *Experimental Neurology* **56**, 553–573.

Siegel, J. M., Breedlove, S. M., and McGinty, D. J. (1979a). Photographic analysis of relation between unit activity and movement. *Journal of Neuroscience Methods* **1**, 159–164.

Siegel, J. M., Wheeler, R. L., and McGinty, D. J. (1979b). Activity of medullary reticular formation neurons in the unrestrained cat during waking and sleep. *Brain Research* **179**, 49–60.

Siegel, J. M., Nienhuis, R., and Tomaszewski, K. S. (1984). REM sleep signs rostral to chronic transections at the pontomedullary junction. *Neuroscience Letters* **45**, 241–246.

Siegel, J. M., Tomaszewski, K. S., and Niehhuis, R. (1986). Behavioral states in the chronic medullary and midpontine cat. *Electroencephalography and Clinical Neurophysiology* **63**, 274–288.

Sitaram, N., Wyatt, R. J., Dawson, S., and Gillin, J. S. (1976). REM sleep induction by physostigmine infusion during sleep. *Science* **191**, 1281–1283.

Steriade, M., and Llinas, R. R. (1988). The functional states of the thalamus and the associated neuronal interplay. *Physiological Reviews* **68**, 649–742.

Steriade, M., Datta, S., Pare, D., Oakson, G., and Dossi, R. C. (1990a). Neuronal activities in brain-stem cholinergic nuclei related to tonic activation processes in thalamocortical systems. *Journal of Neuroscience* **10**, 2541–2559.

Steriade, M., Pare, D., Datta, S., Oakson, G., and Dossi, R. C. (1990b). Different cellular types in mesopontine cholinergic nuclei related to ponto-geniculo-occipital waves. *Journal of Neuroscience* **10**, 2560–2579.

Strumwasser, F. (1958). Long-term recording from single neurons in brain of unrestrained mammals. *Science* **127**, 469–470.

Suzuki, S. S., Siegel, J. M., and Wu, M. F. (1989). Role of pontomedullary reticular formation neurons in horizontal head movements: An ibotenic acid lesion study. *Brain Research* **484**, 78–93.

Szymusiak, R., and McGinty, D. (1986a). Sleep suppression following kainic acid-induced lesions of the basal forebrain. *Experimental Neurology* **94**, 598–614.

Szymusiak, R., and McGinty, D. J. (1986b). Sleep-related neuronal discharge in the basal forebrain of cats. *Brain Research* **370**, 82–92.

Szymusiak, R., and McGinty, D. (1989a). Effects of basal forebrain stimulation on the waking discharge of neurons in the midbrain reticular formation of cats. *Brain Research* **498**, 355–359.

Szymusiak, R., and McGinty, D. (1989b). Sleep–waking discharge of basal forebrain projection neurons in cats. *Brain Research Bulletin* **22**, 423–430.

Szymusiak, R., and McGinty, D. (1990). State-dependent neurophysiology of the basal forebrain: Relationship to sleep, arousal, and thermoregulatory function. *In* "The Diencephalon and Sleep" (M. Mancia and G. Marini, eds.), pp. 111–124. Raven, New York.

Szymusiak, R., McGinty, D., Shouse, M. N., Shepard, D., and Sterman, M. B. (1990a). Effects of systemic atropine sulfate administration on the frequency content of the cat sensorimotor EEG during sleep and waking. *Behavioral Neuroscience* **104**, 217–225.

Szymusiak, R., Tilley, R., Danowski, J., and McGinty, D. (1990b). REM sleep-suppressing effects of atropine in cats vary with environmental temperature. *Sleep Research* **19**, 93.

Szymusiak, R., Danowski, J., and McGinty, D. (1991). Exposure to heat restores sleep in cats with preoptic/anterior hypothalamic cell loss. *Brain Research* **541**, 134–138.

Trulson, M. E. (1985). Simultaneous recording of dorsal raphe unit activity and serotonin release in the striatum using voltammetry in awake, behaving cats. *Life Sciences* **37**, 2199–2204.

Trulson, M. E., Jacobs, B. L., and Morrison, A. R. (1981). Raphe unit activity during REM sleep in normal cats and in pontine lesioned cats displaying REM sleep without atonia. *Brain Research* **226**, 75–91.

Valatx, J. L., Jouvet, D., and Jouvet, M. (1964). Évolution electroencephalographique des différents états de sommeil chez le chaton. *Electroencephalography and Clinical Neurophysiology* **7**, 218–233.

Villablanca, J. (1966). Behavioral and polygraphic study of "sleep" and "wakefulness" in chronic decerebrate cats. *Electroencephalography and Clinical Neurophysiology* **21**, 562–577.

von Economo, C. (1931). Sleep as a problem of localization. *Journal of Nervous and Mental Disease* **71**, 249–259.

Wauquier, A., Gaillard, J. M., Monti, J. M., and Radulovacki, M. (1985). "Sleep: Neurotransmitters and Neuromodulators." Raven, New York.

Wauquier, A., Dugovic, C., and Radulovacki, M., eds. (1989). "Slow Wave Sleep: Physiological, Pathophysiological, and Functional Aspects." Raven, New York.

Webster, H. H., and Jones, B. E. (1988). Neurotoxic lesions of the dorsolateral pontomesencephalic tegmentum–cholinergic cell area in the cat. II. Effects upon sleep–waking states. *Brain Research* **458**, 285–302.

Whitehouse, P. J., Price, D. L., Strable, R. G., Clark, A. W., Coyle, J. T., and DeLong, M. R. (1982a). Alzheimer's disease and senile dementia loss of neurons in the basal forebrain. *Science* **215**, 1237–1239.

Wu, M. F., Mallick, B. N., and Siegel, J. M. (1989). Lateral geniculate spikes, muscle atonia, and startle response elicited by auditory stimuli as a function of stimulus parameters and arousal state. *Brain Research* **499**, 7–17.

Zepelin, H., and Rechtschaffen, A. (1974). Mammalian sleep, longevity and energy metabolism. *Brain, Behavior and Evolution* **10**, 425–470.

Sleep–Wake States, Sucking, and Nursing Patterns in Young Rats

Harry N. Shair and Myron A. Hofer

Department of Psychiatry
College of Physicians and Surgeons
Columbia University
New York, New York 10032
and
Department of Developmental Psychobiology
New York State Psychiatric Institute
New York, New York 10032

I. Introduction

Very little work has been done to investigate systematically the relationship of sleep–wake states and feeding behaviors during development. Each of these areas has been studied extensively, but separately. With a few important exceptions, most observations linking the two behaviors during ontogeny have been casual. However, there are reasons to believe that sleep–wake states and feeding behavior do interact both developmentally and in adult animals. This research is reviewed in the sections below.

One goal of this article is to describe the relationship between sleep–wake states and nursing behavior in infant rats. A particular aspect of feeding behavior, sucking by the pups, is of primary interest, but other aspects are considered as well. Pups were studied with their mothers in normal litters while the pups' sleep–wake states and jaw muscle activity were monitored polygraphically. Pups of 12–14 days of age were chosen for investigation for two reasons. First, this is the earliest age at which slow-wave sleep is fully distinguishable (Jouvet-Mounier *et al.*, 1970). Also, at this age, a very streamlined head implant is possible (Hofer, 1976), which permits the test pups to compete with littermates during normal nursing.

A second goal of the work described here is to begin to understand the controls for any of the relationships discovered. To this end, the mother–pup interactions were manipulated in several ways. Deprivation of the pups from the dam has known effects on both feeding behavior (e.g., Brake *et al.*, 1982a; Hall and Rosenblatt, 1977; Lorenz *et al.*, 1982; see below for more references, and see Lorenz's article in this volume) and sleep–wake states (Hofer, 1976; Hofer and Shair, 1982). Therefore, deprivation and reunion were used to perturb the normal relationships between sleep–wake states and feeding and thus highlight any interactions and control mechanisms. Another manipulation involved testing the pups while they were attached to the teats of their anesthetized mothers both before and after deprivation. In this preparation, the mother's behavior, including milk delivery, was removed from the nursing interaction, allowing more precise focus on the pups themselves.

A. A SELECTIVE REVIEW OF THE LITERATURE ON CONTROL OF INTAKE

For some time, there has been controversy in the literature as to whether young rat pups can, in fact, control their intake while attached to the teat of a nursing mother. Many researchers believe that rat pups are, to a great extent, passive recipients of milk. The dam controls how much milk they ingest. Even the name of the milk delivery process, "milk ejection," suggests such a passive role for the pup: the mother ejects the milk into the nipple-attached pup.

The bases for the controversy over rat pups' control of food intake are two series of deprivation experiments with seemingly different results. In both series of experiments, rat pups of various ages were separated from their dams and thus deprived of food and all other aspects of the mother–infant interaction, including sucking. Upon reunion, most studies found that nondeprived and deprived pups younger than 10–11 days show no differences in latency to attach to the teats of their anesthetized dams or changes in the percentage of time attached during the test session (Cramer et al., 1980; Hall and Rosenblatt, 1978; Brake et al., 1982a; however, see Drewett et al., 1974). Even when returned to normal litters and mothers, deprived and well-fed pups remain attached for equal amounts of time (Lorenz et al., 1982). Also, the deprivation level does not affect the amount of milk ingested by pups younger than approximately 15 days attached to the teat of an anesthetized dam and receiving pulses of milk through a posterior tongue cannula (Cramer and Blass, 1983a,b; Hall and Rosenblatt, 1977). In fact, very young pups remain attached to the nipple and draw in milk until extremely overengorged, often in respiratory difficulty (Cramer and Blass, 1983a,b; Hall and Rosenblatt, 1978).

In contrast to this startling result, when placed together with a normal un-anesthetized dam, the deprived pups ingest more than nondeprived pups (Friedman, 1975; Houpt and Epstein, 1973; Houpt and Houpt, 1975). This increase in ingestion is true even though the attachment time to the teat is not increased (Lorenz et al., 1982). It is also true that very young rat pups show the effects of deprivation on intake when tested in an independent (i.e., not attached to a teat) feeding experiment (Hall and Bryan, 1980). Thus, two lines of study, with different experimental conditions, had seemingly contradictory results. It was these differences in experimental conditions that provided one of the bases for thinking that the differences in experimental results could be resolved.

B. Studies of Sucking Behavior

One measure missing from the above studies is the actual sucking behavior of the pups. Stephen Brake has demonstrated that sucking levels of 11- to 13-day-old rats do change in response to deprivation (Brake *et al.*, 1979). He measured sucking behavior by implanting the digastric muscle of the jaw with an electromyogram (EMG) electrode and recording the EMG on a polygraph. Pups can be attached to a dam's teats for the same length of time, yet be spending more or less time sucking, and they can express different types of sucking. Brake described three different kinds of sucking: rhythmic sucking, treadles, and bursts (for further descriptions, see Section II,C). These three sucking types are differentially influenced by deprivation and by the nutritive consequences of sucking (Brake *et al.*, 1979, 1982a). When tested on an anesthetized nonnutritive dam, rhythmic sucking is increased by deprivation, even if the pups are given a milk preload of 5% of their body weight prior to the test. Arrhythmic (i.e., bursts and treadles) sucking is not increased by deprivation in this test situation. However, if pups are tested on an anesthetized mother, but under nutritive conditions with milk available in a tongue cannula, milk preloads prevent the increase in sucking that is caused by the availability of milk. Thus, the level of the actual sucking behavior itself is influenced both by nutritive status (i.e., deprived or not deprived, preload or no preload) and by whether the sucking produces nutritive results or not.

We decided to use the techniques developed by Brake to examine more natural mother–infant interactions. If the changes in sucking behavior he described are important for intake control, similar changes should be seen during normal nursing bouts. We decided to monitor the pups' sleep–wake state as well, for two reasons: (1) Much work has shown that monitoring sleep behavior is extremely important in assessing the capabilities of young animals. For example, Martinus and Papousek (1970) found habituation of an eye-blink response in 5-day-old infants while in quiet sleep, but not in active sleep. For further discussion of this area, see also Anders (1975, sleep research), Chase (1972, development of reflex activity), Junge (1979, cardiovascular development), and especially Korner (1972, for a theoretical discussion). (2) There is a great deal of evidence linking sleep–wake states and feeding behavior, as reviewed below.

C. Evidence Linking Sleep–Wake States and Feeding

The interactions of sleep–wake states and feeding have been shown in many different species and at many different ages. Four different types of such interactions have been described.

1. We have all had the sensation of feeling sleepy after a heavy meal, known as postprandial sleep. In fact, entering sleep has been described as an important

part of the satiety sequence in adult rats (Young *et al.*, 1974). Lorenz (see his article in this volume) suggests specifically that increased paradoxical sleep causes the termination of nursing bouts in young rats. One of the major findings implicating cholecystokinin as a satiety hormone is that rats go to sleep after cholecystokinin injection (Mansbach and Lorenz, 1983). Postprandial sleep has also been described in infant humans. Infants are more likely to be asleep following a feed than either prior to that feed or following a sham feed (Emde and Metcalf, 1970; Harper *et al.*, 1977; Wolff, 1972). One striking example of postprandial sleep has been described by Emde and Metcalf:

> A characteristic behavioral sequence is: sucking with eyes "bright" and awake-type eye movements, sucking with eyes "glassy" and without gross eye movements, sucking with a horizontal darting of the eyes, and, finally, continued nutritional sucking with horizontal and vertical eye movements indistinguishable from REMs as seen during drowsiness and sleep.

Thus, again, in this situation, sleep could be considered part of the satiety sequence. In fact, this example suggests that the babies may enter a state which is at least similar to paradoxical sleep while continuing nutritional sucking.

Not only is feeding important, but the oral factors involved in feeding are also important in eliciting sleep. Wolff (1972) demonstrated that infants fed through a stomach tube are not as likely to fall asleep following a feed as infants fed by mouth. Feeding can affect other variables besides sleep–wake states, either as correlative phenomena or perhaps due to the influence of the state [e.g., heart rate (Harper *et al.*, 1977)].

2. Feeding behavior may help to regulate sleep–wake state patterning. This has been demonstrated by experiments involving changing meal size, composition, or timing and observing changes in sleep–wake state behavior. The most dramatic change in sleep–wake state behavior occurs following food deprivation. In general, the amount of sleep decreases severely following such deprivation (Danguir and Nicolaidis, 1979; Hockman, 1964; Jacobs and McGinty, 1971). The phase of sleep most depressed, the patterning change, and the amount of this depression all depend on the specifics of the experimental preparation. In adult rats, at least two studies have shown that increasing meal size or changing the timing of the meals can change sleep–wake state cycles (Danguir *et al.*, 1979; Mouret and Bobillier, 1971). Similar findings have been found in human infants. Gaensbauer and Emde (1973) showed that infants who are schedule-fed have different sleep–wake responses to feeding than infants who are demand-fed, even though the average time between feedings is the same. Finally, the composition of the diet can influence the type of sleep in the period after feeding. Diets high in tryptophan cause babies to enter quiet sleep and active sleep more quickly than diets high in valine (Yogman and Zeisel, 1983).

The influence of nutrient on sleep does not depend solely on gastric mechanisms. Intravenous infusions of nutrient also affect sleep–wake states. In lean young adults rats given no other food, intravenous infusions of amino acids increase paradoxical sleep. Neither glucose nor lipid infusions have any significant effect, but a composite solution of all three nutrients increases both paradoxical and slow-wave sleep (Danguir and Nicolaidis, 1980). Both protein and glucose, given intravenously, increase slow-wave sleep at the expense of paradoxical sleep in young women (Lacey *et al.*, 1978).

3. Many studies in animals have demonstrated that there is a very quick-acting link between nutrient and changes in electroencephalogram (EEG) patterns. The general finding is that infusion of nutrient causes the animal to have more slow-wave EEGs. This has been found in response to milk infused into the mouth and the gut in anesthetized cats (Sudakov, 1965), in response to nutrients given via jugular cannulae in adult rats (Rosen *et al.*, 1971), and in infant cats either sucking at the teat of their mother or feeding from a bowl (Anokhin and Shuleikina, 1977). Intraduodenal infusions of fat in the adult cat seem to cause increases in paradoxical sleep (Rubenstein and Sonnenschein, 1971), an effect which is blocked by atropine. Lorenz (1986) suggested that deprived rat pups intragastrically given milk preloads preferentially increase paradoxical sleep time, if allowed to suckle an anesthetized dam.

4. An influence of sleep on subsequent feeding has also been demonstrated. Siegel (1975) found that the amount of rapid eye movement (REM) sleep in one 12-hr period correlated with the amount of food intake in the next 12-hr period in adult cats. Increased REM predicted decreased food intake. The total amount of sleep was not predictive of changes in feeding behavior. Thus, one particular stage of sleep seems to be crucial for this prediction.

These known interactions between sleep–wake states and feeding behavior confirmed our desire to monitor sleep–wake states during natural nursing in the infant rat.

II. General Methods

This article describes three separate sets of experiments. The general methods are given here. The specific methods for each set of experiments are described later.

A. SUBJECTS

Wistar-derived rats (*Rattus norvegicus;* Marland Farms, Hewitt, New Jersey) were born and raised in our laboratories in Plexiglas terraria, 40 × 20 × 24 cm, under a reverse 12-hr light:12-hr dark cycle. Cages were checked for births each morning and afternoon. The day of notation was labeled day 0–1. Litters were culled to eight or nine pups within 2–3 days after birth. Food (Purina Rat Chow, #5001, Memphis, Tennessee) and water were available *ad libitum* to the dams. Bedding material was pine wood chips. Temperature (25–27°C) and humidity (50%) were controlled in the laboratory building. In two of the three experiments, the litters were raised in an animal care room with a population of approximately 25 females near the time of parturition or with litters under 3 weeks of age. No experimental procedures were carried out in this room.

B. PROCEDURES

The procedures and surgical techniques are described here only briefly, since they have been reported elsewhere in detail (Hofer, 1976; Hofer and Shair, 1982; Shair *et al.*, 1984; and extensively in Shair, 1991).

Litters were undisturbed until 11–12 days postnatally, when one member, chosen at random, was implanted with chronic electrodes for recording EEG, neck EMG, digastric EMG, and respiration. After recovery from anesthesia, the pup was intubated with 1 ml of bovine milk and replaced with the litter and the dam.

Two days later, at 1200 hr, in the middark period of the light–dark cycle, the mother was temporarily removed from the cage, the infant was weighed, and its rectal temperature was taken. Only those pups that gained weight since the time of the electrode implantation were included in the experiment. The pup's electrodes were connected via leads to a Grass Instrument Company (Quincy, Massachusetts) Model 7 polygraph, and the pup was reunited with its dam (see below) in its home cage nest area. Two hours was chosen a the time of the recording session, since it is sufficient to include a nursing bout as well as an interbout interval in most cases (Croskerry *et al.*, 1976; Grota and Ader, 1969; Hofer and Grabie, 1971). In addition, it was similar to our previous experiments (Hofer, 1976; Hofer and Shair, 1982). Finally, the pup is unlikely to develop separation effects, since interbout intervals of this length are not unknown in litters of this age.

Depending on the experiment, the pup was recorded while attached to the teat of its urethane-anesthetized dam or with its littermates and its unanesthetized freely moving dam. This recording session was labeled "baseline day." The polygraph was positioned near the home cage terrarium to facilitate concurrent recording of behavioral observations. Because recordings were made during the dark phase of the light cycle, the infant was observed under indirect and minimal light (equal to direct light from a 15-W bulb). The paper speed on the polygraph was 10 mm/sec. At the end of the baseline recording, the lead wires were removed from the pup and its rectal temperature and weight were taken again.

Note that any weight changes during the experiment may not accurately reflect intake or metabolic rate, since excretion was not controlled. The pup may have been stimulated to excrete during the session either by the dam or by the procedures themselves. We decided not to void the pup prior to the recording session for fear that its behavior or the mother's reactions might have been changed.

All test pups were then separated from their mothers. The exact manner of housing for the pup depended on the experiment, but all had at least two littermates as companions, were in a nest of home cage shavings, and had thermoregulated heat supplied (36.5°C delivered to the bottom of the cage). After 22 hr of separation, each test pup was recorded and observed during a 2-hr reunion session. The procedures for the reunion test were exactly the same as on baseline day for that particular experiment.

C. SCORING OF SLEEP–WAKE STATE AND SUCKING BEHAVIORS

Three major states were defined by classical criteria (Anders *et al.*, 1971; Gramsbergen, 1976; Jouvet-Mounier *et al.*, 1970) from polygraph recordings of EEG, neck EMG, respiratory rate, and behavioral observation of activity (see Fig. 1 for EEG and respiration examples). "Awake" was defined by a fast low-

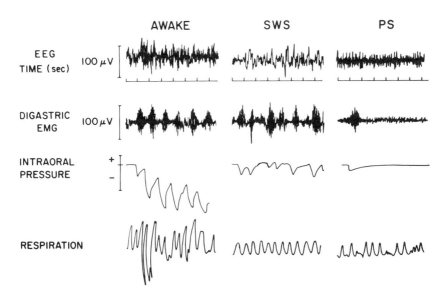

FIG. 1.   Polygraph recordings of a nursing pup in all three arousal states. In the awake and slow-wave sleep (SWS) stages, the pup shows the rhythmic pattern of sucking. During paradoxical sleep (PS), there is a "burst." Top channel, electrocorticogram; channel 2, timing (in seconds); channel 3, digastric muscle electromyogram; channel 4, intraoral pressure changes; channel 5, respiration (by impedance plethysmography). (From "Suckling in the Rat: Evidence for Patterned Behavior during Sleep" by H. Shair, S. Brake, and M. Hofer, 1984, *Behavioral Neuroscience,* **98:**366–370. Copyright by the American Psychological Association, reprinted by permission of the publisher.)

voltage EEG, a high-amplitude neck EMG, variable and fast respiration, and bouts of coordinated behavioral activity. Slow-wave sleep consisted of a slow low-voltage EEG, a moderately low neck EMG amplitude, very regular respirations, and behavioral quiescence. In paradoxical sleep, there was a fast low-voltage EEG, a minimal neck EMG with occasional phasic twitches, an irregular respiratory pattern, and behaviorally sudden movements superimposed on a loss of postural tone.

Note that eye movements were not recorded, because respiratory patterns gave a clearer distinction between the two major sleep states at this age. A pattern of phasic irregularity was seen during paradoxical sleep, whereas during slow-wave sleep the respirations showed almost machinelike regularity. Body movements were also sensitively registered on the polygraph as baseline fluctuations of the impedance respiratory channel. Fifteen-second epochs were classified according to whatever state occupied most of the epoch. A rationale for these criteria for state scoring is discussed in the next section.

Sucking was characterized according to three basic patterns of muscle activity, previously described by Brake *et al.* (1979). The three patterns consist of treadles, bursts, and rhythmic sucking. Bursts were characterized as discrete episodes of high-frequency activity lasting at least 2 sec. Treadles consisted of discrete periods of activity lasting at least 2 sec, with slow and fast waves mixed. The jaw muscle activity was accompanied by a characteristic movement of the forelimbs which suggested the name "treadles." Forelimb movement artifacts were shown to account for the slow-wave activity (Brake *et al.*, 1979). Bursts were unaccompanied by body movements. Bursts and treadles occurring sequentially had to be separated by at least 2 sec to be counted as different episodes. Rhythmic sucking bouts were characterized as brief periods of regularly alternating increases and decreases in activity lasting at least 5 sec, with no more than 2 sec separating each activity peak. The relationship between the three EMG patterns and actual suction on the teat has been verified by measuring intraoral pressure (Brake *et al.*, 1979; see Fig. 1 for examples). The intensity of jaw EMG between sucks was also rated as a measure of the tonic pressure seal developed by the pup. This intensity rank was rated for each epoch of 15 sec on an arbitrary scale of one to four points.

The issue of experimenter bias must be addressed, since the scorer (H.N.S.) of all of the sleep–wake state data was not blind to the experimental condition of the record. There are three factors which we hope lessened the likelihood of experimenter bias. First, there was no change in scoring criteria over time as the experimental results became known. Reliability separated by a 2-year period was 94.5%, with approximately equal results for all three states. The second factor which worked to prevent bias was that there was no strong hypothesis as to the direction of any results. Finally, many of the conclusions depend on the relationship between sucking behavior and sleep–wake states. Stephen Brake scored all of the sucking data and was blind both to experimental condition and to sleep–wake state.

D. Rationale for Sleep–Wake State Scoring Criteria

States are defined operationally by constellations of behaviors which do not always coalesce in exactly the same form (Prechtl *et al.*, 1968). Individuals may vary as to exactly how these behaviors coalesce. In one subject, the respiratory pattern may not discriminate state changes well. In another, differences in EEG may not be as distinct. Thus, recognizing sleep–wake state behavior becomes a problem in pattern recognition. Also, for each individual subject, the particular pattern-recognition criteria must be reset slightly.

No single behavior, even EEG, is enough to define state, particularly when comparing different individuals. For example, in a study of adult rats using spectral analysis of the EEG, Young *et al.* (1978) described most of the spectral power during paradoxical sleep as between six and nine cycles per second. Another study listed most power between 30 and 40 cycles per second (Timo-Iaria *et al.*, 1970). Similar discrepancies in results can be found for the awake and slow-wave sleep states. (The different results for paradoxical sleep can probably be reconciled. In the first study, the EEG is dominated by θ waves, possibly due to electrode placement. The faster waves of paradoxical sleep are of low amplitude, probably superimposed on the θ waves, but with little spectral power.)

Another, but equally difficult, problem relates to the overlap in EEG frequencies in the different states. Waves of all frequencies are seen in all three states. Slow-wave sleep is discriminated from the awake and paradoxical sleep states, in part, by the proportion of slow waves seen. Thus, there can be much overlap in EEG patterns. In fact, the EEG patterns for paradoxical sleep and the awake state are practically indistinguishable, in both adult and young rats (Jouvet-Mounier *et al.*, 1970; Timo-Iaria *et al.*, 1970).

The work described in this article differed from most of the studies in the literature, in that the recordings were often done with the pup attached to its mother's teat. Did this alteration in test setting change the constellation of sleep–wake state behavior such that the state scorings under different attachment conditions were not comparable? We suggest that the answer to this question is no, for four reasons.

1. Emde and Metcalf (1970), Jouvet-Mounier *et al.* (1970), and Ruckebusch (1972) have all monitored young mammals while nipple-attached and made no reference to any need to change state-rating criteria.

2. The polygraph tracings and behavioral observations taken on pups when attached in the present studies appear the same as those recorded from unattached pups in our laboratory (Hofer, 1976; Hofer and Shair, 1982).

3. In the normal mother experiment, pups were recorded both while attached and while unattached. Each individual could be compared in the two conditions. No changes in the behaviors or electrophysiology which make up the criteria for state rating were observed. Respiration was regular, almost machinelike, during slow-wave sleep under both conditions. Irregularity in breathing of the same type was seen in paradoxical sleep. The neck EEG patterns looked similar, attached or unattached.

However, had we used the digastric EMG to help score state, there would have been much confusion. The amplitude of the jaw EMG tracing while nipple-attached and asleep was frequently as high as when awake and unattached.

4. Some preliminary work using spectral analysis of the EEG confirms the similarity of the two test settings. We have now recorded three pups, both while attached and while unattached. After scoring sleep–wake states by the normal criteria, the EEGs from epochs of each of the three states under both conditions were analyzed using a spectral analysis program (Williams and Gottman, 1982). This program counts the EEG waves and sorts it according to frequencies. The pattern of EEG frequencies seen was not significantly influenced in any state by the attachment condition.

E. DATA ANALYSIS

Fifteen-second epochs were scored by the above criteria and measures were derived for the duration and frequency of periods in each state, the percentage of total recording time spent in each state, and the rate and pattern of transitions from one state to the next. We also scored the latency to sleep onset. The total amount of sucking for the three sucking types was measured for each animal. Finally, we also calculated for each animal the rate of sucking per unit of time spent in each sleep–wake state, a state-specific sucking rate.

In this experimental design, each infant served as its own control, with respect to changes in measures from baseline day to reunion day, to changes in measures within different states, and with respect to measures recorded when the pup was attached or unattached to its mother's teat. Dependent t tests (dep t) and one- and two-way analyses of variance (ANOVAs) with repeated measures took into account this strong experimental design. Comparisons across groups without repeated measures were done by independent t test. The correlation of one variable with another was done using Pearson's product–moment parametric correlations. Variation around all mean values are given by the standard errors of the means, in both text and figures. In consideration of space and readability, the ANOVA results are not generally reported. However, all t tests reported in this article have been justified by the ANOVA results or an *a priori* hypothesis.

III. Normal Mother and Litter: Baseline

The purpose of this section is to describe the behavior of 2-week-old rat pups during the normal nursing cycle. For the reasons discussed in Section I, the emphasis is on the relationship between sleep–wake states and sucking behavior. Another goal is to provide normative data on aspects of the mother–infant interaction for comparison with previous studies. Behavioral and physiological recordings of nursing bouts and interbout intervals are examined for differences and similarities between the two situations.

The data are presented in the following fashion. There is a detailed analysis of the behavioral observations of the six experimental litters. Included in these data are such measures as the number and timing of nursing bouts and milk ejections, activity levels of the implanted pups, and weight and temperature changes.

The polygraph results are presented next. Sleep–wake states and sucking patterns are emphasized. Periods during nursing bouts are compared with interbout intervals. Trends in the data over the time of the nursing episodes are also examined.

A. METHODS

Six litters were born and raised near the polygraph machine in the testing room where they would be studied later. This procedure was followed to accustom the mothers to the presence of the investigators. On the day of electrode implantation, the usual procedures were followed, except that the electrodes were made especially long (10 cm) to allow the pups more freedom of movement.

On baseline day, 15 min prior to the test session, the dam was removed from the cage and the implanted pup was connected to leads buried under the nest shavings. After the dam was returned to her litter, care was taken to watch her closely during the first 15 min of the recording session, since she was likely to attack the electrodes during this time, if at all. It was sometimes necessary to distract her attention from the electrodes by touching the top of the cage or occasionally by actually pushing her head away from the electrodes with a long probe. No heat was supplied to the bottom of the cage during the test sessions, since the mother and the littermates were present to provide normal temperature controls to the test pup.

In this experiment, the mother was free to come and go from the litter; thus, the data were analyzed both while the pup was attached to the mother's teat and while the pup was unattached, as well as for an overall analysis of sleep–wake behavior combining both conditions. Gaps in attachment of 1 min or less were included as attachment time. During these short gaps, the pups were frantically nosing their mother's ventrums, in the process of reattaching to the same nipple or a new one. The short gaps usually occurred just following a milk ejection, during which a nipple switch is to be expected. The short gaps did not constitute a termination of the nursing bout itself. Of course, sucking behaviors could only be analyzed when the pup was attached. It must be noted that it was impossible to see the test pup some of the time, since the mother and the littermates would block the view; thus, the behavioral observations were occasionally incomplete.

As is known from the work of two groups of researchers, the mother rat must be in slow-wave sleep for a milk ejection to occur (Lincoln *et al.*, 1980; Voloschin and Tramezzani, 1979). She is generally in a relaxed posture, with the pups quietly attached to her ventrum. The milk ejection activates both mother and pups. The mother wakes and stands on four splayed legs over her litter with her back arched (Drewett *et al.*, 1974; Lincoln *et al.*, 1980). The pups begin to suck vigorously and display a stereotypic "stretch" response, showing a rigid body extension with limbs pressed against the mother's ventrum (Drewett *et al.*, 1974; Lincoln *et al.*, 1973, 1980).

We used these already known behaviors of the mother and the entire litter to rate the occurrence of a milk ejection, as have other workers in the field (e.g., Drewett and Trew, 1978; Voloschin and Tramezzani, 1979). A variety of measures have justified the use of these behaviors as a marker for milk ejection, including their temporal correlation with a rise in intramammary pressure, with the administration of oxytocin to the dam, etc. (for a review, see Drewett, 1983). However, it has not been conclusively proven in the natural nursing situation that these behaviors occur only when the pups receive milk or that the pups never receive milk without their occurrence. Thus, following common practice in the field, when we discuss the pups' response to a milk ejection, we refer to this defined "milk ejection response" behavior.

This problem of definition is especially relevant, since the sucking pattern was also used to define the milk ejection response. The EMG was rated independently by Brake in four categories, ranging from "definite" to "barely possible," as to whether a milk ejection had occurred. Since, in the data analysis, we describe sucking changes during milk ejection responses, it would be circular if we tried to imply that these behaviors were a necessary part of all milk delivery. The two rating systems overlapped very well for 28 cases, and these were called milk ejection responses. In five cases, either the behavioral or EMG rating was so high that these instances were called milk ejection responses despite reservations of the second scoring system. There were another 30 cases with low ratings as milk ejection responses by either system or, more usually, both. These examples were not included in the data analysis. Thus, we used a conservative approach to calling a particular behavior a milk ejection, deliberately accepting the chance of more "misses" than "false positives."

After the baseline recording session, the test pup and two littermates were placed in a new cage overnight. As noted in Section II, home cage shavings and thermoregulated heat were supplied. Four pups were left with the mother in the home cage in order to reduce any changes in the mother's behavior which might be caused by the experimental procedure. Thus, on reunion day, four of the seven pups had not been deprived, while three had been. The observations of the mother–infant interaction of reunion day should be interpreted with the differential experience of the two groups of pups in mind.

B. RESULTS

1. Behavioral Observations

During the 2-hr test session, the implanted pup was able to compete successfully with its littermates. There were no gross behavioral differences between the test pup and its littermates. The head implant did not prevent the pup from burrowing quickly under its dam and attaching to a teat. No test pup ever missed a milk ejection received by its littermates. They were able to attach to their dams 79% ± 4% of the time that she was in the vicinity of the litter, demonstrating the pups' mobility. Also, as seen in 2,a below, the sleep–wake patterns of the pups were quite comparable to the norms described for pups of this age recorded without their dams or littermates (Hofer, 1976; Jouvet-Mounier et al., 1970). Thus, there seems little reason to believe that the following results were an artifact of the recording procedure.

a. Attachment Time. During the 2-hr test session, both the number and the length of the nursing interactions between pups and dams varied among the six litters. This variability is displayed in Fig. 2. Note the irregular patterns of milk ejections as well. A few constants do appear to be true, however. No milk ejections occurred in any nursing bout of less than 5 min. Only rarely was there a milk ejection in the first several minutes after attachment.

The data from Fig. 2 and its derived means (see Table I) are well within the range of results found by other investigators. Two-week-old rats are suckled approximately 40% of the time (Grota and Ader, 1969; Leon et al., 1985). In this study, nipple switches were seen following 22% of the milk ejections (data derived from Table I), as has been reported for pups of this age (Hall et al., 1975). The average length of the nursing bouts in this experiment was a little shorter than the 20 min found by others for pups of this age (Grota and Ader, 1969; Leon et al., 1978). However, these researchers monitored maternal nest time, not actual attachment time. As shown in Fig. 2, nursing bouts were sometimes interrupted by only a few minutes. The dam may not have left the nest area during this time.

b. Milk Ejection Responses. There was a total of 33 milk ejection responses observed during the 4.9 hr of attachment of all implanted pups. The data in Table

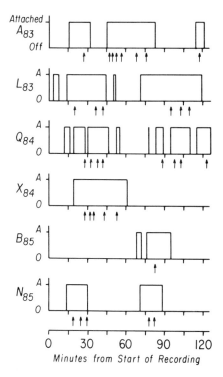

FIG. 2.   Patterns of nursing bouts for all six litters during the 2-hr baseline recordings. These data are based on the times during which each implanted pup either was or was not attached to a teat. The results for any other individual in a litter may vary slightly. Gaps in attachment of 1 min or less are not indicated. Milk ejections are designated by arrows. Designations A_{83} to N_{85} identify each particular litter.

I concerning the defined milk ejection responses are comparable to those in other reports in the literature (Lincoln *et al.*, 1973). These investigators found a very similar range in interejection intervals from about 2 min to over 20 min, with a mean of 6.6 min. Thus, since the present recording procedure did not interrupt the normal pattern of milk letdown, the test procedure must have allowed the mothers to fall asleep (Lincoln *et al.*, 1980; Voloschin and Tramezzani, 1979).

c. Weight and Temperature Data. Pups were within the normal range for weight and temperature at the start of the recording session (Table II) (Hofer and Grabie, 1971; Messer *et al.*, 1969). Pups were equally warm at the end of the session. There was a small but significant increase in weight during the 2-hr period. If the pups had continued to gain weight at that rate for 24 hr, their percentage change in weight would have been $0.8\% \times 12 = 9.6\%$. The normal

TABLE I

DATA FROM BEHAVIORAL OBSERVATIONS OF MOTHER–PUP INTERACTIONS ON BASELINE DAY[a]

	Time attached (min)	% TRT attached	Latency to first NB (min)	No. of NB's	Length of NB's (min)	No. of nipple-switches[b]	No. of ME's	Latency to first ME (min)[c]	Time between later ME's (min)[d]
Mean	51.0	41.0	21.0	3.5	15.5	1.2	5.5	7.5	6.3
SEM	9.1	6.8	9.4	1.0	3.1	0.8	1.5	1.5	0.8
Range	23–84	19–65	3–67	1–8	0.5–48	0–5	1–8	1.8–24	2.8–16

[a]TRT, Total recording time; NB, nursing bout; ME, milk ejection; SEM, standard error of the mean.

[b]A nipple-switch is defined as an event in which a pup detached from a nipple and reattached to the same or another nipple within 1 min.

[c]Latency to the first milk ejection of each nursing bout, not the total recording time.

[d]Figured only for milk ejections within the same nursing bout.

gain in weight for a pup of this age is approximately 11% (Messer *et al.*, 1969). Neither change nor percentage of change in weight was significantly correlated with the amount of time the pup was attached to the nipple, with the number of milk ejection responses, or with the number of nipple switches. Remember, as mentioned in Section II,B, the pups had not been voided prior to the start of the test procedure; thus, variable amounts of elimination might have influenced the weight measures.

   d. Activity Levels. Hofer and Grabie (1971) reported that, for the 2-week-old pup, the distribution of active and inactive episodes did not depend on whether the pup was being nursed. Results in the present experiment were similar. As

TABLE II

BODY WEIGHT AND RECTAL TEMPERATURE: BASELINE DAY[a]

	Body weight (g)			Rectal temperature (°C)	
	Pre	Post	% Change	Pre	Post
Mean	27.6	27.9[b]	0.80	35.90	36.30[c]
SEM	1.0	1.0	0.26	0.16	0.21
Range	24.5–31.6	24.5–31.8	0–1.6	35.4–36.4	35.8–36.9

[a]Pre, preobservation; Post, postobservation; SEM, standard error of the mean.

[b]Significant increase in weight ($p < 0.05$).

[c]No significant change in temperature.

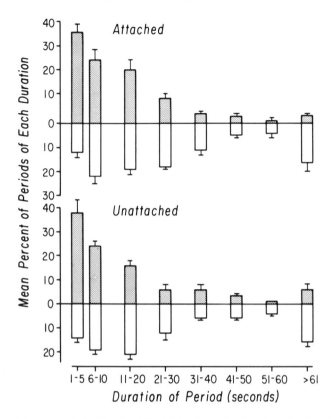

FIG. 3. Histogram analysis of active (stippled bars) and inactive (open bars) periods during nursing (attached) and when the mother was away (unattached), illustrating the relative frequency of occurrence of periods of different durations.

shown in Fig. 3 and confirmed by two-way ANOVAs with repeated measures, there was no influence of attachment condition on the duration of either active or inactive episodes. This confirmation of a previous study gave us more reason to believe that our recording procedure was not too disruptive.

2. Electrophysiological Data

Rat pups not only slept during the internursing bout intervals, but also during most of each nursing bout. A typical example (Fig. 4) shows how quickly one pup fell asleep after grasping the teat. The pup alternated among all three sleep–wake states during the period it was attached to the mother's teat. Note that the pup was asleep at the start of each of the three milk ejections, then awakened briefly during and after the milk ejection. The example also shows that sucking

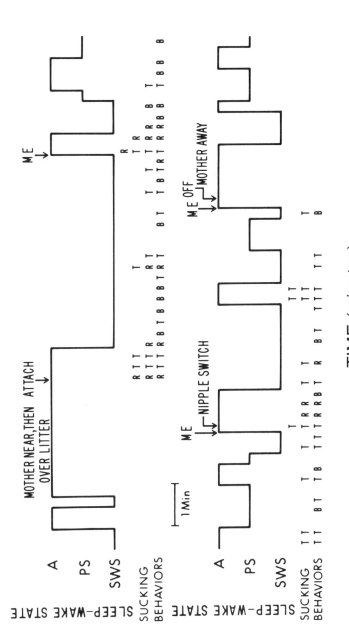

TIME (minutes)

FIG. 4. Sleep–wake state data and sucking behaviors during a typical nursing episode. The height of the top line indicates which state the pup was in at any given time. After the pup was attached, the type and amount of sucking during each 15-sec interval are shown by the letters below the sleep–wake state tracing. Other behaviors of interest are noted above the state tracing. Thus, three R's indicate 11–15 sec of rhythmic sucking. A, Awake; PS, paradoxical sleep; SWS, slow-wave sleep; R, rhythmic sucking; T, treadles; B, bursts; ME, milk ejection. (From "Suckling in the Rat: Evidence for Patterned Behavior during Sleep" by H. Shair, S. Brake, and M. Hofer, 1984, *Behavioral Neuroscience*, **98**:366–370. Copyright by the American Psychological Association, reprinted by permission of the publisher.)

TABLE III

MEASURES OF SLEEP AND WAKEFULNESS OF INFANT RATS RECORDED WITH THEIR NORMAL MOTHER AND LITTERMATES FOR 2 HR ON BASELINE DAY[a]

| | Sleep latency (min) | % Time in state[b] | | | State episode analysis | | | | | | |
| | | | | | Mean duration (min) | | | Frequency/hr | | | State transitions/hr |
		A	PS	SWS	A	PS	SWS	A	PS	SWS	
Overall	2.3	31	39	30	1.02	1.82	1.33	18	13	14	46
Attached	0.8	29	33	38	0.68	1.22	1.18	26	17	20	61
Unattached	2.4	33	43	25	1.34	2.66	1.46	16	10	10	35
					Comparison of attached and unattached						
Dependent t test ($df = 5$)	1.913	0.637	1.347	1.866	2.479[c]	3.104[d]	1.344	5.097[e]	3.008[d]	5.513[e]	7.377[f]

[a] A, Awake; PS, paradoxical sleep; SWS, slow-wave sleep.

[b] The percentage of time in a state is based on the total recording time for the overall condition, the time being nursed in the attached condition, and the time with mother away in the unattached condition.

[c] $p < 0.10$ (not significant).

[d] $p < 0.05$.

[e] $p < 0.01$.

[f] $p < 0.001$.

behaviors occurred in all three states. The rest of this section characterizes these observations in greater detail. First sleep patterns, then sucking data, and finally the periods around milk ejection are analyzed.

a. Sleep–Wake States. As suggested by Fig. 4, rat pups were asleep a high percentage of the time during nursing bouts. In fact, the sleep–wake state percentages were not significantly different whether the pup was or was not attached (see Table III). Other results did show a difference between the two attachment conditions. The sleep latency immediately following nipple attachment was actually shorter than that after the pups had come off the nipple. There is another interesting point having to do with sleep latencies. After initial attachment, pups always entered slow-wave sleep. However, when pups fell asleep following detachment, they showed an equal likelihood of entering into slow-wave or paradoxical sleep.

The duration of episodes was shorter in all three states while pups were nursing than when they were not nursing. These episodes also occurred at a higher frequency, which resulted in the equal percentages of recording time noted above. The fewer number of state transitions per hour of the pups when not attached reflects the data on duration and frequency in a single figure. The more state transitions per hour of the attached animal was probably due to the fact that the pup was being disturbed from external sources—the mother's movements and her milk ejections.

Another characteristic of state behavior is the probability of transition from one particular state to another. In this study, there were no significant changes by two-way ANOVA in these transitional probabilities that depended on whether the pups were being nursed or not (Fig. 5). Under both conditions, the most likely sequence of transitions was from the awake state to slow-wave sleep to paradoxical sleep and back to awake. However, note that only two cases (awake to slow-wave sleep and paradoxical sleep to awake) were above 20% in probability. Thus, these pups did not have the adult pattern of more predictable transitions,

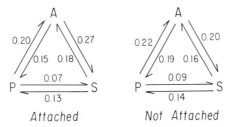

FIG. 5. The probabilities of transitions among the three sleep–wake states during nursing (attached) and while the mother was away (unattached) on baseline day.

Harry N. Shair and Myron A. Hofer

TABLE IV

MEAN (± SEM) SUCKING TIMES IN EACH SLEEP–WAKE STATE OF INFANT
RATS BEING NURSED BY THEIR MOTHER ON BASELINE DAY[a]

State	Rhythmic sucking	Bursts	Treadles
Awake	44 ± 11	19 ± 5	70 ± 15
Paradoxical sleep	2 ± 1	17 ± 5	17 ± 6
Slow-wave sleep	19 ± 4	34 ± 9	30 ± 6

[a]For each of the three sucking types, the time spent sucking was calculated as the number of 5-sec bins in which a suck of that type occurred.

which has also been reported for other young mammals (Meier and Berger, 1965; Shimizu and Himwich, 1968).

b. Sucking Behavior. All six pups engaged in frequent sucking while they were asleep and attached to their mother's nipple. This finding has been noted above in the nursing example illustrated in Fig. 4. Table IV summarizes the mean sucking times for the three sucking types: bursts, treadles, and rhythmic sucking. Overall, almost 50% of all sucking occurred while the pups were asleep. The sucking pattern called "burst" was different from treadles and rhythmic sucking. It was the only sucking pattern predominantly (i.e., 71%) seen during sleep. The other two patterns were seen more in slow-wave than paradoxical sleep, but still less than half as much as while awake.

However, since the proportions of time spent in the three sleep–wake states were different, a rate of sucking in each state gives a better measure of the relationship between sucking pattern and sleep–wake states. In Fig. 6, one can see that all four aspects of sucking behavior occurred at appreciable levels during the two states of sleep as well as during the awake state, with the single exception of rhythmic sucking, which was almost never observed in paradoxical sleep. Bursts actually occurred at a higher rate in slow-wave sleep than while awake. The rate of each type of sucking differed significantly between the sleep–wake states, as shown by ANOVAs whose *post hoc t* tests are given in the legend to Fig. 6.

c. Milk Ejection Responses. The period around the milk ejection responses was analyzed closely in terms of sleep–wake states and sucking patterns. As mentioned above, 33 milk ejections were observed. In Fig. 7, one can see that in all of them, the pups were asleep prior to milk ejection, were awakened by the milk ejection, and in 50% of the cases were asleep again within 15 sec. By 30 sec, the percentage asleep had risen to 74%.

The levels of all three sucking types were not elevated prior to milk ejection responses (see Fig. 8). Treadles and rhythmic sucking both rose during the

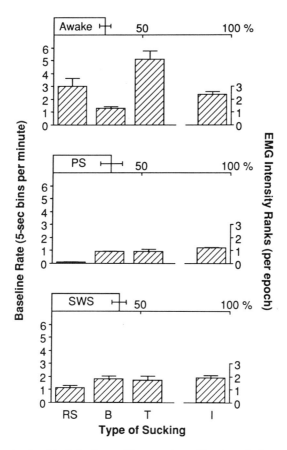

FIG. 6. The rate of sucking behaviors and the percentage of time in each sleep–wake state during nursing on baseline day. Dependent t tests ($df = 5$) demonstrated that there was a characteristic rate of each sucking type within each state.

	A versus PS	PS versus SWS	SWS versus A
RS/min	4.540[a]	4.454[a]	3.245[b]
B/min	2.818[b]	3.658[b]	2.642[b]
T/min	6.539[a]	2.581[c]	6.114[a]
EMG I/epoch	17.294[d]	3.682[b]	10.826[d]

The horizontal bars represent the mean percentage of attached recording time spent in each sleep–wake state (A, awake; PS, paradoxical sleep; SWS, slow-wave sleep). The three left-hand vertical bars give the mean rate of sucking per minute for rhythmic sucking (RS), bursts (B), and treadles (T). The bar to the right (I) measures the amplitude of the digastric EMG recording when no sucking is occurring (an index of the muscle tone involved in maintaining a seal on the nipple). a, $p < 0.01$; b, p 0.05; c, $p < 0.10$; d, $p < 0.001$. (From "Suckling in the Rat: Evidence for Patterned Behavior during Sleep" by H. Shair, S. Brake, and M. Hofer, 1984, *Behavioral Neuroscience*, **98**: 366–370. Copyright by the American Psychological Association, reprinted by permission of the publisher.)

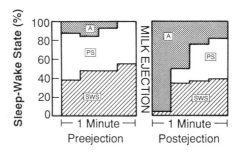

FIG. 7.   The percentage of pups in each sleep–wake state during the minute before (preejection) and the minute after (postejection) milk ejection responses in 28 of 33 cases observed. In five cases, the pups detached from the teat for more than 15 sec and were omitted from this analysis. A, Awake; PS, paradoxical sleep, SWS, slow-wave sleep. (From "Suckling in the Rat: Evidence for Patterned Behavior during Sleep" by H. Shair, S. Brake, and M. Hofer, 1984, *Behavioral Neuroscience*, **98**:366–370. Copyright by the American Psychological Association, reprinted by permission of the publisher.)

minute following milk ejection. Treadles rose to nearly five times normal rates immediately after milk ejection. Considering the entire minute after milk ejection, the overall rate was doubled (see Table V). Thus, treadles and rhythmic sucking are implicated as nutritive sucking types for the rat pup. The rate of bursts appeared to be unchanged by the milk ejection.

When the definition of the "milk ejection response" is expanded to include even those 30 behavioral events rated "barely possible" milk ejections (see

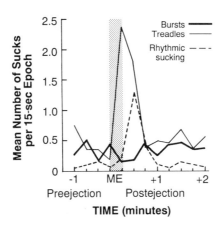

FIG. 8.   Sucking levels for the minute before, during, and 2 min after the milk ejection (ME) response. Mean values are based on the 28 MEs in which the pups did not detach for more than 15 sec.

TABLE V

COMPARISON OF MEAN (± SEM) SUCKING RATES IN THE 2 MIN IMMEDIATELY AFTER MILK
EJECTION TO THE OVERALL SUCKING RATES DURING ATTACHMENT ON BASELINE DAY

	Meaning sucking rate			Dependent t test ($df = 5$)	
	1st min post-ME	2nd min post-ME	Overall	1st min vs. overall	2nd min vs. overall
Rhythmic sucking	2.05 ± 0.35	0.37 ± 0.20	1.22 ± 0.16	2.180[a]	5.751[b]
Bursts	1.09 ± 0.26	1.63 ± 0.48	1.38 ± 0.14	1.641	0.642
Treadles	4.95 ± 0.45	2.13 ± 0.47	2.37 ± 0.37	7.766[c]	1.582

[a] $p < 0.10$ (not significant).
[b] $p < 0.01$.
[c] $p < 0.001$.

Section III,A), the above-described sleep–wake and sucking patterns were not altered dramatically. The pups were still asleep prior to virtually every milk ejection. They returned to sleep even more quickly thereafter. Sucking behavior changed in that neither rhythmic sucking nor treadles rose quite as high during and just after the suspected ejection.

What happened to the sucking rates in each of the three states in this period of milk ejection response (as originally defined)? In general, the rate of sucking in any given state was not significantly changed by a milk ejection. Treadles while awake were an exception. The mean rate for each of the six pups just after milk ejection was significantly higher than the overall awake rate (dep $t = 3.537$, $df = 5$, $p < 0.05$). Note that these data must be considered tentative, since there was a limited number of epochs available for comparison. The problem was especially acute for paradoxical sleep, since two pups did not enter paradoxical sleep in the minute following milk ejections. However, these data suggested that it would be worth examining how fixed the rate of sucking is in each sleep–wake state. This point is addressed further in the studies to follow.

3. Trends over Time within the Nursing Bout

As discussed in Section I, there is a relationship between feeding behavior and sleep–wake cycles (e.g., Danguir and Nicolaidis, 1979; Siegel, 1975; Yogman and Zeisel, 1983). One of the simplest ways to consider this relationship is that young mammals may be awake when hungry and asleep when full, a formulation included as part of what Kleitman (1963) called "wakefulness of necessity." The article by Lorenz in this volume describes a somewhat more complex version of this idea, specifically designed to help understand feeding and satiety in young rats. The illustrated nursing bout (Fig. 4) suggests that a simple explanation cannot be true in all cases, since the pup in this example fell asleep before receiving any milk. Another way to examine the hypothesis is to compare the pups' behavior in the first half of the nursing bouts to their behavior in the second half of the bouts. In Table VI (top), one can see that neither the sleep–wake state percentages nor the time spent sucking showed any significant change between the two halves of the nursing bouts. These data do not fit the predictions that the pups would spend more time asleep after receiving milk.

Did the behavior associated with milk ejections change over the time of the nursing bouts? For the 14 nursing bouts of 5 min or more, there were an average of 1.1 ± 0.3 milk ejections in the first half of the bout, and 1.3 ± 0.1 in the second half [dep $t = 0.763$, $df = 13$, not significant (ns)]. The sleep–wake state percentages in the minute before and the minute after milk ejections did not differ when measured in the first versus the second half of the nursing bout. Neither did the sucking rates show any change over time (Table VI, bottom).

TABLE VI
TRENDS OVER TIME WITHIN THE NURSING BOUT: BASELINE DAY[a]

Comparison of state percentages and sucking behaviors in the first versus the second half of each bout					
	Sleep–wake state (%)			Time sucking	
	A	PS	SWS	RS	B	T
First half	35	23	42	16.4	14.7	23.7
Second half	32	32	36	10.2	13.5	24.0
Dependent t test ($df = 13$)	0.978	1.700	1.188	1.610	0.641	0.125

Comparison of the rates of sucking in the minutes around milk ejection (ME) in the first versus the second half of the nursing bout					
	Minutes prior to ME			Minutes following ME	
	RS	B	T	RS	B	T
First half	0.5	1.8	1.4	2.1	0.8	5.3
Second half	0.3	1.1	1.7	2.3	1.2	4.7
Dependent t test ($df = 5$)	0.753	1.698	0.558	0.172	0.945	0.537

[a]Data are only from the 14 nursing bouts of 5 min or more. A, Awake; PS, paradoxical sleep; SWS, slow-wave sleep; RS, rhythmic sucking; B, bursts; T, treadles.
[b]Data averaged by pup since the number of MEs was not the same in the first and second halves.

4. The Problem of "Indeterminate State"

As discussed in Sections II, C and D, states are defined by a constellation of behaviors. Individuals may vary from each other or within themselves over time in the preciseness of the coherence of the parameters used to define states. Thus, certain epochs may be hard to characterize as one state or another. This problem is often especially acute in young animals, because the parameters that constitute a state may not have developed fully at the time of the recording session (Anders, 1975; Petre-Quadens, 1974; Wolff, 1972). On baseline day, there were difficult-to-score epochs in an average of 9% of each recording session. These have been labeled "indeterminate state" (IDS). Each of these difficult epochs was placed in the state to which, in our best estimation, it belonged. However, these epochs were tracked for further analysis. Sixty-four percent of IDS epochs appeared to be a cross between an awake–drowsy state and slow-wave sleep with movement. This state has been labeled the "intermediate state" (ITS). ITS occurred an average of 6% ± 1.3% of the baseline recording. The range of ITS among the animals went from 0% to 10%. Of these epochs, 69% were scored as slow-wave sleep, 31% as awake state.

If one assumes that these epochs were mislabeled—that the pups were really awake—what would be the effect on the results described in the preceding sections? As can be noted in Table VII, this recalculation caused only a small change in sleep–wake percentages. In fact, the similarities between the attached and unattached conditions in sleep–wake percentages were even more striking when scored in this manner (cf. Table III).

If all ITS epochs in the minute following milk ejections were scored as awake,

TABLE VII

INFLUENCE OF INTERMEDIATE STATE (ITS) SCORING ON SLEEP-WAKE STATE PERCENTAGES[a]

	Mean % of recording time		
	A	PS	SWS
Overall: original scoring	31	39	30
Overall: ITS scored as A	34	39	27
Attached: ITS scored as A	38	33	29
Unattached: ITS scored as A	34	43	24
Comparison of attached and unattached			
Dependent t test ($df = 5$)	0.894 (ns)	1.493 (ns)	0.890 (ns)

[a]A, Awake; PS, paradoxical sleep; SWS, slow-wave sleep.

the speed at which pups fell asleep was still dramatic. In 42% of the cases, the pups were asleep by 15 sec. This figure climbed to 69% by 30 sec. Thus, we calculated that any problem caused by these epochs did not significantly influence the general pattern of our results.

C. Discussion

The results of this experiment demonstrate that there are striking similarities in the behavior of the 2-week-old rat while attached and unattached to its dam's teat. Activity levels do not distinguish between the two conditions, confirming the work by Hofer and Grabie (1971). Most importantly, the basic sleep–wake pattern continues, to a large extent, independently of the attachment condition. For example, there is no change in the percentage of time in each sleep–wake state. The rat pup alternates in a fairly rapid manner among the three basic arousal states, spending approximately two-thirds of the time asleep under both conditions. What does alter is the duration and frequency of the state episodes. While attached, the episodes tend to be shorter and more frequent, possibly due to the mother's behavioral stimulations.

The results also reveal that, during nursing bouts, almost half of all sucking behavior occurs while the infant rat is asleep. Characteristic rates of each sucking type are exhibited in the different states. These rates tend to be highest while the pup is awake, intermediate in slow-wave sleep, and lowest in paradoxical sleep. However, one sucking pattern, the burst, has its highest rates in slow-wave sleep.

The proportions of sleep–wake state percentages and the rates of sucking do not differ between the first and second halves of the nursing bouts. Thus, in the normal suckling situation in the 2-week-old rat, increasing sleepiness and decreased levels of sucking are not found to occur as the nursing bout progresses. In this species, in which milk letdown occurs periodically, sleep–wake state levels do not provide a simple explanation for the termination of feeding. Indeed, termination of nursing bouts has been found to be triggered by increases in the mother's ventral temperature rather than other feeding-related events (Woodside et al., 1980).

After the pup attaches to the teat in our recording sessions, we can predict its state only in the periods of the milk ejection responses. Before each milk ejection, the animal is always asleep; after each milk ejection, the pup awakens briefly. Rhythmic sucking and treadles are both increased during milk ejection responses and are therefore likely to be behaviors that are diagnostic of ingestion during sucking.

Dennis Lorenz kindly sent us an early draft of his article in this volume, on ingestion and satiety in young rats. In this version (based on Lorenz, 1986), he suggested that slow-wave sleep is associated with nipple attachment and suckling. Further, he hypothesized that pups communicate their level of hunger to the dam through the amount of rhythmic sucking per unit of time. As pups ingest more milk during the normal nursing bout, he proposed that they would spend more time in paradoxical sleep, since he had found that the paradoxical sleep levels of deprived pups increased as part of their satiety response. The very low rates of rhythmic sucking during paradoxical sleep toward the end of a nursing bout would not exert a sufficient soporific effect on the dam; thus, she would awaken and terminate the nursing bout.

It is clear that our study of sleep–wake states and sucking behavior during normal nursing with undeprived pups provides little support for Lorenz's ideas as expressed in the draft of article. Although pups did enter slow-wave sleep first following initial nipple attachment, they almost always entered paradoxical sleep prior to receiving any milk. The likelihood of being in paradoxical sleep prior to the first milk ejection of a nursing bout was no different than just before the last milk letdown. We found no decrease in rhythmic sucking or increase in paradoxical sleep as the nursing bout progressed. Also, the sleep–wake state percentages found in this study were quite comparable to earlier work with pups studied with neither sucking nor feeding available (Hofer, 1976; Hofer and Shair, 1982).

It is possible that the discrepancies between our results and those of Lorenz are due to methodological differences. Lorenz's pups were deprived for 9–12 hr and then given large intragastric feedings, whereas ours were not deprived and were fed small amounts with each periodic milk ejection. We have often observed soporific effects of milk loading on deprived pups in many of our studies on the development of heart rate (unpublished observations). However, these pups were in litter piles, without any opportunity to suckle. Perhaps the following experiment on deprivation and reunion with a normal dam will provide some support for Lorenz's theory in the special case of the deprived pup.

IV. Normal Mother and Litter: Reunion after 22-Hour Overnight Separation

The baseline experiment reported above raised some unexpected issues. If satiety is not simply linked with sleepiness, what is the relationship between feeding and sleep–wake states? The pups' sleep–wake patterns were similar whether they were attached or unattached to their mother's teat. Is this similarity evidence that the sleep-wake states are generated internally by the pups and not easily influenced by the environment? How is the sucking behavior which occurs during sleep controlled? What factors influence this behavior?

Deprivation experiments have often been used to perturb normal behaviors and thus highlight any relationships among them. One such deprivation—separation from the mother—has known effects on both sleep–wake states and sucking behaviors in young rats, albeit studied separately and under different experimental conditions (Hofer, 1976; Hofer and Shair, 1982; Brake *et al.*, 1982a). The goal for this experiment was to see how deprivation affected the mother–infant interaction and especially the relationship of sleep–wake states and sucking behaviors.

The data are presented in a format similar to that of the baseline results experiment. First, the behavioral observations are described. Second, the polygraph data are analyzed. Trends in the data over the time of the whole recording session are examined as well as trends over time within the nursing bout. These analyses may be especially important to help understand how the mother and her pups adapt to reunion. Reunion and baseline day comparisons are made throughout the data presentation as needed.

A. BEHAVIORAL OBSERVATIONS

Upon reunion, the pups still showed the alternation of active and quiet periods which was observed on baseline day, both when attached and when unattached. However, implanted pups and their separated littermates appeared more active than their nonseparated littermates. The separated pups were more vigorous in attempting to attach to the dams, occasionally going as far as leaving the litter pile and chasing the dam around the cage. Remember that since only three pups from each litter were separated overnight, the following data do not represent the normal response of mother and litter to deprivation, but comparisons can be made between the test pup's own responses on the baseline and reunion days.

1. Attachment and Milk Ejection Response Data

As can be seen in Fig. 9, there was a great deal of variability in both attachment and milk ejection response patterns among the six litters. There was a significant increase in attachment time over the baseline day (see Table VIII, but this did not translate into an increased number of milk ejections as defined by the criteria in Section III, A. Four pups had more milk ejections on reunion day; two pups had fewer. Neither the latency to the first milk letdown of a nursing bout nor the time between subsequent letdowns was significantly decreased on reunion day.

The milk ejection response data were also examined for each pup in relation to the total recording time (i.e., independent of the variable timings of the nursing bouts). Thus, a mean figure was derived from each pup, and these were used to get an overall mean. This method of analyzing the data allowed us to see whether the pups were getting milk ejections sooner or more frequently on reunion day. The mean latency to the first milk ejection of the recording for each pup on baseline day was 34 ± 7.9 min. On reunion day, it was 26 ± 9.1 min (dep $t =$

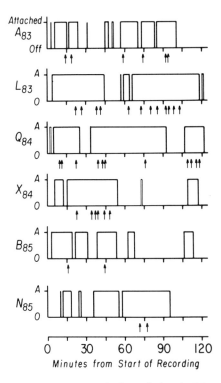

FIG. 9.   Patterns of nursing bouts for all six litters during the 2-hr reunion recordings. Milk ejections are designated by arrows. Data presentation and labels are as in Fig. 2, with which comparisons of reunion and baseline days can be made.

0.538, $df = 5$, ns). In the baseline-to-reunion latency change, four animals decreased latency to the first milk ejection on reunion day, one increased latency, the last showed little change. When considered independently of breaks in attachment, the mean latency between subsequent milk ejections per pup was as follows: baseline mean = 13.3 ± 2.0 min; reunion mean = 8.9 ± 2.0 min (dep t = 1.664, $df = 4$, ns).

The mean latency to the first milk ejection of each nursing bout of each pup was as follows: baseline mean = 8.1 ± 1.5 min; reunion mean = 8.2 ± 1.6 min (dep $t = 0.079$, $df = 5$, ns). Thus, in this experiment, in which only one-half of the litter had been separated, the deprived pups were not able to elicit significantly more or more frequent milk ejections from their dams. These results suggest, among other things, that any changes in the test pup's behavior and electrophysiological data from baseline to reunion were not in response to major shifts in the dam's behavior or milk ejection patterns.

TABLE VIII

DATA FROM BEHAVIORAL OBSERVATIONS OF MOTHER–PUP INTERACTIONS ON REUNION DAY[a]

	Time attached (min)	% TRT attached	Latency to first NB (min)	No. of NB's	Length of NB's (min)	No. of nipple-switches[b]	No. of ME's	Latency to first ME (min)[c]	Time between later ME's (min)[d]
Mean	70	58	3.2	5.3	13.6	2.5	6.5	6.8	5.8
SEM	7.8	5.6	0.5	0.9	2.7	1.2	1.8	1.2	1.2
Range	52–94	43–77	1.0–4.8	4–9	0.5–52	0–7	2–12	1.5–18	1.5–30
			Comparison of means to baseline data (from Table I)						
Dependent t test ($df = 5$)	3.071[e]	3.229[e]	1.913	1.642	0.863	1.164	0.745	0.222	0.334[f]

[a] TRT, Total recording time; NB, nursing bout; ME, milk ejection; SEM, standard error of the mean.

[b] A nipple-switch is defined as an event in which a pup detached from a nipple and reattached to the same or another nipple within 1 min.

[c] Latency to the first milk ejection of each nursing bout, not the total recording time.

[d] Figured only for milk ejections within the same nursing bout.

[e] $p < 0.05$.

[f] Independent t test, $df = 41$ (not significant).

TABLE IX
BODY WEIGHT AND RECTAL TEMPERATURE: REUNION DAY[a]

	Body weight (g)			Rectal temperature (°C)	
	Pre	Post	% Change	Pre	Post
Mean	25.8	26.9[b]	4.3	35.2	36.3[c]
SEM	1.2	1.2	2.4	0.4	0.4
Range	22.4–30.0	22.4–30.2	−2.6–11.6	33.6–36.2	35.6–36.6
	Comparison of means: reunion and baseline (from Table II)				
Dependent *t* test (*df* = 5)	7.129[d]	—	1.521	2.130[e]	—

[a]Pre, preobservation; Post, postobservation; SEM, standard error of the mean.
[b]Not significant
[c]$p < 0.10$ (not significant).
[d]Reunion less than baseline ($p < 0.001$).
[e]Reunion less than baseline ($p < 0.10$, not significant).

2. Weight and Temperature Data

During the 22 hr of deprivation, the test pups lost an average of 2 ± 0.3 g. After reunion, the increase in body weight during the 2-hr period (1.1 g, or 4.3% of body weight) was not consistent enough to be statistically significant (see Table IX), even though the average increase was greater than the change on baseline day. Two pups actually lost weight during the reunion test session. These results are similar to the findings of Brake *et al.* (1988), in which deprived pups had an increased variability in weight gain following reunion. In their studies, although most pups increased sucking amplitude and intake, a minority of deprived pups had very decreased amplitudes of sucking. Despite the increased variability in the present study, neither weight nor percentage changes correlated significantly with attachment time, with the number of milk ejections, or with the number of nipple switches.

The pups' average temperature was $35.2 \pm 0.4°C$ prior to recording. The temperature had not changed significantly due to deprivation, nor did it change significantly during the recording session.

B. ELECTROPHYSIOLOGICAL DATA

1. Sleep–Wake States

Even after 22 hr of separation, when pups were returned to their mothers and littermates, they were asleep a great deal of the time both while attached and while unattached. The percentage of time spent in each of the sleep–wake states did change from baseline day, however. One of these changes, the decreased time spent in paradoxical sleep (see Table X), confirmed similar findings for two strains of Wistar rat pups recorded in isolation (Hofer, 1976; Hofer and Shair, 1982).

In the present study, the amount of time awake also increased significantly on reunion day, while the amount of time spent in slow-wave sleep did not change. There was no difference in the number of state transitions per hour, probably due to the behavioral changes discussed later.

Few baseline-to-reunion correlations of sleep parameters reached significance. However, the animals that showed the least paradoxical sleep on baseline day showed the most such sleep on reunion day, suggesting a possible rebound effect ($r = -0.78$, $df = 4$, $p < 0.05$). There was a strong positive correlation of the mean duration of episodes in slow-wave sleep between baseline and reunion days, possibly indicating the resistance of slow-wave sleep to change ($r = 0.93$, $df = 4$, $p < 0.01$).

Upon reunion, the patterning of sleep–wake states of the pups depended on whether or not they were attached to a teat. Attachment condition influenced the percentage of time spent in each state, as well as the episode mean duration and frequency per hour in many cases (Table X). These differences may be explained by the interaction of the environmental stimuli of reunion and the internal motivational state of the deprived pups. For example, when unattached, the test pups were often observed chasing their dams around the cage, nosing frantically at her ventrum, attempting to attach. It was this type of behavior that led to their being awake 77% of the time, with an average episode duration of 3.3 min.

Of the small amount of paradoxical sleep during the reunion test, less than one-quarter of it occurred while the pups were attached (Table X). Also, while they were attached, any episodes that did occur were of very short duration, and were usually terminated by the awakening of the pup (Fig. 10). When pups were unattached, episodes of paradoxical sleep were not more frequent, but their mean

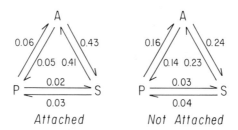

FIG. 10.   The probabilities of transitions among the three sleep–wake states during nursing and while the mother was away on reunion day. Data presentation and labels are as in Fig. 5, with which comparisons of reunion and baseline days can be made.

TABLE X
MEASURES OF SLEEP AND WAKEFULNESS OF INFANT RATS RECORDED WITH THEIR NORMAL MOTHER AND LITTERMATES FOR 2 HR ON REUNION DAY[a]

	Sleep latency (min)	State episode analysis									State transitions/hr
		% Time in state[b]			Mean duration (min)			Frequency/hr			
		A	PS	SWS	A	PS	SWS	A	PS	SWS	
Overall	6.5	57	9	33	1.92	1.02	1.35	19	5	16	40
		Comparison of means: reunion and baseline (from Table III).									
Dependent t test ($df = 5$)	1.787	4.372[c]	7.057[d]	0.834	3.976[e]	3.451[f]	0.234	1.337	3.924[f]	1.234	1.812
		Comparison of attached and unattached									
Attached	1.6	48	4	48	1.24	0.60	1.46	24	4	21	48
Unattached	4.4	77	13	11	3.27	1.62	0.79	17	6	9	30
Dependent t test ($df = 5$)	2.191[g]	2.674[h]	2.091[g]	4.884[i]	2.132[g]	3.030[j]	3.296[k]	1.777	0.552	2.350[g]	1.455

[a] A, Awake; PS, paradoxical sleep; SWS, slow-wave sleep.
[b] The percentage of time in a state is based on the total recording time for the overall condition, the time being nursed in the attached condition, and the time with mother away in the unattached condition.
[c] Baseline less than Reunion ($p < 0.01$).
[d] Baseline greater than Reunion ($p < 0.001$).
[e] Baseline less than Reunion ($p < 0.05$).
[f] Baseline greater than Reunion ($p < 0.05$).
[g] $p < 0.10$ (not significant).
[h] $p < 0.05$.
[i] $p < 0.001$.
[j] $p < 0.10$ (not significant, $df = 3$).
[k] $p < 0.05$ ($df = 2$).

duration was longer. We believe that the low amount of paradoxical sleep observed while pups were attached may be related to the pattern of sucking behavior elicited by reunion. This point is addressed further after the sucking data have been presented. With the demands of the sucking behavior met, a higher percentage of paradoxical sleep occurred while the pups were unattached.

The percentage of slow-wave sleep that occurred while the pups were unattached was significantly lower than when the pups were being nursed (Table X), possibly due to the activity of the pups trying to attach. Another possible explanation is that some element of the reunion nursing itself was crucial. Lorenz suggested that it is the nipple attachment and sucking which induce slow-wave sleep in the pup.

In the data describing the transitional probabilities among sleep–wake states (Fig. 10), there is further evidence of the different demands on the pups in the attached and unattached conditions (demonstrated by a significant ANOVA interaction effect of attachment condition and direction of state transition, $F(5,55)$ $= 7.658, p < 0.001$). When attached, pups were three times more likely to shift from paradoxical sleep to the awake state than to shift from paradoxical sleep to slow-wave sleep. This finding occurred despite the fact that awake and slow-wave sleep percentages of total attached time were equal. When unattached, pups in paradoxical sleep were more likely to shift to slow-wave sleep than would have been predicted by random chance based on the sleep–wake state percentages. In neither attachment condition was the most common adult mammal pattern seen, that of awake to slow-wave sleep to paradoxical sleep to awake.

Comparison of these data with the similar data from the baseline session demonstrates the greater influence of attachment condition on sleep–wake behavior after separation and reunion. Note, especially, that the percentage of time in each state differed with attachment condition after reunion but did not on baseline day. Thus, attachment condition was a more salient stimulus on reunion day than during the baseline session. The above data might lead one to believe that 22-hr-deprived pups were simply hyperaroused, probably because of hunger. Also, it is true that the pups were awake more often after deprivation, even while being nursed (Table XI). However, note that the increased time awake was due to a selective reduction in paradoxical sleep. Slow-wave sleep was once again resistant to change. Neither the percentage of time in slow-wave sleep nor the duration or frequency of episodes differed significantly between baseline and reunion recordings. Also, sleep latency was not significantly increased on reunion day. It is therefore difficult to think of these deprived pups as just hyperaroused by hunger, since they all still fell asleep prior to receiving any milk. The significant decrease in state transitions per hour after separation might be considered evidence against hyperarousal as well, but the very low amount of paradoxical sleep explains this finding. Shifting between two states in a limited amount of time leads to fewer transitions than changing among three.

TABLE XI

COMPARISON OF SLEEP–WAKE STATE MEASURES DURING ATTACHMENT: BASELINE TO REUNION[a]

| | | % TAT in state | | | State episode analysis | | | | | | State transitions/hr |
| | Sleep latency (min) | | | | Mean duration (min) | | | Frequency/hr | | | |
		A	PS	SWS	A	PS	SWS	A	PS	SWS	
Baseline	0.8	29	33	38	0.68	1.22	1.18	26	17	20	61
Reunion	1.6	48	4	48	1.24	0.60	1.46	24	4	21	48
Comparison (dep t, $df = 5$)	1.612	2.667[b]	4.228[c,d]	1.705	2.698[b]	1.581[d]	1.859	1.309	6.852[c,d]	0.329	3.620[b]

[a]TAT, Total attached time; A, awake; PS, paradoxical sleep; SWS, slow-wave sleep.

[b]$p < 0.05$.

[c]$p < 0.01$.

[d]$df = 3$, since two reunion pups had no paradoxical sleep while attached.

The increased percentage of time awake on reunion day was made up from longer, but no more frequent, episodes (Table XI). Many of these longer episodes of wakefulness occurred following milk ejections (discussed below).

2. Sucking Behavior

Upon reunion after deprivation, 2-week-old rat pups increase their intake from the dam (Houpt and Epstein, 1973), or in an artificial feeding test, with milk flow into the mouth (Hall and Rosenblatt, 1978; Lorenz et al., 1982). Privation influences not only attachment time beginning at this age (cf. Tables I and VIII; see also Cramer et al., 1980; Dollinger et al., 1978; Hall and Rosenblatt, 1977), but the time spent sucking as well (Brake et al., 1979; Brake et al., 1982a). As shown in Fig. 11, our data confirmed this previous work. Total instances of treadles and rhythmic sucking and the nipple attachment intensity rating all increased from baseline to reunion day.

However, examination of the sucking rate per unit of time in each state demonstrated a pattern very similar to that of baseline day. High rates for sucking were seen while awake, low rates were present in paradoxical sleep, and intermediate levels were seen in slow-wave sleep (see Fig. 12). Bursts were again the exception, being highest in slow-wave sleep. In fact, the sucking rate per unit of time in each state seemed relatively resistant to change. There were no mean increases in rates per state from baseline to reunion test. Thus, the increase in

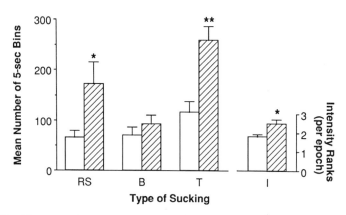

Fig. 11. The average time spent in each sucking type while attached to the teat of a dam during baseline (open bars) and reunion (hatched bars) recordings. Time of sucking is represented as the number of 5-sec periods in which a suck of a given type occurred. Statistical indications compare baseline and reunion results for a given sucking type, and are based on dependent t tests ($df = 5$). *, $p < 0.05$; **, $p < 0.01$; RS, rhythmic sucking; B, bursts; T, treadles; I, EMG intensity rank.

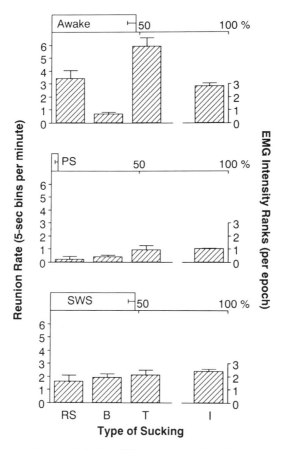

FIG. 12. The rate of sucking behaviors (RS, rhythmic sucking; B, bursts; T, treadles) and the percentage of time in each sleep–wake state (A, awake; PS, paradoxical sleep; SWS, slow-wave sleep) during nursing after reunion from a 22-hr separation. Data presentation and labels are as in Fig. 6, with which comparisons of baseline and reunion days can be made. As on baseline day, dependent t tests demonstrated significant differences in the rates of sucking among the states.

	A versus PS	PS versus SWS	SWS versus A
RS/min	2.963[a,b]	1.860[a]	2.987[c]
B/min	5.421[a,c]	4.525[a,c]	5.322[d]
T/min	6.824[a,d]	3.554[a,c]	6.378[d]
EMG I/epoch	5.081[a,c]	5.290[a,c]	5.267[d]

Reunion versus Baseline comparisons, within a given state, yield:

	A	PS	SWS
RS/min	0.457	0.436[a]	1.397
B/min	9.790[e]	3.502[a,c]	0.622
T/min	1.004	0.245[a]	1.310
EMG I/epoch	1.045	2.449[a]	2.000

$df = 5$, except where noted a, when $df = 3$. b, $p < 0.10$; c, $p < 0.05$; d, $p < 0.01$; e, $p < 0.001$.
I, EMG intensity rank.

total amounts of sucking were not simply due to a generalized increase in sucking
in all three states.

These sucking rate measures were not absolutely fixed, however. The mean
rate of bursts decreased significantly after deprivation both in the awake state and
in paradoxical sleep. Also, individual animals often had either larger or smaller
sucking rates within each state. We are not trying to say that sucking rates per
unit of time within each state never increase. In fact, an increase did occur for
treadles while awake for five of the six experimental pups. However, such an
increase was not a necessary part of the response to deprivation for any type of
sucking. For treadles, one pup had a decreased rate, and for several pups the
magnitude of the increase was quite small.

3. Milk Ejection Responses

The periods surrounding milk ejections were defined and examined closely, as
was done on baseline day. There were 39 observed milk letdowns. In 34 of these,
the pups did not detach from the teat for more than 15 sec. These 34 instances
were used for analysis. As on baseline day, pups were almost always asleep just
prior to milk letdown (see Fig. 13). Deprivation and reunion did shift the ratio of
sleep states dramatically. In only 3% of the cases were the pups in paradoxical
sleep in the 15 sec prior to the occurrence of milk ejections (Fig. 13); in 94%,
they were in slow-wave sleep. After milk ejection, the pups returned to slow-
wave sleep, but more slowly than on baseline day. By 1 min, pups were asleep in
50% of the cases.

As shown in Fig. 14 and Table XII, the rate of treadles rose precipitously after
milk ejection, returning to normal by the end of the second minute. Although
rhythmic sucking was not increased in comparison with its overall rate, it did
show an increase when the minute after milk ejection was contrasted with the
preceding minute (dep $t = 3.595$, $df = 5$, $p < 0.05$). Why didn't rhythmic
sucking increase compared to its overall rate? This may have been due to the high
rate of rhythmic sucking observed during the times of attachment and detachment, as well as during shifts of maternal position. Another explanation may be

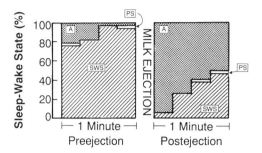

FIG. 13.   The percentage of pups in each sleep–wake state on reunion day during the minute before (preejection) and the minute after (postejection) the milk ejection response in 34 of 39 cases observed. In five cases, the pups detached for more than 15 sec and were omitted from this analysis. Compare to the baseline results in Fig. 7.

that the large body movements of treadling emitted by these pups may have prevented the EMG leads from picking up the underlying rhythmic sucking.

Work by Brake (1991) suggested that treadles and rhythmic sucking may actually be the same sucking type. The EMG activity of the limb movements of treadling may be obscuring the rhythmic sucking pattern on the polygraph tracing. Sucking can also be recorded using a second technique involving a tongue cannula and a pressure transducer (Brake et al., 1986; Brake, 1991). This methodology is not influenced by feeding movements. With the cannula technique, rhythmic sucking appears to be underlying most, if not all, treadling during the milk ejection response. However, it is not yet clear that treadles and rhythmic

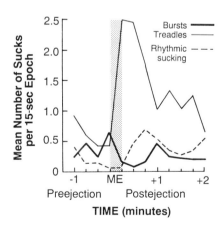

FIG. 14.   Sucking levels on reunion day for the minute before, during, and 2 min after the milk ejection response (ME). Mean values are based on the 34 MEs in which the pups did not detach for more than 15 sec. Compare to the baseline results in Fig. 8.

TABLE XII

COMPARISON OF MEAN (± SEM) SUCKING RATES IN THE 2 MIN IMMEDIATELY AFTER MILK
EJECTION TO THE OVERALL SUCKING RATES DURING ATTACHMENT ON REUNION DAY

	Mean sucking rate			Dependent t test ($df = 5$)	
	1st min post-ME	2nd min post-ME	Overall	1st min vs. overall	2nd min vs. overall
Rhythmic sucking	1.69 ± 0.53	1.37 ± 0.62	2.46 ± 0.54	1.673	3.254[a]
Bursts	0.88 ± 0.40	0.86 ± 0.24	1.29 ± 0.21	1.168	1.315
Treadles	7.36 ± 0.79	4.12 ± 1.26	3.81 ± 0.35	4.456[b]	0.235

[a] $p < 0.05$
[b] $p < 0.01$.

sucking are always the same. Further experiments directed specifically to this point are needed. Also, even if sucking patterns are the same, the presence or absence of treadling motions may be an important difference in the pup's response to milk ejection. Kneading the ventrum may cause more milk to be released or allow the pup to suck better by positioning its body more advantageously. Thus, the distinction between rhythmic sucking and rhythmic sucking with treadles may still be valuable.

As on baseline day, there was a significant increase in the rate of treadles while awake in the minute following milk ejection (8.9 treadles per minute versus the 5.9 treadles per minute overall rate, dep $t = 3.001$, $df = 5$, $p < 0.05$). Unlike on baseline day, the increase in treadles while in slow-wave sleep was significant as well (3.9 treadles per minute versus the 1.9 treadles per minute overall rate, dep $t = 2.727$, $df = 4$, $p = 0.053$). There was a significant decrease in the rates of bursts and rhythmic sucking while awake, probably due to the amount of time taken up by treadling. These data again implicate treadling as the nutritive sucking pattern and demonstrate that the sucking rate per unit of time in a state can change in response to environmental stimuli.

C. TRENDS OVER TIME

The baseline recording session occurred against the background of normal interaction between the pups and their dams. However, on reunion day, the pups were abruptly presented with their mothers, from whom they had been separated for 22 hr. With this in mind, it was especially important to look for changes over the course of the recording session as well as during the nursing bouts. For example, one might expect to see pups awake more at the start of the nursing bouts or recording session and asleep more after having received several milk ejections or having spent time sucking.

As shown in Table XIII, there was such a decrease in the percentage of time awake while attached in the second half of the recording session. Note, however, that neither the percentage of time attached nor the number of milk ejections differed between the two halves. Thus, pups were still actively seeking the mother, attaching and sucking during the second half. The pups also showed a decrease in the rate of treadles from the high rates during the first half of the session (Table XII). When considered in conjunction with the decreased awake time in the second half, shown above, it suggests that the decrease in treadle rate may have been due to the lower level of awake time, not necessarily to a change in the treadle rate per unit of time in each state.

This idea was tested by comparing the treadling rate while awake in the first versus the second half of the total recording time and finding no significant change in rate (dep $t = 1.928$, $df = 5$, ns). In fact, there were no significant changes in the rate for any sucking type within any state from the first versus second half of the recording session.

If attachment to a teat, feedback from sucking, or milk ingestion acted together or individually to reverse quickly the effects of deprivation on the pups, then one might predict a difference in sleep–wake state percentages from the first to second half of each nursing bout. As can be seen in Table XIV, in the initial nursing bout, there was a trend for the pups to be awake more in the first half and in slow-wave sleep more in the second half of the bout. This trend disappeared when all of the nursing bouts within the recording session were analyzed, despite

TABLE XIII

TRENDS OVER TIME DURING THE RECORDING SESSION: COMPARISON OF ATTACHED PUPS FROM THE FIRST VERSUS THE SECOND HALF OF THE REUNION SESSION[a]

	% TRT attached	No. of MEs	Sleep–wake state (%)			Sucking rates		
			A	PS	SWS	RS	B	T
First half mean	61	3.5	53	0.5	46	2.7	1.4	4.4
Second half mean	54	3.0	40	7.2	53	1.8	1.3	3.1
Dependent t test ($df = 5$)	0.457	0.355	3.448[b]	1.834	1.333	1.223	0.084	4.460[c]

[a]Data are only from the 20 nursing bouts (i.e., attached episodes) of 5 min or more. TRT, Total recording time; ME, milk ejection; A, awake; PS, paradoxical sleep; SWS, slow-wave sleep; RS, rhythmic sucking; B, bursts; T, treadles.
[b]$p < 0.05$.
[c]$p < 0.01$.

TABLE XIV

TRENDS OVER TIME WITHIN THE NURSING BOUT: REUNION DAY[a]

	Sleep–wake state (%)			Time sucking		
	A	PS	SWS	RS	B	T
Comparison of state percentages and sucking behaviors in the first versus the second half of the initial nursing bout						
First half	63	0	22	44	5	32
Second half	42	0	44	19	18	29
Dependent t test ($df = 5$)	2.140[b]	—	2.190[b]	2.810[c]	2.330[b]	0.560
Comparison of state percentages and sucking behaviors in the first versus the second half of each bout						
First half	53	1	46	34.0	10.9	39.7
Second half	46	5	49	15.0	16.4	38.6
Dependent t test ($df = 19$)[d]	0.927	2.061[b]	0.451	3.898[e]	1.970[b]	0.348

	Minutes prior to ME			Minutes following ME		
	RS	B	T	RS	B	T
Comparison of the rates of sucking in the minutes around milk ejection (ME) in the first versus the second half of the nursing bout						
First half	0.6	1.2	1,6	1,4	0.5	7.1
Second half	0.8	1.2	2.4	2.8	1.1	7.6
Dependent t test ($df = 4$)[f]	0.386	0.000	0.625	1.737	0.964	0.563

[a]A, Awake; PS, paradoxical sleep; SWS, slow-wave sleep; RS, rhythmic sucking; B, bursts; T, treadles.

[b]$p < 0.10$ (not significant).

[c]$p < 0.05$.

[d]Data are only from the 20 nursing bouts of 5 min or more.

[e]$p < 0.001$.

[f]Data averaged by pup since the number of MEs was not the same in the first and second halves.

the fact that the deprived pups were still avidly pursuing the dam throughout the 2-hr test. Also, none of the test pups had any paradoxical sleep in the first bout, but they did enter paradoxical sleep in later bouts. Therefore, although the reunion may be reversing some of the deprivation effects, this reversal was neither rapid nor total. Even in the second half of the nursing bouts, the pups were awake more and in paradoxical sleep much less than on baseline day (cf. Table VI).

The amount of rhythmic sucking decreased dramatically over time, both in the first nursing bout of reunion and in overall nursing bouts (Table XIV, top). How might this observation be explained? One factor may be that, as we have hypothesized, rhythmic sucking is used to attach to the teat, as well as ingestion. We know that the decrease in rhythmic sucking cannot be explained by a difference in opportunities to respond to milk ejections, since the mean number of milk ejections was the same in each half (first half: 1.3 ± 0.29; second half: 1.3 ± 0.32). Figure 9 provides a visual impression of these data. Third, the decrease in rhythmic sucking may give evidence for the pups' decreasing motivation to ingest, as Lorenz would speculate (see his article in this volume). If this hypothesis were true, one would predict that the amount of weight gained would correlate with the amount of decrease in rhythmic sucking. However, no such correlation was even close to significance. Further, there were no significant changes in rates of sucking behaviors in the periods around milk ejections from the first to the second half of the nursing bouts (Table XIV, bottom). Thus, it seems unlikely that decreasing motivation to ingest explains the difference in rhythmic sucking amounts.

D. Intermediate State

What has been called the "intermediate state" (ITS) was described in the baseline section. During reunion, ITS accounted for an average of 10% ± 1% of the recording session. This amount was a significant increase over baseline day (dep $t = 2.538$, $df = 5$, $p < 0.05$). Of ITS epochs, 74% were scored as slow-wave sleep and 26% were scored as awake. If all such epochs were scored as awake, the overall sleep–wake percentages would become: awake = 64% ± 3.7%; paradoxical sleep = 9% ± 1.9%; slow-wave sleep = 27% ± 2.7%. If the data in the sections above were analyzed with these changes in scoring, the major baseline versus reunion day shifts would still have the same form: that is, an increase in time awake, less time in paradoxical sleep, and no significant change in slow-wave sleep.

E. Discussion

What has been learned from the reunion procedure? First, pups are not simply hyperaroused by the deprivation experience. The pups still fall asleep quickly after attachment to the nipple and before receiving any milk. They spend over half the time asleep while being nursed. There are changes in state behavior, however. The pups do spend more time awake and for longer durations. The amount of paradoxical sleep is reduced, confirming earlier work on pups studied without their dams (Hofer, 1976; Hofer and Shair, 1982). Also, after deprivation, sleep–wake patterns are dramatically changed by attachment condition. When not attached, the pups are awake almost continually, often actively chasing their mother around the cage. (Note that pups studied without their dams present never showed this kind of locomotor behavior or other periods of hyperactivity.) When attached, slow-wave sleep time equals time spent awake, and there is very little paradoxical sleep.

The amount of time spent sucking is increased by deprivation, confirming in this naturalistic procedure the work using an anesthetized dam (Brake *et al.*, 1979). The most intriguing finding about sucking behavior is that the characteristic rates of sucking within each state are not significantly increased by deprivation. One strategy by which pups could increase their total time spent sucking would be to raise sucking rates within one or all of the three states. This strategy was not used. Instead, pups shift sleep–wake states to those states with higher sucking rates (awake and slow-wave sleep) and decrease the state with the lowest rates (paradoxical sleep). Sucking rates per unit of time in each state are not totally fixed, however. There are transient increases in the minute just after milk letdown. Also, the rate of bursts while awake and in paradoxical sleep is decreased by deprivation and reunion.

These results demonstrate that deprivation and reunion influence both sleep–wake states and sucking behavior in an interactive way. The data do not imply that one change is primary and the other secondary. One might imagine that changes in sucking behavior cause the state variations. For example, the increased levels of treadles and rhythmic sucking just following milk ejections may cause the pups to stay awake longer. However, a second explanation is that milk ejections are more stimulating to deprived pups, causing them to remain awake longer, with the consequent higher levels of sucking. Thirdly, milk itself may stimulate both the sleep–wake and sucking changes independently of one another. The small percentage of paradoxical sleep seen while attached post-deprivation is a similar case. The few episodes that did occur often ended with some sucking activity and awakening. Perhaps it was the sucking that woke the pups. If this idea is true, however, it is hard to explain why 24-hr-separated pups recorded without the dam also have decreased amounts of paradoxical sleep postdeprivation (Hofer, 1976; Hofer and Shair, 1982).

What effects does the increase in sucking time have on milk intake? First, in this atypical situation with only three deprived pups in each litter, the pups do not elicit more milk ejections or shorter latencies between the ejections. However, the pups do stay awake longer during the milk ejection responses. They may use this period to ingest more food. In fact, the average weight gain was higher on reunion day, although not significantly (due to increased variability of intake on this second day).

During reunion after deprivation, one expects to find recovery from the deprivation effects. This recovery can occur gradually or rapidly. It may or may not be complete. In the 2-hr reunion period, pups did not spend less time attached or receive fewer milk ejections as time passed. Thus, the pups were still showing the effects of the deprivation at the end of the test session. There was, however, less time awake while attached in the second half of the recording session. Also, the differences between the first and second half of the nursing bouts were greatest in the initial bout following the reunion. These findings may show the beginnings of a recovery process. Something about the reunion must have been influencing the state change. Milk intake and sucking stimulation are two obvious possibilities.

There is some evidence in this reunion study which support Lorenz's theory of the relationship among sleep, rhythmic sucking, and satiety, if it were applied only to deprived pups. Deprived (presumably hungry) pups were found to have a very low level of paradoxical sleep. Those levels did tend to increase over the 2-hr recording time comprising several nursing bouts. Also, rhythmic sucking did decrease over the same period. However, in the initial bout after reunion, when this decrease in rhythmic sucking levels was the greatest, there was no paradoxical sleep at all. Thus, the decreasing levels of rhythmic sucking were not associated with increases in paradoxical sleep, as Lorenz's theory predicts. Clearly, processes other than satiety can decrease rhythmic sucking rates, as is further demonstrated in the experiments with anesthetized dams which follow.

V. Anesthetized Mother: Baseline

The results of the normal mother experiment indicated a relationship between sleep–wake states and sucking behaviors. Each sucking type appeared to have a characteristic rate within each sleep–wake state. Twenty-two hours of maternal deprivation had little effect on these rates. However, as with all naturalistic studies, there was a great deal of variability of the conditions faced by each experimental subject. The number of nursing bouts differed. Each pup received a different (and unknown) quantity of milk. The littermates may have been more (or less) active.

In order to clarify any relationships among states and sucking behaviors, we needed a recording situation that was more easily controlled. One possibility immediately suggested itself, that of recording each pup while it was attached to its anesthetized dam with no littermates. This preparation would minimize any external stimuli that influenced the pup's behavior. There would be no milk ejections (Lincoln *et al.*, 1973), no body movements of the mother or littermates, and no coming and going by the dam. Each pup would be exposed to the same conditions during the test session. The similarity of experimental stimuli should facilitate comparisons among the individual pups.

Clearly, this test situation has the drawbacks of artificiality. The lack of external stimulation might, in essence, be a stimulation in itself. A pup may have learned to associate its mother with periodic milk ejections, with changes in position, and with being licked and manipulated. However, the similarities between the anesthetized dam and the normal dam are also quite striking. During a nursing bout, the normal dam is generally inactive and sleeps through much of the time between milk ejections. This period is irregular, and milk ejections can be as much as 20–25 min apart (Lincoln *et al.*, 1973). Thus, there were grounds to believe that the pup's behavior with an anesthetized dam and with a waking dam should be comparable.

There are three goals in this section. The first is to look at the levels of sleep–wake and sucking behaviors in the anesthetized versus normal mother preparations. This examination not only will help verify the generality of the anesthetized mother findings, but also will aid in understanding the effect on the pups of the mother's behavior, including milk ejections. Second, any interactions of sleep–wake state and sucking behavior that were hidden by the variance resulting from dam and littermate disturbance will be revealed. Are state episode length and sucking rates related? Do states and sucking behaviors change together over the time of the recording session? Do other variables whose influence might have been hidden (e.g., body weight and temperature) influence the sleep–wake and sucking interactions? Finally, these results will provide the baseline day for a deprivation and reunion experiment which was carried out to investigate further the stability of sucking rate per unit of time within each state. The data are presented in an order similar to that of the previous experiments.

A. METHODS

In this experiment, six litters were studied, on both baseline and reunion days. Each implanted pup was recorded for 2 hr without littermates in its home cage while attached to its urethane-anesthetized mother (2–3 mg/kg). After the baseline recording, the pup was separated from the mother overnight with two littermates in the home cage. The mother was placed in another cage with three littermates and home cage shavings. The three pups with the mother often remained attached to nipples overnight, despite the fact that milk ejections were unlikely to have occurred (Lincoln *et al.*, 1973). Just prior to the reunion test, the mother was placed on new bedding from the home cage nest, and two of the separated littermates were placed on her to draw out her teats if necessary. They were then removed before recording from the experimental pup.

B. BEHAVIORAL OBSERVATIONS

When tested with anesthetized mothers, the pups' behaviors were much simplified. Each of the six pups attached rapidly to its dam's teat and remained attached for virtually the entire recording session: mean attachment = 98% ± 0.3% of the total recording time. While attached, the pups showed some patterns of behavior similar to those seen in the normal nursing situation. Pups on the anesthetized dam alternated brief periods of activity—changing postures, treadles—with longer periods of quiet attachment. Four of the six pups rarely switched nipples, but one pup nipple-switched seven times: mean = 2.2 ± 1.0 nipple switches. Of course, in this test situation, nipple-switching could not be a response to milk ejections; therefore, its function is unclear. Correlations between the number of nipple-switches and other pup parameters are reported throughout Section V to help clarify its significance. For example, nipple-switching may be an indicator of feeding motivation.

Weight and Temperature Data

The pups' weights (mean = 29.2 ± 1.0 g) and temperatures (mean = 35.6° ± 0.2°) were normal at the start of the recording sessions (Hofer and Grabie, 1971; Messer *et al.,* 1969). All pups lost a small amount of weight during the 2-hr observation (mean percentage change = −0.9 ± 0.1), as expected, since no milk was available. There was no significant difference in body weight or rectal temperature between anesthetized and normal mother pups (independent t = −1.132 and 1.332, respectively; df = 10).

Neither pretest body weight, percentage of change in weight, nor rectal temperature was significantly correlated with the number of nipple-switches. If one can consider the first two variables as tentative markers for hunger and/or high metabolic rate, the results ruled against a simple link between any of the three parameters and nipple-switching behavior.

C. ELECTROPHYSIOLOGICAL DATA

1. Sleep–Wake States

During the 2-hr recording session, the test pups were asleep over 84% of the time (see Table XV). Pups always went into slow-wave sleep first during the recording session; thus, the sleep latency given in the table is also slow-wave sleep onset. In a previous experiment (Hofer and Shair, 1982), pups of the same strain and age, but monitored while isolated, were awake more and in slow-wave sleep less than these pups. Isolated pups had a much longer sleep latency as well, but also went into slow-wave sleep first.

Transitional probabilities are given in Fig. 15. It is worth noting that the pups were more likely to go from the awake state to paradoxical sleep than to slow-wave sleep, despite the fact that sleep onset after initial attachment was always into slow-wave sleep. Part of this, no doubt, was due to the much larger percentage of paradoxical than slow-wave sleep during the recording session, since

TABLE XV

Measures of Sleep and Wakefulness of Infant Rats Recorded while Attached to Their Anesthetized Dams for 2 Hr on Baseline Day[a]

| | Sleep latency (min) | % TRT in state | | | State episode analysis | | | | | | |
| | | | | | Mean duration (min) | | | Frequency/hr | | | State transitions/hr |
		A	PS	SWS	A	PS	SWS	A	PS	SWS	
Mean	1.7	12	57	30	0.56	2.05	1.95	14	18	10	41
SEM	0.65	1.9	1.0	1.5	0.04	0.18	0.16	2.2	1.3	0.7	3.2
Comparison to normal mother baseline pups (while attached)											
Mean	0.8	29	33	38	0.68	1.22	1.18	26	17	20	61
Independent t test ($df = 10$)	1.362	4.725[b]	4.079[c]	1.511	1.793	2.918[d]	4.519[b]	5.071[b]	0.289	4.221[c]	5.553[b]

[a] TRT, Total recording time; A, awake; PS, paradoxical sleep; SWS, slow-wave sleep; SEM, standard error of the mean.
[b] $p < 0.001$.
[c] $p < 0.01$.
[d] $p < 0.05$.

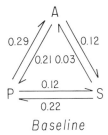

Baseline

FIG. 15. The probabilities of transitions among the three sleep–wake states while attached to the teat of an anesthetized dam. Compare to Fig. 5 (attached) results.

many transitions were brief awakenings with the same sleep state on both sides. Still, as in the normal mother experiment, one sees that, at this age, the sequence of awake state to slow-wave sleep to paradoxical sleep and back to the awake state is not fixed. Note, however, that transitions from the awake state to slow-wave sleep to paradoxical sleep were much more common than the reverse.

Correlations were run to measure the influence of various pup parameters on the percentage of time in each state and on the number of state transitions per hour, a measure of sleep fragmentation. Neither body weight, rectal temperature, nor number of nipple-switches showed any significant relationship with the above measures.

In comparisons of state variables between the anesthetized and normal mother experiments, only the time that pups were attached during the normal mother recordings were considered. This procedure was an attempt to minimize the differences in recording situations between the two experiments. As shown in Table XV, pups studied with their mothers anesthetized were awake less and had fewer state transitions per hour. The length of paradoxical sleep episodes almost doubled. These data suggest that the pups were less activated on the anesthetized dam, probably due to lack of stimulation in the nest or the pacifying effect of nonnutritive sucking. The percentage of time in slow-wave sleep was not different in the two conditions, but consisted of longer and less frequent episodes.

The probabilities of state transition showed many differences between the two test settings (cf. Figs. 5 and 15, normal mother baseline, confirmed by significant ANOVA and *post hoc* results). Only the probability of transition from the awake state to paradoxical sleep was not significantly changed. The most likely transition from the awake state was to paradoxical sleep in this experiment, but was to slow-wave sleep in the previous one. Two factors may have influenced this difference. First, there was a reduced percentage of slow-wave sleep with the dam anesthetized. Second, with the normal dam, pups were twice as likely to enter slow-wave sleep as paradoxical sleep following milk ejections.

2. Sucking Behavior

Sucking behaviors were seen in all three sleep–wake states. Approximately 66% of all sucking took place during sleep. As in the normal mother experiment, bursts were predominantly seen during sleep. The total times spent in treadles and rhythmic sucking were highest when the pups were awake, even though the time awake was so low (Table XV). However, the rate of sucking per unit of time in each state gives a truer picture of the pups' behavior, since the time spent in each sleep–wake state varied. Figure 16 demonstrates that the patterns seen with the anesthetized dam were similar to those seen in the previous experiment:

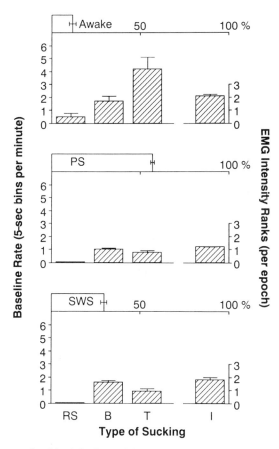

FIG. 16.   The rate of sucking behaviors and the percentage of time in each sleep–wake state while attached to the teat of an anesthetized dam. Data presentation and labels are as in Fig. 6, with which comparisons to the normal mother baseline can be made. PS, Paradoxical sleep; SWS, slow-wave sleep; RS, rhythmic sucking; B, bursts; T, treadles; I, EMG intensity rank.

Sucking rates were generally highest while awake, lowest in paradoxical sleep, and intermediate in slow-wave sleep. When tested on the anesthetized mother, however, the burst rate in the awake state was as high as that in slow-wave sleep. Only the following sucking rates differed significantly when compared among sleep–wake states: The treadles per minute rate was higher while awake than in slow-wave or paradoxical sleep (dep $t = 3.624$ and 3.755, respectively, $df = 5$, $p < 0.05$). Also, the EMG intensity rank was higher while awake than in paradoxical sleep (dep $t = 7.279$, $p < 0.001$).

Statistical comparisons of the two experiments (see Table XVI) demonstrated no significant differences in the rates of bursts in the awake state, paradoxical sleep, or slow-wave sleep. For treadles, only the slow-wave sleep data approached significance, with somewhat lower rates with the mother anesthetized. For rhythmic sucking, the results were very different. There were significantly higher rates of rhythmic sucking in all three states, when the dam was awake and giving milk ejections.

Correlations were performed to determine whether there was a relationship between the length of state episodes and the rate of sucking within the episodes. No significant correlations were found for any state. The relationship between the average length of awake episodes and the rates of both rhythmic sucking and bursts while awake almost reached significance ($r = 0.76$ and -0.75, respectively; $df = 4$ and $p < 0.10$ for both). Thus, the rates of sucking within each state were not affected by episode duration in general, but this result must be examined again after deprivation.

Did any other factors influence sucking behavior? Neither the number of nipple-switches, pretest body weight, nor change in body weight during the test session correlated significantly with any measure of time spent sucking. Pretest rectal temperature, however, positively correlated with one type of sucking: Warmer pups treadled more ($r = 0.83$, $df = 4$, $p < 0.05$). The direction of temperature change during the recording period did not influence sucking totals, since no correlations of sucking and change in body temperature reached significance.

As noted above, temperature did not correlate with sleep–wake state percentages. Thus, its relationship with the total amount of treadling could not be explained by a shift in states to those states with high rates of treadling. For this reason, the relationship of rectal temperature to the rate of sucking by states was analyzed. There were no significant correlations between body temperature and treadle rate within any state. However, in both slow-wave and paradoxical sleep, the correlations were positive and quite high, approaching significance ($r = 0.70$ and 0.74, respectively).

Two correlations between sucking rates by state and body temperature actually reached significance. While the pups were awake, the rate of both rhythmic sucking and bursts had a negative relationship with temperature ($r = -0.87$ and

TABLE XVI

COMPARISON OF MEAN SUCKING RATES WITHIN EACH SLEEP–WAKE STATE FROM THE BASELINE SESSIONS OF THE NORMAL (NM) AND ANESTHETIZED MOTHER (AM) EXPERIMENTS[a]

	Awake			Paradoxical sleep			Slow-wave sleep		
	RS/min	B/min	T/min	RS/min	B/min	T/min	RS/min	B/min	T/min
AM pups	0.5	1.7	4.2	0	1.0	0.8	0	1.6	0.9
NM pups	3.0	1.3	5.1	0.1	0.9	0.9	1.1	1.8	1.7
Independent t test ($df = 10$)	3.532[b]	1.008	0.768	2.591[c]	0.375	0.411	4.331[b]	0.716	2.127[d]

[a] RS, Rhythmic sucking; B, bursts; T, treadles

[b] $p < 0.01$.

[c] $p < 0.05$.

[d] $p < 0.10$ (not significant).

−0.88, respectively; $df = 4$ and $p < 0.05$ for both). Thus, the simplified preparation of the anesthetized mother experiment revealed a relationship between sucking and body temperature. Even the rates of sucking within a state can be modified by temperature, certainly during the awake state and possibly while asleep. Any function of these changes is not immediately evident. However, the effect of deprivation on the relationships may be informative.

D. TRENDS OVER TIME

Examining the experimental results for any changes over time serves a dual purpose. First, variations in state and sucking patterns may interact in ways that are useful in helping to spot any relationships between them. Second, if the pups were reacting to the artificial recording situation, their behavior might show changes over time.

The data were analyzed for the first and second hours separately, as shown in Table XVII. As can be seen, neither sleep–wake percentages nor sucking time changed significantly. However, the rise in paradoxical sleep almost reached significance. Since paradoxical sleep was the state with the lowest rate of sucking, one might suspect that the rates within one or more states may have increased in order for sucking time to remain constant.

This suspicion was not confirmed (see Table XVIII). There were no significant increases in sucking rates. In fact, there was a decrease in the rate of treadles during slow-wave sleep. Correlations of the first and second halves of the session were almost all positive and fairly high (Table XVIII). Once again, the sucking rates by state appeared to be relatively stable, without being invariant.

TABLE XVII

TRENDS OVER TIME DURING THE RECORDING SESSION: COMPARISON OF MEAN STATE PERCENTAGES AND SUCKING BEHAVIORS IN THE FIRST VERSUS THE SECOND HALF OF THE BASELINE TEST[a]

	Sleep–wake state (%)			Time sucking		
	A	PS	SWS	RS	B	T
First half	13	54	32	4	84	90
Second half	12	60	28	4	64	79
Dependent t test ($df = 5$)	0.403	2.006[b]	0.877	0.193	1.749	1.556

[a]A, Awake; PS, paradoxical sleep; SWS, slow-wave sleep; RS, rhythmic sucking; B, bursts; T, treadles.
[b]$p < 0.10$ (not significant).

TABLE XVIII

TRENDS OVER TIME DURING THE RECORDING SESSION: COMPARISON OF THE RATES OF SUCKING WITHIN EACH SLEEP–WAKE STATE IN THE FIRST VERSUS THE SECOND HALF OF THE BASELINE SESSION[a]

	Awake				Paradoxical sleep				Slow-wave sleep			
	RS/min	B/min	T/min	I/epoch	RS/min	B/min	T/min	I/epoch	RS/min	B/min	T/min	I/epoch
First half	0.7	1.5	5.7	2.1	0	1.0	0.8	1.3	0	2.0	1.2	1.7
Second half	0.5	1.8	5.4	2.3	0	0.9	0.8	1.2	0	1.1	0.7	1.8
Dependent t test ($df = 5$)	0.537	0.713	0.314	0.734	0.000	1.450	0.415	1.369	1.581	1.977	2.948[b]	0.192
Pearson's r	0.68	0.69	0.70	0.45	—[c]	0.95[d]	0.87[b]	0.28	—[c]	-0.22	0.76[e]	0.31

[a]RS, Rhythmic sucking; B, bursts; T, treadles; I, EMG intensity rank.
[b]$p < 0.05$.
[c]No comparison is possible due to the lack of rhythmic sucking.
[d]$p < 0.01$.
[e]$p < 0.10$ (not significant).

E. DISCUSSION

The anesthetized mother preparation served the purpose for which it was designed. It was a much less "active" situation than in the normal litter. The test pups remained attached to the teats for almost the entire 2-hr recording session. They spent less time awake, had fewer transitions, and the durations of episodes in paradoxical and slow-wave sleep were longer than in the normal litter situation. Yet, much of the sleep–wake behavior was similar to the previous experiment. Sleep-onset latency did not differ, nor did the percentage of time in slow-wave sleep. Also, there were few changes in state behavior over time. Thus, factors such as hunger or lack of stimulation from littermates or the dam were unlikely to have been a major factor. It is hard to understand how the high percentage of paradoxical sleep, with the tendency to increase in the second hour, could fit with Lorenz's theory linking satiety and paradoxical sleep.

The pattern of sucking in the three sleep–wake states was quite similar between the two experiments. Pups sucked at the highest rate while awake, an intermediate rate in slow-wave sleep, and at the lowest rate in paradoxical sleep. In this experiment, however, the burst rate while awake was as high as that during slow-wave sleep. Almost no rhythmic sucking was seen in any state with the mother anesthetized. This difference between the two experiments accentuates the link between rhythmic sucking and milk ingestion/nipple attachment.

The relationship between sucking and sleep–wake behaviors appears to be relatively stable. The rate of sucking within each state is unaffected by state episode duration. There is not much change in either state or sucking behaviors over the time of the recording session. However, body temperature was correlated with certain sucking rates while the pups were awake, and possibly while they were in slow-wave sleep as well. There were no such correlations between temperature and state measures. Thus, at least one pup parameter influenced sucking without affecting sleep–wake state.

Finally, this experiment provided the baseline data for the next deprivation and reunion study. The issues raised here and in Sections III and IV are examined further in the next section. Special attention is paid to the stability of the sucking rates per unit of time within each state, since so few manipulations have changed these rates.

VI. Anesthetized Mother: Reunion

Twenty-two hours after the baseline recording period, the pups were returned to their anesthetized dams for a 2-hr reunion session. Based on the results of Brake *et al.* (1979, 1982a) and from the pups tested with their normal mothers (described above), we predicted that deprivation would lead to increased time spent sucking during the reunion. Similarly, we predicted that sleep–wake state behavior would change as well. We hoped that the changes in the two systems under study would permit close examination of any interactions between them. Specifically, what would happen to the rates of sucking within each state? Would some interesting variability in the pups' responses to deprivation be revealed that was hidden in the previous experiment by the variability in maternal behavior? Perhaps these responses might highlight any relationships between sleep–wake states and sucking behavior.

A related issue was addressed by this experiment as well. In the normal mother reunion session, pups were beginning to show small evidence of recovery from deprivation effects. Pups were awake less during the second hour of the recording period. Also, the differences between the first and second halves of each nursing bout were most pronounced in the initial bout after the reunion. Reunion with an anesthetized dam might help in understanding the role of behavioral stimulation and food intake on the causes of this recovery.

The data are presented in the same format as the previous sections: first, behavioral observations of the pup; then, electrophysiological data, including sleep–wake states and sucking behavior; and finally, any trends in behavior over the time of the test session. Some figures repeat data from Section V in order to facilitate comparisons.

A. BEHAVIORAL OBSERVATIONS

As on the baseline day, the test pups quickly grasped their mothers' teats. The pups stayed attached for 97% ± 0.9% of the test period. During the reunion session, the pups appeared more active than on the previous day. For example, four of the six pups had many more nipple-switches upon reunion, although the increased number did not quite reach statistical significance. The mean number of nipple-switches during the test period was 6.3 ± 1.1 (dep $t = 2.076$, $df = 5$, $p < 0.1$, ns). Also, the electrophysiological data described below provided more evidence of increased activity on the second day. However, all of the test pups were quietly attached for some period. For five of the six pups, there were long episodes of quiet attachment. One pup (E79) was aberrant in behavior. Although attaching to a nipple quickly and remaining attached 98% of the time, this pup was active for much of the session, especially during the first hour. Data from this pup are considered further below.

Weight and Temperature Data

At the start of the reunion session, the pups were both lighter (26.9 ± 1.0 g) and slightly cooler (34.7° ± 0.3°C) than on baseline day (dep $t = 9.268$, $p < 0.001$ and $t = 2.821$, $p < 0.05$, respectively; $df = 5$). The weight loss was, of course, expected. The temperature loss occurred despite the warming of the pups by placing their cages on heating pads, as described in Section II. Note, however, that these lower temperatures are within the normal range for pups in this series. For example, one of the pups in the normal mother experiment had a temperature of 33.9°C after deprivation. In this study, the pup with the aberrantly high activity level (E79) had both the lowest weight (24.4 g) and the lowest temperature (33.4°C) at the start of the reunion. Its percentage of change in body weight was midrange, however (−8.7%). Thus, after deprivation, the range of weight and temperatures was wide, yet within the normal range, allowing examination for any effects on the other behavioral and physiological parameters. Body weight was correlated with rectal temperature ($r = 0.76$, $df = 4$), which does not quite reach significance ($p < 0.10$). However, the scatter plots of body weight and rectal temperature data (see Fig. 17A) suggest that in the midrange of these parameters the correlation was not significant, but at the extremes the correlation might be valid.

Neither rectal temperature ($r = 0.54$) nor the percentage of change in body weight ($r = 0.33$) was significantly correlated to the number of nipple-switches that pups showed. However, the negative correlation of body weight itself to the number of nipple-switches ($r = -0.78$, $p < 0.10$) was high and approached significance. This could mean that the relatively underfed pups were using nip-

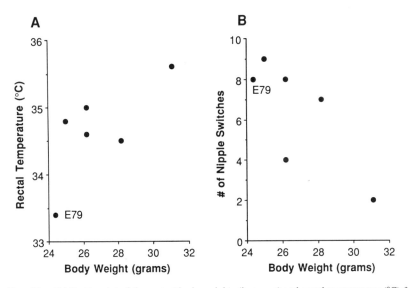

FIG. 17.   (A) Scatter plot of the pretest body weights (in grams) and rectal temperatures (°C) for the six test pups on reunion day. The value for subject E79 is labeled on scatter plots since this pup's values lie in the extremes on so many variables. (B) Scatter plot of the pretest body weights (in grams) and the number of nipple-switches emitted by the six pups during the reunion session.

ple-switching in an attempt to obtain more milk from their dams. Maturation is unlikely to explain these results, since the peak age for nipple-shifting is not until 21 days (Cramer et al., 1980). However, these pups may have low body weights because they are less interested in food. Thus, no firm conclusion on the purpose of nipple-switching can be drawn.

During the 2-hr observation, the pups continued to lose weight (mean change $= -1.5\%$, dep $t = 4.824$, $df = 5$, $p < 0.01$). Rectal temperature did not change significantly. Neither of these changes correlated significantly with each other or with nipple-shifting.

B. ELECTROPHYSIOLOGICAL DATA

1. Sleep–Wake Stages

Even after 22-hr separations, the pups were asleep an average of 64% of the time. As shown in Table XIX, this percentage was a decrease from the baseline. The decrease was due to a large loss in paradoxical sleep time, while slow-wave sleep time tended to increase. Thus, the alterations in sleep–wake state percentages were in similar directions in both the normal and anesthetized mother experiments.

Note that in Table XIX the information for reunion day is compared to the data for baseline day, both with and without pup E79. This procedure was followed since E79 was so aberrant in terms of the percentage of time spent in each state (awake = 82%, paradoxical sleep = 10%, slow-wave sleep = 9%). Despite these results, we have no reason to think there was anything wrong with E79. It was merely on one end of the spectrum of responses to separation and reunion. In a previous study, we also had one extremely insomniac separated pup (Hofer, 1976). Note that in the normal mother experiment, there was increased variability in the weight gain data on reunion day compared to baseline day. In the present experiment, without differences in the mothers' behavior as a variable, the pups had more variability in their state data after deprivation (cf. Tables XV and XIX). Brake (1991) also found increased variability in the responses of young rats to deprivation on measures of sucking behavior and weight gain as well. The varied responses he described had predictive value for long-term growth after reunion with the dam. Thus, deprivation may cause the pups to separate into two (or more?) groups. For this reason, the data that follow are presented both with and without pup E79 when it is important to do so.

As with baseline day, the relationships among sleep–wake state percentages to body weight, percentage of change in weight, number of nipple-switches, and rectal temperature were examined. After separation, some correlations appeared suggestive. The percentage of paradoxical sleep positively correlated with rectal temperature ($r = 0.91$, $df = 4$, $p < 0.05$) and negatively correlated with the

TABLE XIX

MEASURES OF SLEEP AND WAKEFULNESS OF INFANT RATS RECORDED WHILE ATTACHED TO THEIR ANESTHETIZED DAMS FOR 2 HR ON REUNION DAY[a]

| | Sleep latency (min) | % TRT in state | | | State episode analysis | | | | | | State transitions/hr |
| | | | | | Mean duration (min) | | | Frequency/hr | | | |
		A	PS	SWS	A	PS	SWS	A	PS	SWS	
Mean	13.6	36	20	44	1.31	0.72	1.60	21	14	17	52
SEM	10.1	9.4	3.4	7.7	0.61	0.03	0.23	2.4	2.0	2.6	5.6
		Comparison of reunion and baseline (from Table XV)									
Dependent t test ($df = 5$)	1.098	2.708[b]	8.570[c]	2.020[d]	1.226	6.012[e]	1.886	2.020[d]	1.706	2.978[b]	1.546
		Comparison as above without pup E79									
Dependent t test ($df = 4$)	0.770	4.510[b]	7.768[e]	5.332[e]	1.318	7.823[e]	2.444[d]	3.861[b]	1.754	4.733[e]	6.288[e]

[a]TRT, Total recording time; A, awake; PS, paradoxical sleep; SWS, slow-wave sleep; SEM, standard error of the mean.
[b]Reunion greater than baseline ($p < 0.05$).
[c]Reunion less than baseline ($p < 0.001$).
[d]Reunion greater than baseline ($p < 0.10$, not significant).
[e]Reunion less than baseline ($p < 0.01$).

number of nipple-switches ($r = 0.82$, $p < 0.05$). The correlation of the percentage of paradoxical sleep to body weight ($r = 0.80$, $p < 0.1$) did not quite reach statistical significance. After the influence of the outlier E79 was considered, no other correlations were even close to significance.

2. Sucking Behavior

As shown in Fig. 18, the amount of sucking time upon reunion increased after the 22-hr separation, as predicted by the work by Brake *et al.* (1982a) and the results of the normal mother experiment. There was no significant change in bursts, but the other three sucking measures increased dramatically. The increase in rhythmic sucking was significant only by nonparametric tests, due to the extreme variability in the rhythmic sucking seen on day 2. This pattern of change caused by deprivation closely matched the results of the normal mother procedure (cf. Fig. 11).

When the sucking data were analyzed in terms of the rate of sucking per unit of time in each state (see Fig. 19B), the pattern that emerged was generally comparable to the results of the previous experiments. Sucking rates were highest while awake, but appreciable levels of sucking were emitted while asleep, especially in slow-wave sleep. The burst rate was again highest in slow-wave sleep, although not significantly higher than that while awake.

Comparing rates by state on baseline and reunion days, rates of sucking within states were not increased. The only significant change was a decrease in the number of bursts per minute during paradoxical sleep. Once again, the resistance to change of sucking rate within each state was demonstrated. However, the pups

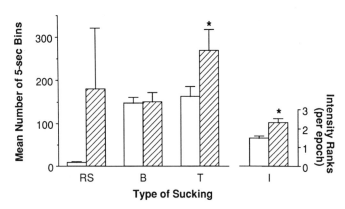

FIG. 18. The average time spent in each sucking type while attached to the teat of an anesthetized dam during baseline (open bars) and then reunion (hatched bars) from a 22-hr separation. Data presentation and labels are as in Fig. 11. ∗, $p < 0.05$.

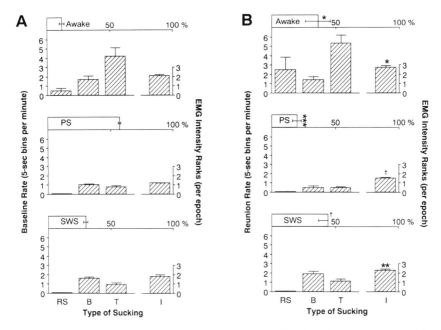

FIG. 19.   The rate of sucking behaviors and the percentage of time in each sleep–wake state while attached to the teat of an anesthetized dam. (A) Baseline. (B) Reunion. During the reunion, the following sucking types differed when compared among sleep–wake states ($df = 5$). Bursts (B)/min: A > PS, dep $t = 2.209$ († , $p < 0.10$); SWS > PS, dep $t = 4.570$ (**, $p < 0.01$). Treadles (T)/min: A > PS, dep $t = 5.321$ (**, $p < 0.01$); A > SWS, dep $t = 5.273$ (**, $p < 0.01$). EMG intensity rank per epoch: A > PS, dep $t = 4.897$ (**, $p < 0.01$); SWS > PS, dep $t = 6.558$ (**, $p < 0.01$); A > SWS, dep $t = 3.053$ (*, $p < 0.05$). Rhythmic sucking (RS)/min: All pups had higher rates of RS when awake (A) than in either slow-wave sleep (SWS) or paradoxical sleep (PS). However, this difference did not reach significance with a dependent t test, due to the high variability in the A data and the number of zeros when asleep. By the nonparametric sign test, A > PS, $p = 0.016$ and A > SWS, $p = 0.016$. Data presentation and labels are as in Fig. 6. Significance indications on the graph are comparisons of the reunion bar to its equivalent baseline bar. These comparisons include the percentage of total recording time of a given state, sucking rates, and EMG intensity within a given state. All significance findings are based on dependent t tests ($df = 5$).

were attached more tightly to the teat after deprivation, as shown by the significant increases in EMG intensity.

If sucking rates in each state were truly fixed for each individual animal, one would expect high positive correlations between the rates by state on baseline and reunion days. As shown in Table XX, while such correlations were positive in general, none of the rates by the state comparisons and only one of the EMG intensity measures reached significance. Removing E79 from the comparisons caused the correlations to become more positive in all cases except one. Clearly, sucking rates within each state were not fixed for each individual. Some pups

TABLE XX

BASELINE-TO-REUNION CORRELATIONS OF SUCKING RATE MEASURES[a]

	Awake				Paradoxical sleep				Slow-wave sleep			
	RS/min	B/min	T/min	I/epoch	RS/min	B/min	T/min	I/epoch	RS/min	B/min	T/min	I/epoch
Pearson's r ($n = 6$)	0.27	0.64	0.13	0.56	—[b]	0.46	−0.25	−0.09	0.56	0.39	0.75[c]	0.81[d]
Pearson's r ($n = 5$; as above, without E79)	0.78	0.92[d]	0.48	0.75	—[b]	0.59	−0.21	−0.06	1.00[e]	0.13	0.77	0.89[d]

[a]RS, Rhythmic sucking; B, bursts; T, treadles; I, EMG intensity rank.
[b]No comparison is possible due to the lack of rhythmic sucking.
[c]$p < 0.10$ (not significant).
[d]$p < 0.05$.
[e]Perfect correlation is based on the following data:

Pup #	Q75	B76	I74	B79	I79
Baseline	0	0	0.1	0	0
Reunion	0	0	0.1	0	0

Thus, while the relationship is statistically significant it is unlikely to have biological relevance.

increased rates; some pups decreased. However, the positive correlations do suggest that some individual stability was present from baseline to reunion. Other variables, including changes in weight and body temperature, may have influenced the sucking rate measures differentially in each pup. Further study with more animals are needed to discover whether the positive correlations truly reflect an underlying individual stability in sucking rates within states.

As on baseline day, the relationships among various pup parameters and sucking measures were examined (Table XXI). As one can see, there was a significant relationship between the EMG amplitude and both pretest body weight and temperature. The smallest and coolest pups clung most firmly to their dam's teats. Even when the data points for E79 were removed, the same high negative correlations were found.

Time spent in rhythmic sucking negatively correlated with two measures as well, but these correlations were due to the outlier. Without E79, the correlation between the time of rhythmic sucking and the percentage of change in body weight dropped precipitously from -0.90 to 0.06.

Unlike baseline day, there was no positive correlation between body weight and the time spent treadling, even when the data for E79 were not included. If the baseline relationship was not due to chance, then some aspect of the deprivation and reunion experience must have overridden or changed this relationship. There is no logical reason to assume that body weight has exactly the same significance to the pups before and after deprivation. Perhaps, after deprivation, all of the pups were hungry, whereas before deprivation only the lighter pups were. Note the high negative correlation between treadling and the percentage of change in body weight during deprivation. Although not quite significant, this datum suggested that, after deprivation, it was the pups that lost the most weight that treadled most. Perhaps this new factor altered the direct correlation between weight and treadling.

Before deprivation, changes in rectal temperature were related to changes in certain sucking rates while awake and possibly while asleep. What happened to those relationships after deprivation? Again, bursts per minute in awake animals correlated significantly with body temperature ($r = 0.86$, $df = 4$, $p < 0.05$). However, the direction of the correlation altered. It had been negative, but was positive on day 2. We have no good explanation for this reversal. The reunion correlation between rhythmic sucking while awake and body temperature was similar to the baseline one, except that after deprivation the correlation did not quite reach significance ($r = -0.74$, $df = 4$, $p < 0.10$). When pups were asleep, no correlations between temperature or body weight and any sucking rate came close to significance. Thus, after deprivation as before, sucking rates while awake were affected by body temperature.

As mentioned earlier, during the baseline recording, there were high negative correlations between the average length of awake episodes and the rates of both

TABLE XXI

PEARSON'S PRODUCT–MOMENT CORRELATIONS: MEASURES OF PUPS' WEIGHTS, TEMPERATURES, AND NIPPLE-SWITCHING BEHAVIORS CORRELATED WITH LEVELS OF SUCKING

	Body weight			Rectal temperature		No. of nipple-switches
	Pretest weight	% Change from baseline	% Change during reunion	Pretest temperature	Change during reunion	
Time spent in rhythmic sucking	−0.54	0.19	−0.90[a] / 0.06[b]	−0.90[a] / −0.44[b]	0.49	0.37
Time spent in bursts	0.36	0.06	0.31	0.64	0.15	−0.28
Time spent in treadles	−0.43 / −0.55[b]	−0.74[c] / −0.73[b]	0.08	−0.06	−0.35	−0.03
EMG intensity rank	−0.82[a] / −0.79[b]	−0.46	−0.60	−0.94[d] / −0.89[a,b]	0.12	0.62

[a] $p < 0.05$.
[b] Correlation run again, without data from pup E79.
[c] $p < 0.10$ (not significant).
[d] $p < 0.01$.

rhythmic sucking and bursts while awake, which almost reached significance. Deprivation and reunion altered these relationships. The awake episode duration was definitely not significantly correlated to burst rate ($r = -0.51$) and positively correlated with the number of rhythmic sucks per minute ($r = 0.96$, $df = 4$, $p < .01$). However, this positive correlation was due to the outlier E79. Without E79, $r = 0.57$. Thus, deprivation did not confirm the tentative relationships seen on day 1. Of course, as noted above, there is no *a priori* reason to assume that baseline and reunion relationships must be the same. When pups were asleep, no state durations significantly correlated with sucking rates within this state. A possible relationship was suggested by the correlations between treadles per minute and episode duration in paradoxical sleep, both with and without E79 ($r = -0.78$, $df = 4$, $p < 0.10$ and $r = -0.82$, $df = 3$, $p < 0.10$, respectively). Therefore, the question of the relationship between state episode duration and any sucking within this episode must remain open.

C. TRENDS OVER TIME

The data were analyzed in the first versus the second hour of recording to see whether there were any changes during the recording session. As shown in Table XXII, the high sucking time upon reunion occurred in both the first and second hours of the recording session. However, the pups did tend to shift the proportions of sleep states as the recording progressed, with very little paradoxical sleep early, but appreciable amounts later in the recording, when it replaced both slow-wave sleep and awake time. This rise in paradoxical sleep percentage over time

TABLE XXII

TRENDS OVER TIME DURING THE RECORDING SESSION: COMPARISON OF MEAN STATE PERCENTAGES AND SUCKING BEHAVIORS IN THE FIRST VERSUS THE SECOND HALF OF THE REUNION TEST[a]

	Sleep–wake state (%)			Time sucking		
	A	PS	SWS	RS	B	T
First half	41	9	50	156	88	148
Second half	32	30	38	56	62	142
Dependent *t* test	1.512	9.561[b,c]	2.022[b,d]	1.700	1.122	0.609

[a]A, Awake; PS, paradoxical sleep; SWS, slow-wave sleep; RS, rhythmic sucking; B, bursts; T, treadles.

[b]The decrease in slow-wave sleep was statistically significant when pup E79 was excluded from the analysis (dep $t = 15.438$, $df = 4$, $p < 0.001$). The change in paradoxical sleep remained significant at the same probability level. Pup E79 had neither slow-wave nor paradoxical sleep during the first hour.

[c]$p < 0.001$.

[d]$p < 0.10$ (not significant).

on reunion day was also seen while pups were attached in the normal mother experiment (Table XIV), although in this case statistical significance was not attained. Unlike the previous study, the decrease in amount of time spent awake did not reach significance. Thus, any recovery from deprivation seen in the present study was not as great as when pups were returned to a normal mother.

Sucking rate changes in treadles per minute in both paradoxical and slow-wave sleep again showed that sucking rates by state were not totally fixed (see Table XXIII). Note that this change in treadles per minute in slow-wave sleep was also seen on baseline day (Table XVIII). However, most of the sucking types showed no alteration in rate by state. Not only that, there were many highly significant positive correlations in rate by state measures between the first and second hours. Thus, within the 2-hr recording period, there was great stability in the rates of sucking within each state for the individuals, as well as for the group as a whole.

D. DISCUSSION

In this experiment, the response of the test pups to deprivation and reunion was very similar to that seen in the normal mother experiment. Sleep–wake state percentages altered so that the pups spent more time awake and less time in paradoxical sleep. The pups also had higher levels of sucking behavior. However, again, there were no increases in the sucking rates within each state. The only significant change in rate was a decrease in bursts per minute during paradoxical sleep, a decrease found in the previous experiment as well. After deprivation, the rat pup has a very different state pattern. The picture is of a pup awake for much more of the time and for longer episodes. Sleep–wake cycles are fragmented. The pup is rarely in paradoxical sleep and wakes rapidly from this state. As the recording session progresses, more paradoxical sleep is seen. Perhaps something about the reunion experience, even with an anesthetized dam, enables the pup to begin a recovery process. This result seems to us quite difficult to reconcile with Lorenz's theory relating increases in paradoxical sleep particularly to ingestion and satiety. Another explanatory hypothesis suggested by the work by Szymusiak and Satinoff (1981) is that the pup gains heat and enters the thermoneutral zone, known to have an influence on the percentage of paradoxical sleep. A positive correlation was found between body temperature and the percentage of time in paradoxical sleep. However, since the pups in this study did not gain temperature over the recording period, some other factor must explain the increase in paradoxical sleep time.

Other findings suggest that individual animals may be affected differentially by deprivation. The amount of variability in state behavior increased dramatically from day 1 to day 2. The variability in sucking time increased as well. There were positive correlations between sucking rates within states from baseline day to reunion day, but few reached significance. Of course, these changes

TABLE XXIII

TRENDS OVER TIME DURING THE RECORDING SESSION: COMPARISON OF THE RATES OF SUCKING WITHIN EACH SLEEP–WAKE STATE IN THE FIRST VERSUS THE SECOND HALF OF THE REUNION SESSION[a]

	Awake				Paradoxical sleep				Slow-wave sleep			
	RS/min	B/min	T/min	I/epoch	RS/min	B/min	T/min	I/epoch	RS/min	B/min	T/min	I/epoch
First half	2.9	1.5	5.2	2.7	0	0.7	0.3	1.7	0.4	1.9	1.4	2.4
Second half	1.9	1.3	5.4	2.6	0	0.4	0.6	1.6	0	1.6	0.7	2.2
Dependent t test ($df = 5$ or 4^d)	1.334	0.450	0.427	1.341	—[b]	1.883	2.982[c]	1.725	0.999	1.677	3.344[c]	1.206
Pearson's r	0.94[e]	0.70	0.96[e]	0.92[e]	—[b]	0.89[c]	0.76	0.85[c]	—[b]	0.60	0.94[e]	0.60

[a]RS, Rhythmic sucking; B, bursts;, T, treadles; I, EMG intensity rank.
[b]No comparison is possible due to the lack of rhythmic sucking.
[c]p < 0.05.
[d]df = 4 for paradoxical and slow-wave sleep measures, since pup E79 was awake the entire first hour.
[e]p < 0.01.

may be clues to shifts in some underlying mechanisms. For example, pups with the lowest body weights and temperatures have the least amount of paradoxical sleep. They also tend to nipple-shift more. Temperature influences the rate of sucking behavior as well, but only when the pup is awake. A final point about sucking rate by state: In both the normal and anesthetized mother experiments, the characteristic sucking rates within each state appeared stable. However, these rates were not totally fixed. There were a few differences from baseline to reunion in each experiment. There were a few differences from baseline to baseline between the two experiments, and there were a few differences between the first and second hours of the anesthetized mother experiment. Temperature can influence sucking rate while awake. Milk ejections bring a transient increase in treadles while awake. However, it is now clear that the general response to deprivation and reunion is *not* one of increasing sucking rates within the various states. The preponderance of the results suggests that pups increase sucking time after deprivation by increasing the percentage of time spent in states with the higher rates of sucking (i.e., the awake state and slow-wave sleep). The final experiment attempts to investigate how tightly coupled the sucking rates and the sleep–wake states are.

VII. Infused Diet Experiment

The purpose of this experiment was to study the connection between particular sleep–wake states and the characteristic sucking rates within these states. The experiments reported above demonstrated that state and sucking rates remained relatively firmly linked. However, a certain lability was seen. How great was that lability? Could rate and state be separated experimentally?

A possible way to dissociate the two variables was suggested by previous research. We knew that normal sleep–wake patterns can be maintained, even after 22 hr of maternal separation (Hofer and Shair, 1982). The method involved infusion of a nutrient formula comparable to rat milk on a periodic schedule similar in timing to the dam's pattern of nursing. Another series of experiments showed that prefeeding does not influence the amounts of nonnutritive sucking of maternally deprived pups (Brake *et al.*, 1982a). Thus, if the two variables are regulated by separate mechanisms, then providing such periodic nutrient during the time between baseline and reunion should affect sleep–wake states, but not sucking amounts. The pups should have a baseline-type sleep–wake pattern and reunion-type sucking time, forcing the states and rates to dissociate.

Certain caveats must be considered. The protocols of the two background studies are different from one another and from the present series of experiments. In the sleep–wake work, pups were tested without their mothers (Hofer and Shair, 1982); thus, no attachment was possible. Brake *et al.* (1982a) gave their rats a single stomach load of 5% of body weight, rather than infusing formula periodically throughout the deprivation period. These caveats suggested that all of the following possible outcomes must be considered.

1. Normal sleep–wake patterns and increased sucking time; therefore, increased sucking rates within some or all of the states;

2. Reunion sleep–wake patterns and increased sucking time; therefore, no change in sucking rates by state;

3. Normal sleep–wake patterns and no increased sucking time; therefore, no change in sucking rates by state;

4. Some interaction of sleep–wake patterning and sucking level change; therefore, no specific prediction of rate by state results.

With these outcomes in mind, the experiment was performed as described in the next section.

The data are presented in two sections. First, to examine whether the gastric cannula implantation influenced the test pups' behavior, comparisons of the baseline days of the infused diet and anesthetized mother experiments are performed. The comparisons include behavioral observations, sleep–wake state patterns, and sucking rates within each state. No comparison was made with the normal mother data, due to the problem of having attached and unattached portions of the recording time.

Second, the influence of the diet infusions on the reunion to baseline comparisons within this experiment is examined. Only sleep–wake patterns, total sucking time, and sucking rates within states are discussed, since these are the key behaviors which distinguish among the possible results listed above.

A. METHODS

In this experiment, six litters were studied. The test procedure was almost the same as that in the anesthetized mother experiment, with the following exceptions. At the time of electrode implantation, each animal was provided with a gastric cannula made of 30-gauge polyethylene tubing (Clay-Adams, PE-10, Becton Dickinson Co., Parsippany, NJ) by techniques modified from the work by Messer *et al.* (1969) and described by Hofer (1973). The tube passed through the ventral surface of the stomach, through a purse-string suture, through a 1.5-mm slit in the peritoneum, and curved laterally and dorsally near the spine. At this point, it curved abruptly in a caudal direction after surfacing in the middle of the pup's back, and the external 3–5 cm lay on the surface along the lower back, extending to the tail. Sutures distal to beads in the wall of the polyethylene tubing at the stomach and abdominal walls, as well as a small patch of collodion at the exit point in the skin prevented the displacement of the cannula by traction. Bends in the polyethylene tubing were formed by heat prior to surgery to conform approximately to body contours. These cannulae remained patent to infusions for several days and were rarely destroyed by the mother.

After the baseline recording, the pup's cannula was connected to tubing (Silastic 602-105, Dow Corning, Midland, Michigan) through which the pup was infused with an enriched formula diet. The major constituent was condensed bovine milk with corn oil, producing a 50% increase in fat. This diet also included small amounts of vitamins, minerals, and amino acids and was diluted with water to mimic, as closely as possible, the composition of rat milk. A detailed comparison between rat milk, condensed bovine milk, and this formula is available (Messer *et al.*, 1969). The diet was infused during the 22-hr of separation on a schedule approximating that of the normal nursing cycle. A timer was used to activate a Harvard Apparatus (South Natick, Massachusetts) infusion pump for 15- or 20-min periods, alternating with 40- to 60-min periods of no infusion. The flow rate of nutrients was adjusted so that the pup received approximately the same amount of milk it would have received from its mother. The tubing was supported in such a way as to prevent tangling by the movement of the test pup or its two littermates. The last infusion occurred approximately 30 min before the reunion test period.

B. Baseline Comparisons: Infused Diet to Anesthetized Mother Experiments

In the previous experiments, the pups showed good recovery from the electrode implantation. Was the addition of a gastric cannula operation enough to hinder complete recovery?

The behavioral observations suggested that the pups with gastric cannulae behaved normally. The cannulae did not inhibit their movements. The pups did not direct any appreciable attention to the cannulae, either scratching or chewing at them. During the baseline recording, the infused diet (ID) pups attached to the dams' teat almost immediately and remained attached an average of 96% of the session. This result did not differ significantly from the attachment percentage of the anesthetized mother (AM) pups (independent $t = 1.601$, $df = 10$). The number of nipple-switches on baseline day did not distinguish between the two groups either: ID pups mean $= 1.7 \pm 0.8$; AM pups mean $= 2.2 \pm 1.0$ (independent $t = 0.707$, $df = 10$). However, between the day of surgery and the baseline recording day, the ID animals gained only an average of $8.5\% \pm 1.8\%$ of body weight. The AM pups in the same length of time gained $17.0\% \pm 1.8\%$ of body weight (independent $t = 2.755$, $df = 10$, $p < 0.05$). Still, the ID pups did not appear stunted; while their pretest weight of 28.0 ± 1.0 g was slightly lower than that of the AM pups (29.2 ± 1.0 g), this difference was not significant (independent $t = 0.717$, $df = 10$). Thus, the gastric cannulae did appear to exert some effect on recovery from surgery, yet the overall behavior of these pups appeared normal.

Next, the ID and AM pups were compared on sleep–wake state variables, as shown in Table XXIV. As can be seen, the average amount of time spent awake did not differ between the two groups, but the ID pups spent less time in slow-wave sleep and tended to spend more time in paradoxical sleep than the pups in the previous experiment. The change in the paradoxical sleep percentage was so small that neither the duration nor the frequency per hour of the episode showed a significant difference between the two groups. The lower slow-wave sleep time was due to the fewer number of episodes per hour. The mean duration of the episodes was not significantly different between the two groups.

The comparison of sucking rates by state also showed some differences between the pups on baseline day in the two experiments. The rates of bursts and treadles in both paradoxical and slow-wave sleep was much lower in the ID experiment baseline (see Table XXV). While awake, ID pups had a higher rate of rhythmic sucking. There were no other significant changes in sucking rates by state between the two experiments.

Whether or not the above changes were a result of the abdominal surgery is uncertain. Another possibility is that the rat's strain and/or rearing conditions may have shifted slightly in the 5 years between the two experiments. Thus, the pups on baseline day were not identical in the AM and ID experiment. However, if we look at the overall picture, the two groups look similar. Sleep–wake state percentages are not much different. The pattern of sucking rates by state was also similar in the two groups: highest while awake, intermediate in slow-wave sleep, lowest in paradoxical sleep. In the ID pups, the distinction between slow-wave and paradoxical sleep was not as great as with the AM experiment, mainly due to the low levels of sucking in slow-wave sleep. With the above differences in mind, we proceeded to separate the ID pups for 22 hr while providing food on a periodic schedule of infusion.

C. Reunion to Baseline Comparisons: Infused Diet Experiment

As intended, the diet infusion caused the pups to gain weight during the maternal deprivation period. The pups received an average of 6.9 ± 0.2 ml of diet and gained an average of $13\% \pm 0.9\%$ of body weight (dep $t = 17.300$, $df = 7$, $p < 0.001$). As predicted previously (Brake et al., 1982a), food intake did not prevent the increase in total nonnutritive sucking time caused by maternal deprivation (see Fig. 20). The amount of treadling doubled upon reunion, while rhythmic sucking almost doubled. Again, bursts did not change significantly. Thus, suggested outcome 3 (introduction to Section VII) was disproved. Sucking totals were increased.

An examination of the sleep–wake state percentage bars in Fig. 21A and B

TABLE XXIV

MEASURES OF SLEEP AND WAKEFULNESS OF INFANT RATS PREVIOUSLY IMPLANTED WITH GASTRIC CANNULAE RECORDED WHILE ATTACHED TO THEIR ANESTHETIZED DAMS FOR 2 HR ON BASELINE DAY[a]

	Sleep latency (min)	% TRT in state			Mean duration (min)			Frequency/hr			State transitions/hr
		A	PS	SWS	A	PS	SWS	A	PS	SWS	
ID Mean	0.5	15	62	24	0.60	2.16	2.21	18	18	7	42
SEM	0.16	1.6	2.1	2.2	0.05	0.20	0.39	1.5	1.3	1.0	3.2
AM Mean	1.7	12	57	30	0.56	2.05	1.95	14	18	10	41
Comparison of ID and AM means											
Independent t test (df = 10)	1.730	0.442	1.924[b]	2.425[c]	0.638	0.438	0.678	1.591	0	2.516[c]	0.297

(State episode analysis spans Mean duration and Frequency/hr columns)

[a]TRT, Total recording time; A, awake; PS, paradoxical sleep; SWS, slow-wave sleep; ID, infused diet experiment; SEM, standard error of the mean; AM, anesthetized mother experiment.

[b]$p < 0.10$ (not significant).

[c]$p < 0.05$.

TABLE XXV

COMPARISON OF MEAN SUCKING RATES WITHIN EACH SLEEP–WAKE STATE FROM THE BASELINE SESSIONS OF THE INFUSED (ID) AND ANESTHETIZED MOTHER (AM) EXPERIMENTS[a]

	Awake			Paradoxical sleep			Slow-wave sleep		
	RS/min	B/min	T/min	RS/min	B/min	T/min	RS/min	B/min	T/min
ID pups	2.1	1.2	2.8	0.1	0.4	0.3	0.1	0.7	0.2
AM pups	0.5	1.7	4.2	0	1.0	0.8	0	1.6	0.9
Independent t test ($df = 10$)	4.419[b]	0.973	1.403	1.672	3.072[c]	3.258[b]	0.914	3.680[b]	3.316[b]

[a]RS, Rhythmic sucking; B, bursts; T, treadles.
[b]$p < 0.01$.
[c]$p < 0.05$.

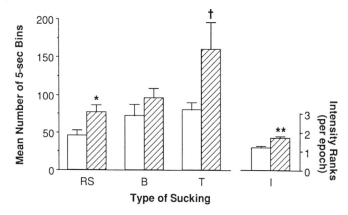

FIG. 20.   The average time spent in each sucking type while attached to the teat of an anesthetized dam during baseline (open bars) and then reunion (hatched bars) from a 22-hr separation. Pups were fed intragastrically during the period of separation. Data presentation and labels are as Fig. 11. RS, Rhythmic sucking; B, bursts; T, treadles; I, EMG intensity rank; $*$, $p < 0.05$; $\dagger$, $p < 0.10$; $**$, $p < 0.01$.

demonstrates that there was a change in the sleep–wake state percentage from baseline day to reunion day. The percentages of total recording time of the awake state and slow-wave sleep were significantly increased, and paradoxical sleep was decreased. Thus, the infused diet did not normalize the sleep–wake state percentage when the pups were tested attached to an anesthetized mother. This result was not predicted from the previous work (Hofer and Shair, 1982), in which the pup was tested without the mother. Since sleep–wake states were not regularized, suggested outcome 1 cannot be true. There was no generalized increase in sucking rates by state that occurred independently of sleep–wake state patterning.

Why wasn't sleep–wake state behavior normalized? If these pups had been studied without their dams, such normalization would have resulted (Hofer and Shair, 1982). One must assume that some aspect of the testing situation, probably attachment to the anesthetized dam, prevented the infused diet from having its predicted effect. Given the series of experiments described in this article, it is tempting to assume that the lack of state normalization was related to the sucking behavior. Perhaps feedback from the sucking activity kept the pups awake more. Alternatively, one can hypothesize that some central mechanism drove both state and sucking behavior. Or this hypothetical mechanism could have driven sleep–wake patterns, which were, in turn, permissive for sucking rates within each state. Any of these speculations appears possible. The hypothesized central mechanism might simply be excitement. Upon reunion, the pup's dam is arousing, whereas on baseline day she may have a pacifying effect. Only further experiments can differentiate among these speculations.

What happened to the sucking rates within each state? The results were a bit equivocal in terms of the predicted possible results. As shown in Fig. 20A and B, the sucking rate by state did not change significantly between baseline and reunion days in either the awake state or paradoxical sleep. However, in slow-wave sleep, there appeared to have been an increase in the rate of treadles, based on the results of a t test (dep $t = 3.310$, $df = 5$, $p < 0.05$). If true, this increase in rate was the first statistically significant *increase* in sucking rate within a state for any comparison from reunion to baseline recordings in any of the three experiments. Why it should occur in this experiment, in which the pups were fed during separation, is unclear. One possibility is that the increase was due to random effects. Why might this possibility be correct? Whereas the t test cited above

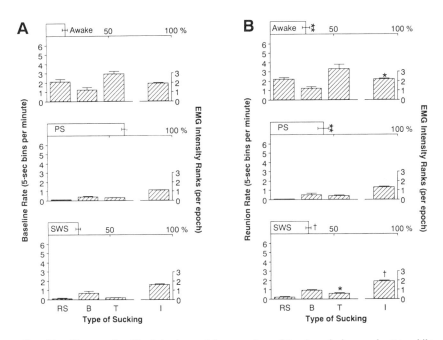

FIG. 21. The rate of sucking behaviors and the percentage of time in each sleep–wake state while attached to the teat of an anesthetized dam. Pups were fed intragastrically during the period of separation. (A) Baseline. (B) Reunion. Significance indications on the graph are comparisons of the reunion bar to its equivalent baseline bar. These comparisons include the percentage of total recording time of a given state, sucking rates, and EMG intensity (I) within a given state. All significance findings are based on dependent t tests ($df = 5$). Data presentation and labels are as in Fig. 6. PS, Paradoxical sleep; SWS, slow-wave sleep; RS, rhythmic sucking; B, bursts; T, treadles; ∗∗, $p < 0.01$; ∗, $p < 0.05$; †, $p < 0.10$.

reached significance, the overall ANOVA on treadles per minute showed only state effects, only a trend for a deprivation effect, and no interaction effect. Note that the results of t tests and ANOVAs for all other variables (rhythmic sucking, bursts, and EMG intensity rank) were concordant. However, this experiment was specifically designed to test the effects of deprivation on the rate of sucking within a state. The hypothesis demanded specific comparisons of the individual cells from baseline to reunion (Winer, 1971, p. 384).

One other explanation for the results is that the treadle rate was somewhat lower on baseline day than in noncannulated pups (see Table XXV). Perhaps the apparent increase in response to deprivation was really a further accommodation by the pups to their implants.

Thus, in general, the results support suggested outcome 2 without totally eliminating outcome 4. Rat pups can change sucking rates within states on occasion. Even increases in rate by state are possible. However, these changes are not the way that pups increase sucking upon reunion after deprivation. Rat pups increase sucking times by switching states. Paradoxical sleep, the state with the lowest sucking rates, decreases in time. The awake state and slow-wave sleep, with their higher rates, both increase.

VIII. General Discussion

A. Summary of Major Findings

One of the principal findings of this study is that 2-week-old rat pups are asleep much of the time while being nursed by their mothers. Tested with normal unanesthetized dams, the percentage of time in each sleep–wake state is equal in the attached and unattached conditions. Rat pups are asleep an even larger percentage of the time while attached to the teats of anesthetized mothers.

Deprivation causes alterations of sleep–wake state behavior in pups tested during reunion with their dam. The percentage of paradoxical sleep is reduced, while awake and possibly slow-wave sleep time are increased, as is also true for pups tested without their mothers present (Hofer, 1976). Even after periodic gastric infusion of nutrient during separation, a procedure that normalizes sleep–wake behavior in young rats tested without their dams (Hofer and Shair, 1982), pups exhibit "deprivation-type" states when tested during reunion. However, despite the increase in awake time, deprived pups still fall asleep as soon after attaching to teats as they did on baseline day, and before receiving any milk. They are asleep for the majority of the 2-hr reunion period. Thus, any arousal caused by the deprivation experience is not a simple phenomenon that causes the pups to remain awake continually.

A second major finding is that pups suck while attached to the teat both while awake and during the two states of sleep. Even when tested with the normal mother, almost 50% of all sucking occurs while the pups are asleep. Characteristic rates of sucking are seen in each sleep-wake state. The pattern of these rates was similar on baseline day in all three experiments. In general, sucking rates are highest while awake, intermediate during slow-wave sleep, and lowest in paradoxical sleep. However, the sucking type called "bursts" actually has its highest rate during slow-wave sleep. Deprivation increases the amount of sucking upon reunion, as previously reported (Brake *et al.*, 1979, 1982a). However, the distribution of sucking rates within each state is similar to that for preseparation. This similarity leads to the third major finding of this research.

The rates at which young rats suck within each state are stable across many of the experimental conditions. In general, deprivation does not change the rates of sucking within each state. Nor do the young pups shift sucking rate by state during the time of the recording session. However, these sucking rates within each state are not totally unchangeable. For example, the treadle rate while awake goes up during the milk ejection response, although no other rate within a state shows a similar increase. Another set of findings from the anesthetized mother experiment is similarly illustrative. Over a short period (within 1 day's recording session), not only does the group show no changes in sucking rates within states, but the individual pups' sucking rates are also stable. This individual stability was demonstrated by the very significant positive correlations for sucking rates by state for the members of the group, from the first to the second hour of the test session. However, this individual stability did not extend over the longer period and the deprivation experience: Few correlations across the 2 days reached significance. Therefore, although deprivation caused few changes in sucking rates within a given state for the group, the rates of any individual may have increased or decreased.

Sleep–wake state behavior has a very characteristic pattern during the defined milk ejection responses. In fact, the only times one can accurately predict what states pups will be in are during the nipple attachment process (awake) and in the period around the milk ejections. Two-week-old rat pups are always asleep just before milk ejection. If state behaviors in the pups were randomly related to milk ejections from the dam, one would expect the pups to be asleep prior to only 70% of the milk ejections. Possible explanations for this relationship are discussed below. The young pups are aroused briefly by the milk ejection and return quickly to sleep afterward. Thus, it is possible that milk or some other aspect of the milk ejection experience has arousing properties. Even after deprivation, the rat pups show the same pattern. In this case, however, the sleep prior to milk ejection is almost exclusively slow-wave sleep. Also, the pups stay awake longer during the milk ejection response. Possible reasons for this longer period awake are considered below.

The sucking behavior also shows characteristic changes during milk ejection responses. Treadles and rhythmic sucking are implicated as nutritive sucking types, in that they both increase. Also, these increases, especially in treadles, are longer lasting after deprivation.

B. RELATIONSHIP OF SUCKING LEVELS AND STATE: POSSIBLE IMPLICATIONS FOR MOTIVATIONAL PROCESSES

As has been shown in this series of experiments, the rate for each type of sucking within each of the three sleep–wake states is a stable phenomenon. This idea does not imply that sucks are emitted at precise intervals within each state, under the control of some central pattern generator. Rather, the implication is that the relative frequency at which sucks of a certain type are distributed in time is related to the state of the animal. This frequency appears to be highest in the awake state for rhythmic sucking and treadling, but highest in slow-wave sleep for bursts.

Changes in state have been linked to changes in the frequency of many behavioral and physiological events. The behaviors used to define the states themselves certainly fit this category. For example, phasic twitches, one of the defining characteristics of paradoxical sleep, are seen during other states as well, but at a much lower frequency (Petre-Quadens, 1974). Other kinds of behavior also have state-linked frequencies. In infant humans, rhythmic mouthing is highest during slow-wave sleep; reflex smiles are highest during paradoxical sleep (Korner, 1969). The regulation of the cardiovascular system changes during the different states (Combs, 1982). In fact, the amount of heart rate variability, which is largest during paradoxical sleep, has been used as a way of monitoring behavioral states in fetuses (Junge, 1979). Chase (1972) demonstrated that the amplitude of the reflex responses of the jaw muscles of the cat is modulated differently, depending on state. The masseter muscle EMG is greatest while awake, intermediate in quiet sleep, and lowest in active sleep. The digastric reflex response has its peak amplitude during quiet sleep, is smaller while awake, and is smallest in active sleep.

The rate of sucking itself has previously been linked to the behavioral state of the animal. In a study of the effect of food satiation and auditory stimulation on the nonnutritive sucking of human infants, Kaye (1966) stated "It would appear that within the current testing procedures the sucking rates are 'locked' by the general level of arousal, the latter being determined in part by pretest ingestional factors. Only stimuli altering the level of arousal will change the sucking rate." Wolff (1972) made similar points based on his study of healthy and neurologically impaired infants. He even suggested that the basic sucking frequency "is controlled by central oscillatory mechanisms which can operate independent of peripheral input." He went on to say, "Nowhere was it assumed, however, that such hypothetical oscillators would actually function independent of environmental or peripheral influences in the intact organism." Despite differences in methodologies and species, their observations agree very well with the results described here. In the rat, levels of sucking also seem set by behavioral state. But, environmental and/or peripheral influences can alter these levels (e.g., the rate of rhythmic sucking in all three sleep–wake states is higher in the normal mother experiment than in the anesthetized mother experiment).

The present results extend the findings by Wolff (1972) and Kaye (1966) by showing the stability of the sucking rates within each state in response to deprivation. This stability may have implications for understanding how changes in motivation affect an animal's behavior.

Any discussion of motivation has a certain circularity built into it. Motivational levels are defined in terms of the response of an animal. It is assumed that rat pups, upon reunion from deprivation, have a high motivation to get milk and to suck. The evidence for this assumption is the increased levels of sucking (Brake et al., 1979) and intake (e.g., Houpt and Houpt, 1975). The rat pups could respond to deprivation by showing increased levels of sucking in all states, or even just while awake. In fact, evidence for central coding of motivational state in response to hunger has been found during both paradoxical and slow-wave sleep (Jacobs et al., 1970). These authors recorded single-unit activity in the lateral and medial hypothalami in adult cats during food deprivation and postsatiation. Approximately one-half of the cells recorded changed firing rates during both paradoxical and slow-wave sleep following satiation. In the medial hypothalamus, firing rate generally increased. However, the pups described in the present experiments suck at the same rate within each state in response to a deprivation stress. The way their behavior does change with deprivation is to shift sleep–wake states. Paradoxical sleep is reduced while the awake state and slow-wave sleep are increased. This shift is away from the state with the lowest rates of sucking.

Which comes first: the state change or the sucking change? Our research supplies no answer to this question. However, state changes in rats tested without mothers are almost identical to our results with rats tested attached to their mother's teat (Hofer, 1976; Hofer and Shair, 1982). It is tempting to think that the state change is the primary response to deprivation and that change sets the level of sucking.

Wolff (1972) had a similar speculation. He stated, "Hunger satiation has remarkably little influence on the temporal organization of nonnutritive sucking; the changes of sucking rate observed in the course of gastrostomy feeding were probably due to changes in state rather than the direct effects of gastric loading."

C. How Pups Regulate Feeding Based on Deprivation Levels

As discussed in Section I, there has been a controversy in the literature about deprivation effects on feeding in young rats. Young pups (prior to approximately 2 weeks of age) attached to a teat and with unlimited milk supply continue to

ingest until seriously overengorged, even to the point of respiratory distress
(e.g., Hall and Rosenblatt, 1978). Also, stomach loading has been reported to
affect neither attachment nor sucking levels on nonnutritive nipples (e.g., Brake
et al., 1982a). However, rats of the same age tested while unattached do regulate
intake (Hall and Bryan, 1980). Also, rats of these young ages increase intake
over nondeprived pups when returned to normal litter nursing situations (e.g.,
Houpt and Houpt, 1975; Lorenz *et al.*, 1982).

The more recent work by Brake and colleagues contributes to a resolution of
this controversy, some of which has been well described by Hall and Williams
(1983). In the natural nursing situation, there is a limited amount of milk available and it comes only periodically. Based on the defined milk ejection responses, deprived pups suck longer and generate greater negative pressure following milk pulses (Brake *et al.*, 1982b, 1988), presumably extracting more
milk from each letdown. In the tongue cannula preparation, the pup is not only
being required to ingest milk, but also it is required to demonstrate satiation by
detaching from the nipple. This is a very different requirement than being asked
to extract more or less milk from a teat. Young rats do not frequently leave the
teat, even when milk letdown is prevented; for example, pups younger than
approximately 14 days remain attached to an anesthetized dam for 6 hr and even
longer (Brake and Hofer, 1980; Drewett, 1983). In the natural nursing situation,
the dam terminates the nursing bout in a process probably controlled by maternal
thermoregulation (Leon *et al.*, 1985).

The results presented here have shown that maternal deprivation regulates the
rat pup's sleep–wake states in ways that interact with and may help control food
intake during natural nursing upon reunion. Both baseline and deprived pups
were asleep prior to milk ejection, but deprived pups remained awake longer
following letdown. They were then more likely to enter slow-wave than paradoxical sleep. The awake state and slow-wave sleep are the states with the highest
rates of sucking. In studies in which milk is infused continuously through a
tongue cannula, another factor may be involved. Milk has arousing properties. It
increases sucking levels, wiping out the distinction between deprived and nondeprived pups (Brake *et al.*, 1982a). Milk also wakes the pups up, as demonstrated in this article. Further, in pilot work, we have demonstrated that pups
sleep through very small and/or slow infusions of milk through a tongue cannula,
but wake up to larger or more rapid infusions (Shair *et al.*, 1983). In response to
large or long pulses through a tongue cannula, the pups are probably awakened
for long periods due to the stimulation of the milk. Thus, tongue cannula studies
may introduce a ceiling effect. The pups may all be awake and sucking at a
maximum rate, and therefore unable to show a distinction between deprived and
nondeprived states.

Another speculation can be made about the possible effects of deprivation
levels on the feeding interaction. It is known that sucking stimulation by the pups

is necessary to induce milk letdown by the dam (Drewett and Trew, 1978). It is possible that deprived pups, with their decreased time in paradoxical sleep and increased amount of time spent sucking, may stimulate larger and/or more frequent milk ejections (for similar speculations, see Lorenz's article in this volume). In the experiments described in this article, only three pups in the litter were deprived. These litters did not elicit more frequent milk ejections. If the entire litter had been deprived, the results might have been different.

Unfortunately, an attempt to substantiate a linkage of deprivation-increased sucking and increased number of milk letdowns produced negative results in our laboratory (Zmitrovich, 1991). Entire litters separated for 18 hr (or nonseparated controls) were returned either to separated or nonseparated dams for 2 hr. Behavioral interactions and weight changes were carefully monitored. Independent of the dam's condition, the separated litters neither gained more weight, decreased the latency to the first milk ejection, nor shortened the inter-milk ejection interval when compared to the nonseparated litters.

D. Possible Functions of Sucking during Sleep

Why do rat pups suck during the two sleep states? One idea is based on the work showing that sucking is necessary to induce milk ejection (Drewett and Trew, 1978). The mother rat must be asleep for milk ejections to occur (Lincoln *et al.*, 1980; Voloschin and Tremezzani, 1979). Perhaps the optimal stimulus for the mother rat is quiet (i.e., sleeping) pups who are, nevertheless, sucking actively. The sleeping pups do not disturb their mother and thus allow her also to go to sleep. It is possible to imagine that, for this reason, sucking evolved during sleep. Such speculation provides an "ultimate" evolutionary reason for the finding that rat pups were always asleep prior to the milk ejection response on both baseline and reunion days. How this ultimate function was translated into the physiology and behavior of the individual pup is, of course, unknown. One explanation is based on statistical probabilities and the idea of the optimal stimulus described above. When the entire litter is asleep, the dam is most likely to be able to enter slow-wave sleep herself. Therefore, milk ejections should be most probable at these times.

Sucking during sleep might also be explained as an aid to digestion. Sucking stimulates saliva production. It has also been suggested that sucking may increase gastrointestinal motility. It would be interesting to test the digestive capabilities of animals given equal amounts of food intragastrically. If one-half of the pups were allowed to suck normally and the other half were prevented from sucking, would the food be digested better or more quickly by the pups allowed to suck?

Finally, sucking during sleep may allow pups to extract every drop of milk available from the mother's teat. Even though milk ejections are periodic, small amounts of milk may be available between milk ejections. Whether milk is available in these intervals has yet to be tested directly. However, an anesthetized mother who has been deprived of her pups for 1 day prior to anesthesia has milk in her teats that can be withdrawn prior to any oxytocin injection (Lincoln *et al.*, 1973). Thus, it is possible that milk does build up in the teats in the normal situation. If such milk is available, our pilot work demonstrates that pups can suck and swallow milk in either paradoxical or slow-wave sleep (Shair *et al.*, 1983). However, the amount that can be ingested while the pups remain asleep would be approximately twice as large in slow-wave than in paradoxical sleep, due to the higher rates of sucking in the former state. This fits very well with the reduction in paradoxical sleep seen after deprivation. Whether or not the two findings are actually related more than coincidentally is still unknown.

E. EFFECT OF FEEDING ON STATE BEHAVIOR

As discussed in Section I, many studies have shown that state regulation and feeding behavior are linked. This is true at many different ages, in many different species, and in many different experimental preparations. One typical finding is that the amount of paradoxical sleep is decreased in food-deprived animals (Danguir and Nicolaidis, 1979). Similar results have been described in this article in the normal mother and anesthetized mother experiments. However, food deprivation is not the only cause for this reduction in paradoxical sleep. Giving pups nutrient on a periodic schedule during maternal deprivation causes pups to gain weight at normal levels, and, when tested without the mother present, normalizes sleep-wake state behavior (Hofer and Shair, 1982). However, if the pups are tested attached to an anesthetized dam, delivery of food during the deprivation period has no effect on state patterns (infused diet experiment). This finding leads one to postulate the greater arousing properties of the dam to a sucking-deprived pup. In future experiments, pups will be given sucking experience during deprivation either with or without the infused diet, then tested while attached to an anesthetized mother.

Short-term linkages between feeding and sleep have also been reported. In fact, falling asleep after feeding has been described as part of the satiety sequence in rats (e.g., Mansbach and Lorenz, 1983). Also, infusion of nutrient into the gut causes almost immediate changes in the EEG (e.g., Sudakov, 1965). In the normal mother experiment as well, a link between feeding and sleep was also found. The pups were always asleep *prior to* milk ejection, even after the deprivation experience. They were awakened by milk ejections and quickly fell back to sleep. Perhaps the milk ejection and/or the nursing bouts serve as *zeitgebers* for the setting of the sleep–wake cycles. Milk in the gut may cause animals to go to sleep. This could either be an immediate mechanism of taste or some sensation in the gut coursing over a neural pathway to the brain. Also, there could be postabsorptive effects of food on the stomach and digestion which influence the sleep–wake state cycles. (For other speculations, see Lorenz's article in this volume.)

Another possibility is that, rather than milk causing sleep, milk may wake the pup due to its arousing properties. The milk may keep the pup awake as long as it is flowing. This awake time may reset the sleep–wake cycles. This idea is not often considered by researchers in the field. For example, Wolff (1972) describes a study of the effects of feeding on state in normal infants versus infants fed through gastrostomy. Infants fed in a normal fashion are more frequently asleep 30 min after feeding than infants fed through a stomach tube. Wolff takes this as evidence that the sucking as well as feeding has an influence on sleep–wake states. However, he does not comment on the fact that one-half the gastrostomy infants are asleep during the feeding, whereas all of the normal infants are awake. Thus, it seems likely that the normal operation of the sleep–wake cycle would cause fewer gastrostomy infants to be asleep in the period following feeding.

It is even possible that the sleep–wake and feeding interaction is learned or partly learned during development. In the young rat, each milk ejection appears to be associated with a very specific change in sleep-wake states. The temporal pairing of milk in the mouth and/or the gut with the rapid transition into sleep may provide the substrate for Pavlovian conditioning. It is also possible that instrumental processes may be involved. Perhaps the more rapidly the pups return to sleep, the quicker the dam can reenter slow-wave sleep and provide another milk ejection. Thus, the pups' rapid return to sleep may be a conditioned anticipatory response. In older animals in which feeding takes place independently, the response of postprandial sleep may have been learned in part by this earlier association of falling asleep on the teat. It is possible to test these speculations by raising pups fed on different schedules using artificial rearing techniques that minimize or eliminate suckling from the dam, often called "pup-in-cup" techniques (Diaz, 1991).

F. Interaction of Sleep States with Other Behavioral Processes: Implications and Speculations

Learning has been shown to occur during feeding in the young rat (Brake, 1981; Martin and Alberts, 1979). However, the present work has shown that pups are awake only briefly following a milk ejection. How can learning occur in this very brief time? First, it may be that not all of the learning that has been demonstrated experimentally could actually occur under natural conditions. Experimental paradigms using milk through tongue cannulae as a reward often utilize infusions of longer duration than those the pups receive during milk ejections. Pups may be kept awake longer by longer infusions of milk. Alternatively, the possibility exists that milk is so arousing that it causes attention to other stimuli in the environment, even during a brief period of waking. The work by Sullivan *et al.* (1986a,b) has shown that stimulation can be important in promoting learning in the young rat.

Attachment between the young rat pup and its dam is assumed to develop, at least in part, as a result of the nursing experience. As in the paragraph above, how can such experiences be integrated in the brief period of awake time? Again, the arousing properties discussed above may be important in the attachment phenomenon as well. Also, one must remember that milk ejection experience and awakening thereafter are repeated over and over as the pup grows. This repetition may allow attachment to develop.

In adults, many physiological processes are linked to sleep–wake states in a circadian or ultradian manner. Among these are hormone secretion (Åkerstedt, 1984), cardiovascular regulation (Combs, 1982), and thermoregulation (Obal, 1984). Often, these processes are not linked very early in development. Perhaps the milk ejection and/or nursing bouts are entraining stimuli for these processes as well. This could be through either immediate or longer (i.e., postingestive) consequences of milk ejection. For example, a blood pressure increase always accompanies milk ejection, and no blood pressure changes of similar magnitude are seen at any other point in the normal behavior of the young pup (Shair *et al.*, 1986). Thus, the milk ejection has been shown to be linked to both sleep–wake state changes and cardiovascular changes. This link may provide the substrate by which sleep–wake states and the cardiovascular system become linked during development.

What is the relationship between the phenomena described in the young rat to similar processes in humans and other species? One similarity is that many species show sucking behavior while asleep (Emde and Metcalf, 1970; Jouvet-Mounier *et al.*, 1970). However, whether such sucking while asleep will occur in and around a nutritive feeding situation remains to be tested systematically. Second, as discussed above, many species, including humans, fall asleep soon after feeding. One difference is that humans and many other species get milk in a more continuous flow. During a 10-min feed, breast-fed human infants take in almost 90% of all the milk within 4 min. The last half of the feed is almost nonnutritive (Lucas *et al.*, 1979). This difference in milk flow may have important consequences for the response of the baby to the feeding situation. Perhaps human infants are kept awake longer during the continuous flow by the arousal properties of milk. They may then sleep longer afterward. It is even possible that the length of the sleep–wake cycle may, in part, be set by the feeding experience. A more continuous flow may be too great to allow any sleep during the feeding situation, at least in the beginning of the nursing bout. In goats (Ruckebusch, 1972), the young are awake while receiving milk. To the best of my knowledge, sleep–wake states have not been studied systematically in any other species during the actual intake of food. We encourage the reader to begin work of this kind in his or her favorite species.

Acknowledgments

Much of this work was carried out at Montefiore Medical Center, Bronx, New York, and was supported by a project grant from the National Institute of Mental Health. These studies were in partial fulfillment of the doctoral requirements (H.N.S.) in the Biopsychology Program, City University of New York at Hunter College.

Our thanks to the many colleagues and students who have contributed to this research over the years. Special thanks to Dr. Stephen Brake, whose own work helped to initiate these experiments and whose creative ideas helped to guide them. Dr. Brake also scored all of the digastric EMG records. Special thanks are due as well to Phyllis Blackman for typing, editing, and proofreading beyond the call of duty.

We also thank Drs. Epstein and Morrison for the opportunity to present these experimental results in much greater depth than the usual journal article allows. Dr. Epstein was one of the founders of developmental psychobiology. His recent tragic death was a great loss to the field and a personal loss for both authors.

References

Åkerstedt, T. (1984). Hormones and sleep. *Experimental Brain Research, Supplementum* **8,** 193–204.

Anders, T. (1975). Maturation of sleep patterns in the newborn infant. *Advances in Sleep Research* **2,** 43–66.

Anders, T., Emde, R., and Parmelee, A. (1971). "A Manual of Standardized Terminology, Techniques and Criteria for Scoring of States of Sleep and Wakefulness in Newborn Infants." UCLA Brain Information Service/BRI Publications Office, Los Angeles.

Anokhin, P., and Shuleikina, K. (1977). System organization of alimentary behavior in the newborn and the developing cat. *Developmental Psychobiology* **10,** 385–419.

Brake, S. (1981). Suckling infant rats learn a preference for a novel olfactory stimulus paired with milk delivery. *Science* **211,** 506–508.

Brake, S. (1991). New information about early feeding and motivation: Techniques for recording sucking in infant rats. *In* "Developmental Psychobiology: New Methods and Changing Concepts" (H. Shair, G. Barr, and M. Hofer, eds.). Oxford University Press, New York.

Brake, S., and Hofer, M. (1980). Maternal deprivation and prolonged suckling in the absence of milk alter the frequency and intensity of sucking responses in neonatal rat pups. *Physiology and Behavior* **24,** 185–189.

Brake, S., Wolfson, V., and Hofer, M. (1979). Electromyographic patterns associated with non-nutritive sucking in 11–13-day-old rat pups. *Journal of Comparative and Physiological Psychology* **93,** 760–770.

Brake, S., Sager, D., Sullivan, R., and Hofer, M. (1982a). The role of intraoral and gastrointestinal cues in the control of sucking and milk consumption in rat pups. *Developmental Psychobiology* **15,** 529–541.

Brake, S., Sullivan, R., Sager, D., and Hofer, M. (1982b). Short- and long-term effects of various milk delivery contingencies on sucking and nipple attachment in rat pups. *Developmental Psychobiology* **15,** 543–556.

Brake, S., Tavana, S., and Myers, M. (1986). A method for detecting and analysing intra-oral negative pressure in suckling rat pups. *Physiology and Behavior* **36**, 575–578.

Brake, S., Shair, H., and Hofer, M. (1988). Exploiting the nursing niche: The infant's sucking and feeding in the context of the mother–infant interaction. *In* "Handbook of Behavioral Neurobiology" (E. Blass, ed.), Vol. 9. Plenum, New York.

Chase, M. (1972). Patterns of reflex excitability during the ontogenesis of sleep and wakefulness. *In* "Sleep and the Maturing Nervous System" (C. Clemente, D. Purpura, and F. Mayer, eds.). Academic Press, New York.

Combs, C. (1982). Behavioral modulation of arterial baroreflexes. *In* "Circulation, Neurobiology and Behavior" (O. Smith, R. Galosy, and S. Weiss, eds.). Elsevier, New York.

Cramer, C., and Blass, E. (1983a). Mechanisms of control of milk intake in suckling rats. *American Journal of Physiology* **245**, R154–R159.

Cramer, C., and Blass, E. (1983b). Rate versus volume in the milk intake of suckling rats. *In* "The Neural Basis of Feeding and Reward" (B. Hoebel and D. Novin, eds.). Haer, Brunswick, Maine.

Cramer, C., Blass, E., and Hall, W. (1980). The ontogeny of nipple-shifting behavior in albino rats: Mechanisms of control and possible significance. *Developmental Psychobiology* **13**, 165–180.

Croskerry, P., Smith, G., Leon, M., and Mitchell, E. (1976). An inexpensive system for continuously monitoring maternal behavior in the laboratory rat. *Physiology and Behavior* **16**, 223–225.

Danguir, J., and Nicolaidis, S. (1979). Intravenous infusions of nutrients and sleep in the rat: An ischymetric sleep regulation hypothesis. *American Journal of Physiology* **238**, E307–E312.

Danguir, J., and Nicolaidis, S. (1980). Dependence of sleep on nutrients' availability. *Physiology and Behavior* **22**, 735–740.

Danguir, J., Nicolaidis, S., and Gerard, H. (1979). Relations between feeding and sleep patterns in the rat. *Journal of Comparative and Physiological Psychology* **93**, 820–830.

Diaz, J. (1991). Experimental rearing of rat pups using chronic gastric fistulas. *In* "Developmental Psychobiology: New Methods and Changing Concepts" (H. Shair, G. Barr, and M. Hofer, eds.). Oxford University Press, New York.

Dollinger, M., Holloway, W., and Denenberg, V. (1978). Nipple attachment in rats during the first 24 hours of life. *Journal of Comparative and Physiological Psychology* **92**, 619–626.

Drewett, R. (1983) Sucking, milk synthesis, and milk ejection in the Norway rat. *In* "Parental Behaviour of Rodents" (R. Elwood, ed.). Wiley, London.

Drewett, R., and Trew, A. (1978). The milk ejection of the rat, as a stimulus and a response to the litter. *Animal Behaviour* **26**, 982–987.

Drewett, R., Statham, C., and Wakerley, J. (1974). A quantitative analysis of the feeding behaviour of sucking rats. *Animal Behaviour* **22**, 907–913.

Emde, R., and Metcalf, D. (1970). An electroencephalographic study of behavioral rapid eye movement states in the human newborn. *Journal of Nervous and Mental Disease* **150**, 376–386.

Friedman, M. (1975). Some determinants of milk ingestion in suckling rats. *Journal of Comparative and Physiological Psychology* **89**, 636–647.

Gaensbauer, T., and Emde, R. (1973). Wakefulness and feeding in human newborns. *Archives of General Psychiatry* **28**, 894–897.

Gramsbergen, A. (1976). The development of the EEG in the rat. *Developmental Psychobiology* **9**, 501–515.

Grota, L., and Ader, R. (1969). Continuous recording of maternal behaviour in *Rattus norvegicus*. *Animal Behaviour* **17**, 722–729.

Hall, W., and Bryan, T. (1980). The ontogeny of feeding in rats: II. Independent ingestive behavior. *Journal of Comparative and Physiological Psychology* **94**, 746–756.

Hall, W., and Rosenblatt, J. (1977). Suckling behavior and intake control in the developing rat pup. *Journal of Comparative and Physiological Psychology* **91**, 1232–1247.

Hall, W., and Rosenblatt, J. (1978). Development of nutritional control of food intake in suckling rat pups. *Behavioral Biology* **24**, 413–427.

Hall, W., and Williams, G. (1983). Suckling isn't feeding, or is it? A search for developmental continuities. *In* "Advances in the Study of Behavior" (J. Rosenblatt, R. Hinde, R. Beer, and M. Busnell, eds.), Vol. 13, pp. 219–254. Academic Press, New York.

Hall, W., Cramer, C., and Blass, E. (1975). Developmental changes in suckling of rat pups. *Nature (London)* **258**, 318–320.

Harper, R., Hoppenbrouwers, T., Bannett, D., Hodgman, J., Sterman, M., and McGinty, D. (1977). Effects of feeding on state and cardiac regulation in the infant. *Developmental Psychobiology* **10**, 507–517.

Hockman, C. (1964). EEG and behavioral effects of food deprivation in the albino rat. *Electroencephalography and Clinical Neurophysiology* **17**, 420–427.

Hofer, M. (1973). The role of nutrition in the physiological and behavioral effects of early maternal separation on infant rats. *Psychosomatic Medicine* **35**, 350–359.

Hofer, M. (1976). The organization of sleep and wakefulness after maternal separation in young rats. *Developmental Psychobiology* **9**, 189–205.

Hofer, M., and Grabie, M. (1971). Cardiorespiratory regulation and activity patterns of rat pups studied with their mothers during the nursing cycle. *Developmental Psychobiology* **4**, 169–180.

Hofer, M., and Shair, H. (1982). Control of sleep–wake states in the infant rat by features of the mother–infant relationship. *Developmental Psychobiology* **15**, 229–243.

Houpt, K., and Epstein, A. (1973). Ontogeny of controls of food intake in the rat: GI fill and glucoprivation. *American Journal of Physiology* **225**, 58–66.

Houpt, K., and Houpt, T. (1975). Effects of gastric loads and food deprivation on subsequent food intake in suckling rats. *Journal of Comparative and Physiological Psychology* **88**, 764–772.

Jacobs, B., and McGinty, D. (1971). Effects of food deprivation on sleep and wakefulness in the rat. *Experimental Neurology* **30**, 212–222.

Jacobs, B., Harper, R., and McGinty, D. (1970). Neuronal coding of motivational level during sleep. *Physiology and Behavior* **5**, 1139–1143.

Jouvet-Mounier, D., Astic, L., and Lacote, D. (1970). Ontogenesis of the states of sleep in the rat, cat, and guinea pig during the first postnatal month. *Developmental Psychobiology* **2**, 216–239.

Junge, H. (1979). Behavioral states and state related heart rate and motor activity patterns in the newborn infant and the fetus antepartum—A comparative study. I. Techniques, illustrations of recordings, and general results. *Journal of Perinatal Medicine* **7**, 85–107.

Kaye, H. (1966). The effects of feeding and tonal stimulation on non-nutritive sucking in the human newborn. *Journal of Experimental Child Psychiatry* **3**, 131–145.

Kleitman, N. (1963). "Sleep and Wakefulness." University of Chicago Press, Chicago.

Korner, A. (1969). Neonatal startles, smiles, erections and reflex sucks as related to state, sex, and individuality. *Child Development* **40**, 1028–1053.

Korner, A. (1972). State as variable, as obstacle, and as mediator of stimulation in infant research. *Merrill–Palmer Quarterly* **18**, 77–94.

Lacey, J., Stanley, P., Hartmann, M., Koval, J., and Crisp, A. (1978). The immediate effect of intravenous specific nutrients on EEG sleep. *Electroencephalography and Clinical Neurophysiology* **44**, 275–280.

Leon, M., Croskerry, P., and Smith, G. (1978). Thermal control of mother–young contact in rats. *Physiology and Behavior* **21**, 793–811.

Leon, M., Adels, L., and Coopersmith, R. (1985). Thermal limitation of mother–young contact in Norway rats. *Developmental Psychobiology* **18**, 85–105.

Lincoln, D., Hill, A., and Wakerley, J. (1973). The milk-ejection reflex of the rat: An intermittent function not abolished by surgical levels of anesthesia. *Journal of Endocrinology* **57,** 459–476.

Lincoln, D., Hentzen, K., Hin, T., Vander Schoot, P., Clarke, G., and Summerlee, A. (1980). Sleep: A prerequisite for reflex milk ejection in the rat. *Experimental Brain Research* **38,** 151– 162.

Lorenz, D. N. (1986). Alimentary sleep satiety in suckling rats. *Physiology and Behavior* **38,** 557– 562.

Lorenz, D., Ellis, S., and Epstein, A. (1982). Differential effects of upper gastrointestinal fill on milk ingestion and nipple attachment in the suckling rat. *Developmental Psychobiology* **15,** 309–330.

Lucas, A., Lucas, P., and Baum, J. (1979). Pattern of milk flow in breast-fed infants. *Lancet* **2,** 57– 58.

Mansbach, R., and Lorenz, D. (1983). Cholecystokinin (CCK-8) elicits prandial sleep in rats. *Physiology and Behavior* **3,** 179–183.

Martin, L., and Alberts, J. (1979). Taste aversions to mother's milk: The age-related role of nursing in acquisition and expression of a learned association. *Journal of Comparative and Physiological Psychology* **93,** 430–435.

Martinus, J., and Papousek, H. (1970). Response to optic and exteroceptive stimuli in relation to state in the human newborn: Habituation of the blink response. *Neuropaediatrie* **1,** 452–460.

Meier, G., and Berger, R. (1965). Development of sleep and wakefulness patterns in the infant rhesus monkey. *Experimental Neurology* **12,** 257–277.

Messer, M., Thoman, E., Terrasa, A., and Dallman, P. (1969). Artificial feeding of infant rats by continuous gastric infusion. *Journal of Nutrition* **98,** 404–410.

Mouret, J., and Bobillier, P. (1971). Diurnal rhythms of sleep in the rat: Augmentation of paradoxical sleep following alterations of the feeding schedule. *International Journal of Neuroscience* **2,** 265–270.

Obal, F., Jr. (1984). Thermoregulation and sleep. *Experimental Brain Research, Supplementum* **8,** 157–172.

Petre-Quadens, O. (1974). Sleep in the human newborn. *In* "Basic Sleep Mechanisms" (O. Petre-Quadens and J. Schlag, eds.). Academic Press, New York.

Prechtl, H., Akiyama, Y., Zinkin, P., and Kerr-Grant, D. (1968). Polygraphic studies of the full term newborn: I. Technical aspects and qualitative analysis. *Clinics in Developmental Medicine* **27,** 1–25.

Rosen, A., Davis, J., and LaDove, R. (1971). Electrocortical activity: Modification by food ingestion and a humoral satiety factor. *Communications in Behavioral Biology* **6,** 323–327.

Rubenstein, E., and Sonnenschein, R. (1971). Sleep cycles and feeding behavior in the cat: Role of gastrointestinal hormones. *Acta Cientifica Venezolana, Suplemento* **22,** 125–128.

Ruckebusch, Y. (1972). Development of sleep and wakefulness in the foetal lamb. *Electroencephalography and Clinical Neurophysiology* **32,** 119–128.

Shair, H. (1991). Physiological recording during normal mother–infant interactions. *In* "Developmental Psychobiology: New Methods and Changing Concepts" (H. Shair, G. Barr, and M. Hofer, eds.). Oxford University Press, New York.

Shair, H., Gottschalk, A., Brake, S., and Hofer, M. (1983). Two-week-old rat pups can ingest small quantities of milk while asleep. Program abstract from the annual meeting of the International Society for Developmental Psychobiology, Hyannis, Massachusetts.

Shair, H., Brake, S., and Hofer, M. (1984). Suckling in the rat: Evidence for patterned behavior during sleep. *Behavioral Neuroscience* **98,** 366–370.

Shair, H., Brake, S., Hofer, M., and Myers, M. (1986). Blood pressure responses to milk ejection in the young rat. *Physiology and Behavior* **37,** 171–176.

Shimizu, A., and Himwich, H. (1968). The ontogeny of sleep in kittens and young rabbits. *Electroencephalography and Clinical Neurophysiology* **24,** 307–318.

Siegel, J. (1975). REM sleep predicts subsequent food intake. *Physiology and Behavior* **15**, 399–403.

Sudakov, K. (1965). The electroencephalogram and neurohumoral mechanisms of satiety. *Bulletin of Experimental Biology and Medicine (English Translation)* **59**, 103–106.

Sullivan, R., Brake, S., Hofer, M., and Williams, C. (1986a). Huddling and independent feeding of neonatal rats can be facilitated by a conditioned change in behavioral state. *Developmental Psychobiology* **19**, 625–635.

Sullivan, R., Hofer, M., and Brake, S. (1986b). Olfactory-guided orientation in neonatal rats is enhanced by a conditioned change in behavioral state. *Developmental Psychobiology* **19**, 615–623.

Szymusiak, R., and Satinoff, E. (1981). Maximal REM sleep time defines a narrower thermoneutral zone than does minimal metabolic rate. *Physiology and Behavior* **26**, 687–690.

Timo-Iaria, C., Negrao, N., Schmidek, W., Hoshino, K., Lobato de Menezes, C., and Leme de Rocha, T. (1970). Phases and states of sleep in the rat. *Physiology and Behavior* **5**, 1057–1062.

Voloschin, L., and Tramezzani, J. (1979). Milk ejection reflex linked to slow wave sleep in nursing rats. *Endocrinology (Baltimore)* **105**, 1202–1207.

Williams, A., and Gottman, J. (1982). "A User's Guide to the Gottman–Williams Time-Series Analysis Computer Programs for Social Scientists" Cambridge University Press, London.

Winer, B. J. (1971). "Statistical Principles in Experimental Design," 2nd ed. McGraw-Hill, New York.

Wolff, P. (1972). The interaction of state and non-nutritive sucking. *In* "Third Symposium on Oral Sensation and Perception: The Mouth of the Infant." (J. F. Bosma, ed.) Thomas, Springfield, Illinois.

Woodside, B., Pelchat, R., and Leon, M. (1980). Acute elevation of the heat load of mother rats curtails maternal nest bouts. *Journal of Comparative and Physiological Psychology* **94**, 61–68.

Yogman, M., and Zeisel, S. (1983). Diet and sleep patterns in newborn infants. *New England Journal of Medicine* **309**, 1147–1149.

Young, G., Steinfels, G., and Khazan, N. (1978). Cortical EEG power spectra associated with sleep–wake behavior in the rat. *Pharmacology, Biochemistry and Behavior* **8**, 89–91.

Young, R., Gibbs, J., Antin, J., Holt, J., and Smith, G. (1974). Absence of satiety during sham feeding in the rat. *Journal of Comparative and Physiological Psychology* **87**, 795–780.

Zmitrovich, A. (1991). "The Effects of Separation on the Mother–Infant Interaction during Reunion in Ten to Twelve Day Old Rat Litters," unpublished doctoral dissertation. City University of New York, New York.

Taste, Feeding, and Pleasure

Thomas R. Scott
Department of Psychology
University of Delaware
Newark, Delaware 19716

I. Introduction

Feeding is laced with danger. Most organisms prefer not to be consumed, and defend themselves by physical or chemical means. Physical defenses (e.g., inaccessibility, size, speed, quills, shells, thorns, and bark) are countered with physical weapons not germane to this article. More relevant here is the need for the forager to detect and avoid chemical defenses (e.g., toxins and extremes of pH) and to identify nutrients, a pressure that has led to the evolution of the chemical senses, smell, and taste. These are the most primitive of specialized sensory systems, with an evolutionary history of some 500 million years. Accordingly, they deal with the two most fundamental requirements of life: the acquisition of nutrients to sustain the individual, and reproduction to sustain the species. Smell has become more specialized for the latter; taste, the former. It is the sense of taste, poised at the threshold between the external and internal milieux, that must evaluate the acceptability of a chemical in the mouth and serve as the final arbiter in the digital decision to swallow or reject.

A decision to swallow is binding for a rat. The composition of its gastric wall does not permit the violent contractions necessary to regurgitate a toxin, and so the digestive sequence proceeds, regardless of consequences. Thus, the rat must select wisely from its chemical environment. While it must not accept toxins, it cannot afford to bypass nutrients. Moreover, feeding, as opposed to the maintenance of fluid balance, places multiple demands on the omnivore. Diverse nutrients are called for, and the mix among them may change with disease (Carson and Gormican, 1977), age (Murphy, 1986), or nutritional (Beauchamp *et al.*, 1987) or reproductive status (DiLorenzo and Monroe, 1989). However, rats and other animals do select a proper diet over time, an ability termed "body wisdom" by Curt Richter. The thesis I advance here is that *body wisdom is the outcome of fulfilling a simple and constant goal: to maximize hedonic reward. The flexibility of matching that which is needed to what the animal finds desirable is provided by alterations in the sensitivity of the taste system.* As a corollary to this thesis, I hold that *taste responses are influenced not only by chemicals that are taken into*

231

the mouth but also by the past experiences and the momentary physiological status of the animal.

Decisions about the acceptability of a potential food are based largely on gustatory afferent activity. This input has four consequences: Somatic reflexes are activated either for swallowing or rejection, autonomic reflexes are released to facilitate the impending digestive processes, a hedonic appraisal of the chemical is made, and stimulus quality and intensity are evaluated. Each of these may be mediated by a distinct anatomical branch of the taste system.

The neural mechanisms of taste and the reflexive and hedonic sequelae of taste-evoked activity that guide food selection are the subjects of this article.

II. Characterization of Taste

The questions researchers have asked regarding the sense of taste are those that have served well in the study of vision, hearing, and somesthesis. First, what are the physical characteristics of stimuli that determine taste quality? Second, are there primary taste qualities, each independent of the others, that may be combined in various proportions to create any taste? Third, are taste neurons divisible into functional types, one corresponding to each primary quality, such that neurons within each type are nearly identical in their sensitivities? Fourth, is the code for quality carried in the pattern of activity of all taste neurons, or is it restricted to a channel composed of cells most responsive to that quality? Finally, is there a topographic organization in taste whereby the taste quality to which a cell is most responsive is a function of its physical location? If corresponding questions were put to investigators of retinal color vision mechanisms, the answers would be definitive: (1) stimulus wavelength; (2) yes; (3) yes; (4) all neurons; (5) no. For pitch discrimination, they would be nearly reversed, yet equally definitive.

In taste, however, the accumulation of data and the application of analytical approaches more sophisticated than those required to achieve the preceding answers have not provided such clarity. First, physical characteristics: A number of stimulus attributes have been associated with particular taste qualities. These include pH, hydrophobicity, and molecular weight and configuration. At best, these pertain only to specific qualities and fail to relate to the entire range of taste sensations (McBurney, 1978).

Second, primary tastes: There are cogent arguments for four or five independent classes of taste stimuli that may be established at the receptor level, maintained throughout the processing chain, and experienced as qualitatively distinct perceptions. Most, though not all, of the supporting data derive from psychophysical studies which are not always free of cultural and linguistic biases. When these effects are minimized by the use of semantic differential scales or licking in rodents, the independence of the classes is less obvious (Pritchard and Scott,

1982; Schiffman and Erickson, 1971). Similarly, it is not clear that the appropriate combination of stimuli prototypical of each class could mimic any taste experience.

Third, neuron types: Taste neurons may be categorized by any of several criteria: location, size, connections, response profiles, or function. Investigators have relied on these, singly or in combination, to partition cells into discrete types that correspond to the putative primary tastes. The most quantitative data regarding this issue derive from analyses of the relative similarities among neuronal response profiles. The conclusion these analyses promote is that most taste cells may be assigned to a small number of groups, each of which is statistically independent of the others, but within which the constituent neurons are not identical. Thus, by a liberal definition (statistical independence among groups), the concept of gustatory neuron types is acceptable; by a more stringent one (uniformity of cells within each group), the notion largely fails (Scott and Chang, 1984; Scott et al., 1986a,b; Smith et al., 1983; Woolston and Erickson, 1979).

An alternative strategy is to monitor the changes that the taste system undergoes to accommodate the transient physiological needs of the animal. When a rat is salt deprived, responses of peripheral (Contreras and Frank, 1979) and central (Jacobs et al., 1988) gustatory neurons to sodium declines, presumably to encourage a restorative increase in salt consumption. Other modifications in taste-evoked activity have been reported as a consequence of conditioning (Chang and Scott, 1984), the manipulation of satiety factors (Giza and Scott, 1983, 1987b; Glenn and Erickson, 1976), and the use of taste modifiers (Hellekant et al., 1981). If there are neuron types and they function independently, these alterations should be fully mediated by activity changes within the type that is responsible for the relevant taste quality, and should not be manifested among other neuron types. Four applications of this strategy have indicated that changes in gustatory activity are indeed limited to identifiable subtypes of cells, and so provide convincing support for the existence of both peripheral and central gustatory neuron types (Chang and Scott, 1984; Contreras and Frank, 1979; Jacobs et al., 1988; Scott and Giza, 1990).

Fourth, coding channels: If there are primary tastes and neuron types, there is the further possibility that they function independently, composing four or five discrete sensory channels. The results of one study suggest that it is the activity in a putative "sweet channel," not the response of the entire system, that encodes sweetness (Pfaffmann, 1974). The quality of saltiness has also been associated with activity in a particular gustatory channel (Giza and Scott, 1991; Scott and Giza, 1990). However, there are complications. At a theoretical level, the broad sensitivity of individual taste cells to a variety of qualities would render a channel strategy quite inefficient. A majority of each neuron's spikes would be contributing noise. In practical terms, the best response of a neuron, and so the channel to which it should be assigned, can change with stimulus concentration (Erickson,

1967) or with location of the stimulus within the mouth (Norgren, 1985). These considerations enhance the appeal of a coding strategy that recognizes patterns of activity generated by all taste cells (Erickson *et al.*, 1965). Still, the weight of evidence favors the existence of coding channels in taste.

Finally, topography: Sensitivity to taste quality is not uniformly distributed throughout the oral cavity. Thresholds to sweet and salty stimuli are lowest at the tip of the tongue; to acids, on the posterior tongue; and to quinine, on the soft palate (Collings, 1974; Hanig, 1901). This chemotopic arrangement is preserved to some degree at each successive gustatory relay (Funakoshi *et al.*, 1972; Halpern and Nelson, 1965; Ishiko and Akogi, 1972; Ishiko *et al.*, 1967; Scott *et al.*, 1986a,b; Yamamoto and Kawamura, 1975, 1977; Yamamoto *et al.*, 1980, 1984). However, a topographic organization of sensitivities is nowhere so clear as in the nonchemical senses, and appears too ill defined to support taste quality discriminations.

Answers to questions designed to investigate vision, hearing, and somesthesis emerge as black or white in those systems. In taste, it is increasingly apparent that the corresponding answers are gray. Thus, conclusions rest on how dark the gray must be to be defined as black, or how light to be white, and the issues persist unresolved.

A possible shortcoming lies with the model. The sense of taste is an intermediary between the traditional nonchemical sensory systems and visceral sensation. It possesses typical features of nonchemical senses, such as identification of stimulus quality and intensity through spatiotemporal codes. However, taste may be classified as a visceral afferent system according to its embryological, anatomical, and functional characteristics (Herrick, 1922, 1944). The sense of taste may be viewed as the beginning of a body-long chemosensory system with receptors throughout that are sensitive to the molecules being liberated by the digestive process. Chemicals stimulating taste receptors, however, are only candidates for ingestion—they have not yet been swallowed. Therefore, it is the obligation of the taste system to assess the desirability of consuming a prospective food relative to the momentary physiological needs of the animal it serves. Taste is well suited to this task by its anatomy and function, which I describe now in a chemically oriented mammal, the rat, and in another mammal more reliant on vision for its diet, the macaque monkey.

III. Gustatory Anatomy

A. THE RAT

The role of taste as a mediator between the external and internal chemical milieux is reflected in its anatomy. In the hindbrain, the special visceral afferent fibers of taste run in close apposition to both somatosensory and visceral afferents. Beyond the pons, taste axons bifurcate, sending one projection to the thalamocortical axis in conjunction with oral somesthesis, and the other into ventral forebrain areas associated with autonomic processes (Fig. 1).

1. Peripheral and Hindbrain Connections

Cranial nerves V, VII, IX, and X convey taste information to the central nervous system (CNS). Afferent axons of taste receptors in the anterior lingual epithelium carry gustatory and somesthetic information together in the lingual branch of the trigeminal nerve. Several millimeters centrally, a slender thread diverges from the main nerve to form the chorda tympani, composed of only 1000 fibers, of which perhaps 300 are gustatory (Miller, 1971). This nerve courses across the upper margin of the eardrum (hence, its name) and joins the greater superficial petrosal nerve, which innervates the palate, to form the intermediate nerve of Wrisberg, the sensory component of nerve VII (Norgren, 1984; Whitehead and Frank, 1983). From the posterior tongue, both taste and somesthetic information passes through the lingual–tonsillar branch of nerve IX. The superior laryngeal branch of nerve X innervates receptors for both modalities in the larynx. Thus, a close anatomical relationship between taste and somesthesis is established in the periphery, to be maintained at each synaptic relay in the CNS.

Second-order taste cells are located in the rostral nucleus tractus solitarius (NTS). They fill the mediolateral extent of the nucleus at the rostral pole, but as

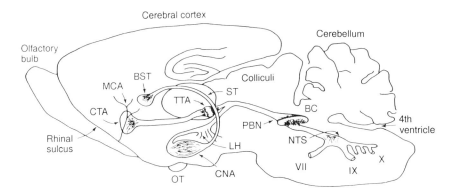

FIG. 1. Parasaggital section showing the centripetal gustatory anatomy of the rat. BC, Brachium conjunctivum; BST, bed nucleus of the stria terminalis; CNA, central nucleus of the amygdala; CTA, cortical taste area; LH, lateral hypothalamus; MCA, middle cerebral artery; NTS, nucleus of the solitary tract; OT, optic tract; PBN, parabrachial nucleus; ST, stria terminalis; TTA, thalamic taste area; VII, IX, and X, cranial nerves VII, IX, and X. [Courtesy of Dr. Carl Pfaffmann. Reprinted from Norgren (1977) with permission.]

the NTS broadens caudally, they are confined mainly to the lateral division (Hamilton and Norgren, 1984; Norgren, 1981, 1984, 1985; Whitehead and Frank, 1983). The percentage of gustatory neurons declines with posterior progression, to become negligible in the caudal half of the nucleus. Throughout its rostrocaudal extent, the taste region is infiltrated by somesthetic axons terminating on touch- and temperature-sensitive neurons whose distribution extends into the lateral NTS from the spinal trigeminal nucleus (Halpern and Nelson, 1965; Makous *et al.*, 1963; Pfaffmann *et al.*, 1961). Within the region of overlap are cells responsive to both gustatory and somesthetic stimulation.

The medial and caudal aspects of the NTS are dominated by nongustatory vagal afferents (Fig. 2). A small region is devoted to respiratory and cardiac function, but the majority of the caudal half of the NTS receives visceral input from the gastrointestinal tract (Kalia and Sullivan, 1982). No direct communication has been established between viscerosensory and gustatory regions of the NTS (Norgren, 1985; Novin, 1986), although the dendrites of cells in the rostral portion do spread into the caudal division, and an indirect link by way of the

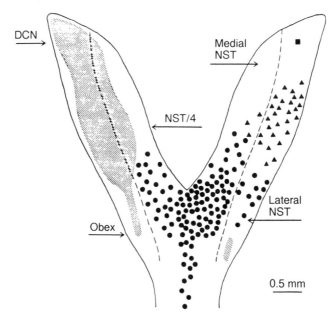

FIG. 2. Horizontal section through the solitary tract nucleus (NTS) of the rat, indicating the distribution of gustatory and nongustatory afferent nerves. The hatched region represents the area of termination of nerves carrying taste information. Symbols indicate the distribution of nongustatory afferents: ▲, lingual; ●, cervical vagus; ■, inferior alveolar. DCN, Caudal boundary of the dorsal cochlear nucleus; NST/4, level at which the NTS meets the fourth ventricle. [Reprinted from Hamilton and Norgren (1984) with permission.]

subjacent reticular formation has been hypothesized (Hermann and Rogers, 1985).

The dorsal motor nucleus and nucleus ambiguus are the primary sources of parasympathetic motor fibers that control ingestive processes and regulate the musculature of the larynx, pharynx, and esophagus. Taste axons from the NTS project to both nuclei, as well as to the salivatory nuclei of the intervening reticular formation and the hypoglossal and facial nuclei. It is estimated that only 20% of NTS cells project rostrally to the pons (Ogawa *et al.*, 1982; Ogawa and Kaisaku, 1982); the remainder either form intranuclear connections or contribute to the pathways serving parasympathetic and somatic motor nuclei (Loewy and Burton, 1978; Norgren, 1978). These projections constitute the major output of the gustatory NTS.

Such rich anatomical connections provide the basis for independent control of both reflexive and regulatory processes by the hindbrain. Rats decerebrated at the supracollicular level lose most of their spontaneous behavioral sequences, yet autonomic and somatic reflexes are largely intact (Grill and Norgren, 1978a). Moreover, many regulatory mechanisms associated with ingestion survive decerebration. These include the cephalic phase insulin release occasioned by gustatory stimulation (Grill and Berridge, 1981), the sympathoadrenal response to glucoprivation (DiRocco and Grill, 1979), insulin-induced hyperphagia (Flynn and Grill, 1983), and satiety and anorexia induced by the gut hormone cholecystokinin (Grill *et al.*, 1983).

Thus, taste afferents are shown to overlap somesthetic fibers on their lateral boundary and to project to autonomic areas medially. Studies of physiology confirm that these interactions with both exteroceptive and interoceptive processes are important in guiding the animal's behavior.

Third-order neurons in the rat's gustatory system are concentrated in the caudal and medial parabrachial nuclei (PBN) (Norgren, 1978; Norgren and Leonard, 1971, 1973; Ricardo and Koh, 1978). A region of tongue-touch sensitivity lies at their lateral border in the principal sensory nucleus of the trigeminal nerve, to which some NTS cells project (Norgren, 1981; Norgren and Pfaffmann, 1975). Within the taste areas itself, many gustatory neurons are also activated by cooling, and inhibited by warming the tongue (Norgren, 1984). Viscerosensory fibers from the caudal NTS also project to the PBN, terminating in its dorsolateral quadrant (Norgren, 1981). Tracing studies indicate a convergence of projections from the rostral and caudal NTS onto a common neuronal pool in the caudal PBN, thus providing the basis for gustatory–autonomic integration (Novin, 1986). Moreover, the gustatory region of the PBN sends a substantial projection centrifugally to the nucleus ambiguus and the salivatory nuclei. The anatomical organization of the rat's hindbrain, then, involves taste fibers with the exteroceptive somesthetic system serving the oral cavity and with visceral afferents primarily mediating digestive processes.

2. Thalamocortical Connections

Pontine gustatory neurons send axons through the central tegmental tract to terminate in the wedge-shaped medial tip of the ventrobasal complex (Ables and Benjamin, 1960; Benjamin, 1963; Benjamin and Akert, 1959; Ganchrow and Erickson, 1972). This small densely packed parvocellular nucleus contains the fourth-order neurons of taste. Although the most medial cells are responsive exclusively to chemical stimulation of the oral cavity, a lateral progression of the recording electrode quickly identifies multimodal cells sensitive to taste and temperature, taste and oral touch, and—still only a millimeter from the medial border—solely to touch.

Projections from the gustatory thalamus pass to the agranular insular cortex, a region that borders on and overlaps the lingual representation of the primary somatosensory cortex (Benjamin and Akert, 1959; Benjamin and Pfaffmann, 1955; Kosar et al., 1985). The electrode documents the preservation of the gustatory–somesthetic sequence identified in the thalamus, with a rostrocaudal progression revealing a gradual transition from lingual tactile to temperature to taste sensitivity. Thus, the anatomical relationship between taste and somesthesis is fulfilled through the cortical level, paralleling the pattern of the exteroceptive senses. Classical notions ascribe to the thalamus the task of analyzing quality–intensity information to the exclusion of a hedonic evaluation. Accordingly, destruction of thalamic or cortical gustatory areas alters taste sensitivity (Benjamin, 1959; Oakley, 1965; Oakley and Pfaffmann, 1962), but not preference–aversion functions (Grill and Norgren, 1978a).

3. Afferents to Ventral Forebrain

Gustatory neurons in the PBN project at least as massively to a second series of targets independent of the thalamocortical axis: those situated throughout the ventral forebrain (Norgren, 1974, 1976; Norgren and Leonard, 1973). The densest termini include the lateral hypothalamus, central nucleus of the amygdala, and bed nucleus of the stria terminalis, although other ventral forebrain sites are also implicated. These structures are associated with motivation, emotion, reinforcement, and particularly ingestion. Their damage disrupts normal responsiveness to exteroceptive input, a syndrome known as sensory neglect, which may contribute to the aphagia consequent to hypothalamic lesions (Marshall and Teitelbaum, 1974; Marshall et al., 1971). Lesions also interfere with taste-mediated interoceptive functions, such as sodium appetite (Wolf, 1964) and the acquisition (Kemble and Nagel, 1973; Roth et al., 1973) or retention of conditioned taste aversions. Thus, there appears to be a functional distinction between the two major targets of PBN fibers in the rat. Projections to the thalamocortical axis may mediate the discriminative capacity of the taste system, an exteroceptive function in the same category as oral somesthesis whose mediating fibers accompany those of taste. Connections to the ventral forebrain may permit the integration of taste with interoceptive and exteroceptive information to guide and regulate feeding behavior (Pfaffmann et al., 1977). Such a hypothesis, now implied primarily by lesion studies, awaits electrophysiological confirmation.

4. Centrifugal Connections

The thalamocortical and ventral forebrain taste systems both send centrifugal projections to hindbrain relays in the NTS and the PBN (Norgren and Grill, 1976; Saper, 1982; Shipley and Sanders, 1982; Van der Kooy et al., 1984). In addition, the gustatory cortex projects heavily back to the thalamic taste relay, while ventral forebrain nuclei reciprocate the connections they receive from hindbrain parasympathetic nuclei (Berk and Finkelstein, 1982; Conrad and Pfaff, 1976; Hosoya et al., 1984). Thus, routes are established by which such factors as motivation or conditioning could at least influence taste-mediated acceptance–rejection reflexes. These connections also imply that the very taste activity that helps guide feeding may be differentially biased at an early synaptic level to accommodate the transient physiological needs of the animal, as suggested below.

B. THE MACAQUE MONKEY

1. Peripheral and Hindbrain Connections

Cranial nerves V, VII, IX, and X also carry gustatory afferents to the monkey NTS, which, however, extends father rostrally than in the rat to approach the caudal border of the main sensory nucleus of the trigeminal nerve. All of the nerves send fascicles rostrally upon reaching the NTS to innervate gustatory cells in this prefacial NTS (Beckstead and Norgren, 1979). The monkey NTS is organized similarly to that of the rat. The rostral and lateral divisions receive fibers mainly from nerves VII and IX, and these areas are known to contain neurons responsive to gustatory stimuli (Scott et al., 1986a). Vagal axons innervate primarily the medial segment of the NTS, although a portion of the fibers terminate more laterally. Thus, there is some degree of overlap among all three taste nerves that reach the lengthy rostrocaudal extent of the lateral NTS.

2. Thalamocortical Connections

Projections from the NTS differ among species. Although all levels of the rat NTS project to the PBN, a corresponding pathway rises only from the caudal

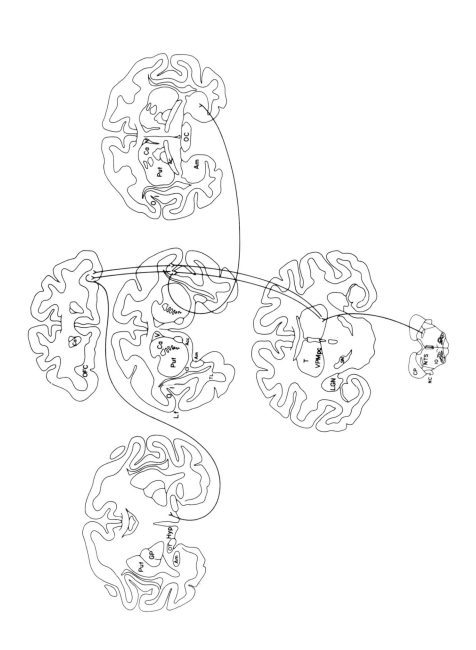

NTS in the monkey. Axons from the rostral areas associated with taste bypass the PBN and travel by way of the ipsilateral central tegmental tract to terminate in the medial ventrobasal complex, as some do eventually in the rat as well (Beckstead *et al.*, 1980) (Fig. 3). Therefore, projections from both the gustatory and visceral NTS to the PBN in rats provide a basis for possible viscerogustatory integration (Novin, 1986), whereas the projections from the rostral and caudal NTS in the monkey appear to separate taste from visceral inputs.

From the thalamic taste area, axons project to the frontal operculum and the anterior insula of the monkey (Benjamin and Burton, 1968; Burton and Benjamin, 1971; Jones and Burton, 1976). Autoradiographic tracing indicates that these fibers may also ramify into the posterior orbitofrontal cortex (Pritchard *et al.*, 1986), although retrograde tracing studies (Wiggins *et al.*, 1987) and the unique functional character of neurons in this region (Rolls *et al.*, 1985) make this finding less certain. The involvement of the insular–opercular cortex in taste reception is well documented by both clinical and experimental studies. A dozen patients who suffered damage in this region from bullet wounds were ageusic or dysgeusic (Bronstein, 1940a,b). Lesions in the same region in monkeys caused reliable, if temporary, elevation of taste thresholds (Bagshaw and Pribram, 1953; Patton, 1960; Ruch and Patton, 1946). Also, stimulation of the peripheral taste nerves resulted in evoked potentials both on the lateral convexity of the postcentral gyrus and, with slightly longer latency, in the frontal operculum and the anterior insula (Bagshaw and Pribram, 1953; Benjamin and Emmers, 1968). The latter area was interpreted to be the primary cortical taste area. Finally, single neurons in the insular–opercular cortex have been shown to be responsive to taste solutions on the tongue (Ogawa *et al.*, 1989; Scott *et al.*, 1986b; Sudakov *et al.*, 1971; Yaxley *et al.*, 1990). Whether this region represents a single continuous relay or two adjacent taste-sensitive sites has not been established yet, although the insula and the operculum have been shown to be cytoarchitectonically distinct (Jones and Burton, 1976; Mesulam and Mufson, 1982; Mufson and Mesulam, 1982; Roberts and Akert, 1963; Sanides, 1968, 1970). It is also notable that the thalamic somatosensory relay projects to the somatosensory cortex of both pre- and postcentral gyri, but not to the insular–opercular cortex (Pritchard *et al.*, 1986). Therefore, the anatomical separation of taste and touch is maintained to a greater degree in monkeys than in the rat.

FIG. 3.   Transverse sections summarizing the afferent limb of central gustatory projections in the cynomolgus monkey. AC, Anterior commissure; Acc, nucleus accumbens; Am, amygdala; Ca, caudate; Cl, claustrum; CP, cerebellar peduncle; GP, globus pallidus; Hyp, hypothalamus; I, insula; IO, inferior olive; LF, lateral fissure; LGN, lateral geniculate nucleus; NC, cuneate nucleus; NTS, nucleus of the solitary tract; O, operculum; OC, optic chiasm; OFC, orbitofrontal cortex; OT, optic tract; Put, putamen; SN, substantia nigra; T, thalamus; TL, temporal lobe; V, ventricle; VPMpc, ventroposterior medial nucleus of the thalamus, pars parvocellularis. [Reprinted from Scott and Yaxley (1989) with permission.]

3. Intracortical and Corticofugal Connections

Interconnections among the frontal operculum, anterior insula, and lateral posterior orbitofrontal cortex have been demonstrated consistently, although details of the different anatomical studies have varied (Nauta, 1964). Initially, strychnine neuronographic techniques indicated that all three areas were reciprocally interconnected (Pribram and MacLean, 1953). Subsequently, a lesion study confirmed the projection from the operculum to the dorsal insula, but not the converse (Turner *et al.*, 1980). Most recently, retrograde tracing using horseradish peroxidase in the orbitofrontal cortex indicated direct projections from both the frontal operculum and the anterior insula, but not from the thalamic taste nucleus (Wiggins *et al.*, 1987). These authors concluded that both the operculum and the insula may be considered the primary gustatory cortex, while the orbitofrontal region includes a second-order cortical taste area. The latter region receives a robust projection from the amygdala, which receives fibers from the gustatory insula (Aggleton *et al.*, 1980; Mufson and Mesulam, 1982) and itself contains taste-responsive neurons. The amygdala also communicates reciprocally with the lateral hypothalamus and the basal forebrain, in which taste responses are known to be modulated by hunger level (Burton *et al.*, 1976; Wilson *et al.*, 1984). In addition, the amygdala projects back to the NTS, establishing the possibility of a lengthy and open circuit through which gustatory information could interact with feeding, hedonics, and motivation, as in the rat. However, on the basis of available knowledge, the anatomical connections in the primate suggest serial processing of taste information (NTS to the thalamus to the cortex), followed by integration of this analysis with motivational–hedonic components. This is in contrast to the implied situation in the rat, in which parallel processing along the thalamacortical axis and in the ventral forebrain occurs beyond the PBN. The rat's anatomy, then, suggests a more intimate and lower-order relationship between taste and motivational systems.

IV. Organization of the Taste System

No issue is more basic to the characterization of a sensory system than a definition of the dimensions on which perceptions are based. The study of auditory perception may proceed in a logical fashion because it is known that the perception of pitch derives largely from the frequency of the incident pressure waves. Therefore, stimuli may be applied in an orderly fashion, and the relationship between the independent variable (stimulus frequency) and the dependent variable (neural response) may be determined. Similarly, the relationships between stimulus wavelength and color perception, locus of retinal stimulation and form perception, and locus of skin deformation and pressure sensation may be defined. Taste perceptions are also a product of the physical characteristics of relevant stimuli, and our appreciation of the receptor mechanisms underlying these perceptions is advancing briskly.

A. RECEPTOR MECHANISMS

The investigation of receptor function has presumed the existence of four basic tastes. Transduction mechanisms associated with salty, sour, sweet, and bitter stimuli have been studied independently by researchers who often specialize in only one or two of these processes, despite the fact that individual receptor cells, like their CNS counterparts, typically respond to a variety of taste stimuli (Kimura and Beidler, 1961). Each cell, then, is presumed to maintain sites for multiple transduction processes on its apical (receptive) membrane, with the proportion of sites determining its response profile.

The interaction of a sapid chemical with a receptor site leads, through a variety of mechanisms summarized in Fig. 4, to a change in membrane conductance and depolarization of the receptor cell. This depolarization spreads from the apical to the basolateral region of the cell, where it induces an increase in intracellular Ca^{2+} either by permitting Ca^{2+} influx through voltage-gated channels or by releasing Ca^{2+} from internal stores through second messengers (Kinnamon and Getchell, 1991).

1. Salty

The mechanism associated with the transduction of Na^+, Li^+, and K^+ is perhaps the simplest and most readily explained. As their concentration rises on the tongue, these ions flow passively down their concentration gradients into receptor cells through channels in the apical membrane (Fig. 4A). The resulting depolarization may spread passively to the basolateral portion of the cell, to induce an increase in Ca^{2+} and so initiate synaptic transmission (DeSimone et al., 1981; Heck et al., 1984). Only a portion of the signal for saltiness results from this mechanism, however. When passive Na^+ transmission is blocked by the agent amiloride, these salts continue to generate neural (Brand et al., 1985; DeSimone and Ferrell, 1985; Ninomiya et al., 1985) and psychophysical (Schiffman et al., 1983) responses. Moreover, amiloride does not affect the activity evoked by other salts, despite their "salty" components (Brand et al., 1985); nor does it block the Na^+ response in neonatal rats in whom this mechanism presumably is not yet developed (Hill and Bour, 1985) or in adult rats, sodium deprived since birth, whose lack of experience with salt may deny them the environmental confirmation necessary for amiloride-sensitive channels to be expressed (Przekop et al., 1990).

It is possible that the theory of salt transduction is complete, but tests of it are

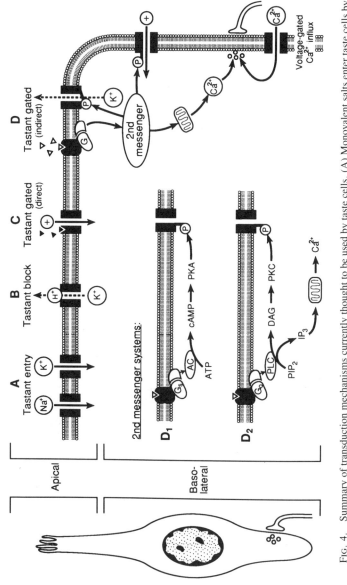

FIG. 4. Summary of transduction mechanisms currently thought to be used by taste cells. (A) Monovalent salts enter taste cells by passing through ion channels on the apical membrane (B) Hydrogen ions (sour) block apical K^+ channels. (C) Amino acids (not discussed here). (D) Sugars and some bitter compounds bind to an apical receptor coupled to a second messenger system. Second messenger-generating enzymes in taste cells include adenylyl cyclase (AC) and PIP_2 phospholipase C (PLC). [Reprinted from Kinnamon and Getchell (1991) with permission.]

flawed. Amiloride may not bind tightly enough to the ion channel to prevent all Na^+ transport. The highly specific analog of amiloride, phenamil, totally blocks the gerbil's neural response to NaCl, while 30% remains after amiloride treatment (Schiffman et al., 1990). Alternatively, the remainder of the response to these salts may derive from Cl^- transport into the cell (Formaker and Hill, 1988).

2. Sour

The perception of "sour" depends, to some degree, on the concentration of hydrogen ions in the bathing medium. There are, however, other considerations. As a group, organic acids are perceived as more intensely sour than inorganic acids of corresponding pH. The effects of more specific properties of the anion on sourness have also been reported (Beidler, 1969, 1971).

At rest, there is a small but significant outward current from the apical membrane, carried by K^+. An increase in H^+ concentration blocks the K^+ channel and so reduces this current, causing a decrease in K^+ conductance and receptor depolarization (Teeter et al., 1989) (Fig. 4B).

There is also evidence that acid-induced receptor potentials decline in the absence of Ca^{2+} (Sato et al., 1984). This may implicate Ca^{2+} conductance as a second transduction mechanism. Alternatively, it may merely reflect the fact that K^+ conductance depends partly on the presence of Ca^{2+}, without which K^+ would be less activated and so less subject to H^+ blockade (Avenet and Lindemann, 1987). Even in an ion-free environment, however, the acid response is only attentuated, not abolished. This suggests that changes in surface potential may mediate a portion of the acid-induced activity.

3. Sweet

Only a minute portion of the molecules available to animals elicit sweetness, but these comprise a surprising diversity of molecular structures. A common physical property of these molecules is the possession of at least one site where two anions are separated by 3 Å, with one of them bound to a H^+ (Shallenberger and Acree, 1967, 1971). It is hypothesized that such a stimulus molecule interacts with a complementary complex on a sweet receptor site to form a pair of hydrogen bonds—the requisite physical condition for sweetness. While this complex can be identified on nearly all molecules that evoke a sweet sensation, its presence is no guarantee of sweetness. Thus, the theory lacks predictive power, and its utility is limited.

On the receptor side, protein fractions that undergo conformational changes in the presence of sweet-tasting compounds have been derived from homogenates of bovine (Dastoli and Price, 1966) and rat and monkey (Hiji *et al.*, 1968) tongues. Since proteolytic enzymes applied to the tongue selectively abolish sweet-evoked neural activity (Hiji, 1975), the identification of sweet-sensitive proteins was indeed suggestive. The derived fractions contain proteins that respond specifically to sweet molecules within appropriate concentration ranges, and are obtained only when the taste buds are intact (Price and DeSimone, 1977). However, they also bind compounds that are not sweet and have been identified in nongustatory epithelium (Nofre and Sabadie, 1972), raising doubts about their status as the transduction sites for sweetness.

While humans report sweet sensations in response to several types of compounds, an individual's sensitivity to one class is not predictive of sensitivity to others (Faurion *et al.*, 1980a,b). Moreover, if a subject is adapted to one sweet stimulus, other chemicals can still elicit undiminished sensations of sweetness (Schiffman *et al.*, 1981). These results, combined with the wide variation in responses to sweet compounds across species, require the existence of multiple receptor sites for sweetness. These sites remain to be discovered.

Whatever the sites, the transduction of sweet tastes requires the presence of GTP, thus implicating GTP-binding proteins (Striem *et al.*, 1989). With binding, adenylyl cyclase activity is stimulated, allowing cAMP-dependent phosphorylation, and so blockade, of K^+ channels (Fig. 4D). The blockade of K^+ channels through this second messenger system would lead to the observed depolarization of receptor cells with an increase in membrane resistance—just the outcome that accompanies the application of saccharides to taste cells (Tonosaki and Funakoshi, 1984, 1988a,b).

4. Bitter

The chemical requirements for bitterness are as general as those for sweetness are specific. There may be multiple transduction mechanisms to account for the variety of chemical structures that are effective in evoking a bitter sensation (Teeter and Brand, 1987). The lipophilicity of many bitter compounds suggests a nonspecific recognition mechanism. The molecules may be absorbed within the lipid layer of the apical membrane (Koyama and Kurihara, 1972), there to alter surface potential (Kumazawa *et al.*, 1985) or activate a second messenger system. The degree of lipophilicity has been shown to correlate with the intensity of bitterness for a wide variety of compounds (Gardner, 1980; Greenberg, 1980), but it does not satisfy all observations: The genetic trait of taste "blindness" to thiourea compounds implies the existence of a specific molecule for the recognition of at least this class of bitter substances (Kalmus, 1971).

While the molecular structures and binding mechanisms associated with bitter taste transduction are still unclear, the subsequent step—generation of a receptor potential—is better defined. Bitter alkaloids such as quinine elicit depolarization accompanied by an increase in membrane resistance (Akaike and Sato, 1976; Ozeki, 1971; Sato and Beidler, 1982), the signal, subsequently confirmed by patch–clamp recordings, that K^+ current is being blocked (Avenet and Lindemann, 1987; Kinnamon and Roper, 1988). In addition, depolarization has been shown to result from the efflux of Cl^- from taste cells upon stimulation by quinine (Okada *et al.*, 1988). Finally, denatonium chloride, the most bitter substance known to humans, works through an unidentified second messenger to release intracellular Ca^{2+} and so evoke transmitter release (Akabas *et al.*, 1988) (Fig. 4D). The relative contribution of these three mechanisms may vary with the bitter stimulus.

Since the processes by which sapid molecules are recognized and coded are not well defined, they may yet prove not to be as independent of one another as they now appear to be. It is doubtless, however, that the receptor mechanisms associated with various categories of taste qualities are rather distinct, certainly more so than the differences between receptor mechanisms for low versus high pitches, red versus green colors, or visual patterns generated by Pollock versus Mondrian.

B. STIMULUS CHARACTERISTICS

The foregoing makes it clear that stimulus characteristics are largely unrelated for each of the basic tastes. Lipophilicity may partly explain bitterness; however, it relates not at all to saltiness. There is no apparent single physical dimension on which the study of the sense of taste may be organized. This lack has hampered progress in nearly all aspects of taste research. If stimuli cannot be applied in an orderly manner—as one might step, for example, through wavelengths or sound pressure levels—responses cannot be evaluated in the proper context. Each stimulus–response pair must be treated as an isolated event, its relationship to other pairs gleaned only from subjective criteria. The inability to reveal a single dimension for gustation has even led to the suggestion that taste is not an integrated sensory system, but a series of independent modalities sensitive to different aspects of the chemical environment.

The introduction of multidimensional scaling techniques into taste research (Erickson *et al.*, 1965; Schiffman and Erickson, 1971) permitted a direct approach to this issue. A wide range of sapid stimuli could be applied, and the profile of either neural or behavioral activity that characterizes each chemical could be determined. Similarity measures among the profiles, provided, for example, by correlation coefficients, could then be used in a multidimensional scaling routine to generate a spatial representation of relative stimulus similarity.[1] The axes of the space must represent those stimulus characteristics that underlie gustatory discriminability, for the amount of each characteristic a stimulus possesses is what determines its taste quality, and hence its position in the space. Therefore, the dimensions along which taste quality is organized may be determined by finding the optimal match between a stimulus characteristic and each relevant axis of the multidimensional space. The importance of any characteristic in determining taste quality is proportional to the total data variance accounted for by the axis with which it is matched.

This approach has now been used to interpret both psychophysical (Schiffman and Erickson, 1971) and electrophysiological (Scott and Mark, 1987) data. The common result of these studies is that a major dimension along which taste stimuli may be organized relates not to any one physical feature of the molecule, but rather to a physiological characteristic: its effect on the welfare of the animal. Figure 5 shows a two-dimensional space in which 16 chemicals are placed according to the relative similarities of the neuronal response profiles they evoked from a sample of 42 taste cells in the rat NTS. The two dimensions of Fig. 5a account for 95% of the data variance, the preponderance of which—91%—pertains to dimension 1 alone. Thus, the stimulus characteristic that corresponds to this dimension is the major factor in permitting these chemicals to be neurally distinguished by the taste system. Stimulus placement on this dimension correlates 0.83 ($p < 0.001$) with stimulus toxicity, as indexed here by the rat oral LD_{50}. Stimulus toxicity, then, provides an excellent basis for predicting relative taste quality across a wide range of chemicals. This dimension is shown in isolation in Fig. 5b. Dimension 2, accounting for 4% of the variance, corresponds to differences in the effectiveness of various solutions in driving the system. The mean number of spikes evoked across all 42 neurons during the 5-sec response period correlates 0.76 ($p < 0.001$) with placement on this dimension, implying that it is a measure of total response magnitude.

While the relationship between LD_{50} and stimulus position on the dominant first dimension is highly significant, there are anomalies. Most notably, the organic acids—citric (LD_{50} = 11,700 mg/kg), lactic (3730 mg/kg), and acetic (3310 mg/kg)—all generate patterns that correlate about 0.90 with that of

---

[1] For example, the activity evoked from perhaps 50 single neurons by the application of saline to the subject's tongue would constitute the profile for NaCl. This profile may be compared with that representing each of the other stimuli by computing Pearson's product–moment correlation. The list of correlation coefficients so obtained offers a measure of the similarity of NaCl to each of the other stimuli used. Performing the same calculation between all possible pairs of profiles yields a full matrix of coefficients relating the relative taste qualities of all stimuli. This is similar to behavioral data, in which neuronal spikes may be replaced by the number of licks from a spout containing each stimulus, and human psychophysical data, in which a stimulus profile may be generated by the subject's level of agreement with each of a series of adjectives (adjectives replace neurons; level of agreement replaces spikes).

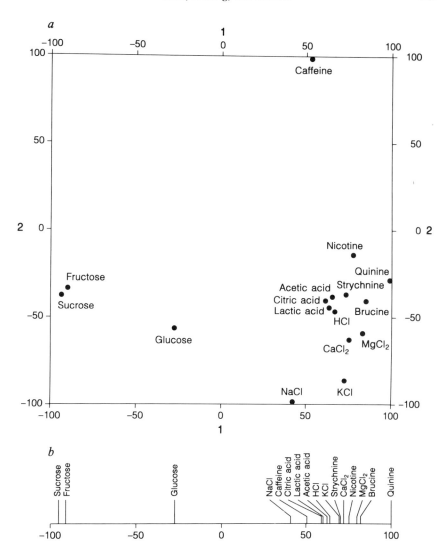

FIG. 5. (a) A two-dimensional space representing relative similarities among taste qualities, as determined by activity profiles across neurons. Dimension 1 accounts for 91% of the data variance, and the position of a stimulus on it correlates 0.83 ($p < 0.001$) with stimulus toxicity (rat oral LD_{50}). Dimension 2 accounts for 4% of the variance, and the position of a stimulus on it correlates 0.76 ($p < 0.001$) with total activity evoked across all neurons by each stimulus. Five percent of the variance is unaccounted for by these two dimensions. (b) Dimension 1 is shown in isolation. [Reprinted from Scott and Mark (1987) with permission.]

strychnine (5 mg/kg), despite the obvious difference in toxicity and the fact that behaving rats easily discriminate between strychnine and the acids. Thus, the animal has access to more information than is assayed by this analysis. This additional input may derive from the temporal character of the evoked response. In the analysis above, only the total spikes that accumulated from each stimulus application during 5 sec of evoked activity were considered. However, the neural response to each basic stimulus has a distinctive time course (Fig. 6) that not only carries reliable information regarding taste quality (DiLorenzo and Schwartzbaum, 1982; Nagai and Ueda, 1981) but may also be sufficient to activate appropriate reflexive responses to chemicals in behaving rats (Covey and Erickson, 1980). Therefore, temporal profiles, each composed of 50 100-msec bins, collapsed across neurons, were generated for every stimulus, and the correlation matrix and multidimensional representation were calculated as before. The result is shown in Fig. 7a. Dimension 1 is again dominant, accounting for 89% of the variance, and placement on it correlates 0.85 with LD_{50} ($p < 0.001$). It is represented in isolation in Fig. 7b. Dimension 2, accounting for 5% of the variance, is undefined.

The temporal analysis provides a solution to the confusion between strychnine and the organic acids, all of whose temporal discharge patterns correlate only in the low 0.40's with that of the alkaloid. It also introduces coefficients that would

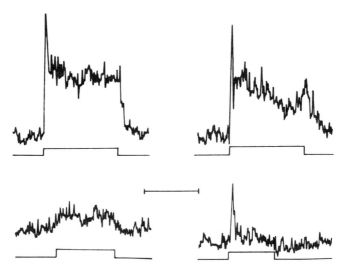

FIG. 6. Integrated multiunit activity evoked from lower-order neurons in the nucleus of the solitary tract by the four basic taste stimuli: (top left) 0.1 M NaCl; (top right) 30 mM HCl; (bottom left) 1.0 M sucrose; (bottom right) 10 mM quinine HCl. Time bar, 10 sec. [Reprinted from Scott (1981) with permission.]

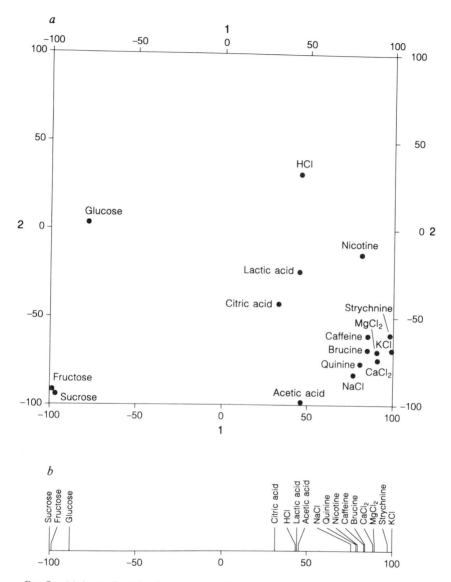

FIG. 7. (a) A two-dimensional space representing relative similarities among taste qualities, as determined by activity profiles across time. Dimension 1 accounts for 89% of the data variance, and the position of a stimulus on it correlates 0.85 ($p < 0.001$) with stimulus toxicity. Dimension 2 accounts for 5% of the variance and is undefined. Six percent of the variance is unaccounted for by these two dimensions. (b) Dimension 1 is shown in isolation. [Reprinted from Scott and Mark (1987) with permission.]

be troublesome (the temporal pattern of salty NaCl correlates in the high 0.80's with those of bitter $MgCl_2$ and $CaCl_2$) if the earlier analysis (in which these coefficients reach only the mid-0.50's) were not available. Certain stimulus pairs, then, are clearly discriminable based on the response distribution across either neurons or time. Other pairs (e.g., quinine and sucrose) are readily discriminable by both means. When neither factor provides separation, however— as with $MgCl_2$ and $CaCl_2$, whose across-neuron correlation is 0.91 and whose temporal correlation is 0.93—the rat cannot easily make a behavioral discrimination. The conclusion is that taste quality information in the hindbrain of the rat is carried in a spatiotemporal code, both the spatial and temporal aspects of which are organized predominantly along dimensions that relate to the rat's welfare.

By what mechanism does the code operate that signals LD_{50}? With regard to the spatial distribution of the response, this is undetermined, because our knowledge of the distribution of neurons within the NTS is limited. There is some suggestion of a chemotopic arrangement of neural sensitivity across the nucleus (Halpern and Nelson, 1965; Ishiko and Akogi, 1972; Scott et al., 1986a), such that the first dimension of Fig. 5a might correspond to a rostrocaudal progression across the NTS, but the evidence is not yet sufficiently precise to evaluate this notion. The basis for distinctions among temporal aspects of the responses, however, is more apparent: the phasic–tonic ratio of the evoked activity. The more toxic a chemical, the sharper the phasic burst of activity that initiates the evoked response. The ratio of evoked activity during the first second (phasic portion) to the mean activity during the next 4 sec (tonic portion) ranges from a mean of 0.64 for the three sugars to 2.34 for five alkaloids. Across all 16 stimuli, the phasic–tonic ratio correlates 0.75 ($p < 0.001$) with position on the first dimension of Fig. 7a. This time course corresponds to the sharp taste of toxins, in contrast to the smooth onset of tastes associated with carbohydrates, as reported in psychophysical studies (Schiffman and Erickson, 1971).

The discovery of a dimension of physiological welfare underlying the organization of taste quality coding is not simply the recreation of a sweet–bitter dichotomy. It is a more fundamental *physiological* dimension, on which the *psychological* dimensions of sweetness and bitterness may be based. Chemicals in the environment promote or disrupt physiological functions in animals, providing nutrition or causing illness or death. Selection among foragers, then, favors the taste system that activates the appropriate hedonic tone (viz., attraction to nutrients and revulsion by toxins) to match the physiological consequences of ingestion. The evolution of a system designed to distinguish the beneficial from the harmful is hardly unique to taste. The nonchemical senses permit the detection of predator and prey, and so promote escape from the former and capture of the latter. However, predator and prey are not coded as a survival dimension in the optic, trigeminal, or auditory nerves of mammals, as a welfare dimension is in the rat hindbrain. For this is the primary function of taste: not to provide a continuous record of the surroundings, but to sample the chemical environment discretely, to predict in each case the consequences of ingestion, and so to activate both hindbrain reflexes to ingest or expel and powerful hedonic components to motivate consumption or withdrawal. The sense of taste looks not just beyond the body, but within it. Its unifying organization is not physical, but physiological.

C. RESPONSES TO NUTRIENTS AND TOXINS

The effectiveness of the gustatory neural code in protecting the biochemical welfare of the animal has been demonstrated in a behavioral study in which naive rats under 18-hr fluid deprivation were offered free access to the same series of chemicals used in the electrophysiological study. Rats rejected these chemicals in direct proportion to stimulus toxicity ($r = 0.78$). The more strictly a stimulus was rejected by rats, the more likely it was to be described by humans as "bitter" or "nauseous"; chemicals avidly accepted by rats were labeled "sweet" or "pleasant." Thus, the neural dimension of nutrition–toxicity is directly related to the acceptance–rejection behavior of rats and is perceptually coded in the hedonics of pleasant or unpleasant sensations. With only a few exceptions, the better something tastes, the more nutritious it is.

The neural machinery to manage some of these reactions has been identified (Norgren, 1978; Travers, 1988). Gustatory input has at least four manifestations: (1) control of somatic reflexes for the immediate decision to swallow or expel, (2) if the former, then activation of parasympathetic reflexes to anticipate and aid the digestive process, (3) arousal of hedonic appreciation that sustains feeding, extending a bite into a meal, and a meal to a diet, and (4) determination of the quality and intensity of a stimulus.

1. Somatic Reflexes

Clusters of neurons in the ventral regions of gustatory NTS send their projections not rostrally, but ventrolaterally. These paths lead to salivatory and pharyngeal efferents in reticular formation, to the hypoglossal nucleus, and toward the facial and ambiguus nuclei, through which acceptance–rejection reflexes could be orchestrated. These reflexes are fully integrated in the hindbrain. They are stereotypical to each of the basic taste qualities and are unaltered by the loss of tissue rostral to the brain stem. In an exhaustive series of experiments, Steiner and colleagues studied orofacial responses to taste stimuli in normal adult humans, full-term and premature human neonates (Steiner, 1973), anencephalic and hydroanencephalic human neonates (Steiner, 1979), blind adolescents, patients with craniofacial abnormalities, retarded humans, and subhuman primates (Steiner and Glaser, 1985), mammals (Steiner, 1973), and birds. To the extent permitted by their various limitations, subjects across these phylogenetic, on-togenetic, and pathological ranges all reacted similarly to the application of basic taste stimuli. Steiner and co-workers concluded that facial expressions are adapt-ive both in dealing with the chemical (swallowing, if appetitive; clearing the mouth, if aversive) and also in communicating a hedonic dimension to other members of the species. Moreover, this chemical monitor is neurally intact by the seventh gestational month in humans (Steiner, 1979).

The same conclusion is obtained from studies in which the orofacial ex-pressions of intact and decerebrate rats (supracollicular plane of section) were monitored during the application of diverse taste stimuli (Grill and Norgren, 1978a). The reactions of decerebrates were nearly identical to those of normal rats to all taste qualities. Thus, the reflexes that support the acceptance or rejection of a taste solution are complete in the hindbrain.

2. Parasympathetic Reflexes

A second projection from the ventral NTS goes caudally, to ramify through the viscerosensory NTS and the dorsal motor nucleus of the vagus (DMNX), through which it may influence the autonomic processes of digestion. There are several cephalic phase pancreatic and gastrointestinal reflexes associated with ingestion, the best understood being the cephalic phase insulin response (CPIR) (Powley, 1977). Thousands of β cells in the rats' islets of Langerhans are stimulated to release insulin by fewer than 200 fibers coursing through the gastric and hepatic branches of the vagus (Powley et al., 1987). These fibers originate in the ros-tromedial section of the DMNX, which, in turn, is overlaid by the gustatory NTS as a cloth lies on an arm (Fig. 8). Neurons in the DMNX send apical dendrites into the NTS, effectively fusing the two structures (Powley and Berthoud, 1991) and offering gustatory input direct influence over autonomic reflexes. Accord-ingly, a sweet taste stimulus elicits insulin secretion, and this effect is blocked by vagotomy (Louis-Sylvestre and LeMagnen, 1980; Louis-Sylvestre et al., 1983). The CPIR is also eliminated if the sweet stimulus is paired with gastrointestinal distress to generate a conditioned taste aversion. As discussed in Section V,A, such a conditioning paradigm alters the gustatory code of a sweet stimulus, replacing the normal temporal character of a sugar response with a phasic burst of activity usually reserved for bitter stimuli (Chang and Scott, 1984). The loss of the CPIR following conditioning implies a parasympathetic manifestation of this change in the gustatory code.

3. Hedonic Appreciation

From dorsal areas of the gustatory NTS, axons proceed rostrally to the PBN, and then to the thalamus and the ventral forebrain. Parabrachial projections

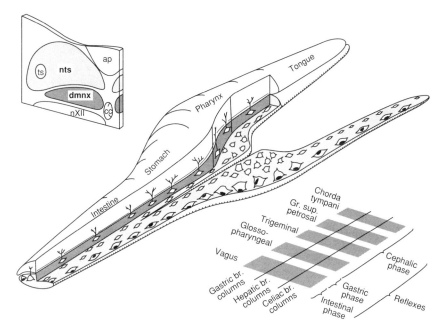

FIG. 8. Schematic illustration of the anatomical relationship between the dorsal motor nucleus of the vagus (dmnX) and the nucleus of the solitary tract (nts). Structures are shown from dorsal, caudal, and right lateral perspectives. The horizontal view shows the dmnX ventrally (shaded) on both sides of the brain stem, while the nts is dorsal (unshaded) and appears only on the left. A corresponding frontal view of a section through the left side of the vagal trigone is included in the upper left. In the lower right, the lattice arrangement between the dmnX and the nts is formalized. The longitudinal columns of the dmnX are orthogonal to the afferent fibers of the five nerves that serve the nts. The afferent nerves are listed on the left, and the corresponding reflexes are shown on the right. The afferent fibers are also translated into a viscerotopic map and expressed in terms of organs on the dorsal surface of the nts in the central drawing. ap, area postrema; cc, central canal. [Reprinted from Powley and Berthoud (1991) with permission.]

include the lateral hypothalamus, substantia innominata, central nucleus of the amygdala, and bed nucleus of the stria terminalis in their itinerary (Norgren, 1976). Moreover, the connections are reciprocal, with forebrain areas returning centrifugal projections to brain stem taste nuclei (Bereiter et al., 1979; Saper et al., 1976). Therefore, the rat's taste system communicates directly and reciprocally with structures associated with hedonics, feeding, and emotions.

It is not surprising, then, that taste input carries a hedonic tag, whose neural substrates have now been the subject of several studies. The preponderance of hypothalamic activity evoked by saccharin in rats shifted from the lateral to the ventromedial nucleus with formation of a conditioned taste aversion to saccharin (Aleksanyan et al., 1976). Presumably, the taste signal that formerly would have

256   **Thomas R. Scott**

provided the reinforcement implied by lateral hypothalamic activation had, through conditioning, acquired aversive sensory and motivational properties associated with the ventromedial nucleus. Accordingly, two groups of hypothalamic neurons have been identified in the alert rabbit: a rostral group at the anteroposterior level of the ventromedial nucleus that responded to aversive tastants and to conditioned stimuli that predicted them, and a group in the caudal lateral hypothalamus that was activated by hedonically positive stimuli (Schwartzbaum, 1988).

Moreover, taste-sensitive and visual lateral hypothalamic neurons in alert macaque monkeys gave decreasing responses to the taste of glucose as the monkeys consumed a glucose solution to satiety (Burton *et al.,* 1976) (Fig. 9). As the originally appetitive glucose became aversive, evoked activity ceased. Responsiveness to other appetitive stimuli remained, however, implying that satiety results from the suppression of activity to a specific stimulus in neurons that sustain positive hedonics—hence, the term "sensory-specific satiety" (Rolls *et al.,* 1981). The implication of all of these studies is that hedonic valence is represented topographically in the hypothalamus and that neural activity parallels, and may be responsible for, changes in hedonic appeal that result from conditioning or satiety.

Endogenous opioids may be implicated as the neurochemical basis for lateral

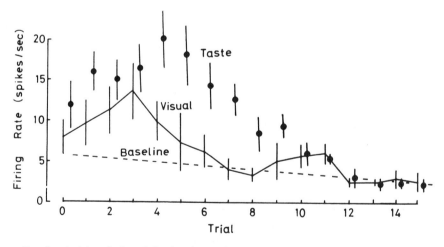

FIG. 9. Activity of a hypothalamic unit recorded in the squirrel monkey. The neuron was activated by the taste of glucose and by the sight of the glucose syringe if the monkey was hungry (trials 0–6), but not when satiated (trials 12–14). The taste-evoked response represents the mean ± SEM during the 5-sec period immediately following the application of 2 ml of 20% glucose on each trial. The baseline discharge rate is indicated by its regression line. [Reprinted from Burton *et al.* (1976) with permission.]

hypothalamic activation by appetitive tastes. There is a substantial body of evidence that sucrose elicits opioid release in the lateral hypothalamus that is not only responsible for its positive effect, but is also available to reduce stress. Therefore, sucrose is seen as transcending its role in feeding and taste to become a medication, and a plausible basis for stress-induced feeding is established (Bertiere *et al.*, 1984; Blass, 1986). These effects, and the intake of sucrose itself, are suppressed by the opioid antagonists naloxone and naltrexone (Ostrowski *et al.*, 1980).

Regions of the rat's lateral hypothalamus that sustain stimulus-bound feeding project to the PBN and the NTS, activating taste-sensitive neurons much as they would be driven by gustatory stimuli (Murzi *et al.*, 1986). Therefore, the hypothalamus has the capacity to impose a bias on taste input, presumably according to the animal's nutritional state. These descending influences may underlie changes in gustatory activity that have been reported in the rat with sodium deprivation (Jacobs *et al.*, 1988) or with increasing satiety (Giza and Scott, 1983, 1987b; Glenn and Erickson, 1976).

Other limbic areas are also involved in mediating the hedonic consequences of taste. Positive reinforcement is associated with increased dopamine (DA) activity in the limbic system (Hoebel, 1984; Wise *et al.*, 1978) and with declines in acetylcholine (Ach) concentration in the nucleus accumbens (Rada *et al.*, 1991) and serotonin (5-HT) in the hypothalamus (Stanley *et al.*, 1989). Therefore, the release of DA is thought to be related to hedonically positive experiences, while the reverse is true for ACh and 5-HT. A saccharin solution placed on the rat's tongue evoked DA release in the nucleus accumbens, in accordance with its reinforcing value (Mark *et al.*, 1991a). If the saccharin had been paired with nausea to create a conditioned taste aversion, however, the same taste stimulus, now aversive to the rat, caused a reduction in DA (Mark *et al.*, 1991b), and instead released ACh in the nucleus accumbens (Mark *et al.*, 1991a) and 5-HT in the lateral hypothalamus (West *et al.*, 1991). Thus, the neurochemical basis for the reinforcing value of saccharin was lost. Conversely, it has been possible to form a conditioned taste *preference* by pairing a neutral taste with intragastric infusions of carbohydrates, such that the taste became associated with nutritional repletion (Sclafani, 1991a). The acquired taste subsequently evoked an increase in DA activity in the nucleus accumbens (Mark *et al.*, 1991c), in accord with its rewarding properties.

Other ventral forebrain regions, notably those associated with motivation and reward, are undoubtedly engaged in the hedonic coding of taste stimuli as well, although their involvement has yet to be documented. However, hedonic appreciation is not the exclusive province of the ventral forebrain. Even the impassive cortex has been shown to encode the appeal of tastants. In recordings from the gustatory cortex of licking rats, a small number of cells was found whose discharge rates were a function of hedonic appeal (Yamamoto *et al.*, 1984, 1989).

As detailed in Section V,B,2, hedonically driven neurons may not exist in the primary gustatory cortex of the macaque monkey (Rolls *et al.*, 1988). However, cells in the secondary (orbitofrontal) cortex reacted in the same manner as did those in the hypothalamus, responding with declining vigor as an initially appetitive glucose solution lost its appeal with repeated offering (Rolls *et al.*, 1989). As in the hypothalamus, cortical responses to other taste qualities were undiminished.

4. Discrimination of Quality and Intensity

Humans do appear to make discriminations among the qualities and concentrations of gustatory stimuli, independently of hedonic evaluations (Rolls *et al.*, 1981). Electrophysiological recordings from the primary (insular–opercular) taste cortex of the alert macaque monkey suggest that quality and intensity information is represented here. Concentration–response functions for all basic taste stimuli except HCl are in good accord with those reported in human psychophysical experiments. Thus, evoked discharge rates in the monkey cortex accurately predict the taste intensity perceived by a human observer (Scott *et al.*, 1991). Taste quality, as indexed by the correlations among patterns of activity evoked by a wide range of tastants in the monkey cortex, matched well with the perceived similarity of the same stimuli, as reported by humans (Kuznicki and Ashbaugh, 1979; Schiffman *et al.*, 1980; Smith-Swintosky *et al.*, 1991) (Fig. 10). The same close association between neural and psychophysical data extended to investigations of amino acids (Plata-Salaman *et al.*, 1992a; Schiffman and Dackis, 1979) and to the subtle distinctions among stimuli, all of which were predominantly sweet (Plata-Salaman *et al.*, 1992b; Schiffman *et al.*, 1979), salty (Plata-Salaman *et al.*, 1990; Schiffman *et al.*, 1980), or sour (Settle *et al.*, 1986; Smith *et al.*, 1990). Therefore, activity in the primary taste cortex of the alert macaque monkey appears to serve the gustatory discriminative capacity of the primate.

Together, the hindbrain, limbic, and cortical sequelae of gustatory input manage the reflexes, hedonic appreciation, and discriminative capacity, respectively, associated with taste.

V. Alterations in the Taste Signal

In the preceding section, I proposed that the taste system is organized to perform a general differentiation of toxins from nutrients, and that this ability is genetically endowed on animals that foraged successfully in a chemically inhospitable environment. Moreover, this analysis is accomplished at a lower-order neural level and directly influences hindbrain somatic and autonomic reflexes,

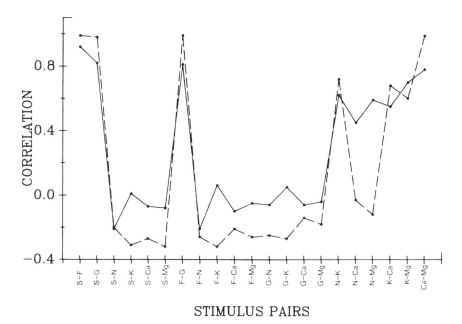

STIMULUS PAIRS

FIG. 10. Relationship between response profiles of stimulus quality generated from human psychophysical responses (dashed line) and from electrophysiological data from the monkey's taste cortex (solid line). The correlation between each stimulus pair is nearly identical by these two approaches, with the exception of those between bitter and salty salts (NaCl versus CaCl₂ and MgCl₂). [Human psychophysical data are from Kuznicki and Ashbaugh (1979); monkey electrophysiological data are from Smith-Swintosky *et al.* (1991), from which the figure is reprinted with permission.]

powerful limbic hedonic mechanisms, and cortical discriminative processes. While providing a broad and effective system for maintaining the biochemical welfare of the species, this organization would not recognize the idiosyncratic allergies or needs of the individual or be sensitive to changes in these needs over time. Physiological needs are in constant flux. In just hours or days, the definition of which chemicals are acceptable may be subject to modification as the dangers of malnutrition weigh against those of toxicity. Thus, a starving animal will accept a wider variety of tastes than one that is sated. After only minutes of feeding, the balance may reverse again. If taste is to provide the information on which the digital decision to swallow or expel is based, its signals should be modifiable to reflect these changing conditions. There is now a body of experimental data demonstrating that taste activity can indeed be modified to accommodate the individual experiences and momentary physiological needs of an animal.

A. PLASTICITY BASED ON EXPERIENCE

An animal's experience has a pronounced and lasting influence on its behavioral reaction to taste stimuli. The gustatory history of suckling rats establishes taste preferences that persist into adulthood (Capretta and Rawls, 1974). Preferences also develop through the association of taste with positive reinforcement, particularly with a visceral reinforcement such as occurs with the administration of a nutrient of which the animal has been deprived (Revusky et al., 1971). Compensatory feeding behavior has been demonstrated in cases of experimentally induced deficiencies of thiamine (Seward and Greathouse, 1973), threonine (Halstead and Gallagher, 1962), and histidine (Sanahuja and Harper, 1962). It is hypothesized that the physiological benefits of dietary repletion are paired with the taste that preceded these benefits, creating a conditioned taste preference.

Even in freely feeding rats, tastes that are paired with intragastric nutrients quickly come to be preferred, a process that can overwhelm and reverse innate aversions to sour or bitter substances (Sclafani, 1991a). Whether this increased acceptance implies a more positive hedonic valence for the tastant has not yet been determined. It has been argued that rats might accept a formerly aversive stimulus because they associate it with beneficial consequences, rather than because they have come to "like" it (Rozin and Zellner, 1985).

There is evidence supporting both possibilities. Even after developing a strong preference for a stimulus, rats showed no change in their orofacial reactions to its administration. Therefore, the somatic reflexes driven by taste quality were unaltered, implying that the gustatory signal was unaffected by conditioning (Sclafani, 1991b). This is not a definitive result, however, because of both the insensitivity of the test as applied in this study and the undetermined relationship between orofacial reactivity and hedonic appreciation. A more direct assessment of a possible change in hedonic value is offered by the finding, cited earlier, that the taste stimulus causes augmented dopamine release in the nucleus accumbens following preference conditioning (Mark et al., 1991b). It would be instructive to monitor the gustatory neural code evoked by the taste in naive and conditioned rats to determine whether it assumes a closer relationship with hedonically positive chemicals.

Since effective procedures for creating conditioned taste preferences have only recently been developed, little is known of their effects on the nervous system. Not so, however, for conditioned taste aversions (CTAs). The CTA involves an especially efficient form of conditioning in which an intense aversion may be developed through a single pairing of a novel taste [the conditioned stimulus (CS)] with gastrointestinal malaise [the unconditioned stimulus (US)] (Garcia et al., 1955). The aversion to a conditioned taste solution is so readily established, so potent and resistant to extinction, that the CTA protocol itself has become a standard tool for studying physiological processes and taste-related behavior (Smotherman and Levine, 1978).

The neural substrates of conditioned taste aversions have been investigated in scores of experiments, most of which have involved ablating selected structures and testing the ability of subjects to retain former CTAs or develop subsequent aversions. Although these studies have implicated the cortex, amygdala, hippocampus, hypothalamus, thalamus, olfactory bulb, and area postrema as having some involvement in aversion learning, only amygdaloid and hypothalamic participation seems unequivocal. Rarely have recordings been made from neurons of conditioned animals to determine the effects of a CTA on taste-evoked activity. Aleksanyan *et al.* (1976) reported that the preponderance of hypothalamic activity evoked by saccharin in rats shifted from the lateral to the ventromedial nucleus with formation of a saccharin CTA. Thus, the nature of the taste stimulus was presumed to shift from appetitive to aversive. DiLorenzo (1985) recorded the responses evoked by a series of taste stimuli in the PBN of rats, then paired the taste of NaCl with gastrointestinal malaise and repeated the recordings. The response to NaCl increased significantly and selectively in a subset of gustatory neurons.

Chang and Scott (1984) recorded single-unit gustatory-evoked activity from the NTS of three groups of rats: unconditioned (exposed only to the taste of the saccharin CS with no induced nausea), pseudoconditioned (experienced only the US, nausea, with no gustatory referent), and conditioned (taste of saccharin CS paired with nausea). Comparisons were performed among the groups' responses to an array of 12 stimuli, including the saccharin CS, a more concentrated saccharin solution, and saccharides, salts, acids, and an alkaloid, through which alterations in the entire gustatory code resulting from this taste experience could be evaluated.

In Fig. 11, the 50 neurons of each group are ranked according to their responsiveness to the CS. There was a 65% increase in evoked activity that was restricted to the 13 cells that gave the largest saccharin responses in conditioned rats. Temporal analyses of the activity evoked from this subgroup of saccharin-sensitive neurons revealed that nearly the entire increase in discharge rate was attributable to a burst of activity that diverged from control group levels 600 msec following stimulus onset, reached a peak at 900 msec, and returned to control levels by 3000 msec (Fig. 12). Thus, the major consequence of the conditioning procedure was to increase responsiveness to the saccharin CS through a well-defined peak of activity. The same enhanced response and temporal pattern were evoked to a lesser extent by other sweet stimuli—fructose, glucose, and sucrose—providing a likely neural counterpart to generalization of the aversion.

Since a range of taste stimuli was used in this study, the effect of an increased response to the CS and related chemicals could be evaluated in terms of taste quality. The pattern of activity evoked by saccharin was altered by the conditioning procedure. How did the new pattern relate to those of other chemicals? Correlation matrices were calculated, and multidimensional spaces were con-

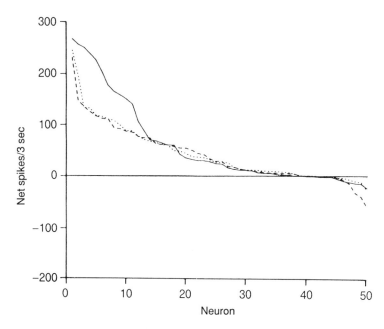

FIG. 11.   Responses of 50 individual neurons in each of three groups of rats to 0.0025 M sodium saccharin, the conditioned stimulus. The control group (dotted line) experienced only the sodium saccharin taste with no malaise; the pseudoconditioned group (dashed line) experienced malaise with no clear gustatory referent; the conditioned taste aversion group (solid line) experienced three pairings of sodium saccharin taste with lithium-induced nausea. Only the neurons most sensitive to sodium saccharin were influenced by the conditioning procedure. [Reprinted from Chang and Scott (1984) with permission.]

structed (as described earlier) in three dimensions from the response profiles of unconditioned and conditioned rats (Fig. 13). In the former group (Fig. 13a), representing a normally functioning taste system, the stimulus arrangement was similar to that seen by others (Doetsch and Erickson, 1970). The basic distinction between sweet and nonsweet chemicals was apparent, as was the precise arrangement of stimuli within the nonsweet group: The four Na–Li salts should have been virtually indistinguishable by the neural patterns they elicited here. The complex sweet–salty–bitter taste of concentrated (0.25 M) sodium saccharin was represented appropriately between the sweet and nonsweet clusters. The consequence of the conditioning procedure was to disrupt this clear organization (Fig. 13b). The relative similarity among nonsweet qualities was reduced; the sharp distinction between sweet and nonsweet was blurred. Moreover, the relative increase in similarity between sweet and nonsweet chemicals was differential, with the greatest increase between the saccharin CS and bitter quinine. The rearrangement was so decisive that quinine was nearly as close to the sweet CS as it was to the acids, a finding that would be quite aberrant in a normally functioning taste system.

This convergence of the afferent profiles for the saccharin CS and quinine may offer a neural basis for the similar behavioral reaction evoked by quinine and sweet chemicals to which an aversion has been conditioned (Berridge *et al.*, 1981; Grill and Norgren, 1978b; Pelchat *et al.*, 1983). The altered gustatory code for the formerly sweet CS may also underlie the abolition of the CPIR observed after aversive conditioning (Louis-Sylvestre and LeMagnen, 1980; Louis-Sylvestre *et al.*, 1983) as well as the decline in dopamine release at the nucleus accumbens (Mark *et al.*, 1991c).

There are other implications of these findings for the interrelationship between taste and feeding. First, they reinforce the reports by others that the responses of brain stem, and indeed hindbrain, taste neurons are subject to modification by experience. Second, conditioned aversions, which, in humans, affect primarily the hedonic evaluation of the CS rather than its perceived quality, caused a rearrangement of the neural taste space that was based on responses from the

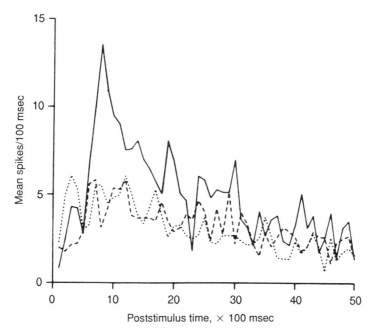

Fig. 12.   Poststimulus time histograms of the mean responses among sweet-sensitive neurons to the conditioned stimulus, 0.0025 *M* sodium saccharin. Activity is shown for control (dotted line), pseudoconditioned (dashed line), and conditioned (solid line) rats. The enhanced activity during the first 3 sec of the evoked response in conditioned animals may represent the increased salience of the sodium saccharin taste. [Reprinted from Chang and Scott (1984) with permission.]

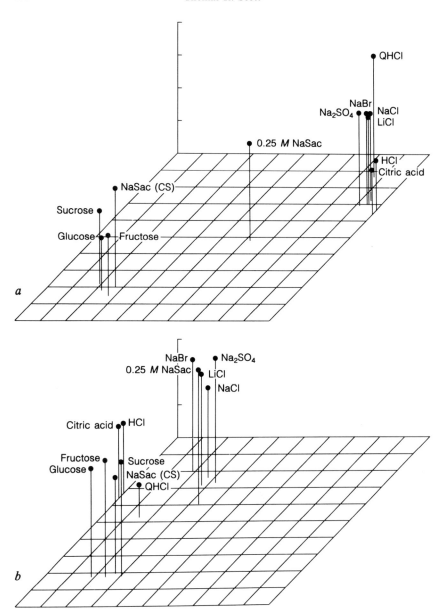

FIG. 13. Three-dimensional spaces representing relative similarities among stimuli, as determined from neural responses in (a) the control group and (b) the conditioned group of rats. Sodium
saccharin [NaSac (CS)] is fixed at the same coordinates in each space. QHCl, Quinine HCl.
[Reprinted from Chang and Scott (1984) with permission.]

NTS in rats. This suggests that the hindbrain code in rats combines sensory discrimination with a hedonic component in a way that it does not in humans, a point to which I return in Section V,B. Finally, activity in these intact animals was modified in ways appropriate for mediation of the behavioral aversion, yet decerebrate rats—with NTS and its vagal afferents intact—are incapable of learning or retaining a CTA (Grill and Norgren, 1978b). This implies hypothalamic or amygdaloid involvement in the processes expressed in the NTS, given the association of these areas with motivation and hedonics, their required integrity for aversion learning to proceed (Kemble and Nagel, 1973), and their close reciprocal anatomical relationship with the NTS. A direct test of this implication, however, refuted it. Decerebrate rats were treated with the same conditioning protocol as were the intact animals. Subsequent recordings from the NTS disclosed a peak of activity to the CS with virtually the same relative amplitude and time course as reported above (Mark and Scott, 1988). Thus, the source of the modification must be located caudal to the colliculi (the plane of decerebration).

Finally, the persistence of these neural effects was assessed in a group of rats in whom an aversion to saccharin was conditioned and then extinguished over several weeks. Despite the fact that these recovered animals were behaviorally indistinguishable from unconditioned controls, the 900-msec peak of activity that served as the neural signature of the conditioning remained, albeit in attenuated form (Nolan and Scott, 1992). Thus, a neural trace of the earlier experience persisted, and with it a basis for the ease with which such an aversion may be reconditioned.

The formation of a conditioned taste aversion to saccharin resulted in a modification of the gustatory code from one that resembled those of sugars to one more akin to the code for quinine. Accordingly, (1) somatic orofacial reflexes reversed from acceptance to rejection, (2) autonomic reflexes that would normally have evoked a CPIR were no longer engaged, and (3) the presumed neurochemical basis for the hedonic reward of sweetness—dopamine release in limbic areas—was lost. The consequences of replacing a "sweet" with a "bitter" signal were manifested throughout the various components of the ingestive process. The remarkable plasticity of the gustatory afferent code at the level of the medulla was sufficient to explain all of the reflexive and hedonic consequences of a conditioned aversion.

B. Plasticity Based on Physiological Need

The momentary nutritional status of an animal has a major impact on feeding behavior. Since physiological needs are complex and in constant flux, the hedonic value of the taste perceptions that guide feeding may be correspondingly labile.

1. Long-Term Needs: The Taste for Sodium

A constant and perhaps innate preference exists for sodium. Evolving in so-dium-deficient environments, most mammals seek out and consume salt wherev-er it is to be found and, when plentiful, consume it in excess of need. Both rats and humans select sodium salts in their diets even when sodium replete (Denton, 1976; Richter, 1936). This preference becomes exaggerated under conditions of salt deficiency. Humans depleted by pathological states (Wilkins and Richter, 1940) or by experimental manipulations (McCance, 1936) often show a pro-nounced craving for salt. Rodents subjected to uncontrolled urinary sodium loss following adrenalectomy (Clark and Clausen, 1943; Epstein and Stellar, 1955), to dietary sodium restrictions (Fregley et al., 1965), or to acute loss of plasma volume (Stricker and Jalowiec, 1970) show sharp increases in salt consumption. This compensatory response to the physiological need for salt results from a change in the hedonic value of tasted sodium. Concentrations of NaCl that had been evaluated negatively and rejected under conditions of sodium repletion evoke a positive hedonic response and acceptance in deprivation. The hedonic change has been thought to follow from a decreased gustatory sensitivity to salt that accompanies sodium depletion (Contreras, 1977). The responses of single fibers in the chorda tympani nerve to NaCl were analyzed in replete and sodium-deficient rats. Depletion was accompanied by a specific reduction in salt respon-siveness among the 40% of fibers that were most sodium sensitive (Contreras and Frank, 1979). This decreased sensitivity could result in the observed shift of the acceptance curve to higher concentrations.

This intensity-based interpretation has recently been recast by Jacobs et al. (1988). Recording from central taste neurons in the NTS, these researchers confirmed a moderate overall reduction in responsiveness to sodium in salt-deprived rats. Separate analyses of activity among different neuron types, how-ever, revealed that the responsiveness of the salt-sensitive group of cells to NaCl was profoundly depressed and that this effect was partially offset by a remarkable increase in sensitivity to NaCl among sweet-sensitive neurons. This reversal of roles was so decisive that the proportion of NaCl-evoked activity carried through the salt-sensitive gustatory channel plummeted from 60% to 7%, while the proportion in the sweet-sensitive channel rose from 1% to 46%. The net effect was to transfer the burden of coding sodium from salt- to sweet-sensitive neu-rons. This implies a change not so much in perceived intensity as in perceived quality in sodium-deficient rats: Salt should now taste "sweet" or, if sweetness is only a human construct, perhaps "good" to such an animal. Multidimensional spaces based on the responses of replete and sodium-deprived rats confirm the shifts in the neural codes for sodium and lithium salts toward those of sucrose and fructose (Fig. 14). This interpretation explains the eagerness with which deprived rats consume sodium, an avidity not shown for any concentration of NaCl, but usually reserved for the ingestion of sugars. Accordingly, the aversive

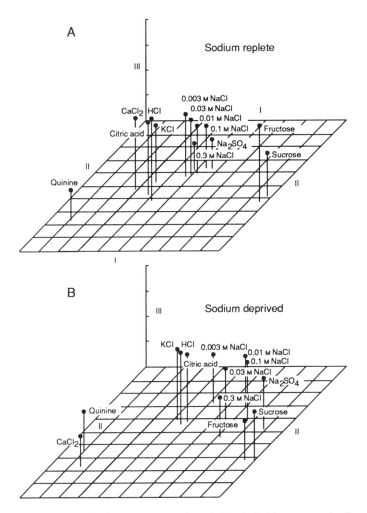

FIG. 14.   Three-dimensional spaces representing relative similarities among stimuli, as determined from neural responses in (A) sodium-replete and (B) sodium-deprived rats. (A) The space
derived from replete rats is typical of a normally functioning taste system. A major division is
between sweet and nonsweet stimuli. Within nonsweet compounds, distinctions are possible among
salts, acids, and quinine. (B) The space representing stimulus quality in sodium-deprived animals
differs in that sodium salts make a closer approach to the sugars. [Reprinted from Jacobs *et al.* (1988)
with permission.]

reactions normally associated with the taste of concentrated NaCl were replaced
by a full sequence of ingestive reflexes (Berridge *et al.*, 1984) and by a significant release of DA in the nucleus accumbens of sodium-deficient rats (Chang *et
al.*, 1988).

We saw in the previous section that a conditioned taste aversion could shift the sensory profile of the conditioned stimulus from one highly correlated with sugars to one more like quinine. In consequence, somatic reflexes reversed from acceptance to rejection, autonomic reflexes associated with foods were suppressed, and limbic DA, whose release is associated with reward, was blocked. Here, we see the converse. Sodium deprivation shifted the profile of concentrated NaCl toward those of the sugars. Reflexive behavior switched from rejection to acceptance, and limbic DA was elicited in conjunction with the powerful reinforcement now evoked by salt. In both the negative and positive cases, changes in gustatory afferent activity in the hindbrain were sufficient to account for the subsequent feeding behavior and the reward derived from it.

2. Serving Transient Needs

While the appreciation of amino acid or sodium deficiency occurs over a period of days, the availability of glucose is of almost hourly concern in a small homeothermic mammal. There must be accommodation of the decision to swallow or reject, and in the hedonic evaluation that drives this decision, as the danger of malnutrition weighs more heavily against the risk of ingesting a toxin. Common experience reinforces the results of psychophysical studies: With deprivation, foods become more palatable; with satiety, less so (Cabanac, 1971; Campbell, 1958; Rolls et al., 1981). The following body of evidence suggests that these effects are also mediated by alterations in gustatory afferent activity.

a. Peripheral Nervous System. Gastric distension is associated with a reduction in the responsiveness of gustatory receptor cells in undeprived frogs (Sharma and Doss, 1973). Conversely, only mild deprivation correlates with increases in the size and decreases in the latency of taste-evoked activity in the glossopharyngeal nerve. Physical distension of the stomach abolishes this effect within 1 min (Dua-Sharma et al., 1973), while chemical stimulation with peptone suppresses the amplitude of peripheral taste-evoked activity (Sharma et al., 1977). Brush and Halpern (1970) monitored glossopharyngeal responses in food-deprived toads and noted variable effects of gastric distension, involving either increases or decreases to specific taste stimuli. All modulatory effects were lost with bilateral transection of the glossopharyngeal nerve, implying that the influence of physiological state on gustatory activity may be mediated by efferent fibers in peripheral taste nerves. Accordingly, Hellekant (1971) suggested that receptor inhibition could result from alterations in efferent activity of the chorda tympani nerve, which he found to be induced by gastric distension in rats. An alternate path of influence may be through the vagus nerve, whose bilateral transection reduces or abolishes these phenomena (Sharma et al., 1977).

b. Central Nervous System. The effects of deprivation and satiety extend to the CNS. Recordings of multiunit activity in the NTS of freely fed rats show a pattern of differential modification similar to that seen in the periphery (Glenn and Erickson, 1976). Gastric distension by air or by 0.3 M NaCl selectively depressed responses in the NTS, with the greatest effect on activity evoked by sucrose, followed, in diminishing order, by NaCl, HCl, and quinine HCl, the responses to which were unmodified. Relief from distension reversed this effect within 45 min. If the rats were severely deprived, however, the influence of gastric distension was lost, suggesting that the modulating processes may be sensitive to the overall nutritive state of the animal.

The effects of other satiety factors on taste-evoked activity in the NTS have also been investigated (Giza and Scott, 1983). Multiunit responses to the four basic stimuli were recorded before and after intravenous loads of 0.5 g/kg of glucose or a vehicle. The glucose infusion had a selectively suppressive effect on taste activity. Elevated blood glucose was associated with a significant reduction in gustatory responsiveness to glucose, with the maximum effect occurring 8 min following the intravenous load (Fig. 15). Recovery took place over 60 min as blood glucose approached normal levels. Responsiveness to NaCl and HCl was suppressed to a lesser degree and for a briefer period, while quinine-induced activity was unaffected.

Hyperglycemia induces a rise in insulin levels through endogenous release. Insulin itself has been reported to depress feeding when it is administered in physiological doses that fall short of causing pronounced hypoglycemia (Lovett and Booth, 1970; VanderWeele et al., 1980, 1982). Thus, the effects of mild hyperinsulinemia on taste responses were also monitored (Giza and Scott,

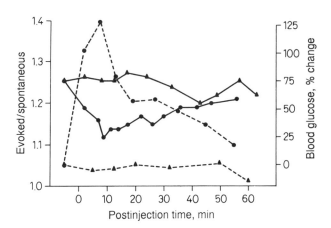

FIG. 15.   Mean blood glucose levels (dashed lines) and gustatory evoked responses (solid lines) to the taste of glucose. The values for vehicle-injected control rats are represented by triangles; those for glucose-injected experimental animals are indicated by circles. Responsiveness to tasted glucose declines, and then recovers in a mirror image of the animals' blood glucose levels. [Reprinted from Giza and Scott (1983) with permission.]

1987b). An intravenous load of 0.5 U/kg of regular insulin caused a sharp rise in plasma insulin, with a return to baseline over 90 min. This was accompanied by a modest decline in plasma glucose levels that was insufficient to initiate hypoglycemic feeding (Steffans, 1969). Concomitantly, glucose-evoked taste activity was significantly suppressed, returning to baseline levels within 20 min. Responses to fructose were similarly affected, but activity evoked by NaCl, HCl, and quinine was unaltered.

Pancreatic glucagon induces glycogenolysis in the liver, and therefore an increase in circulating glucose levels. Its administration is associated with a reduction in appetite and food intake in humans (Schulman *et al.*, 1957; Stunkard *et al.*, 1955) and several other species (Geary and Smith, 1982a; Levine *et al.*, 1984; VanderWeele *et al.*, 1980). The effects of glucagon are specific to feeding, for grooming, exploratory behavior, motor coordination, and fluid intake are unaffected (Geary and Smith, 1982a,b). Therefore, the effects of intrahepatic portal injections of 40 μg/kg of glucagon on taste activity in the rat NTS were explored. Plasma glucose levels rose within 5 min of glucagon administration, and remained elevated for 30 min. During this period, taste responsiveness to glucose declined significantly, then returned to baseline levels after 35 min. Responses to NaCl, HCl, and quinine did not change (Giza *et al.*, 1992).

Cholecystokinin has also been shown to decrease food intake (Gibbs *et al.*, 1973) and to elicit the full behavioral sequence that accompanies satiety (Antin *et al.*, 1978). However, the intravenous administration of 2 and 6 μg/kg of cholecystokinin had no effect on taste activity in the rat NTS (Giza *et al.*, 1990).

Therefore, the exogenous administration of glucose, insulin, and glucagon—but not cholecystokinin—was associated with reductions in the afferent activity evoked by hedonically positive tastes (Fig. 16).[2] This implies that the pleasure that sustains feeding is reduced, making termination of the meal more likely.

As taste responsiveness decreased with satiety, so the parasympathetic reflexes elicited by chemosensory stimulation declined in parallel. Both salivary secre-

[2]A common attribute of the three effective agents is that they increase the availability of utilizable glucose. Direct glucose infusions raise circulating glucose levels, stimulate insulin secretion, and thereby increase glucose availability. Insulin administration promotes glucose absorption from the blood into peripheral tissues. Infusions of both insulin and glucose raise glucose utilization rapidly at several peripheral sites. In fed animals, glucagon increases plasma glucose through liver glycogenolysis and stimulates insulin secretion.

Bradley (1973) has shown that vascular glucose, in sufficient concentration, may stimulate gustatory receptors, raising the possibility that the suppressed responses to sugars may have resulted from receptor adaptation. Such a mechanism is improbable. Circulating glucose concentrations never exceeded 25% of the 0.5 *M* threshold for receptor stimulation, and background activity in the NTS did not increase with injections of glucose, insulin, or glucagon, as would be expected if intravascular glucose were stimulating taste receptors. Moreover, hepatic vagotomy reduces the influence of glucose infusions on taste responsiveness, implying that vagal input to the NTS is a necessary feature of the link between circulating glucose and taste.

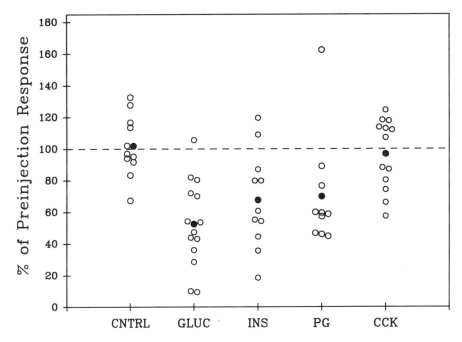

FIG. 16.   A summary of the influence of satiety factors on taste. The mean response during the 10-min intervals in which each injected chemical reached its maximum effect is shown as a proportion of the rat's preinjection response (open circles). Mean values for each group are represented by solid circles. CNTRL, Vehicle injection only; GLUC, 0.5 g/kg of glucose; INS, 0.5 U/kg of insulin; PG, 40 μg/kg of pancreatic glucagon; CCK, 2.0 μg/kg of cholecystokinin-8. Every chemical that resulted in the delivery of utilizable calories to the brain was associated with a suppression of taste responsiveness to glucose. [Reprinted from Giza *et al.* (1992) with permission.]

tions and the CPIR were suppressed as a direct function of the level of satiety in humans (Sahakian *et al.*, 1981).

If taste activity in NTS is affected by the rat's nutritional state, then intensity judgments should change with satiety. Psychophysical studies of human subjects, while not fully consistent among themselves, generally do not support this position. Humans typically report that the hedonic value of appetitive tastes declines with satiety, but that intensity judgments are affected to a lesser extent, if at all (Rolls *et al.*, 1981; Thompson *et al.*, 1976). There are at least three levels of ambiguity that cloud the interpretation of these conflicting results: the neural level from which the data derive, anesthetic effects, and species differences. The electrophysiological data were taken from the hindbrains of anesthetized rats; the psychophysical responses presumably reflected some involvement of cortical processes in alert humans. A resolution of the implied conflict, then, requires an analysis of both intensity perceptions in the rat and taste-evoked activity in the human hindbrain.

To examine intensity perception in the rat, a conditioned taste aversion paradigm was used (Scott and Giza, 1987). Rats were presented with 1.0 M glucose for 15 min, then were injected intraperitoneally with LiCl. Following recovery, they were briefly exposed to test concentrations of glucose ranging from 0.0 to 4.0 M, and lick rates were determined. With increasing test concentrations of glucose, acceptance was sharply reduced, yielding a measure of perceived intensity (Fig. 17, dashed line). This acceptance gradient, derived from normal rats, was then compared to a gradient generated by identical means in rats with intravenous glucose loads (Fig. 17, solid line). Hyperglycemic rats showed greater acceptance at all concentrations from 0.6 to 2.0 M glucose, indicating that they perceived these stimuli to be less intense than did conditioned rats with no glucose load (Giza and Scott, 1987a). Thus, the neural suppression in the hindbrain that results from an intravenous glucose load appears to be manifested in the perception of reduced intensity.

While it is reassuring that the rat's behavior conforms to the implications of its neural responsiveness, the original conflict remains unresolved. To complete the puzzle, information is needed on the influence of satiety on taste-evoked activity at various synaptic levels in humans. The closest available approximation to these data may be supplied by subhuman primates. First, the response characteristics of taste neurons in the NTS of cynomolgus monkeys were defined (Scott

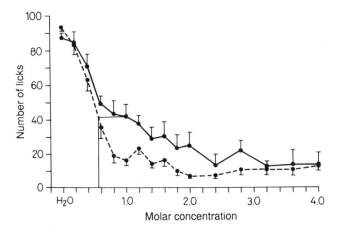

Fig. 17.   Number of licks as a function of glucose stimulus concentration in control rats (dashed line) and in those who received an intravenous glucose load (solid line). The horizontal and vertical lines indicate that animals under a glucose load reacted to 1.00 M glucose, as did control rats to 0.54 M glucose, implying a 46% reduction in perceived intensity at this concentration. [Reprinted from Scott and Giza (1987) with permission.]

et al., 1986a). Then, the activity of small clusters of these cells was monitored as mildly food-deprived monkeys were fed to satiety with glucose (Yaxley *et al.*, 1985). Satiety was measured behaviorally as the monkeys progressed from avid acceptance to active rejection of glucose, typically consuming 200–300 ml (Fig. 18, bottom of each frame). Despite the effects of gastric distension and elevated blood glucose levels this procedure was designed to induce, the responsiveness of NTS neurons to the taste of a range of solutions, including glucose, was unmodified (Fig. 18, top of each frame). These results are in stark contrast to those reported in anesthetized rats, in which similar physiological manipulations caused a reduction of up to 50% in responsiveness to sugars (Giza and Scott, 1983; Glenn and Erickson, 1976).

The same approach has been extended to single cells in cortical taste areas of the frontal operculum (Rolls *et al.*, 1988) and the anterior insula (Yaxley *et al.*, 1989, 1990) with similar results. Therefore, it appears that the decreased acceptance and the reduced hedonic value associated with satiety do not result from a decrement in gustatory responsiveness at any level up to and including the primary gustatory cortex. Rather, activity here was related to sensory quality, independent of the monkey's physiological state.

The situation changed when neurons of the monkey's orbitofrontal cortex (OFC) were studied (Rolls *et al.*, 1985). Taste-responsive cells showed vigorous activity to preferred solutions if the monkey was deprived. As satiety increased—and acceptance turned to rejection—responsiveness declined to near the spontaneous rate (Fig. 19). Activity elicited by other stimuli, however, even those to whose qualities the taste of the satiating stimulus would readily generalize, was unmodified (Fig. 20). Together, these results help clarify the neural mechanisms that underlie sensory-specific satiety. Apparently, this phenomenon cannot be attributed to receptor adaptation nor to reduced activity in peripheral taste nerves or in central taste cells through the primary gustatory cortex. Rather, it rests with higher-order cortical processes of the lateral orbitofrontal area and beyond. Sensory information is kept separate from hedonic and motivational influences until it reaches the OFC. There, the association between a stimulus and its reward value can occur, depending on the need state of the animal. Cells in the OFC have been implicated in behavioral alterations to stimuli that have lost their reinforcing value or which have become associated with punishment (Thorpe *et al.*, 1983). Thus, lesions in this area prevent monkeys from learning extinction (Jones and Mishkin, 1972). Perhaps taste-responsiveness neurons in the OFC are involved in maintaining the association between a taste stimulus and its reward value (Sanghera *et al.*, 1979). Through alterations in OFC activity, the animal could modify its behavior according to the availability of environmental resources in relation to its own needs. Separate populations of neurons have also been identified in the monkey's lateral hypothalamic area that responded either to the taste (Burton *et al.*, 1976) or sight (Rolls and Rolls, 1982) of preferred foods

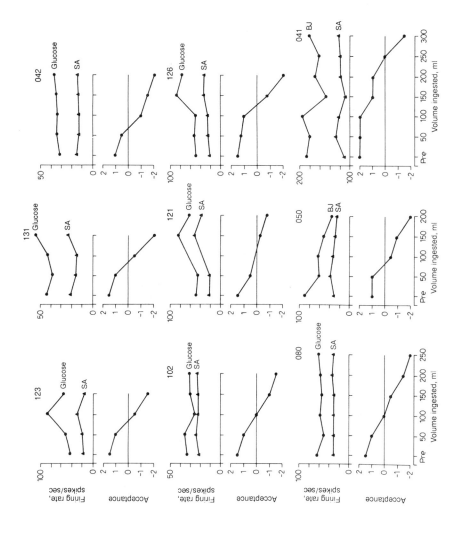

if the animal was hungry. Other cells responded to both taste and vision, implying a convergence of sensory modalities concerned with finding food. As in the OFC, the induction of satiety suppressed this activity (Rolls and Rolls, 1982; Rolls *et al.*, 1986). Responses to the sight of food were unmodified, however, in the inferotemporal cortex, where an advanced stage of visual processing occurs. Nor did physiological state affect globus pallidus activity associated with swallowing (Burton *et al.*, 1976). Thus, the electrophysiological evidence supports the position that both visual and gustatory incentives for the initiation and maintenance of feeding may be modulated by momentary physiological needs. In the primate, however, this influence is evident only after several stages of synaptic processing, including cortical relays at which the quality–intensity evaluation is held independent of hedonic appreciation. It would not be surprising if the macaque monkey joined humans in their ability to evaluate the sensory aspects of food separately from its appeal. A resolution to the conflict between rat electrophysiological and human psychophysical data, then, lies not in whether hedonic evaluations are part of the gustatory neural code—they are in both species—but in the neural level at which the interaction occurs.

VI. Conclusion

I propose that the sense of taste is like a Janus head placed at the gateway to the city. One face is turned outward to its environment, to warn of and resist the incursion of chemical perils, while recognizing and encouraging the receipt of required goods. The other looks inward to monitor the effects of admitted wares on the city's activity and to remain current with its needs.

The outward face of taste signals the quality and intensity of chemicals through a spatiotemporal code, both the spatial and temporal aspects of which are organized on a dimension of physiological welfare. This analysis offers a first approximation of the appropriateness of consuming a chemical. The capacity to perform it is genetically endowed, and, one supposes, derives from evolutionary pressures to avoid chemicals that are toxic and to consume those that provide nutrients. The afferent signals elicited by nutrients drive hindbrain feeding re-

FIG. 18. Spontaneous activity (SA) and multiunit neural responses evoked from the nucleus of the solitary tract by the taste solution on which the monkey was fed to satiety. Each graph represents the results of a separate experiment during which the monkey consumed the satiating solution in 50-ml aliquots, as labeled on the abscissa. Represented below the neural response data for each experiment is a behavioral measure of acceptance of the satiating solution on a scale of 2.0 (avid acceptance) to −2.0 (active rejection), as evaluated independently by three observers. The satiating solution is labeled for each graph. BJ, Blackcurrant juice. The gastric distension, hyperglycemia, and hyperinsulinemia that this protocol was designed to elicit had no effect on gustatory responsiveness in the monkey's solitary tract nucleus. [Reprinted from Yaxley *et al.* (1985) with permission.]

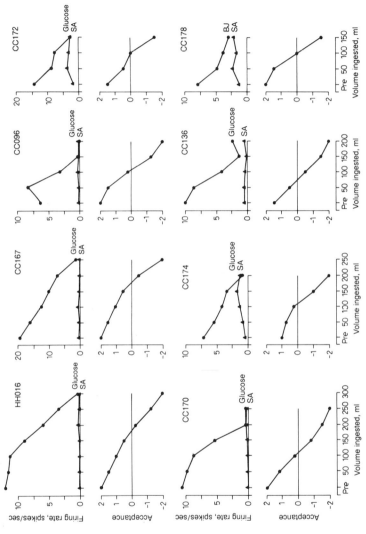

Fig. 19. The same format is used as in Fig. 18, except that responses are derived from single neurons in the lateral caudal orbitofrontal cortex of the monkey. At this level of processing, discharge rate is related to the level of satiety rather than the purely sensory aspects of the stimulus. The letters and numbers in each frame identify the monkey and the recording track, respectively. SA, Spontaneous activity. [Reprinted from Rolls et al. (1989) with permission.]

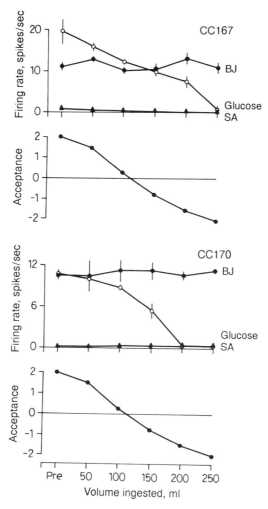

FIG. 20. Demonstration of the specificity of the response to satiation. Satiety to one sweet chemical does not generalize to another stimulus, even though the correlation between the response patterns evoked by glucose and blackcurrant juice (BJ) in the monkey's orbitofrontal cortex is 0.74, implying rather similar gustatory quality. SA, Spontaneous activity. [Reprinted from Rolls *et al.* (1989) with permission.]

flexes and activity in forebrain areas that mediate reward, while those of toxins activate withdrawal reflexes and forebrain neurons associated with avoidance. Thus, a first approximation of body wisdom is inherited through taste.

While the mechanisms that underlie these processes are just now yielding to experimental investigation, their very existence should offer no surprise. We are the descendants of animals who properly identified, were attracted to, and competed successfully for carbohydrates, fats, proteins, and salt. The more pleasure our ancestors derived from the consumption of these substances, the more likely they were to survive to become our progenitors. Ancient creatures who delighted in the taste of toxins would have left few offspring. Since the search for nutrients is the most primitive of all motives, the hedonic appeal of these chemicals may be our most basic pleasure. Cloaked though it may be in cultural trappings, the pure biological reward of consuming nutrients is irresistible to many.

The plasticity of the system requires both faces of taste and permits finer adjustments. The acceptability of a food must be verified by its physiological consequences. If a taste that arouses feeding reflexes and reward is followed by nausea, the gustatory signal is altered—by as yet unknown mechanisms—toward one of a toxin. Conditioning occurs on a time scale that relates to visceral, rather than operant, processes. From the neural level of the gustatory alteration (the hindbrain in a rat) onward, nothing need change, for the afferent code now activates reflexes and hedonics associated with a poison. Whereas the effects of conditioning apply only to the individual, the mechanism that permits this privileged association between taste and physiological consequences is inherent to the structure of the gustatory–visceral complex.

Conversely, an inherently unappealing or neutral taste that is paired with nutritional repletion gains in hedonic appeal. The rat pup with garlic in its mother's milk (Domjan, 1976; Kalia and Sullivan, 1982), the Italian child with tomato sauce on his pasta, and the Japanese with soy on her rice each develop a preference for the tastes that precede postprandial satisfaction. Thus, body wisdom is extended from the level of the species to that of both the culture and the individual.

Finally, within each individual, taste responses and their reflexive and hedonic sequelae are in flux to match the animal's preferences to its momentary physiological needs. The match may be unique and ongoing, as when a pathological state of sodium depletion led to an intense and constant salt appetite (Wilkins and Richter, 1940). More commonly, it reflects the animal's circadian feeding patterns. With nutritional deficiency, feeding reflexes are skewed toward the ingestive, and taste responsiveness to nutrients is heightened, as is the pleasure derived from eating. Repletion brings a suppression of the gustatory signal for reward for that taste, yet other chemicals may still arouse pleasure. It follows that a diet selected purely according to the reinforcing value of its components will be a varied one, perhaps skewed this way or that by the age or metabolic idiosyncrasies of the individual. This variability need not reside in hindbrain reflexes or forebrain reward systems, but only in the form of the gustatory code that drives them. Thus, the animal has one simple goal to fulfill: to maximize hedonism. What tastes best to it is what will best serve its physiological needs at the moment.

Why, then, is the sense of taste perceived in modern society as an enemy to good health? Technical advances of the past few centuries have allowed industry to provide carbohydrates, fats, proteins, and salt in unprecedented quantities. The orgy of consumption that has followed revealed a whole new set of pathologies that had never played into our evolutionary development: cardiovascular stress, diabetes, and hypertension. The chemical senses, tuned so exquisitely to the environment in which we have evolved, clashed with the very society that had learned to pander to them. The intense biological pleasure of consumption had been dulled by the social disgrace of gluttony and by the deleterious effects on health that appear only at ages our ancestors never achieved. The physiologist's recognition that what tastes good is good for you has been reversed in the dieter's lament "everything that tastes good is bad for you."

The dieter is mistaken.

Acknowledgments

During the preparation of this manuscript, the author was supported by research grants from the National Institutes of Health (DK 30964) and the National Science Foundation (BNS 9001213). Stuart McCaughey was instrumental in organizing the references.

This contribution was invited by Dr. Alan Epstein, to whose memory it is dedicated.

References

Ables, M. F., and Benjamin, R. M. (1960). Thalamic relay nucleus for taste in albino rat. *Journal of Neurophysiology* **23**, 376–382.

Aggleton, J. P., Burton, M. J., and Passingham, R. E. (1980). Cortical and subcortical afferents to the amygdala of the rhesus monkey (*Macaca mulatta*). *Brain Research* **190**, 347.

Akabas, M. H., Dodd, J., and Al-Awqati, Q. (1988). A bitter substance induces a rise in intracellular calcium in a subpopulation of rat taste cells. *Science* **242**, 1047–1050.

Akaike, N., and Sato, M. (1976). Mechanism of action of some bitter-tasting compounds on frog taste cells. *Japanese Journal of Physiology* **26**, 29–40.

Aleksanyan, Z. A., Buresova, O., and Bures, J. (1976). Modification of unit responses to gustatory stimuli by conditioned taste aversion in rats. *Physiology and Behavior* **17**, 173–179.

Antin, J., Gibbs, J., and Smith, G. P. (1978). Cholecystokinin interacts with pregastric food stimulation to elicit satiety in the rat. *Physiology and Behavior* **20**, 67–70.

Avenet, P., and Lindemann, B. (1987). Patch–clamp study of isolated taste receptor cells in the frog. *Journal of Membrane Biology* **97**, 223–240.

Bagshaw, W. H., and Pribram, K. H. (1953). Cortical organization in gustation (*Macaca mulatta*). *Journal of Neurophysiology* **16**, 499–508.

Beauchamp, G. K., Vazquez de Vaquera, M., and Pearson, P. B. (1987). Dietary status of human infants and their sensory responses to amino acid flavor. *In* "Umami: A Basic Taste" (Y. Kawamura and M. R. Kare, eds.), pp. 125–138. Dekker, New York.

Beckstead, R. M., and Norgren, R. (1979). An autoradiographic examination of the central distribution of the trigeminal, facial, glossopharyngeal, and vagal nerves in the monkey. *Journal of Comparative Neurology* **184**, 455–472.

Beckstead, R. M., Morse, J. H., and Norgren, R. (1980). The nucleus of the solitary tract in the monkey: Projections to the thalamus and brainstem nuclei. *Journal of Comparative Neurology* **190**, 259–282.

Beidler, L. M. (1969). Anion influences on taste receptor response. *In* "Olfaction and Taste III" (C. Pfaffmann, ed.), pp. 504–534. Rockefeller University Press, New York.

Beidler, L. M. (1971). Taste receptor stimulation with salts and acids. *In* "Handbook of Sensory Physiology" (L. M. Beidler, ed.), Vol. IV, Part 2, pp. 200–220. Springer-Verlag, Berlin.

Benjamin, R. M. (1959). Absence of deficits in taste discrimination following cortical lesions as a function of the amount of pre-operative practice. *Journal of Comparative and Physiological Psychology* **52**, 255–258.

Benjamin, R. M. (1963). Some thalamic and cortical mechanisms of taste. *In* "Olfaction and Taste" (Y. Zotterman, ed.), pp. 309–329. Pergamon, New York.

Benjamin, R. M., and Akert, K. (1959). Cortical and thalamic areas involved in taste discrimination in the albino rat. *Journal of Comparative Neurology* **3**, 231–260.

Benjamin, R. M., and Burton, H. (1968). Projection of taste nerve afferents to anterior opercular–insular cortex in squirrel monkey (*Saimiri sciureus*). *Brain Research* **7**, 221–231.

Benjamin, R. M., and Emmers, R. (1968). Localization of separate cortical areas for taste and tactile tongue afferents in squirrel monkey. *Federation Proceedings, Federation of American Societies for Experimental Biology* **19**, 294.

Benjamin, R. M., and Pfaffmann, C. (1955). Cortical localization of taste in albino rat. *Journal of Neurophysiology* **18**, 56–64.

Bereiter, D. A., Berthoud, H. R., and Jeanrenaud, B. (1979). Oropharyngeal hypothalamic input to the same NTS neurons. *Society for Neuroscience Abstracts* **5**, 125.

Berk, M. L., and Finkelstein, J. A. (1982). Efferent connection of the lateral hypothalamic area of the rat: An autoradiographic investigation. *Brain Research Bulletin* **8**, 511–526.

Berridge, K. C., Grill, H. J., and Norgren, R. (1981). Relation of consummatory responses and preabsorptive insulin release to palatability and learned taste aversions. *Journal of Comparative and Physiological Psychology* **95**, 363–382.

Berridge, K. C., Flynn, F. W., Schulkin, J., and Grill, H. J. (1984). Sodium depletion enhances salt palatability in rats. *Behavioral Neuroscience* **98**(4), 652–660.

Bertiere, M. C., Sy, T. M., Baigts, F., Mandenoff, A., and Apfelbaum, M. (1984). Stress and sucrose hyperphagia: Role of endogenous opiates. *Pharmacology, Biochemistry and Behavior* **20**, 675–679.

Blass, E. M. (1986). Opioids, sweets and a mechanism for positive affect: Broad motivational implications. *In* "Sweetness" (J. Dobbing, ed.), pp. 115–126. Springer-Verlag, Berlin.

Bornstein, W. S. (1940a). Cortical representation of taste in man and monkey. I. Functional and anatomical relations of taste, olfaction and somatic sensibility. *Yale Journal of Biology and Medicine* **12**, 719–736.

Bornstein, W. S. (1940b). Cortical representation of taste in man and monkey. II. The localization of the cortical taste area in man and a method of measuring impairment of taste in man. *Yale Journal of Biology and Medicine* **13**, 133–156.

Bradley, R. (1973). Electrophysiological investigations of intravascular taste using perfused rat tongue. *American Journal of Physiology* **224**, 300–304.

Brand, J. G., Teeter, J. H., and Silver, W. L. (1985). Inhibition by amiloride of chorda tympani responses evoked by monovalent salts. *Brain Research* **334**, 207–214.

Brush, A. D., and Halpern, B. P. (1970). Centrifugal control of gustatory responses. *Physiology and Behavior* **5**, 743–746.

Burton, H., and Benjamin, R. M. (1971). Central projections of the gustatory system. *In* "Handbook of Sensory Physiology" (L. M. Beidler, ed.), Vol. IV, Part 2, pp. 148–164. Springer-Verlag, Berlin.

Burton, M., Rolls, E., and Mora, F. (1976). Effects of hunger on the response of neurons in the lateral hypothalamus to the sight and taste of food. *Experimental Neurology* **51,** 668–677.

Cabanac, M. (1971). Physiological role of pleasure. *Science* **173,** 1103–1107.

Campbell, B. A. (1958). Absolute and relative sucrose preference thresholds in hungry and satiated rats. *Journal of Comparative and Physiological Psychology* **51,** 795–800.

Capretta, P. J., and Rawls, L. H. (1974). Establishment of a flavor preference in rats: Importance of nursing and weaning experience. *Journal of Comparative and Physiological Psychology* **86,** 670–673.

Carson, J. S., and Gormican, A. (1977). Taste acuity and food attitudes of selected patients with cancer. *Research* **70,** 361–365.

Chang, F.-C. T., and Scott, T. R. (1984). Conditioned taste aversions modify neural responses in the rat nucleus tractus solitarius. *The Journal of Neuroscience* **4,** 1850–1862.

Chang, V. C., Mark, G. P., Hernandez, L., and Hoebel, B. G. (1988). Extracellular dopamine increases in the nucleus accumbens following rehydration or sodium repletion in rats. *Society for Neuroscience Abstracts* **14,** 527.

Clark, W. G., and Clausen, D. F. (1943). Dietary "self-selection" and appetites of untreated and treated adrenalectomized rats. *American Journal of Physiology* **139,** 70–79.

Collings, V. B. (1974). Human taste response as a function of locus of stimulation on the tongue and soft palate. *Chemical Senses* **1,** 169–176.

Conrad, L. C. A., and Pfaff, D. W. (1976). Efferents from medial basal forebrain and hypothalamus in the rat. *Journal of Comparative Neurology* **169,** 221–262.

Contreras, R. (1977). Changes in gustatory nerve discharges with sodium deficiency: A single unit analysis. *Brain Research* **121,** 373–378.

Contreras, R., and Frank, M. (1979). Sodium deprivation alters neural responses to gustatory stimuli. *Journal of General Physiology* **73,** 569–594.

Covey, E., and Erickson, R. P. (1980). Temporal neural coding in gustation. Paper delivered at the second annual meeting of the *Association for Chemoreception Sciences,* Sarasota.

Dastoli, F. R., and Price, S. (1966). Sweet-sensitive protein from bovine taste buds: Isolation and assay. *Science* **154,** 905–907.

Denton, D. A. (1976). Hypertension: A malady of civilization? *In* "Systemic Effects of Antihypertensive Agents" (M. P. Sambhi, ed.), pp. 577–583. Stratton Intercontinental, New York.

DeSimone, J. A., and Ferrell, F. (1985). Analysis of amiloride inhibition of chorda tympani taste response of rat to NaCl. *American Journal of Physiology* **249,** R52–R61.

DeSimone, J. A., Heck, G. L., and DeSimone, S. K. (1981). Active ion transport in dog tongue: A possible role in taste. *Science* **14,** 1039–1041.

DiLorenzo, P. M. (1985). Responses to NaCl of parabrachial units that were conditioned with intravenous LiCl. *Chemical Senses* **10,** 438.

DiLorenzo, P. M., and Monroe, S. (1989). Taste responses in the parabrachial pons of male, female and pregnant rats. *Brain Research Bulletin* **23,** 219–227.

DiLorenzo, P. M., and Schwartzbaum, J. S. (1982). Coding of gustatory information in the pontine parabrachial nuclei of the rabbit: Temporal patterns of neural response. *Brain Research* **251,** 245–257.

DiRocco, R., and Grill, H. J. (1979). The forebrain is not essential for sympathoadrenal hyperglycemic response to glucoprivation. *Science* **204,** 1112–1114.

Doetsch, G. S., and Erickson, R. P. (1970). Synaptic processing of taste-quality information in the nucleus tractus solitarius of the rat. *Journal of Neurophysiology* **33,** 490–507.

Domjan, M. (1976). Determinants of the enhancement of flavored-water intake by prior exposure. *Journal of Experimental Psychology, Animal Behavior Processes* **2**, 17–27.

Dua-Sharma, S., Sharma, K. N., and Jacobs, H. L. (1973). The effect of chronic hunger on gustatory responses in the frog. *Physiologist* **16**, 300.

Epstein, A. N., and Stellar, E. (1955). The control of salt preference in adrenalectomized rat. *Journal of Comparative and Physiological Psychology* **46**, 167–172.

Erickson, R. P. (1967). Neural coding of taste quality. *In* "The Chemical Senses and Nutrition" (M. Kare and O. Maller, eds.), pp. 313–327. The Johns Hopkins University Press, Baltimore.

Erickson, R. P., Doetsch, G. S., and Marshall, D. A. (1965). The gustatory neural response function. *Journal of General Physiology* **49**, 247–263.

Faurion, A., Bonaventure, L., Bertrand, B., and MacLeod, P. (1980a). Multiple approach of the sweet taste sensory continuum: Psychophysical and electrophysiological data. *In* "Olfaction and Taste VII" (H. Van der Starre, ed.), pp. 86–89. Information Retrieval, London.

Faurion, A., Saito, S., and MacLeod, P. (1980b). Sweet taste involves several distinct mechanisms. *Chemical Senses* **5**, 107–121.

Flynn, F. W., and Grill, H. J. (1983). Insulin elicits ingestion in decerebrate rats. *Science* **221**, 188–189.

Formaker, B. K., and Hill, D. L. (1988). An analysis of residual NaCl taste response after amiloride. *American Journal of Physiology* **255**, R1002–R1007.

Fregley, M. J., Harper, J. M., and Radford, E. P., Jr. (1965). Regulation of sodium chloride intake by rats. *American Journal of Physiology* **209**, 287–292.

Funakoshi, M., Kasahara, Y., Yamamoto, T., and Kawamura, Y. (1972). Taste coding and central perception. *In* "Olfaction and Taste IV" (D. Schneider, ed.), pp. 336–342. Wissenschaftliche Verlagsgesellschaft, Stuttgart.

Ganchrow, D., and Erickson, R. P. (1972). Thalamo–cortical relations in gustation. *Brain Research* **36**, 289–305.

Garcia, J., Kimmeldorf, D. J., and Koelling, R. A. (1955). Conditional aversion to saccharin resulting from exposure to gamma radiation. *Science* **122**, 157–158.

Gardner, R. J. (1980). Lipid solubility and sourness of acids: Implications for models of the acid taste receptor. *Chemical Senses* **5**, 185–194.

Geary, N., and Smith, G. P. (1982a). Pancreatic glucagon fails to inhibit sham feeding in the rat. *Peptides* **3**, 163–166.

Geary, N., and Smith, G. P. (1982b). Pancreatic glucagon and postprandial satiety in the rat. *Physiology and Behavior* **28**, 313–322.

Gibbs, J., Young, R. C., and Smith, G. P. (1973). Cholecystokinin decreases food intake in rats. *Journal of Comparative and Physiological Psychology* **84**, 488–495.

Giza, B. K., and Scott, T. R. (1983). Blood glucose selectively affects taste-evoked activity in rat nucleus tractus solitarius. *Physiology and Behavior* **31**, 643–650.

Giza, B. K., and Scott, T. R. (1987a). Blood glucose level affects perceived sweetness intensity in rats. *Physiology and Behavior* **41**, 459–464.

Giza, B. K., and Scott, T. R. (1987b). Intravenous insulin infusions in rats decrease gustatory-evoked responses to sugars. *American Journal of Physiology* **252**, R994–R1002.

Giza, B. K., and Scott, T. R. (1991). The effect of amiloride on taste-evoked activity in the nucleus tractus solitarius of the rat. *Brain Research* **550**, 247–256.

Giza, B. K., Scott, T. R., and Antonucci, R. F. (1990). The effect of cholecystokinin on taste responsiveness in the rat. *American Journal of Physiology* **258**, R1371–R1379.

Giza, B. K., Scott, T. R., and VanderWeele, D. A. (1992). The effect of satiety factors on taste-evoked activity in the nucleus tractus solitarius of the rat. *Brain Research Bulletin* **28**, 637–639.

Giza, B. K., Deems, R. O., VanderWeele, D. A., and Scott, T. R. (1993). Pancreatic glucagon suppresses gustatory responsiveness to glucose. Submitted.

Glenn, J. F., and Erickson, R. P. (1976). Gastric modulation of gustatory afferent activity. *Physiology and Behavior* **16**, 561–568.

Greenberg, M. J. (1980). The importance of hydrophobic properties of organic compounds on their taste intensities: A quantitative structure–taste-intensity study. *Agriculture and Food Chemistry* **28**, 562–566.

Grill, H. J., and Berridge, K. C. (1981). Chronic decerebrate rats demonstrate preabsorptive insulin secretion and hyperinsulinemia. *Society for Neuroscience Abstracts* **7**, 29.

Grill, H. J., and Norgren, R. (1978a). The taste reactivity test. II. Mimetic responses to gustatory stimuli in chronic thalamic and chronic decerebrate rats. *Brain Research* **143**, 281–297.

Grill, H. J., and Norgren, R. (1978b). Chronically decerebrate rats demonstrate satiation but not bait shyness. *Science* **201**, 267–269.

Grill, H. J., Ganster, D., and Smith, G. P. (1983). CCK-8 decreases sucrose intake in chronic decerebrate rats. *Society for Neuroscience Abstracts* **9**, 903.

Halpern, B. P., and Nelson, L. M. (1965). Bulbar gustatory responses to anterior and posterior tongue stimulation in the rat. *American Journal of Physiology* **209**, 105–110.

Halstead, W. C., and Gallagher, B. B. (1962). Autoregulation of amino acids intake in the albino rat. *Journal of Comparative and Physiological Psychology* **55**, 107–111.

Hamilton, R. B., and Norgren, R. (1984). Central projections of gustatory nerves in the rat. *Journal of Comparative Neurology* **222**, 560–577.

Hanig, D. P. (1901). Zur Psychophysik des Geschmackssinnes. *Philosophy Studies* **17**, 576–623.

Heck, G. L., Mierson, S., and DeSimone, J. A. (1984). Salt taste transduction occurs through an amiloride-sensitive sodium transport pathway. *Science* **233**, 403–405.

Hellekant, G. (1971). The effect of stomach distension on the efferent activity in the chorda tympani nerve of the rat. *Acta Physiologica Scandinavica* **83**, 527–531.

Hellekant, G., Glaser, D., Brouwer, J., and van der Wel, H. (1981). Gustatory responses in three prosimian and two simian primate species (*Tupaia glis, Nycticebus coucang, Galago senegalensis, Callithrix jacchus jacchus* and *Saguinus midas niger*) to six sweeteners and miraculin and their phylogenetic implications. *Chemical Senses* **6**, 165–173.

Hermann, G. E., and Rogers, R. C. (1985). Convergence of vagal and gustatory afferent input within the parabrachial nucleus of the rat. *Journal of the Autonomic Nervous System* **13**, 1–17.

Herrick, C. J. (1922). What are viscera? *Journal of Anatomy* **56**, 167–176.

Herrick, C. J. (1944). The cranial nerves. A review of fifty years. *Journal of Laboratory Science* **38**, 41–51.

Hiji, Y. (1975). Selective elimination of taste responses to sugars by proteolytic enzymes. *Nature (London)* **256**, 427–429.

Hiji, Y., Kobayashi, N., and Sato, M. (1968). A "sweet-sensitive" protein from the tongue of the rat. *Kumamoto Medical Journal* **21**, 137–139.

Hill, D. L., and Bour, T. C. (1985). Addition of functional amiloride-sensitive components to the receptor membrane: A possible mechanism for altered taste responses during development. *Developmental Brain Research* **20**, 310–313.

Hoebel, B. G. (1984). Neurotransmitters in the control of feeding and its rewards: Monoamines, opiates and brain–gut peptides. *In* "Eating and Its Disorders" (A. J. Stunkard and E. Stellar, eds.), pp. 15–38. Raven, New York.

Hosoya, Y., Matsushita, M., and Sugihara, Y. (1984). Hypothalamic descending afferents to cells of origin of the retrograde HRP and anterograde autoradiographic techniques. *Brain Research* **290**, 141.

Ishiko, N., and Akogi, T. (1972). Topographic organization of gustatory nervous system. *In* "Olfaction and Taste IV" (D. Schneider, ed.), pp. 343–349. Wissenschaftliche Verlagsgesellschaft, Stuttgart.

Ishiko, N., Amatsu, M., and Sato, M. (1967). Thalamic representation of taste qualities and temperature change in the cat. *In* "Olfaction and Taste II" (T. Hayashi, ed.), pp. 563–572. Pergamon, New York.

Jacobs, K. M., Mark, G. P., and Scott, T. R. (1988). Taste responses in the nucleus tractus solitarius of sodium-deprived rats. *Journal of Physiology (London)* **406,** 393–410.

Jones, E. G., and Burton, H. (1976). Areal differences in the laminar distribution of thalamic afferents in cortical fields of the insular, parietal, and temporal regions of primates. *Journal of Comparative Neurology* **168,** 197.

Jones, B., and Mishkin, M. (1972). Limbic lesions and the problems of stimulus–reinforcement associations. *Experimental Neurology* **36,** 362.

Kalia, M., and Sullivan, J. M. (1982). Brainstem projections of sensory and motor components of the vagus nerve in the rat. *Journal of Comparative Neurology* **211,** 248.

Kalmus, H. (1971). Genetics of taste. *In* "Handbook of Sensory Physiology" (L. M. Beidler, ed.), Vol. IV, Part 2, pp. 165–179. Springer-Verlag, Berlin.

Kemble, E. D., and Nagel, J. A. (1973). Failure to form a learned taste aversion in rats with amygdaloid lesions. *Bulletin of the Psychonomic Society* **2,** 155–156.

Kimura, K., and Beidler, L. M. (1961). Microelectrode study of taste receptors of rat and hamster. *Journal of Cellular and Comparative Physiology* **58,** 131–139.

Kinnamon, S. C., and Getchell, T. V. (1991). Sensory transduction in olfactory receptor neurons and gustatory receptor cells. *In* "Smell and Taste in Health and Disease" (T. V. Getchall, R. L. Doty, L. M. Bartoshuk, and J. B. Snow, eds.), pp. 145–172. Raven, New York.

Kinnamon, S. C., and Roper, S. D. (1988). Membrane properties of isolated mudpuppy taste cells. *Journal of General Physiology* **91,** 351–371.

Kosar, E., Norgren, R., and Grill, H. J. (1985). Delimitation of rat gustatory cortex. *Chemical Senses* **10,** 436.

Koyama, N., and Kurihara, K. (1972). Mechanism of bitter taste reception: Interaction of bitter compounds with monolayers of lipids from bovine circumvallate papillae. *Biochimica et Biophysica Acta* **288,** 22–26.

Kumazawa, T., Kashiwayanagi, M., and Kurihara, K. (1985). Neuroblastoma cell as a model for a taste cell: Mechanism of depolarization in response to various bitter substances. *Brain Research* **333,** 27–33.

Kuznicki, J. T., and Ashbaugh, N. (1979). Taste quality differences within the sweet and salty taste categories. *Sensory Processes* **3,** 157–182.

Levine, S., Sievert, C. E., Morley, B. A., Gosnell, B. A., and Silvis, S. E. (1984). Peptidergic regulation of feeding in the dog (*Canis familiaris*). *Peptides (New York)* **5,** 675–679.

Loewy, A. D., and Burton, H. (1978). Nuclei of the solitary tract: Efferent projections to the lower brain stem and spinal cord of the cat. *Journal of Comparative Neurology* **181,** 421–450.

Louis-Sylvestre, J., and LeMagnen, J. (1980). Palatability and preabsorptive insulin release. *Neuroscience and Biobehavioral Reviews* **4** (Suppl. 1), 43–46.

Louis-Sylvestre, J., Giachetti, I., and LeMagnen, J. (1983). Vagotomy abolishes the differential palatability of food. *Appetite* **4,** 295–299.

Lovett, D., and Booth, D. A. (1970). Four effects of exogenous insulin on food intake. *Quarterly Journal of Experimental Psychology* **22,** 406–419.

Makous, W., Nord, S., Oakley, B., and Pfaffmann, C. (1963). The gustatory relay in the medulla. *In* "Olfaction and Taste" (Y. Zotterman, ed.), pp. 381–393. Pergamon, New York.

Mark, G. P., and Scott, T. R. (1988). Conditioned taste aversions affect gustatory evoked activity in the NTS of chronic decerebrate rats. *Society for Neuroscience Abstracts* **14,** 1185.

Mark, G. P., Blander, D. S., and Hoebel, B. G. (1991a). A conditioned stimulus decreases extracellular dopamine in the nucleus accumbens after development of a learned taste aversion. *Brain Research* **551,** 308–310.

Mark, G. P., Rada, P., Weinberg, J. B., Pothos, E., and Hoebel, B. G. (1991b). Effects of feeding, drinking and learned taste aversion on acetylcholine release in the nucleus accumbens of freely-moving rats. *Society for Neuroscience Abstracts* **17**, 782.

Mark, G. P., Smith, S. E., Ackroff, K., Sclafani, A., and Hoebel, B. G. (1991c). An appetitively conditioned taste elicits a preferential increase in mesolimbic dopamine output. *International Journal of Obesity* **15** (Suppl. 3), 34.

Marshall, J. F., and Teitelbaum, P. (1974). Further analysis of sensory inattention following lateral hypothalamic damage in rats. *Journal of Comparative and Physiological Psychology* **86**, 375–395.

Marshall, J. F., Turner, B. H., and Teitelbaum, P. (1971). Sensory neglect produced by lateral hypothalamic damage. *Science* **174**, 523–525.

McBurney, D. H. (1978). Psychological dimensions and perceptual analyses of taste. *In* "Handbook of Perception" (E. C. Carterette and M. P. Friedman, eds.), Vol. VI, Part A, pp. 125–155. Academic Press, New York.

McCance, R. A. (1936). Experimental sodium chloride deficiency in man. *Proceedings of the Royal Society of London, Series B* **119**, 245–268.

Mesulam, M.-M., and Mufson, E. J. (1982). Insula of the Old World monkey. III. Efferent cortical output and comments on function. *Journal of Comparative Neurology* **212**, 38–52.

Miller, I. J., Jr. (1971). Peripheral interactions among single papilla inputs to gustatory nerve fibers. *Journal of Physiology (London)* **51**, 1–25.

Mufson, E. J., and Mesulam, M.-M. (1982). Insula of the Old World monkey. II. Afferent cortical input and comments on the claustrum. *Journal of Comparative Neurology* **212**, 23.

Murphy, C. (1986). The chemical senses and nutrition in the elderly. *In* "Interaction of the Chemical Senses with Nutrition" (M. R. Kare and J. G. Brand, eds.), pp. 87–105. Academic Press, Orlando, Florida.

Murzi, E., Hernandez, L., and Baptista, T. (1986). Lateral hypothalamic sites eliciting eating affect medullary taste neurons in rats. *Physiology and Behavior* **36**, 829–834.

Nagai, T., and Ueda, K. (1981). Stochastic properties of gustatory impulse discharges in rat chorda tympani fibers. *Journal of Neurophysiology* **45**, 574–592.

Nauta, W. J. H. (1964). Some efferent connections of the prefrontal cortex in the monkey. *In* "The Frontal Granular Cortex and Behavior" (J. M. Warren and K. Akert, eds.), pp. 397–409. McGraw-Hill, New York.

Ninomiya, Y., Mizukoshi, T., Higashi, T., and Funakoshi, M. (1985). Differential responsiveness of two groups of rat chorda tympani fibers to ionic chemical and electrical stimulations. *Chemical Senses* **10**, 140.

Nofre, C., and Sabadie, J. (1972). À propos de la protéine linguale dit "sensible aux sucres." *Comptes Rendus Hebdomadaires des Seances de l'Academie des Sciences, Serie D: Sciences Naturelles* **274**, 2913–2915.

Nolan, L. J., and Scott, T. R. (1992). The effects of a conditioned taste aversion on gustatory evoked activity in the rat nucleus tractus solitarius remain after behavioral extinction. *Chemical Senses* in press.

Norgren, R. (1974). Gustatory afferents to ventral forebrain. *Brain Research* **81**, 285–295.

Norgren, R. (1976). Taste pathways to hypothalamus and amygdala. *Journal of Comparative Neurology* **166**, 17–30.

Norgren, R. (1977). A synopsis of gustatory neuroanatomy. *In* "Olfaction and Taste IV" (J. LeMagnen and P. MacLeod, eds.), pp. 225–232. Information Retrieval, London.

Norgren, R. (1978). Projections from the nucleus of the solitary tract in the rat. *Neuroscience* **3**, 207–218.

Norgren, R. (1981). The central organization of the gustatory and visceral afferent systems in the nucleus of the solitary tract. *In* "Brain Mechanisms of Sensation" (Y. Katsuki, R. Norgren, and M. Sato, eds.), pp. 143–160. Wiley, New York.

Norgren, R. (1984). Central neural mechanisms of taste. *In* "Handbook of Physiology" (I. Darian-Smith, ed.), Sect. 1, pp. 1087–1128. American Physiological Society, Bethesda, Maryland.

Norgren, R. (1985). Taste and the autonomic nervous system. *Chemical Senses* **10**, 143–152.

Norgren, R., and Grill, H. J. (1976). Efferent distribution from the cortical gustatory area in rats. *Society for Neuroscience Abstracts* **2**, 124.

Norgren, R., and Leonard, C. M. (1971). Taste pathways in rat brainstem. *Science* **173**, 1136–1139.

Norgren, R., and Leonard, C. M. (1973). Ascending central gustatory pathways. *Journal of Comparative Neurology* **150**, 217–238.

Norgren, R., and Pfaffmann, C. (1975). The pontine taste area in the rat. *Brain Research* **91**, 99–117.

Novin, D. (1986). The control of feeding: A reassessment. *In* "Emotions: Neuronal and Chemical Control" (Y. Oomura, ed.), pp. 3–13. Scientific Societies Press, Tokyo.

Oakley, B. (1965). Impaired operant behavior following lesions of the thalamic taste nucleus. *Journal of Comparative and Physiological Psychology* **59**, 202–210.

Oakley, B., and Pfaffmann, C. (1962). Electrophysiologically monitored lesions in the gustatory thalamic relay of the albino rat. *Journal of Comparative and Physiological Psychology* **55**, 155–160.

Ogawa, H., and Kaisaku, J. (1982). Physiological characteristics of the solitario-parabrachial relay neurons with tongue afferent inputs in rats. *Experimental Brain Research* **48**, 326–331.

Ogawa, H., Imoto, T., and Hayama, T. (1982). Responsiveness of solitario-parabrachial relay neurons to taste and mechanical stimulation applied to the oral cavity in rats. *Experimental Brain Research* **48**, 362.

Ogawa, H., Ito, S., and Nomura, T. (1989). Oral cavity representation at the frontal operculum of macaque monkeys. *Neuroscience Research* **6**, 283–298.

Okada, Y., Miyamoto, T., and Sato, T. (1988). Ionic mechanism for generation of receptor potential in response to quinine in frog taste cell. *Brain Research* **450**, 295–302.

Ostrowski, N. L., Foley, T. L., Lind, M. D., and Reid, L. D. (1980). Naloxone reduces food intake: Effects of water and food deprivation. *Pharmacology, Biochemistry and Behavior* **12**, 431–435.

Ozeki, M. (1971). Conductance change associated with receptor potentials of gustatory cells in rat. *Journal of General Physiology* **58**, 688–699.

Patton, H. D. (1960). Taste olfaction and visceral sensation. *In* "Medical Physiology and Biophysics" (T. C. Ruch, ed.), 18th Ed., p. 369. Saunders, Philadelphia.

Pelchat, M. L., Grill, H. J., Rozin, P., and Jacobs, J. (1983). Quality of acquired responses to tastes by Rattus norvegicus depends on type of associated discomfort. *Journal of Comparative Psychology* **97**, 140–153.

Pfaffmann, C. (1974). Specificity of the sweet receptors of the squirrel monkey. *Chemical Senses* **1**, 61–68.

Pfaffmann, C., Erickson, R., Frommer, G., and Halpern, B. (1961). Gustatory discharges in the rat medulla and thalamus. *In* "Sensory Communication" (W. A. Rosenblith, ed.), pp. 455–473. MIT Press, Cambridge, Massachusetts.

Pfaffmann, C., Norgren, R., and Grill, H. J. (1977). Sensory affect and motivation. *Annals of the New York Academy of Sciences* **290**, 18–34.

Plata-Salaman, C. R., Smith, V. L., and Scott, T. R. (1990). Coding of sodium and lithium salts in the gustatory cortex of the alert cynomolgus monkey. *Chemical Senses* **15**, 625–626.

Plata-Salaman, C. R., Scott, T. R., and Smith-Swintosky, V. L. (1992a). Gustatory neural coding in the monkey cortex: L-Amino acids. *Journal of Neurophysiology* **67**, 1552–1561.

Plata-Salaman, C. R., Scott, T. R., and Smith-Swintosky, V. L. (1992b). Gustatory neural coding in the monkey cortex: The quality of sweetness. *Journal of Neurophysiology* in press.

Powley, T. L. (1977). The ventromedial hypothalamic syndrome, satiety, and a cephalic phase hypothesis. *Psychological Reviews* **84**, 89–126.

Powley, T. L., and Berthoud, H.-R. (1991). Neuroanatomical bases of cephalic phase reflexes. *In* "Appetite and Nutrition: Chemical Senses IV" (M. I. Friedman, M. G. Tordoff, and M. R. Kare, eds.), pp. 391–404. Dekker, New York.

Powley, T. L., Fox, E. A., and Berthoud, H.-R. (1987). Retrograde tracer technique for assessment of selective and total subdiaphragmatic vagotomies. *American Journal of Physiology* **253**, R361–R370.

Pribram, K. H., and MacLean, P. D. (1953) Neuronographic analysis of medial and basal cerebral cortex. II. Monkey. *Journal of Neurophysiology* **16**, 324.

Price, S., and DeSimone, J. A. (1977). Models of taste receptor cell stimulation. *Chemical Senses & Flavour* **2**, 427–456.

Pritchard, T. C., and Scott, T. R. (1982). The taste of amino acids. II. Quality and neural coding. *Brain Research* **253**, 93–104.

Pritchard, T. C., Hamilton, R. B., Morse, J. R., and Norgren, R. (1986). Projections of thalamic gustatory and lingual areas in the monkey, *Macaca fascicularis*. *Journal of Comparative Neurology* **244**, 213–228.

Przekop, P. R., Mook, D. G., and Hill, D. L. (1990). Functional recovery of the gustatory system following sodium deprivation during development: How much sodium and where. *American Journal of Physiology* **259**, R786–R791.

Rada, P., Mark, G. P., Pothos, E., and Hoebel, B. G. (1991). Systemic morphine simultaneously decreases extracellular acetylcholine and increases dopamine in the nucleus accumbens of freely moving rats. *Neuropharmacology* **30**, 1133–1136.

Revusky, S. H., Smith, M. H., and Chalmers, D. V. (1971). Flavor preferences: Effects of ingestion contingent intravenous saline or glucose. *Physiology and Behavior* **6**, 341–343.

Ricardo, J. A., and Koh, E. T. (1978). Anatomical evidence of direct projections from the nucleus of the solitary tract to the hypothalamus, amygdala, and other forebrain structures in the rat. *Brain Research* **153**, 1–26.

Richter, C. P. (1936). Increased salt appetite in adrenalectomized rats. *American Journal of Physiology* **115**, 155–161.

Roberts, T. S., and Akert, K. (1963). Insular and opercular cortex and its thalamic projection in *Macaca mulatta*. *Schweizer Archiv fuer Neurologie, Neurochirurgie und Psychiatrie* **92**, 1–43.

Rolls, E. T., and Rolls, B. J. (1982). Brain mechanisms involved in feeding. *In* "Psychobiology of Human Food Selection" (L. M. Barker, ed.), pp. 33–62. AI Publishing, Westport, Connecticut.

Rolls, B. J., Rolls, E. T., Rowe, E. A., and Sweeney, K. (1981). Sensory specific satiety in man. *Physiology and Behavior* **27**, 137–142.

Rolls, E. T., Yaxley, S., Sienkiewicz, Z. J., and Scott, T. R. (1985). Gustatory responses of single neurons in the orbitofrontal cortex of the macaque monkey. *Chemical Senses* **10**, 443.

Rolls, E. T., Murzi, E., Yaxley, S., Thorpe, S. J., and Simpson, S. J. (1986). Sensory-specific satiety: Food-specific reduction in responsiveness of ventral forebrain neurons after feeding in the monkey. *Brain Research* **368**, 79–86.

Rolls, E. T., Scott, T. R., Sienkiewicz, Z. J., and Yaxley, S. (1988). The responsiveness of neurons in the frontal opercular gustatory cortex of the macaque monkey is independent of hunger. *Journal of Physiology (London)* **397**, 1–12.

Rolls, E. T., Sienkiewicz, Z. J., and Yaxley, S. (1989). Hunger modulates the responses to gustatory stimuli of single neurons in the caudolateral orbitofrontal cortex of the macaque monkey. *European Journal of Neuroscience* **1**, 53–70.

Roth, S., Schwartz, M., and Teitelbaum, P. (1973). Failure of recovered lateral hypothalamic rats to learn specific food aversion. *Journal of Comparative and Physiological Psychology* **83**, 184–197.

Rozin, P., and Zellner, D. (1985). The role of pavlovian conditioning in the acquisition of food likes and dislikes. *Annals of the New York Academy of Sciences* **443**, 189–202.

Ruch, T. C., and Patton, H. D. (1946). The relation of the deep opercular cortex to taste. *Federation Proceedings, Federation of American Societies for Experimental Biology* **5**, 89–90.

Sahakian, B. J., Lean, M. E. J., Robbins, T. W., and James, W. P. T. (1981). Salivation and insulin secretion in response to food in non-obese men and women. *Appetite* **2**, 209–216.

Sanahuja, J. C., and Harper, A. E. (1962). Effect of amino acid imbalance on food intake and preference. *American Journal of Physiology* **202**, 165–170.

Sanghera, M. K., Rolls, E. T., and Roper-Hall, A. (1979). Visual responses of neurons in the dorsolateral amygdala of the alert monkey. *Experimental Neurology* **63**, 610.

Sanides, F. (1968). The architecture of the cortical taste nerve areas in squirrel monkey (*Saimiri sciureus*) and their relationships to insular, sensorimotor and prefrontal regions. *Brain Research* **8**, 97–144.

Sanides, F. (1970). Functional architecture of motor and sensory cortices in primates in the light of a new concept of neocortex evolution. *In* "The Primate Brain" (C. R. Noback and W. Montagna, eds.), pp. 137–208. Appleton-Century-Crofts, New York.

Saper, C. B. (1982). Reciprocal parabrachial–cortical connections in the rat. *Brain Research* **242**, 33.

Saper, C. B., Loewy, A. D., Swanson, L. W., and Cowan, W. M. (1976). Direct hypothalamo–autonomic connections. *Brain Research* **177**, 305–312.

Sato, T., and Beidler, L. M. (1982). The response characteristics of rat taste cells to four basic taste stimuli. *Comparative Biochemistry and Physiology A: Comparative Physiology* **73A**, 1–10.

Sato, T., Okada, Y., and Miyamoto, T. (1984). Effect of various anions on receptor membrane surface upon acid-induced receptor potential in frog taste cell. *Nippon Seirigaku Zasshi* **46**, 460.

Schiffman, S. S., and Dackis, C. (1979). Taste of nutrients: Amino acids, vitamins, and fatty acids. *Perception and Psychophysics* **17**, 140–146.

Schiffman, S. S., and Erickson, R. P. (1971). A psychophysical model for gustatory quality. *Physiology and Behavior* **7**, 617–633.

Schiffmann, S. S., Reilly, D. A., and Clark, T. B., III (1979). Qualitative differences among sweeteners. *Physiology and Behavior* **23**, 1–9.

Schiffmann, S. S., McElroy, A. E., and Erickson, R. P. (1980). The range of taste quality of sodium salts. *Physiology and Behavior* **24**, 217–224.

Schiffmann, S. S., Cahn, H., and Lindley, M. G. (1981). Multiple receptor sites mediate sweetness: Evidence from cross adaptation. *Pharmacology, Biochemistry and Behavior* **15**, 377–378.

Schiffmann, S. S., Lockhead, E., and Maes, F. W. (1983). Amiloride reduces the taste intensity of Na and Li salts and sweeteners. *Proceedings of the National Academy of Sciences of the United States of America* **80**, 6136–6140.

Schiffmann, S. S., Hopfinger, A. J., and Mazur, R. H. (1986). The search for receptors that mediate sweetness. *In* "The Receptors" (P. M. Conn, ed.). Academic Press, Orlando, Florida.

Schiffmann, S. S., Suggs, M. S., Crajoe, E. J., and Erickson, R. P. (1990). Inhibition of taste responses to Na$^+$ salts by epithelial Na$^+$ channel blockers in gerbil. *Physiology and Behavior* **47**, 455–459.

Shulman, J. L., Carleton, J. L., Whitney, J. C., Whitehorn, J. C. (1957). Effect of glucagon on food intake and body weight in man. *Journal of Applied Physiology* **11**, 419–421.

Schwartzbaum, J. S. (1988). Electrophysiology of taste, feeding and reward in lateral hypothalamus of rabbit. *Physiology and Behavior* **44**, 507–526.

Sclafani, A. (1991a). Conditioned food preferences. *Bulletin of the Psychonomic Society* **29**, 256–260.

Sclafani, A. (1991b). Conditioned food preferences and appetite. *Appetite* **17**, 71–72.

Scott, T. R. (1981). Brain stem and forebrain involvement in the gustatory neural code. *In* "Brain Mechanisms of Sensation" (Y. Katsuki, R. Norgren, and M. Sato, eds.), pp. 177–196. Wiley, New York.

Scott, T. R., and Chang, F.-C. T. (1984). The state of gustatory neural coding. *Chemical Senses* **8**, 297–313.

Scott, T. R., and Giza, B. K. (1987). A measure of taste intensity discrimination in the rat through conditioned taste aversions. *Physiology and Behavior* **41**, 315–320.

Scott, T. R., and Giza, B. K. (1990). Coding channels in the taste system of the rat. *Science* **249**, 1585–1587.

Scott, T. R., and Mark, G. P. (1987). The taste system encodes stimulus toxicity. *Brain Research* **414**, 197–203.

Scott, T. R., and Yaxley, S. (1989). The interaction of taste and ingestion. *In* "Neural Mechanisms of Taste" (R. H. Cagan, ed.), pp. 147–177. CRC Press, Boca Raton, Florida.

Scott, T. R., Yaxley, S., Sienkiewicz, Z. J., and Rolls, E. T. (1986a). Gustatory responses in the nucleus tractus solitarius of the alert cynomolgus monkey. *Journal of Neurophysiology* **55**, 182–200.

Scott, T. R., Yaxley, S., Sienkiewicz, Z. J., and Rolls, E. T. (1986b). Gustatory responses in the frontal opercular cortex of the alert cynomolgus monkey. *Journal of Neurophysiology* **56**, 876–890.

Scott, T. R., Plata-Salaman, C. R., Smith, V. L., and Giza, B. K. (1991). Gustatory neural coding in the monkey cortex: Stimulus intensity. *Journal of Neurophysiology* **65**, 76–86.

Selkurt, E. E. (1971). "Physiology," p. 742. Little, Brown, Boston.

Settle, R. G., Meehan, K., Williams, G. R., Doty, R. L., and Sysley, A. C. (1986). Chemosensory properties of sour tastants. *Physiology and Behavior* **36**, 619–623.

Seward, J. P., and Greathouse, S. R. (1973). Appetitive and aversive conditioning in thiamine-deficient rats. *Journal of Comparative Physiology* **83**, 157–167.

Shallenberger, R. S., and Acree, T. E. (1967). Molecular theory of sweet taste. *Nature (London)* **216**, 480–482.

Shallenberger, R. S., and Acree, T. E. (1971). Chemical structure of compounds and their sweet and bitter taste. *In* "Handbook of Sensory Physiology" (L. M. Beidler, ed.), Vol. IV, Part 2, pp. 221–277. Springer-Verlag, Berlin.

Sharma, K. N., and Doss, M. J. K. (1973). Excitation and control of gustatory chemoreceptors. *Proceedings of the 10th International Conference of Medical and Biological Engineering* **3**, 53.

Sharma, K. N., Jacobs, H. L., Gopal, V., and Dua-Sharma, S. (1977). Nutritional state/taste interactions in food intake: Behavioral and physiological evidence for gastric/taste modulation. *In* "The Chemical Senses and Nutrition" (M. R. Kare and O. Maller, eds.), pp. 167–187. Academic Press, New York.

Shipley, M. T., and Sanders, M. S. (1982). Special senses are really special: Evidence for a reciprocal, bilateral pathway between insular cortex and nucleus parabrachialis. *Brain Research Bulletin* **8**, 493.

Smith, D. V., van Buskirk, R. L., Travers, J. B., and Bieber, S. L. (1983). Gustatory neuron types in hamster brain stem. *Journal of Neurophysiology* **50**, 522–540.

Smith, V. L., Scott, T. R., and Plata-Salaman, C. R. (1991). Coding of acids in the gustatory cortex of the alert cynomologus monkey. *Chemical Senses* **15**, 640–641.

Smith-Swintosky, V. L., Plata-Salaman, C. R., and Scott, T. R. (1991). Gustatory neural coding in the monkey cortex: Stimulus quality. *Journal of Neurophysiology* **66**, 1156–1165.

Smotherman, W. P., and Levine, S. (1978). ACTH and ACTH4–10 modification of neophobia and taste aversion responses in the rat. *Journal of Comparative and Physiological Psychology* **92**, 22–23.

Stanley, B. G., Schwartz, D. H., Hernandez, L., Leibowitz, S. F., and Hoebel, B. G. (1989). Patterns of extracellular 5-hydroxyindoleacetic acid (5-HIAA) in the paraventricular hypothalamus (PVN): Relation to circadian rhythm and deprivation-induced eating behavior. *Pharmacology, Biochemistry and Behavior* **33**, 257–260.

Steffens, A. B. (1969). The influence of insulin injections on eating and blood glucose levels in the rat. *Physiology and Behavior* **4**, 823–828.

Steiner, J. E. (1973). The gustofacial response: Observation on normal and anencephalic newborn infants. *In* "Symposium on Oral Sensation and Perception IV" (J. F. Bosma, ed.), pp. 254–278. National Institutes of Health–Department of Health, Education and Welfare, Bethesda, Maryland.

Steiner, J. E. (1979). Human facial expressions in response to taste and smell stimulation. *In* "Advances in Child Development" (H. W. Reese and L. Lipsett, eds.), Vol. 13, pp. 257–295. Academic Press, New York.

Steiner, J. E., and Glaser, D. (1985). Orofacial motor behavior-patterns induced by gustatory stimuli in apes. *Chemical Senses* **10**, 452.

Stricker, E. M., and Jalowiec, J. E. (1970). Restoration of intravascular fluid volume following acute hypovolemia in rats. *American Journal of Physiology* **218**, 191–196.

Striem, B. J., Pace, U., Zehavi, U., Naim, M., and Lancet, D. (1989). Sweet tastants stimulate adenylate cyclase coupled to GTP-binding protein in rat tongue membranes. *Biochemistry Journal* **260**, 121–126.

Stunkard, A. J., Van Itallie, T. B., and Reis, B. B. (1955). The mechanism of satiety: Effect of glucagon on gastric hunger contractions in man. *Proceedings of the Society for Experimental Biology and Medicine* **89**, 258–261.

Sudakov, K., MacLean, P. D., Reeves, A., and Marino, R. (1971). Unit study of exteroceptive inputs to claustrocortex in awake, sitting, squirrel monkey. *Brain Research* **28**, 19–34.

Sudsaneh, S., and Mayer, J. (1959). Relation of metabolic events to gastric contractions in the rat. *American Journal of Physiology* **197**, 269–273.

Teeter, J. H., and Brand, J. G. (1987). Peripheral mechanisms of gustation: Physiology and biochemistry. *In* "Neurobiology of Taste and Smell" (T. E. Finger and W. L. Silver, eds.), pp. 299–330. Wiley, New York.

Teeter, J. H., Sugimoto, K., and Brand, J. G. (1989). Ionic currents in taste cells and reconstituted taste epithelial membranes. *In* "Receptor Events and Transduction in Taste and Olfaction. I. Chemical Senses" (J. G. Brand, J. H. Teeter, R. H. Cagan, and M. R. Kare, eds.), pp. 151–170. Dekker, New York.

Thompson, D. R., Moskowitz, H. R., and Campbell, R. G. (1976). Effects of body weight and food intake on pleasantness for a sweet stimulus. *Journal of Applied Physiology* **41**, 77–83.

Thorpe, S. J., Rolls, E. T., and Maddison, S. P. (1983). The orbitofrontal cortex: Neuronal activity in the behaving monkey. *Experimental Brain Research* **49**, 93–115.

Tonosaki, K., and Funakoshi, M. (1984). The mouse taste cell response to five sugar stimuli. *Comparative Biochemistry and Physiology A: Comparative Physiology* **79A**, 625–630.

Tonosaki, K., and Funakoshi, M. (1988a). Voltage– and current–clamp recordings of the receptor potential in mouse taste cell. *Brain Research* **445**, 363–366.

Tonosaki, K., and Funakoshi, M. (1988b). Cyclic nucleotides may mediate taste transduction. *Nature (London)* **331**, 354–356.

Travers, J. B. (1988). Efferent projections from the anterior nucleus of the solitary tract of the hamster. *Brain Research* **457**, 1–11.

Turner, B. H., Mishkin, M., and Knapp, M. (1980). Organization of the amygdalopetal projections from modality-specific cortical association areas in the monkey. *Journal of Comparative Neurology* **191**, 515.

Van der Kooy, D., Koda, L. Y., McGinty, J. F., Gerfen, C. R., and Bloom, F. E. (1984). The organization of projections from the cortex, amygdala, and hypothalamus to the nucleus of the solitary tract in rat. *Journal of Comparative Neurology* **224**, 1–24.

VanderWeele, D. A., Pi-Sunyer, F. X., Novin, D., and Bush, M. J. (1980). Chronic insulin infusion suppresses food ingestion and body weight gain in rats. *Brain Research Bulletin* **5** (Suppl. 4), 7–11.

VanderWeele, D. A., Haraczkiewicz, E., and Van Itallie, T. B. (1982). Insulin and satiety in obese and normal-weight rats. *Appetite: Journal for Intake Research* **3,** 99–109.

Waldbillig, R. J. (1984). Sensitivity of hindbrain circumventricular neurons to pancreatic hormones. *Society for Neuroscience Abstracts* **10,** 582.

West, H. L., Mark, G. P., and Hoebel, B. G. (1991). Effect of conditioned taste aversion on extracellular serotonin in the lateral hypothalamus and hippocampus of freely moving rats. *Brain Research* **556,** 95–100.

Whitehead, M. C., and Frank, M. E. (1983). Anatomy of the gustatory system in the hamster: Central projections of the chorda tympani and the lingual nerve. *Journal of Comparative Neurology* **220,** 378–395.

Wiggins, L. L., Rolls, E. T., and Baylis, G. C. (1987). Afferent connections of the caudolateral orbitofrontal cortex taste area of the primate. *Society for Neuroscience Abstracts* **13,** 1406.

Wilkins, L., and Richter, C. P. (1940). A great craving for salt by a child with corticoadrenal insufficiency. *JAMA, Journal of the American Medical Association* **114,** 866–868.

Wilson, F. A. W., Rolls, E. T., Yaxley, S., Thorpe, S. J., Williams, F. V., and Simpson, S. J. (1984). Responses of neurons in the basal forebrain of the behaving monkey. *Society for Neuroscience Abstracts* **10,** 128.

Wise, R. A., Spindler, J., DeWit, H., and Gerber, G. J. (1978). Neuroleptic-induced "anhedonia" in rats; pimozide blocks reward quality of food. *Science* **201,** 262–264.

Wolf, G. (1964). Effect of dorsolateral hypothalamic lesions on sodium appetite elicited by desoxycorticosterone and by acute hyponatremia. *Journal of Comparative and Physiological Psychology* **58,** 396–402.

Woolston, D. F., and Erickson, R. P. (1979). Concept of neuron types in gustation in the rat. *Journal of Neurophysiology* **42,** 1390–1409.

Yamamoto, T., and Kawamura, Y. (1975). Cortical responses to electrical and gustatory stimuli in the rabbit. *Brain Research* **94,** 447–463.

Yamamoto, T., and Kawamura, Y. (1977). Physiological characteristics of cortical taste area. *In* "Olfaction and Taste VI" (J. Le Magnen and P. MacLeod, eds.), pp. 257–264. Information Retrieval, London.

Yamamoto, T., Matsuo, R., and Kawamura, Y. (1980). Localization of cortical gustatory area in rats and its role in taste discrimination. *Journal of Neurophysiology* **44,** 440–455.

Yamamoto, T., Yuyama, N., Kato, T., and Kawamura, Y. (1984). Gustatory responses of cortical neurons in rats. I. Response characteristics. *Journal of Neurophysiology* **51,** 616.

Yamamoto, T., Matsuo, R., Kiyomitsu, Y., and Kitamura, R. (1989). Taste responses of cortical neurons in freely ingesting rats. *Journal of Neurophysiology* **61,** 1244–1258.

Yaxley, S., Rolls, E. T., Sienkiewicz, Z. J., and Scott, T. R. (1985). Satiety does not affect gustatory activity in the nucleus of the solitary tract of the alert monkey. *Brain Research* **347,** 85–93.

Yaxley, S., Rolls, E. T., and Sienkiewicz, Z. J. (1989). The responsiveness of neurons in the insular gustatory cortex of the macaque monkey is independent of hunger. *Physiology and Behavior* **42,** 223–229.

Yaxley, S., Rolls, E. T., and Sienkiewicz, Z. J. (1990). Gustatory responses of single neurons in the insula of the macaque monkey. *Journal of Neurophysiology* **63,** 689–700.

Author Index

Numbers in italics refer to the pages on which the complete references are listed.

A

Ables, M. F., 238, *279*
Ackroff, K., 257, 263, *285*
Acree, T. E., 245, *289*
Adams, J. E., 88, *135*
Adels, L., 61, 62, 69, 71, *80*, 153, 220, *227*
Ader, R., 19, 62, 78, 146, 153, *226*
Adey, W. R., 107, *133*
Adolph, E. F., 46, 59, *75*
Aggleton, J. P., 242, *279*
Agren, H., 123, *133*
Aguayo, D., 32, *81*
Aguilar-Jimenez, E., 59, 72, *82*
Akabas, M. H., 247, *279*
Akaike, N., 247, *279*
Akerstedt, T., 224, *225*
Akert, K., 238, 241, *280, 287*
Akiyama, Y., 149, *228*
Akogi, T., 234, 252, *283*
Al-Awaqati, Q., 247, *279*
Alberts, J., 223, *228*
Alberts, J. R., 60, 71, *75*
Aleksanyan, Z. A., 255, *279*
Allin, J. T., 60, *75*
Allison, T., 102, *133*
Amatsu, M., 234, *283*
Anders, T., 143, 147, 165, *225*
Anderson, R. R., 5, 8, 41, *80*
Anika, S. M., 43, 45, *75*
Anokhin, P., 145, *225*
Antelman, S. M., 70, *75*
Antin, J., 144, *229*, 270, *279*
Apfelbaum, M., 257, *280*
Armstrong, D. M., 115, 117, 118, *137*
Ashbaugh, N., 258, 259, *284*
Astic, L., 52, 53, *79*, 141, 147, 149, 153, 224, *227*
Aston-Jones, G., 117, *133*
Avenet, P., 245, 247, *279*

B

Babicky, A., 36, *75*
Baghdoyan, H. A., 118, *135*
Bagshaw, W. H., 241, *279*
Baigts, F., 257, *280*
Banks, E. M., 60, *75*
Bannett, D., 144, *227*
Baptista, T., 257, *285*
Barfield, R. J., 61, *82*
Barnes, C. A., 88, 101, *136*
Barnes, C. D., 101, *136*
Barnett, S. A., 71, *75*
Bateman, N., 8, 10, 11, 12, 19, *75*
Batshaw, M. L., 19, *77*
Baum, J., 224, *228*
Baverstock, P., 36, *75*
Baylis, G. C., 241, 242, *291*
Beahm, E. K., 102, 104, 105, *136*
Beauchamp, G. K., 231, *279*
Beckstead, R. M., 239, 241, *280*
Beidler, L. M., 243, 245, 247, *280, 284, 288*
Bell, R. W., 60, *75*
Benedek, G., 126, *134*
Benjamin, R. M., 238, 241, *279, 280, 281*
Bereiter, D. A., 255, *280*
Berger, R., 160, *228*
Berk, M. L., 239, *280*
Berkowitz, A., 117, 118, *137*
Bernal-Pedraza, J., 59, 72, *77, 82*
Bernstein, I. L., 43, 46, 47, *76*
Berridge, K. C., 237, 263, 267, *280, 283*
Berthoud, H.-R., 254, 255, *280, 287*
Bertiere, M. C., 257, *280*
Bertrand, B., 246, *282*
Bibr, B., 36, *75*
Bieber, S. L., 233, *289*

293

Subject Index

A

Activity levels in studies of sleep–wake states and feeding, 155–156
Afferents to ventral forebrain in rat, 238–239
Alimentary satiety, sleep as index of, 53–59
Anabolism, brain, in theory of ingestion and satiety, 71–73
Appreciation, hedonic, in response to nutrients and toxins, 254–258
Attachment time in studies of sleep–wake states and feeding
  in normal mother and litter, 153
  upon reunion, 168

B

Basal forebrain, SWS and, 126–131
Behavioral functional neuroanatomy of brain site, 86
Behavioral observations in studies of sleep–wake states and feeding
  in anesthetized mother and litter
  baseline, 186–187
  upon reunion, 196–198
  in normal mother and litter, 153–156
  upon reunion, 168
Bitter taste, transduction mechanisms for, 246–247
Brain, neuronal unit discharge in, 85–133; *see also* Neuronal unit discharge; Neuronal unit-recording method
Brain anabolism in theory of ingestion and satiety, 71–73
Brain stem cholinergic neurons, 118–121

C

"Ceiling effect" and milk availability, 10–11
Central nervous system, taste signals and, 268–275
Centrifugal connections in rats, 239
Cephalic phase of insulin release in ingestion studies, 47

D

Cholecystokinin (CCK)
  effects of, in ingestion studies, 42–45
  taste responses and, 270
Coding channels in taste, 233–234
Communication
  sucking, in stimulation of mammary gland, 32–33
  ultrasonic, temperature changes and, 60–61
Consumptive act in theory of ingestion and satiety, 66–67
Corticofugal and intracortical connections in macaque monkey, 242

D

Deprivation
  effects of, on sleep and thermoregulation, 53
  in ingestion studies, 337–39
  levels of, regulation of feeding by pups based on, 219–221
  state of, in theory of ingestion and satiety, 66
Disparity, definition of, $4n$
Dorsolateral pontine cells in REMS, 115–117

E

Electrodes, microwire, in neuronal unit-recording system, 88–93
Electrophysiological data in studies of sleep–wake states and feeding
  in anesthetized mother and litter
  baseline, 187–193
  upon reunion, 198–205
  in normal mother and litter, 156–163
  upon reunion, 171–180
Experience, plasticity of taste signals based on, 260–265

F

Feeding
  effect of, on state behavior, 222–223
  regulation of, by pups based on deprivation levels, 219–221

ISBN 0-12-542115-X